Sad Earth, Sweet Heaven

THE DIARY OF
LUCY REBECCA BUCK

DURING
THE WAR BETWEEN THE STATES

Front Royal, Virginia
December 25, 1861 - April 15, 1865

BUCK PUBLISHING COMPANY
Birmingham, Alabama, USA
1992 Edition Includes Index and Supplement

Published and Distributed throughout the World by
BUCK PUBLISHING COMPANY
2409 Vestavia Drive, Birmingham, Alabama 35216

Edited by
Dr. William P. Buck

FIRST EDITION 1973
SECOND EDITION 1992

Copyright© 1973 by Dr. William P. Buck
ISBN 0-934530-07-6
Library of Congress Catalogue Card Number: 73-85753
All Rights Reserved
Printed in Republic of Singapore

DEDICATED

TO

Lucy's Lord and Savior, Jesus Christ.

INTRODUCTION

Diaries are the "candid cameras" of their day catching and preserving a mien of history that enthralls us most. This Lucy Buck has done with literary skill and rare perception in her daily record of the martial sixties in the Shenandoah Valley of Virginia - its military, political and economic aspects as well as the domestic and social. With two brothers and many cousins in the Confederate Army, the 19-year-old lass was fiercely patriotic and although Yankees by the thousands marched and fought over, occupied and vandalised the Valley, they never conquered the irrepressible Lucy. "The tyrant's heel may be upon us," she wrote, "but although he may restrain speech and action, he cannot shackle the thoughts and feelings that glow within us and which, like all suppressed flames, will burn all the more fiercely when they blaze into action." As these pages, sparkling with fire and brimstone, are a fascinating revelation of the "thoughts and feelings that glowed within" a Christian patriot, the prevailing mood is indeed as sad as the earthly tribulations of a family, town and country caught up in the "angry billows of political and military strife", but it is also as "sweet as the blessed hope of heaven" that sustained the devout diarist through her "fiery trials." Her spirits rise and fall with the fortunes of the Confederacy, running the gamut from "frantic delight" over the recapture of the town from the Yankees, to the flowing tears into which she melted at church when the floodgates of emotion, pent up during weeks of depressing news and enemy occupation, were opened by the "soul-stirring old hymn,'How Firm A Foundation'," which had been her "favorite lullaby and the strain in which the family had united their voices on Sunday evenings at Bel Air." But gleeful or gloomy, she is ever voluble, whether describing a "very exciting. very exhilarating" battle "with bullets and shells passing near enough to whisper confidential messages;" the encircling campfires of "our fiendish foes couched in their lairs, ready to spring upon us;" merry gatherings around tea table, piano, or fireside with soldiers camped nearby or home on leave, hungry for food, flirtation and family; Christmas and holidays celebrated as joyfully as the heartaches and privations of war allowed; days of fasting and prayer with "solemn impressive sermons" that moved her to "foreswear dancing for the rest of the war;" the "glorious day" when "the Grand Old Chief", General Lee, stopped at Bel Air to rest and drink buttermilk while the girls played and sang for him. There are graphic pen-portraits of the prominent people who "preempted" or were entertained at Bel Air, including Generals Lee, Longstreet, Shields and Kimball.

As a rail and crossroads town, Front Royal was often a hive of military operations and excitement, lying in the path of armies advancing "with bands playing and flags flying," and in the wake of the wounded and weary backwash of such tragic encounters as Antietam and Gettysburg. Bel Air, home of the influential Buck Family for over a century, was a center of local affairs from the time it was built about 1795 by Capt. Thomas Buck, a Founding-Father of Front Royal and commander of "Buck's Minute Men" in the Revolutionary militia. As the mansion house of a productive farm of 100 acres, a mill, and orchard in the 1860's it often was occupied as headquarters for military staffs and a campground for armies, Blue and Gray. Lucy's diary resounds with the marching feet and rollings wheels of "mighty multitudes" filing past Bel Air, their "martial music and soul-burning shouts mingled in one unbroken, thrilling volume of sound." Continuous streams of "straved, dusty fellows called at the house for milk, bread and water." When Front Royal was held as headquarters of the Federal Department of the Rappahannoch, the whole area was "white with the tents and wagons of McDowell, Shields and Banks." The volatile Lucy echoes the rage and dismay of the citizens, helpless before the swarming masses "ravenous for food and fuel, tramping over the waving wheat and blooming clover." But her bitter-best vocabulary was reserved for the raiding hordes of Milroy, Sigel, Hunter and Sheridan, who came to search, plunder, steal and burn - "barbaric campaigns of torch and torture. Cowardly crews on pitiful business," she scoffed, "brutally investigating ladies' wardrobes and bureaus. We had to keep up a perfect system of picketing the porches, lest they steal everything." And again: "I hear a strange footfall ... and spring up to leave the room as I always did when the Yankees came ... a huge anathema hangs pendant on my lips and a big wave of indignation rolls over me."

Lucy Buck was born at Front Royal, Va., Sept. 25, 1842, the daughter of William Mason Buck and Elizabeth Ashby Buck. She was reared at Bel Air in the finest religious and cultural heritage of "the old South". As the eldest daughter among thirteen children, she assumed loving responsibility for many family and household duties that sorely taxed her young prowess and patience after all the servants ran off with the Yankees. To a revered and trusted Christ she committed her burdens of anxiety for the adored absent brothers, for her aging father bowed under the weight of economic ruin, for the future of the impoverished land. Charming, vivacious and popular, she had many beaux but never married. Continuing her diary, she was a long-remembered and beloved figure as she sat with a pad on her knee, in the midst of a chattering group of young relatives or in the quiet of her room, exerting herself to write despite pain and fatigue until her death in 1918. She was equally articulate in prose and poetry, winning first prize for her poem, "The Sunset," in a national newspaper contest. Her diary, abiding proof of her narrative skill, won the coveted Marian Perdue Cup awarded by the United Daughters of the Confederacy for "the most outstanding contribution to Southern history."

Laura Virginia Hale

Foreword

Upon looking at the worn edges and faded ink, the loose pages and defaced paper of the original diaries of Lucy Rebecca Buck, written in the war years of 1861–1865, the task of transcribing them into a legible form would seem a hopeless one. Col. Lawrence Neville Buck, U.S.A. (retired) made it a labor of love, and due to his efforts and the cooperation of Orville M. Buck these pages are now made accessible. The late William R. Buck, the last of the Bel Air household, gave the benefit of his knowledge and memories, which helped to clear up many doubtful passages.

William Pettus Buck was responsible for the present edition. His research produced the inserts (in italics) to bring about the chronological history. (Words that were illegible in the original diary are indicated as such by ellipsis points.) Credit is also due Welford Ashby Buck and Gray Carroll Buck whose influence and guidance encouraged the present edition, and to Mary Wallace Buck Rowe who edited the first edition and supplied much information for the present text. All the above mentioned are descendants of the Bel Air family. Miss Laura Virginia Hale; presently of Front Royal, Virginia; read and corrected the various inserts. Also credit is due Mabel Locke Donaldson for the typing and proofreading of this edition.

The amount of material is too great to justify reproducing the diary in its entirety. To avoid monotonous repetition, many entries have been eliminated even though by so doing it was necessary to mar the complete picture of the peaceful days at Bel Air intervening between the more exciting episodes, and to omit references to many of the relatives and friends who were guests at The Old Home during that period.

It may be that some readers of this volume will remember "Miss Lucy" in her later years as she sat with her writing pad on her knee, sometimes in the midst of a chattering group of younger relatives, sometimes in the quiet of her room, exerting herself to write in spite of pain and fatigue. These may have some idea of the effort she put forth to keep this record, which, needless to say, she intended to be seen by no eye but her own. Nevertheless, we are indeed grateful to her for having shown us to what extent life could continue in the presence of repeated invasions by both Confederate and Union armies.

The Shenandoah Valley of Virginia (See map, illustration number 12) stretches northeast from the eminence of land between Staunton and Lexington in the south to the Potomac River in the north, a distance of more than 100 miles. It lies between the Blue Ridge Mountains to the east and the Alleghany Mountains to the west. The width varies from twenty to thirty miles. The Massanutten Mountain rises abruptly out of the valley a few miles east of Harrisonburg and runs northeast where it falls away as suddenly at Strasburg, twelve miles west of Front Royal. The 3000-foot Massanutten is closer to the Blue Ridge than to the Alleghanies and thus divides the valley unequally. The narrow valley to the east is the Luray or Page Valley and the broader valley to the west is known as the "Main Valley."

Two rivers, the North Fork west of the Massanutten Mountain and the South Fork to the east, flow northwardly down their respective valleys and meet near Front Royal to become the Shenandoah River. The Shenandoah continues a northeasterly course to empty into the Potomac River at Harper's Ferry.

Bel Air (figure 6 and 7), the home of Lucy Rebecca Buck, is located on an elevation less than a quarter mile east of Front Royal, Virginia. It was a happy home always buzzing with guests and activity and the two-story structure built in 1795 is the focal point of the diary.

Fifty yards in front and to the right side of the house at the base of a sloping grassy hill runs Happy Creek. The Hope family lived on the west bank of this creek and nearby was the mill. The front of the house faces southward toward the town and beyond it the beautiful panorama of the Blue Ridge Mountains. Lucy gave the best description of this view in the winter of 1861.

> "The evening was lovely and I turned to look on the landscape spread before me. In the foreground the smooth, lawn-like meadows and the little Happy Creek like a silver thread meandering through them. Then the quiet village with the crimson sunset on its windows, and its bright wreaths of curling smoke, and beyond the undulating hill—and in the distance like a fitting frame to this sweet picture stretched the blue mountains all with a cloudless heaven overhead, painted with the sunset pencils...."

Lucy's father, William Mason Buck, age fifty-one (figure 2) was a merchant and a leading citizen of Front Royal. His great grandfather was one of the first settlers in that part of the valley. Mr. Buck and his wife, Elizabeth Ann Ashby, (figure 3) age forty, had eleven children. His mother-in-law, Rebecca Ashby, (figure 5) age 68, also lived at Bel Air. Mr. Buck lived to the year 1895 and it has been written in a Front Royal paper that William Mason Buck was "the last of that generation of old Virginia gentlemen, of whom we have read."

The children at Bel Air were:

> Alvin, the eldest was 23 years old in 1861 and served under Beauregard during the war. (Figure 13)
>
> Irving, 21, and served on Cleburne's staff until wounded at Atlanta. (Figure 14)
>
> Lucy Rebecca, 19, and the oldest daughter. (Figure 1)
>
> Nellie, 17. (Figure 1)
>
> Laura, 14.
>
> Orville, 12.
>
> Carey, 10.
>
> Nannie, 8.
>
> Willie, 5.
>
> Evred was born January 9, 1860 and the baby, Frank (Dixie) was born November 27, 1861.

Mr. Buck had three brothers, one uncle and many other kinsmen living in Front Royal. The population, including slaves, was approximately 500 inhabitants. (Figures number 9, 10, and 11.)

A list of the homes and families in the Front Royal area, during 1861-1865, can be found at the back of this book.

See reference page for resources of historical information contained in editor's notes.

Dr. William P. Buck

Contents

Chapter		Page
	Foreword	5
I	PRE-INVASION *December 25, 1861 - March 26, 1862*	11
II	INVASION AND OCCUPATION *March 27, 1862 - May 22, 1862*	42
III	LIBERATION *May 23, 1862 - May 29, 1862*	77
IV	SECOND OCCUPATION *May 30, 1862 - August 16, 1862*	88
V	FIRST INVASION OF NORTH *August 17, 1862 - December 31, 1862*	130
VI	CHANCELLORSVILLE AND SECOND INVASION OF NORTH *January 1, 1863 - July 13, 1863*	160
VII	RETREAT *July 16, 1863 - June 19, 1864*	214
VIII	EARLY'S VALLEY CAMPAIGN *June 21, 1864 - September 21, 1864*	263
IX	DEFEAT *February 13, 1865 - April 15, 1865*	287
	Homes In The Front Royal Area *1861-1865*	300
	Bibliography	304
	Photographs and Maps	305

I

PRE-INVASION

December 25, 1861 - March 26, 1862

The First Battle of Bull Run (First Manassas) was fought on July 21, 1861. After this first great battle of the Civil War both forces began to prepare for a long war. The spring of 1862 would usher in renewal of the bloody conflict.

On Christmas Day, 1861, a nineteen year old Virginia girl living in the Shenandoah Valley at Front Royal, Virginia, began to write in her diary.

Christmas Morning—1861
   A sweet day that seems woven of the spirit of the Christmas benediction—"Peace on earth—good will to men." The anniversary of the birth of the holy Christ-Child, the anniversary of so many pleasant hours that have vanished never to return, but the memories of which come back to us "as sad as earth, as sweet as heaven."
   I cannot but feel a little sad this morning for my thoughts continually revert to those dear absent brothers who were wont to share our Christmas cheer and gladden the hours of this festive season for us. Poor boys! I wonder if they think of the blazing hearthstone at old Bel Air and wish for a place in the home-circle. When I think of the unexpected changes that have occurred in the last year I feel as if I could not count upon ever having them with us again as of yore with any degree of certainty. I think of how many hands that wreathed the bowl and twined the holly last year are now mouldering in the dust. The bright locks that were then crowned with roses, now dabbled in gore and covered with the turf of the battlefield. I think of the bright eyes that softened neath the

love glances of fond friends then, how they look forth now with a yearning, hopeless gaze from the close grating of the gloomy prison window. I think of it all and sicken when I think. Thus far we have been peculiarly blest; our friends have been strangely preserved and protected from death and suffering through the war; our homes uninjured or unpolluted and we enjoying comparative tranquility and repose. But ere another revolution of the wheel of time, and who of "those we love and those who love us" may not have ceased to speak with us on earth. And oh!—who can tell how we may be called to pass through the "deep waters" and endure the fiery trials in the interval of another year. And how many of us will sink weakly under the heat and burthen of the day; and how many of us who now "cherish noble longings for the strife" may not—

"By the wayside fall and perish
Weary with the march of life."

But oh God forbid! May He give us "Strength as our day" and be to us the "Great Rock in a weary land" when we feel nigh unto fainting. And ere the dawn of another Christmas morning may His "Peace, Be still!" be spoken to angry billows of political strife—calming and restraining their fury; and may our loved country be restored to tranquility and we the happier and better for this refining process which shall consume the dross of selfishness and leave us the truer and purer.

Evening
This has been quite a pleasant day despite its rather gloomy retrospective beginning. Henry Buck came down about eleven o'clock to beg Nellie and me to make up one of a party which was to spend the holidays at Clover Hill—said party consisting of the Misses Tyler–Menie Leech, Nannie Ford, Smith Turner and some others. We had made a prior engagement with Aunt Betty Ashby and so declined Henry's invitation, though I knew they would enjoy themselves so much. We made our toilettes and went over to Oakley about half-past eleven. Found Aunt B and Mr. Brerwood awaiting us and very soon Mr. Hoblitzell came in looking as usual satisfied with himself and the world in general. He had invited a young friend, Mr. Wilson of Baltimore, to meet him at dinner and the young fellow when he came proved to be a very great addition to our company. We finished drinking our toasts and then Mr. B. and I had quite a discussion with Mr. Hoblitzell upon the extent to which the command "children obey parents" was to be obeyed, particularly where matrimony was concerned. 'Twas all very unprofitable though, for at the close of the debate we all retained precisely the opinions as at the commencement. After dinner we had cards and "consequences" and enjoyed ourselves very much. Heard "My Maryland" today for the first time—'tis a beautiful song. Returned home before six and to our great surprise and delight found Emma Cloud there. We were invited

to Mrs. Stewart's tonight but did not go.

December 26, 1861

The early part of the day which was cold and disagreeable, was spent about the fire laughing, talking and eating nuts. In the afternoon Emma and I called at Mrs. Cloud's and there met with Miss Martha Simpson and Mrs. Hamp Miller. Was glad to find the former amicably disposed, for 'tis so unpleasant to meet with one of whose sentiments with regard to yourself you are doubtful. I do not like to feel unkindly to anyone.

I noticed while at Mrs. C's that Miss Mary's pictures were all wreathed with Christmas garlands of evergreens and upon examining them I was particularly attracted by one of them—Evangeline. Although I had previously often seen and examined the picture, yet I had never felt it so before. It seemed that with her the artist must have "grieved for one whose imagine lay too deep for tears" else he could not so faithfully have conceived and depicted the expression of countenance of the crushed world-weary girl.

There was such a depth of sorrowing despair in the dark eyes, such a wistful, longing gaze and yet withal such a chastened meek look about the gentle face, that I felt my own heart throb in painful sympathy and tears come into my eyes, just as if she had been a real human being loving and grieving. 'Tis indeed a wonderful art that which transfers to blank canvas the warm life-hues, the endless variety of passionate expressions that belong to our breathing glowing spirits enshrined in their flesh and blood caskets. What a talismanic power does the artist possess! How he rifles the tombs of the past and bids the forms of beauty, those mighty spirits of old—men of genius, strength and goodness—come forth from the dust of ages and awake to life-likeness—re-enacting their sufferings, their loves and their triumphs upon the cold canvas neath his magic touch! How we reverently bow before them, those heroes and martyrs of old as he brings their image to our gaze. How he revives memories of every age and country! How he leads our fancies with him through distant lands! How we gaze with awe and wonder upon the mighty relics of by-gone eras! How the treasures of every clime, all that is sublime in nature or in art are revealed to us by his potent spell, from the glowing, gorgeous tropics to the sterile, ghostly region of the iceberg! He even leads us into those bright realms of fancy where revels his own poet-soul. Oh 'tis a glorious talent entrusted to man! One which enables him to wield untold influence over the hearts and minds of his fellow beings in every age and condition of life.

Father went over to the cars hoping to receive some report of the anticipated convivialities at Centreville, but the boys did not write and we were forced to be content with Charley Brown's verbal testimony that they were well and enjoying themselves.

After the First Manassas or First Bull Run, the Confederates settled down into winter quarters at Centreville, Virginia. Two of Lucy's brothers, Alvin and Irving, (figures 13 and 14) were there. Many of the wounded Confederates from the Manassas battle were sent to hospitals in Front Royal.

December 27, 1861

What unimpeachable weather we are having—cold, 'tis true, but bright and fair as midsummer. I rejoice in it for the sake of our poor Southern boys in camp.

Charley Brown came in for a couple of hours this morning and amused us much with his droll account of "life in camp." Received a note from Mr. B. soliciting the "pleasure of our company" for the evening and presently the amiable trio—Messrs. H., W., and B. came in person to renew the request, but we were not in tune and declined. Willie Buck came in to play draughts and backgammon with Nellie tonight while I read aloud to Father. Received by cars a note from Irving—short but welcomed bringing an assurance of their well-doing.

December 29, 1861

No service in any of the churches and we spent a quiet morning at home. Uncle Newton said he thought he heard heavy cannonading in the distance. Nellie and I went out of the house and listened to what did indeed closely resemble the bombing of artillery. The evening was lovely and I turned to look on the landscape spread before me. In the foreground the smooth, lawn-like meadows and the little Happy Creek like a silver thread meandering through them. Then the quiet village with the crimson sunset on its windows, and its bright wreaths of curling smoke, and beyond the undulating hills—and in the distance like a fitting frame to this sweet picture stretched the blued mountains all with a cloudless heaven overhead, painted with the sunset pencils forming altogether a scene of surpassing loveliness. So tranquil did everything seem that I could scarce persuade myself of the fact that just beyond those mountain barriers lay the encampments of an invading foe cruel and relentless, who had come with avowed purpose of deluging this beautiful land with the blood of the noblest and best of its sons. They were our enemies who would fain see the dun-cloud of the battlefield or the sombre smoke from our pillaged burning homes ascending to the blackened heavens instead of the sweet Sabbath atmosphere which pervaded the scene now. Those who would ensanguine that little stream with human gore, those who would mar and devastate the face of the earth that they might thus blot out from remembrance everything of beauty from our now beautiful Virginia. Then my thoughts reverted to our own little bands of patriots, and my heart thrilled gratefully as I remembered how gallantly they had hitherto repelled the advances of the insolent foe, and I felt an exulting confidence that ere another winter's frost should have browned the woodlands with the blessing of heaven we should have been welcomed into the family of nations, an honored and respected member of the vast fraternity. And now the evening star "lit its silver lamp" and the sight brought to mind the dear ones who had so often looked with me upon it and I wondered if we should ever meet together again, as in the long ago at twilight and sing the happy songs of our childhood. Dear Brothers! —'tis doubtful very, and even if we were permitted another such reunion, and such a long weary time must first intervene I felt as if I could not wait—as if I could not possess my soul with patience. Ah, well-a-day!

December 31, 1861

I concluded to watch the advent of the New Year and Grandma decided to keep vigil with me. I felt as if this year just being ushered in was to form an important period in the annals of our country, and while waiting for the waning moments to sink into the great abyss of the past, while watching for the last grains dropping from the hour-glass of the year, I recalled the last New Year and the stirring scenes and events that had transpired since its first-dawn. I saw a great and glorious government, which had erst been the pride and the boast of a free and happy people, in that brief period become a by-word of hissing and reproach "a thing of scorn and contempt" through the faithlessness of those who administered the laws made for the blessing and protection of the governed. I saw how one portion of the people became rich and prosperous under the government, but cruel and avaricious too and with all its wealth, jealous and envious of the possessions of the weaker part of the nation. And I saw it stretch forth its greedy power to snatch from the few the inheritance, the privileges and birth-rights which that government had endeavored to secure to them by wise and just laws. I saw this people that waxed strong grow proud and boastful too. I saw it trample upon the laws, desecrate the symbols and outrage every principle upon which this government was founded. Then I saw the oppressed rise up and assert its rights. I saw it plead with the oppressor for equal privileges as brothers of one household. I saw concessions made and efforts for compromise, but the strong would none of it. Might was right, and the only compromise to be accepted was entire submission and resignation of self-respect by the weak. Then I saw the oppressed sorrowfully yield to the force of circumstances. I saw it prepare to leave a home when the authority of the ruling powers was not strong enough to prevent the strong from imposing on the weaker of the nation. I saw it strive to quietly go its way alone where it might worship under its own "vine and fig tree" with "none to vex or make it afraid." But a factorum was not to be given up thus tamely and the oppressor raised a great furor and with threats and chastisements and scourges tried to force the little one into subjection. I saw a young republic born into the family of nations which like Hercules was in its infancy attacked by a monster-serpent that endeavored to crush the bantling in its crib. But like Hercules it courageously grasped its enemy and held it at bay till its muscles could cope with it in strife. I saw the deadly assailant writhe in the hands of its youthful adversary, and still the contest continued. I thought of this all and vainly questioned the future as to the issue of this conflict. That the unholy designs of the aggressor would be brought to naught I did not doubt, but there was so much of uncertainty in the future that with my utmost penetration I could not fathom. Well 'tis best perhaps that we cannot know what is before us in our onward way—better far trust in the goodness of God and rest assured that He will not give us more trials to bear than strength to bear them.

My fleeting fancy next brought before me a picture of the domestic revolutions and changes that this eventful year had produced in the sweet homes of the "Sunny South." I saw the proud mansions that were wont to be glad with mirth and music as each New Year sped on with fleet wings, now shrouded in gloom and darkness. I thought how the warm light had died out from the hearthstones and from the eyes that had beamed brightly around them. I thought of the sad silences of those ancestral halls that erst rang with the music of footfalls that would stray on earth never more now. I knew how many happy a mother had been called to yield up her "Cornelian jewel"—her all and had sent him forth to the battlefield with blessings on this bright young head—knew the hapless anguish of her spirit when they told her the gory grave held now the dear form so often clasped to her bosom. I thought of the gentle sister who resigned the play-fellow of her childhood, the dear protector of her youth to be sacrificed on the altar of his country never again to know the joy of a brother's love. I thought of the young bride who had torn from her brow the nuptial wreath and folded about her the sable weeks of her widowhood. I thought of the babe orphaned ere it could lisp a father's name. Thought of the helpless ones deprived of parents when they most needed a parent's watchful care. Of the maiden who listened and thrilled as she listened to the vows of love from lips stilled in death ere the burning words grew cold upon them. I thought of the hardships endured, the cold and hunger and the harshness to the brave and noble young Southerners whose cradle had been rocked in luxury—who knew of nothing but gentle words and loving smiles in the dear home far away. I thought of the delicate forms of the boys tenderly nurtured now rent with anguish resting on the loathsome hospital couches, no gentle hands to minister to their wants, no dear voice to whisper comfort and cheer when the dark shadows from the Valley of Death closed about them, none to smooth the pillow, none to drop a tear when that wasted form was borne off to the stranger's rude grave. There was none to hear the last whispered message breathed by the dying for those who waited his coming in the home he had left and who might never know where the loved one slept. I thought of the lonely pinings in the gloomy, deadly prison. I thought of the friendships formed, of the loves that had blossomed, of the ties that had been rudely sundered. I thought of the fire and the sword of the rapine and pillage that had devastated the land. And I thought of the profound depths of wickedness and deceit that had been revealed, of the hypocrisy and falsehood of the human heart that had been unveiled to the gaze of the most artless, the purest and most innocent. Oh, the deeds for good or evil that may be concentrated within the period of one little year! How the heart may grow old and cold, how the sympathies, the sensibilities may become dulled and deadened in that little time!

Then I remembered all these things and knew that we could judge of the future but by the past, I felt how perfectly impotent we were in the hands of the Almighty Ruler, how entirely dependent upon Him we were for happiness, and I realized how that we could not do better than say, "Now as the old year with all its deeds is slowly waning—the last sands dropping from the glass, help Thou me! Oh God, to make this resolve, as Thou hast genuinely protected, blessed and preserved me in this year that has just passed, and has shown me that I know not what is good for me, so do Thou be with me in the coming new year, help me to resign myself to Thy will, to commit to Thee issues of coming events and to only be careful that I discharge my duties to Thee and to my fellow-beings to the extent of my ability."

Commenced writing a letter but laid it by unfinished at one o'clock and retired.

January 1, 1862

All hail to thee, New Year! Year destined as thou art to be fraught with events of vast import—events that leave an ineffaceable impression on the world—events that shall reshape influences through the destinies of nations to remote ages. What deeds of high-souled daring, what sacrifices of life and fortunes and affections will not thy sun shine upon. What examples of chivalrous devotion to country will not be set to the nations of the earth.

Surely season never dawned more beautifully. Summer's sunshine, Autumn's soft sky and Spring's balmy breath with the bracing influences of a Winter's morning—a combination of all the seasons to welcome the advent of '62. Nellie, Laura and myself could not sufficiently enjoy it indoors, so we went on the housetop and watched the lifting of the mist from the valley. How beautiful it looked, soft and white as a snow-wreath and braided with the gold and crimson of the sunshine. It rose slowly from the earth and the higher it ascended the more graceful and beautiful it seemed—just like our thoughts and desires that become ever more pure the nearer they lead to heaven.

Mailed my letter and went over to Mrs. Stewart's. Saw Alice, Fannie and Miss Boyd and was introduced to one of the young disciples of Esculapius.

Mrs. Stewart was Miss Belle Boyd's aunt and was the proprietor of Fishback Hotel "The Strickler House."

> *Miss Boyd was a famous Confederate spy and carried on much of her activities in Front Royal where she visited with her aunt. She gathered important information from Union soldiers living in the hotel, "Strickler House."*

Tho' not at all favorably impressed with the two latter individuals, one seemed all surface, vain and hollow; the other rude and evasive. It was my first acquaintance with Alice, and I was much pleased with her. Chatted awhile and had some music, and we then went down to Dr. Brown's where we spent a most pleasant hour. I never knew the Misses B. so agreeable and friendly.

Felt very much dissatisfied with myself tonight when reviewing the events of the day—there was a consciousness of having compromised my dignity in mingling upon terms of equality and apparent friendship with persons whom in my heart I despise—persons whom I felt to be false and heartless. I never am brought in contact with such persons without feeling a conviction that if forced to confine myself to their society I shall become as frivolous apparently as they. Received a petite epistle from dear Irvie after retiring.

January 2, 1862

In the afternoon Fannie Stewart called with two soldiers, acquaintances of hers. They were by no means prepossessing and I was duly glad when, after singing the song they came to hear I had the pleasure of receiving their adieux. Fannie however left assuring us that she intended next accompanying the young doctor over to see us. I sincerely trust though she will not. Would be glad to see her but could not conscientiously extend a warm welcome to her proposed "appendages." Read, wrote and sewed until bedtime.

January 4, 1862

Woke very early and found it had been sleeting during the night. Put my shawl over my head and walked the pavement until it was light enough to read; then practiced on the piano and read and wrote till breakfast. Was very busy all day—sewing for Irving. At dusk Nellie and I went into the parlor and amused ourselves singing and playing. Mason and Slidell have really been yielded up to the demands of the British Government. False-hearted cravens! If the Yankee cabinet did not direct their seizure it endorsed it at the time and now to think of their backing down in that manner. To think of their once vaunted eagle trailing its plumage in the dust at the very feet of the British lion! We read today the correspondence between Seward and Lord Lyons in relation to the affair, and I do think for a man with any reputation for ability, Mr. S. did make the most paltry attempt at playing the diplomatist and his letter the most juvenile effort at display of legal knowledge that I ever saw. Degraded sycophant! There is, I think reason for believing that Old

England has not finished her reckoning with the administration yet. No news of importance tonight.

> *James M. Mason and John S. Slidell on November 8, 1861, were taken from the English ship* Trent *on the high seas, en route to England and France as commissioners from the Confederate States of America. They were released December 26, 1861. Lord Lyons was the British minister at Washington and Seward was Secretary of State of the United States.*

January 5, 1862
So glad to see Mr. Wilson had returned last night very unexpectedly on a long furlough and seems delighted to be back. He's a nice fellow. Mr. Brerwood seemed unusually cheerful. While they were yet here, Mack Richardson, Willie Buck, Jacquie and "Allie" came in and we had quite a levee until dusk. Read aloud to Father after they left. Oh!—this bitter weather, what trials and sufferings does it not bring the poor soldier. May God "temper the wind to the poor fellows."

January 6, 1862
Found a slight fall of snow on the ground this morning and the sky looking very wintry, though it did not snow as we expected.

January 8, 1862
Clear and cold this morning—health and spirits much renovated by a night's rest. Heard that the "Warren Rifles" were ordered to Evansport—hope the report is groundless—suppose we will hear the truth tomorrow.

How well I remember this day year, or rather this night. We were at Dr. Turner's—a small company of as merry young people as ever assembled. Cousin Sam, Emma, Jule, Nellie and Miss Tensia every one of us. Irvie and Will Richardson too. Wonder where we will all be this time next year.

January 9, 1862
Worked hard till ten o'clock this morning cleaning the parlor, putting up curtains, etc. Expected company to dinner but indisposition prevented them from complying with their engagement. Later in the evening and wrapping a shawl about my head went on the porch to enjoy the sunset. It was very beautiful, the air soft and balmy and the sky so blue—mellowed into a rich orange and then burning a bright gold in the west where floated a few glowing clouds like sentinels guarding the sunset chamber. Then a gentle breeze stole out and drew a curtain of mist over the brightness and set in its fleecy folds a single watch star. While sitting intensely enjoying the tranquil scene I heard footsteps on the pavement and turning saw Mr. Cook and Mr. Berry approaching. Invited them in the parlor,

where I entertained them until Father appeared and then Nellie sang a little. I do so enjoy the society of social elderly gentlemen sometime—there is so much benefit to be gleaned from their individual experiences. They are war-scarred veterans on the battlefield of life—they know all the trials and privations to be endured in that long campaign—understand all the maneuvers, can instruct us how to avoid this and that foe, what is necessary in emergencies arising. They can advise much better than the novices in the service, and hence are often preferable companions to the unsophisticated. I fear though that the lessons thus conned are often too soon forgotten to be productive of as good results with me as they should.

I have been sitting here tonight thinking of the last ninth of January. I remember it so well. Irvie was with us and there was a company of mirthful friends in the evening collected about the parlor fire at old Bel Air, and the gleeful games in the dining room. I recollect the philopena gift, the wish and the songs and music. All those pleasant scenes are traced in golden characters on my memory pages. I wonder if the record will ever again be as bright.

> *Philopena was a game with a romantic background, in which each of two persons tried to draw the other into paying a forfeit. When one would come across a nut, like an almond, in which the kernel was in two parts instead of one, a boy and girl would each keep a half. Upon meeting later one of them would say "philopena" and the other would have to produce his or her half nut. If he could not, then he was supposed to pay a forfeit of some kind. Lucy's reward was a ring received from Scott Roy (see April 27, 1862.)*

January 11, 1862

Had just brushed my hair and settled myself down when Messrs. Brerwood and Wilson were announced. Mr. W. told us he had come to leave his adieux as he was to take his departure in the morning for O——. We spent a couple of pleasant hours chatting and singing and then they left. Ma came home about noon and brought me a letter from Dick, saucy fellow! Made a cravat for Mr. Wilson and sent it to him with the cap which Nellie finished for him tonight. And in return she received a very nice note of thanks and assurances of remembrances. I feel very much interested in the boy and hope he may do well whether he returns to military service or receives an appointment in the civil departments—nothing from Irvie—no war news.

January 12, 1862

We all walked up to "Soldiers' Rest" late in the afternoon. It was the first time I had ever been there and it saddened me to see already the number of graves there—mere heaps of earth with rough head and foot boards upon which were inscribed the names and dates of the deceased with the companies to which they had belonged. And there under my very feet they rested so still, so silent, those men who had for the love of country and freedom risked their lives and lost them in battling the usurper of their sacred rights—lost them, not gloriously fallen on the field bathed in their own heart's blood, but stricken with disease they had languished in agony upon friendless couches and at last died no less martyrs to their cause. I could scarce realize that those whose arms had been strong in the conflict, whose feet had been so swift in the battle, were now lying all so powerless, that I, weak girl that I was, might boast of a giant's strength in comparison. I thought so much of the distant homes from which their never-returning footsteps had departed and longed to send some word of comfort to the bereaved hearts there—to say to each mourner "Weep not, he rests well and though he slumbers on, apparently unknown and unnoted, yet in far after years the children he assisted in freeing from bondage shall lean over the grave of the sleeping patriot and drop the tribute of a sigh or tear and call him 'blest' who died in defense of such a cause."

It was quite late when we returned to Oakley and the soldiers in camp were singing their evening hymns, and very sweet it sounded as it came mellowed by the distance to our ears. We sat on the portico and Nellie and I sang for Uncle Tom—went to tea and while we were at table Father walked in to accompany us home. We had spent a delightful day and had a pleasant walk home in the moonlight. Found George Williams here, he had come to tell us good-bye as he was to start on the morrow for the seat of war—had obtained a situation in Beauregard's headquarters. He will doubtless have a merry time of it with old friends there. Saw Henry and Jule from a distance today. No news.

January 13, 1862

Nellie and Laura started to school again today, much to my sorrow, for I do miss them so much when they are away and fear I shall get to moping. Busied myself recording, writing and nursing the little Dixie in the forenoon. In the afternoon sewed and practiced some little. Kattie Boone has sent me a special invitation to visit her tomorrow, and I mean to go if the weather is favorable. Read aloud to Father until he went to the cars tonight; when he returned bringing a nice letter from Irvie containing a number of generals' autographs for me. Dear fellow, how pleased I am to hear from him and know that he and Alvin are well and comfortable. Am afraid though he does not write as cheerfully as usual.

January 21, 1862

Received a long letter from dear Irvie telling me how much engaged they all were in the office. I am so glad he is going to remain there instead of going West next spring. Practiced some time this evening and after tea read aloud to Father a dissertation upon law. I have heretofore imagined that the study of law must be the most unmitigatedly, dull, uninteresting thing in the world, but in this my first glimpse into its mysteries I was agreeably surprised to find the subject a most interesting one treated in this way.

January 22, 1862
Oh such a time as I had this morning with my pupils! I'm convinced my forte is not the management of juvenile masculinity and my patience waxes weaker and weaker at every trial. The fact is I would like to know what my sphere here is—sometimes I'm afraid my "leaf by some o'er hasty angel is misplaced in Fate's eternal volume." I am sure that I am not fitted for any vocation to which I have yet turned attention.

Wrote Uncle John this evening. How quiet everything seems in the military line—they do not seem to have the excitement of an occasional skirmish.

January 27, 1862
Father came in and had a pacquet of letters brought from Centreville the night before by Benton Roy. Upon breaking the seal, we found letters from Alvin and Irving to Father and myself, and from George Williams to Cousin Sue announcing that General Beauregard was ordered to Kentucky and they as clerks would accompany Colonel Jordan, and requesting that their clothes might be put in a state of perfect repair so that everything might be ready for their departure at a moment's warning.

> *General Beauregard fell into controversies with Jefferson Davis and Judah Benjamin, then Secretary of War of the Confederacy after First Manassas. On January 26, 1862, he was ordered to Kentucky under Gen. Albert Sidney Johnston. The command of the army of northern Virginia rested in the hands of Gen. Joseph Johnston. Johnston was superior to Beauregard at First Manassas, but the former had moved from the Shenandoah Valley and was not as familiar with the battleground.*
>
> *Stonewall Jackson was elevated to major general in the provisional army of the Confederacy in October, 1861, and was assigned to command the Shenandoah Valley. He established headquarters at Winchester, November 5, 1861.*

The intelligence was unexpected and sudden as a thunder bolt, and I was so stunned as for a time to lose the power of speech and volition—but soon I realized the whole force of the unwelcomed news. My darling brothers were going to a distant State with no prospect of our seeing them for a long, long time and no chance of ever hearing from them except at long weary intervals. They were to go where they must be surrounded by hostile armies liable to be cut off from communication with us; going among entire strangers who knew nothing and cared nothing for them, going where they could not be gently and tenderly nursed in sickness as we ever had nursed them. It was so hard. I knew many, very many in the Southern army who were much less pleasantly situated than they would probably be, but I never before realized so fully what it was for the poor fellows to be separated from home and friends until thus brought home to me. As soon as we recovered from the shock occasioned by the tidings we fell straightway to work renovating the cast-off undergarments of the boys as requested. Cousin Sue had some sewing to do for Cousin George and, therefore, went down to Rose Hill that she might have the benefit of the sewing machine there.

Benton Roy came over between eleven and twelve and sat a short time—looked badly. He told us the boys would be up to see us before they take their departure. Thank goodness! We will have the pleasure of once more having them together with us under the old homestead roof for a short time though it be.

January 28, 1862

Mrs. Morehead and her brother, Dr. Rixey, came in about four o'clock and after tea Benton came also and remained till after the cars went out when he went over to get the news. Found upon closer acquaintance that he was really much more sociable than I had fancied him in the morning yesterday, then I thought, like most of the boys who had been in the army, that he had become so pugnacious that he could talk, think, or breathe nothing but war and military. It's so stupid when that's the case.

We went to the office but heard nothing from the boys. Neither was there any news by paper.

January 30, 1862

A very disagreeable winter day, snowing and sleeting. Resumed my teaching this morning with Nellie as assistant. She has not been to school this week and consequently I have not been so lonely as usual, though I did feel right blue today attributable to the snowy weather and physical indisposition. Nellie and I had a nice long practice on the piano before tea and after tea prepared ourselves for a game of backgammon when Benton was announced. He had come over to say good-bye preparatory to leaving in the morning—looked sad, seems to be grieved to see his mother's distress at his going away from her. We had a long old-fashioned talk and quarreled a little, and I played and sang a little, then about nine o'clock he left to go to the cars. Nellie and I played our game of backgammon until the cars came in when we went out to watch for the boys who did not come, neither did they write. I do feel so anxious about them. Irvie promised he would write before he came up and I hoped he would. Tomorrow, certainly they will come unless something unusual has occurred to prevent them. Patience!

January 31, 1862
We none of us heard the cars come in at the regular hour this morning and so concluded they were detained by some accident. Sure enough about nine o'clock we saw a crowd assembled at the depot and heard the whistle of the cars. Saw Benton in the train as it passed by and he waved to us. The engine had gotten off the track, which caused the detention. Father went over to the cars at about ten o'clock. We saw him coming up the yard with the lantern, though we could not distinguish any of his companions. Out we rushed and found ourselves in the midst of them—Alvin and Irving and Cousin George W. Oh, it was a happy reunion!—and we sat up until after twelve listening to their accounts of "adventures by fire and flood" by their companions. They met Benton en route for Centreville and when he learned the general and his staff had left there he concluded to return home with them. I think the poor boys all look pale and haggard, but I hope a few days at home will restore them. They have all, excepting Irvie, a furlough until Monday—he is to spend a day in Richmond and will therefore have to leave here a day earlier. Oh, dear!

February 1, 1862
It snowed this morning, but we were all too happy indoors to heed the wild play of the elements without. I was up early and had a fire in the parlor. After breakfast we adjourned to Ma's room and we had a thorough review and renovation of the boys' trunks and respective wardrobes—a mighty task it proved occupying us 'til dinner time. Meanwhile Uncle Tom came in and carried Irvie home with him—Cousin George leaving at the same time. Cousin Bettie Richards of Riverside came in to dinner, Irvie also returning, we had a merry meal of it. After dinner we all went into the parlor and sang and played for the boys and then Ma, Nellie, Laura and myself sat down and had a nice cozy chat with them all to ourselves. Had not enjoyed it long though when the door opened and Messrs. Roy and Williams were announced and very soon after, Cousin Will Cloud was ushered in and Cousin Bettie came from downstairs, so the room was pretty well filled and such chattering as they kept up. It reminded me so much of last winter when the same pleasant circle gathered about the blazing hearth in light-hearted enjoyment, and then when they all gathered about the piano while we played it seemed so natural I could almost imagine the wheel of time had been reversed and we were re-enacting the pleasures of that memorable winter of '61. I was so provoked because too hoarse to sing as I wished. What a queer piece of humanity Scott Roy is—I like him, but can't exactly understand his varied and variable moods—this evening he was sarcastic and humorous, gave a very graphic description of camp life before he left and seemed very sociable, and then took his departure

with the others at five o'clock without so much as a bow or a good-evening. I do believe I like him for his eccentricities for they afford considerable variety in the study of his character and constantly lend piquancy to that study. If I could only get some clue to his disposition.

A very amusing incident occurred just as Irvie was projecting a sky rocket (it went around the corner of the west end and frightened all the colored folks looking on) which kept us all in convulsions of laughter until M. left. But notwithstanding our lively enjoyment of the fun, I cannot help but wish we could have had the boys more to ourselves and have had more unrestrained intercourse with them. Dear fellows! It's the last time they may be together with us for a long, long time and I do not feel as if I had had any of their society at all. Poor Irvie looks unusually sad tonight, more so than the fact even of his departure tomorrow would account for, but he will not acknowledge that anything troubles him or that he's unwell. He went over to the cars tonight and returned after tea saying he and Benton would certainly leave in the morning. So we have been sitting up with him till after eleven, making some final preparations and having some farewell talk with him, bless him!

February 2, 1862

Was up at three o'clock to see dear Irvie off and when the cars passed by went out on the pavement to wave the light to him. It was hard to see him go away from us looking so depressed and unhappy—I know I shall think of it enough after he's gone—perhaps he is more unwell than he would have us believe. Oh me!—tomorrow Alvin goes too.

Cousin George Williams came in to spend the evening and make arrangements for their departure tomorrow. They were in a dilemma as Irvie went down this morning unaccompanied by Colonel Jordan, chief of staff to Beauregard, and did not send home their transportation tickets as he expected to have done.

Thomas Jordan later became a brigadier general.

They finally concluded to go over to the cars in the morning and see Colonel J. and advise with him. Benton Roy did not go down this morning as he had expected to do.

February 3, 1862

Alvin went over to the cars at four o'clock this morning and soon returned stamping the snow from his feet and shivering with the cold. He had seen Colonel Jordan who told him that he would go on to Richmond and remain there two days which time Alvin might, if he liked, spend at home! Benton went on with the colonel and George went to the junction where he would procure tickets for Alvin and himself and return tonight. I am so glad George is coming back. He has already improved so much on nearer acquaintance that I am glad to have an opportunity of knowing him better. We hovered about the fire all day listening to Alvin's merry account of the sayings and doings of the mess at Centreville, and reading, laughing, and singing. It was altogether a very pleasant day. In the afternoon A. walked over to town with Cousin Will. We all sat in Ma's room, Father and I listening to Alvin's interesting conversation and Nellie and Cousin Will playing draughts and backgammon until late.

February 4, 1862

Went into the parlor with Nellie this morning and commenced playing and singing when the door opened and entered Cousin Will, Alvin, and George who had arrived last night after we retired and unknown to us. He reported Irvie well, but very much vexed at having missed connection with the Richmond train. After breakfast Cousin Will left, Alvin went to resting and George and I played backgammon and draughts until eleven o'clock, and then I commenced making a cap, which I finished by the time he came over after tea and for which I received his gracefully expressed thanks. How I have enjoyed this last day of Alvin's stay at home, we were all well and with nothing to mar our happiness but the thoughts of tomorrow's separation. Mr. Brerwood came in at twilight to tell him good-bye and wish a pleasant journey. George came in about nine o'clock while we were sitting about the fire and thereupon he and Alvin commenced a running fire of retort and repartee which lasted until they unwillingly took leave for the night. Poor Alvin! He does all he can to conceal his reluctance at leaving.

February 5, 1862

Was up at three o'clock this morning to see our travelers off. They came in and sat with us a few moments and then with warm farewells and hearty good wishes they left us in the house very lonely.

I had the recitations to hear and then spent the remaining part of the forenoon in reducing my writing drawer to some appearance of order. Henry B. came in at eleven and remained until about three o'clock in the evening. We all had a social confab and altogether he seemed more natural than I have known him since he came home. I do wish I could comprehend him, that I might know if he is really as cold and cynical as he seems.

Cousin Will C. came home from school with Laura this evening. The latter said that Mr. Brerwood with some friends would be over after tea. Had a fire made in the parlor and whiled away the evening playing backgammon with Cousin W. and singing and playing on the piano. The guests were not forthcoming to my great satisfaction, for I felt neither particularly bright nor agreeable.

I have thought so much of the dear absentees today and each hour I have wondered where they were, what they were doing and missing them so much all the time and longing for another season of happy communion with them. O!—when will that be ever again. When! When!

February 8, 1862

We fully expected to hear from the boys tonight and what a disappointment it was when our eager inquiries were answered with the, "No letters." We sat up late—twelve o'clock laughing and talking. The news by the papers was very discouraging. The enemy had free access to the Tennessee River and there is no knowing when their ravages will cease. I trust that their occupation of Fort Henry may not enable them to interfere with the sailing of boats between Kentucky and the Southern States.

> *On September 13, 1861, Maj. Gen. Leonidas Polk, C.S.A., seized Columbus, Kentucky. Brig. Gen. U. S. Grant counter attacked by taking Paducah, Kentucky.*
>
> *Early in February, Commodore Foote, U.S.A. and Brigadier General Grant moved up the Tennessee River and after a naval bombardment, Fort Henry fell on February 6, 1862. Its garrison moved to Fort Donelson on the Cumberland River.*

Sunday, February 9, 1862

Was so uneasy at not hearing from the boys—will not probably hear from them now until they reach Columbus, Kentucky. By eleven o'clock my feelings were wrought up to such a pitch that I stole upstairs to indulge in a good cry. Felt better after that and went downstairs to try and make myself agreeable. Uncles Tom and Mack were there discussing the perils of the times. Took a walk all by myself about sunset. Went down to the creek and stood upon the bare rocks looking down into the water where were reflected the dull gray of the sky, the dry rustling grass and leafless trees among the branches of which the wind sighed so mournfully in low fitful gusts. It was a dreary scene and harmonized well with my own sad spirit, but I really enjoyed it as though I had been holding communion with a congenial friend—and felt better on returning to the house. Had a little chat with Father before tea and read aloud to him until bedtime. Poor Alice!—my heart aches for her tonight as she has had one of her passionate gusts of weeping and it required all our eloquence and soothing united to restore her to anything like tranquility. She has enough to make her very sad and I don't wonder that she thinks the world dark now. I hope there is a better day dawning for her, and I only wish I could do something to dispel the shadows over her life.

February 10, 1862

I was sitting by the fire reading to Father when the door opened and Scott Roy and Charley Richardson came in. Such a time as we had laughing and talking, singing and playing until ten o'clock. Scott seemed so much the boy of other days and I felt so easy and unrestrained with him—he's a clever, good boy despite his mischievous propensities. Whilst turning my rings about on my finger, I fractured the little black one placed on my finger with a wish a year ago. Was so sorry for it.

Heard such dreadful news by papers. The Yankees have possession of the Tennessee River and are carrying everything with a high hand in Alabama. They have taken possession of Roanoke Island and threatening Norfolk.

Roanoke Island, off the coast of North Carolina, fell to General Burnside, U.S.A., February 8, 1862.

It is distressing to hear of such disasters and the worst of it is that they are probably but the forerunners of other greater evils, but we can only trust in God for the issue.

February 11, 1862

Was late at breakfast this morning. Alice and I concluded to spend the day at Rose Hill and commenced preparations for an early walk when Walter Buck came in very unexpectedly. Dear boy how glad I was to see him! Said he was at home on two weeks' furlough and intended making his holiday one of pleasure. While chatting with him there was a knock at the door and very soon Scott was ushered in. Came to bring us a letter from Irvie, which was brought the night before by private hand from Richmond. Upon reading it, we found his impressions of Richmond anything but pleasant. Said they would leave the next Sunday for Lynchburg, to rejoin the other boys. S. also brought me the miniature which B. told me he would send from Rd. We had a game of draughts and backgammon and then he undertook to mend my ring and we had quite a romp over it. I am so sorry he is going away tomorrow, and wish he could have been over more frequently during his stay at home.

February 12, 1862

We opened our eyes on a bright morning and were a light-hearted party that met in the breakfast room. Father came in directly after breakfast and brought such an important account of our military affairs that we experienced quite a ... feeling. We started home while the ground was still frozen and the jalking practicable. Saw a stranger riding on horseback along the street—upon his approaching and saluting us several times, I finally recognized Captain Simpson, although his beard has outgrown my recollection. Bowed coolly to him. Found the family rather blue on reaching home. They had gotten the papers the night before giving an account of the extended ravages of the Hessians, their progress southward, etc., all of which depressed them very much. Indeed, the clouds seemed to be lowering very darkly over our country now and a prospect of settlement more distant than ever before. Yet I do not fear for the ultimate success of our cause. I but fear me for the fiery ordeal through which we must pass first. We can only trust in "One Who can give us strength as our day."

> Capt. Robert Simpson (later major) was commander of "Warren Rifles", Co. B., Seventeenth Virginia Infantry. This was the first company of Confederate soldiers recruited in Warren County. Before the war, Captain Simpson conducted a school known as the Front Royal Academy on Crescent Street.

Cousin Mary C. came in late in the afternoon and not long after Mr. Boyd, Irvie's employer, (store in Baltimore.) We were so glad to see him for Irvie's sake and the family assembled in full conclave to welcome him—he made a favorable impression probably as much on account of his evident esteem for I. as for any intrinsic merit of his own. He left us about ten o'clock. Cars did not come in till four A.M.

Sunday, February 16, 1862
Read aloud to Father a dissertation upon language until he left for church. The walking was so disagreeable as not to admit of our accompanying him. Aunt Letitia Blakemore came in about eleven o'clock and concluded to remain several days. Allie and Mr. Hoblitzell came in while we were at dinner and stayed until about four in the afternoon. Then Dr. Dorsey came in and sat some time. Went upstairs and had a nice long dreaming spell for myself. Heard Emma repeat the "Raven" for the first time this evening.

Latest advices from the seat of war announced a glorious victory at Fort Donelson—the enemy repulsed upon every side. We were on the qui vive for another attack at the latest dispatches.

> On February 14, 1862, Fort Donelson's guns drove off the Federal gunboats, but the fort fell after four days of siege on the sixteenth to General Grant. Richmond had received news of the first day of battle when the Federal gunboats were driven off and the South rejoiced with a victory.

February 17, 1862
Papers bring a full account of the victory at Donelson, but the conflict has been renewed. We have evacuated Bowling Green and the enemy shelled and burned the place.

> The whole line across Kentucky gave way after the fall of the forts on the Tennessee and Cumberland rivers. Bowling Green, Kentucky, fell February 14–15, 1862. Gen. Albert Sid-

ney Johnston retreated to Murfreesboro, Tennessee; Nashville was occupied by the Union troops.

February 18, 1862

Sewing, reading, and teaching all day. No letters by mail, but there were the sad tidings of the fall of Donelson—learned nothing of the particulars of the unexpected calamity, but 'tis enough to know its capture gives the foe command of the Cumberland River and access to the heart of Tennessee. Another item this, in the "Geng. debt" we are "piling" for the brutal foe.

'Tis strange we hear nothing from the boys and can learn naught of the whereabouts of Beauregard. Trust he was not at Fort Donelson.

February 20, 1862

Was arranging the contents of my "treasury" this morning when Nellie came bounding in bidding Emma and me "guess who was married last night" at the same time answering her own question—"Kattie Boone and Mr. Samuels."

Kathleen Boone and Green Berry Samuels were married February 19, 1862, by the Reverend Robert T. Berry.

What a surprise! The ceremony strictly private, no invitations, no attendants, no kind of demonstration. Well, it does seem strange when I think of my old schoolmates making for themselves homes thus when I cannot learn to regard them or myself as anything but children. Heigh-ho—so wags the world—marrying and giving in marriage unto the end.

Walter knocked at the door—just arrived from Centreville and reported all things well. No letters but most dreadful news by papers. Our loss at Fort Donelson incredibly great, Beauregard sick at Nashville and that city itself menaced by the enemy—and our prospects in Kentucky altogether very dark. Heaven help us!

February 22, 1862

Jefferson Davis was inaugurated provisional president on February 18, 1861 in Montgomery, Alabama. The Confederate capital was moved to Richmond after the secession of Virginia. Elections were held in November, 1861 and he was elected president for a six year term. On February 22, 1862, Jefferson Davis was again inaugurated President of the Confederacy.

The glorious twenty-second!—rendered doubly dear to every Southern heart witnessing as it will the inauguration of our first Confederate president—the establishment of a new and independent government. May the God of nations smile approval upon this, our country's natal day, may He bless and consecrate it and make of us a great and happy people, and may wisdom from on high descend upon the ruler this day chosen to minister over us and may his administration be a happy and a prosperous one!

Walter and Henry came in—the latter left early, the former remained all night. We had such a nice confab together in the twilight, just like those we have so often enjoyed together long ago, talked about my darling Alvin and about himself. I told him how I had thought him so changed and how glad I was to find my mistake. He explained the apparent inconsistency of his behavior to my entire satisfaction. Messrs. B and Hoblitzell came in after tea and Father came home from Capon in all the darkness and rain.

> *Capon Springs was quite a noted resort. It was owned by the Bucks and the Richards. The main structure was burned during the Civil War, but the annex is still used as a hotel.*

February 23, 1862

Raining and dreary. Had a most stupid two hours entertaining the "guard" stationed at the parlor fireplace. They left as soon as it cleared off,—Mr. Hoblitzell bidding us a final adieux as he expects to rejoin his regiment tomorrow. Walter left before breakfast with the promise of returning to say good-bye after awhile. Accordingly about noon in he came with a saucy speech, a kiss and a caress for each of us, and then was gone away in a twinkling. He's a dear fellow to be sure!

February 25, 1862

After Cousin E. and W. left this morning, attended to my pupils. Father again left for Capon at noon. He has gone to remove what he can of bed linen as it is unsafe where it is—will pack the articles in bales and keep them here until he can send them off. In the afternoon I had commenced quite a long letter to the dear boys when Mr. Brerwood came in to protect us in Father's absence tonight. Papers brought news of the burning of the Lynchburg bridge.

February 27, 1862

Had a disagreeable time with my scholars this morning. Mr. Brerwood came in at noon and said there was current in town a rumor that Winchester would be evacuated by our forces—we did not believe it—'twas too startling for credence. In the afternoon Cousin Mary came in and after tea while we were sitting about the candle discussing recent events the door opened and Father walked in—had just returned from Capon—much earlier than he had expected on account of hearing there was sickness in the family. And alas!—he confirmed the report of the evacuation of W. Oh, how shocking! What a calamity it will prove to us. The enemy will then have possession of the railroad as far as Manassas Junction which affords them great facilities for transporting to flank our army or Centreville. Then they could with some justice cry "On to Richmond!" Surely, surely, our condition must be a desperate one to hazard such a movement!—and then the individual inconvenience if they take Winchester our mails will be interrupted and then adieux to letters or papers. Dear brothers, they are so far from us that we shall be unable to hear anything at all from them, and how pillaged and—oh, I can't bear to think of it all.

February 28, 1862
Our president has appointed this day for one of humiliation and prayer and our spirits were very much in consonance with such a decree. Intended going to church, but though I had my bonnet on ready for attending the summons of the bell, Grandma and Father vetoed the resolution in consideration of the inclement weather. We were all sick in consequence of the prolonged fast and retired to bed quite early. The cars did not get in until eleven o'clock and we did not therefore hear from the office.

March 1, 1862
Felt better this morning and was dressing for breakfast when Laura rushed in exclaiming, "Come into Ma's room all of you and hear Irvie's letter read." In we went and there sure enough was a letter from the dear fellow. He wrote from Columbus where they all with the exception of Alvin had arrived safely after many "hairbreadth scrapes." A. had left them at a wayside station en route for Hopkinsville and they had not heard from him since. I very much fear he will have serious difficulty in getting to his place of destination. But we were so rejoiced at getting a letter from them that I would not long harbor the thought of danger to them.

March 4, 1862
Anniversary of the inauguration of the arch-fiend Lincoln and the anniversary of the inauguration of a despotism as atrocious as ever the fair sun shorn upon. Truly will it be a day memorable in the annals of our nation's woes.

Cousin Bettie is in deep distress and not without cause. They have heard through a letter received from a friend that Cousin Marcus and Dick Blakemore were certainly at Donelson during the battle there, and as nothing has been heard from them since, the probability is that they are either killed, wounded, or prisoners. Heaven forbid that either should be the fact, poor fellows!

March 6, 1862
Had Mrs. Morehead and Cousin Mount Cloud with us this morning. Was very unwell all day and consequently felt but little like entertaining

company. We were very much surprised tonight by the entrance of Mr. James LaRue (*stepson of Aunt Cattie, sister of William Buck.*) He and his brother both being invalids had been at home for some time, but they were forced to flee from the Yankees who have possession of Charlestown and were arresting and abusing the citizens generally. We were very much amused until ten o'clock listening to his accounts of affairs in Clark. Cars brought no mail.

March 8, 1862

Had settled myself to my sewing when Cary came in to tell me that "COUSIN JULE was in the other room." In I went and was delighted to see her really there. We were chatting away at a great rate when Father came in bringing a letter from Benton to his mother dated from Jackson, Tennessee. They had been ordered down from Columbus to rejoin Beauregard, who was sick in J. He describes the town as a perfect little paradise—says the party is in good plight and that they enjoy themselves much. It was so thoughtless in him not to have mentioned whether or not Alvin had rejoined them—if he has not done so ere this the probability is that he is a prisoner and that's too dreadful to think of. Oh, if Irvie would but write!

Saw a large number of horses and wagons coming from Winchester today. What does it all mean I wonder?

March 9, 1862

Such a day of tumultuous excitement as we have endured! This morning whilst putting on my bonnet for church I heard a knock at the door which I soon discovered proceeded from Mr. Brerwood—he stood there perfectly white and trembling with excitement. Upon inquiring the cause of his perturbation, he said that advices had been received to the effect that both Winchester and Manassas were being evacuated by our troops, who were falling back towards Staunton on the one hand and Richmond on the other.

When we went to church everyone seemed stupified by the intelligence and discussed it in suppressed whispers even in church. Mr. Berry preached a beautiful sermon from the text "Faint, yet pursuing."

The Confederate army at Centreville was in an exposed position and was faced, it was felt, by a better equipped and numerically superior army of the United States. General Johnston was ordered to withdraw and establish a defense line further south. This withdrawal from March 8 to 10, 1862, resulted in the destruction of much needed equipment. The Yankees did not reach Bull Run until March 11, 1862, and did not leave Alexandria until the Confederates had withdrawn.

Jackson's army in the Shenandoah Valley was the left flank of Johnston's command and evacuated Winchester March 11,

1862. He made his camp at Mount Jackson, but in two weeks, March 23, 1862, he was in Kernstown. The evacuation was necessitated because of the Manassas withdrawal.

The "tyrant's heel" will be upon us, but although he may restrain speech and action he cannot shackle the thoughts and feelings that glow within us, and which, like all suppressed flames will burn all the more fiercely when they blaze into actions.

March 10, 1862
Rather a pleasant day—went through my usual routine of teaching and reading.

Regular school classes were held in the homes in those days and were conducted for the younger children by the older and more experienced ones.

Late in the evening Scott came in and sat an hour, said he was going in a day or two to rejoin his regiment although not yet fit for service—feared to remain lest the Yankees should dash in and capture him. We went into the parlor, had music—singing some of our old songs that served to remind us pleasantly of "by-gone hours." Scott was so like himself and so like the nice fellow he really is, we enjoyed his society very much. Left promising to call and say good-bye tomorrow.

March 11, 1862
Charley and Nannie Buck came in, the former to say good-bye previous to leaving for the army. Poor fellows!—'tis so hard for them to be forced to flee their homes for fear of imprisonment, to be forced by such a villainous crew of cowardly Yankees.
After Charley went away Cousin Mary and Emma Cloud came in and they seeing us equipped for the walk insisted on our going and leaving them here to "make themselves at home." So we had a merry walk to town, Nellie, Nannie, Scott and myself—first went to pay my bridal call on Kattie Samuels. Found her in her room dressing for dinner—she was looking well—full of chat and is evidently of the opinion that all the virtues pertaining to manhood are concentrated in one individual—that individual Mr. Samuels. Ah!—well-a-day. I hope she may ever think thus but I feel sad to hear young brides indulging in such bright anticipations as these—I think of the contrast between married life as they imagine it to be and married life as they will find it to be ten years hence.
From Mrs. Boone's went to the hotel to see Miss Pollie Haynie—was seized on my way by Alice S. and Belle Boyd who insisted on carrying us captive into the parlor—made our escape but were recaptured in Miss Pollie's room and forced in self-defense to comply with their request to sing and play. Our audience consisted of Dr. Dorsey, the young physi-

cian and some of the ladies—made Dr. Blackford's acquaintance—not at all favorably impressed. Fannie Stewart and her father leaving tomorrow for the South fleeing the enemy. Will write to the boys by them to be mailed at some intermediate point. The cars have ceased running to town and we have no other way of sending letters now than by private hand.

My visit to town saddened me so—there was so much excitement—each one has a different tale to tell, a different opinion to advance, but all agreeing in one particular viz—in being as wild and as insane as possible. Among other rumors they had it that General Beauregard was dead—don't believe it though just because Dr. Kennedy told me.

Father came home about four o'clock P.M. He was directly from Strasburg and stated that the wires had been cut between that place and Winchester, but seemed to think the citizens unnecessarily alarmed as Jackson was still in W.

Heard a rumor of a victory achieved by Price in Missouri. Also a successful brush by Magruder at Newport News. Hope it is true.

March 12, 1862

Bright morning. Emma, Ma, Laura and Willie went down to Rose Hill and soon after they left Mr. Richards called by to say that Jackson had fallen back from Winchester and the enemy were in possession of the place—one of the river bridges had been burned. So we might look for our guests expectant any day. Eliza Hope came in to sit with us in the morning, but was very soon summoned home. In the afternoon Nellie and I made some preparations looking to the advent of the Yankees. We opened our writing drawers and had a general review of old letters and notes—burning some and putting others in a place of security (*tied in packages and hung from wire hoops in their skirts*.) Such a time as we had with these pleasant mementoes of a happy past—with the souvenirs of absent friends, miniatures, locks of hair, faded flowers, little poems, etc. While surrounded with this heterogeneous mass, a rap at the door was followed by the entrance of Scott—his face flushed and eyes dancing with excitement as he exclaimed: "Good news!" "Guess what it is!" Not being Yankee enough to accomplish this, he told us that the "Warren Rifles" were at Gaines' X roads and that Willie R. had come across from thence home where he would remain a whole day and two nights. Johnston's army was moving across country thru Page—it was supposed towards Staunton. Scott thought as the Rifles would probably go in that direction, he would join them in Luray. While discussing the matter, the little children came running in to say that the "Yankees were coming." Upon looking in the direction indicated, we really did see a cavalry company entering town, but it proved to be portions of Ashby's regiment, and Ma coming home from Rose Hill soon after told us Walter was among them and would be over in the morning to see us. Jackson had retired from Winchester and the Seventh Regiment, being the rear guard, were very near being cut off by the enemy, who had already possession of W. Oh dear, what commotion!

Scott sat until sunset singing and playing with us and then took his final leave—poor fellow. I wonder shall we ever see him again. A Mr. Pendleton from Clarke dined with us today—he is very young and looks so delicate. Has been at home, an invalid, but is forced to flee before the advance of the foe. I am afraid poor fellow he is not very well fitted to endure hardship and privations of an active campaign.

March 13, 1862

Walter came in with such a cheerful face this morning. Gave us a hearty injunction not to be discouraged by present unpromising appearances—assured us "all was well," we would "soon be free" and with a kiss and embrace had vanished like a ray of sunlight. His company is stationed as advance picquet at Nineveh—poor fellow, he deserves a nobler foe than these hound Yankees.

Scotty, Giles, and Charley left for C. this morning as it proved a mistake about the Rifles going to L., they were at C.

Father learned from the paper smuggled in today that Beauregard had evacuated Columbus bag and baggage, and was fortifying Island Number Ten in the Mississippi—can it be true? The reported victory at Norfolk is confirmed—our vessel, the *Merrimac*, sunk two of the Federal craft. Glorious!

> The U.S.S. Merrimac *was scuttled when Norfolk was evacuated by the United States fleet. It was raised by the Confederates March 8, 1862. As the Confederate ironclad* Virginia, *it sank the U.S.S.* Cumberland *and the U.S.S.* Congress *was burned.*
>
> Columbus, Kentucky, *described as the "Gilbraltar of the West," was evacuated by Beauregard's forces on March 2, 1862. The defense of the Mississippi River was to be made at Island Number Ten, sixty miles below Columbus.*

March 16, 1862

Though cold and muddy this morning, we concluded to go to church. Found Eltie, Cousins Mary and Emma there almost alone, it being quite early. Eltie leaned over pew and told that our bogus military governor appointed by U.S. "Pierpont" had issued an edict to the effect that every man within the Yankee lines who refused to bear arms for the North should be arrested and imprisoned—perhaps excuted. This intelligence proved one drop too many in my cup of sorrow, and when they just then commenced singing "How Firm a Foundation," that old soul-stirring hymn, which even in childhood had the power to melt and subdue my heart as nothing did, my heart overflowed with the fulness of conflicting feelings. I cried as if my heart would break. The first tears shed since our army deserted us. It was not fear that affected me so much as pain at the contrast between our present situation and the times when we were wont to hear and sing that old familiar hymn. It used to be my favorite "lullaby" and then it was the strain we brothers and sisters always were wont to sing with united voices when together assembled those Sabbath evenings at dear old Bel Air—an unbroken home circle and so happy. Later, I remembered it as it used to ascend from the congregation collected together in the old church where we all went, still an unbroken bond—still happy. And now—oh, the change! Separated from those dear members of our household by more than mere distance of miles—by circumstances that might well preclude our ever hearing from them again. Our country overrun by our remorseless foes—there we sat, completely in the power of our implacable enemies whom we were hourly expecting—enemies who would pillage and destroy our homes, imprison or exile all our natural protectors and leave us poor females and children defenseless, without the means of subsistence and at the mercy of these St. Bartholomew assassins. Oh, it was all so terrible and everything seemed so much darker than ever before. Cried until relieved by giving vent to long-pent-up feelings and then composed myself to listen to the most impressive and comforting sermon from the text "Let not him that girdeth on his armor boast as him that putteth it off." So appropriate to the occasion and so applicable to the state of our country that it was a whole sermon within itself, and then Mr. Berry made it the source of so much comfort to us. Felt quite calm by the time church was dismissed and after exchanging greetings with our friends came home. Father laughed at the idea of our distressing ourselves so needlessly about the retrograde motion and quite reassured us by saying he was convinced it was a false alarm.

March 17, 1862
Saw Miss Tensia Tyler in the store this morning—she was making preparation for immediate departure. Her brother—Colonel Tyler—with his family were following our army to Culpeper and she would accompany them in their pilgrimage. I felt really grieved at bidding her good-bye with so little prospect of seeing her again for a long, long time and almost wish circumstances admitted of our leaving in the same way.

March 18, 1862
Father had a large lot of Capon cutlery and silver, which he wished to have assorted and inspected so as to be sent off before the arrival of the "land sharks." So Nellie and I went to work and we were busy until four o'clock when Kattie Samuels came in to spend an hour. Father soon entered and told us that heavy cannonading had all day been heard in the direction of Strasburg. We all flocked to the old trysting tree and could distinctly hear each heavy booming report, rolling and reverberating through the mountains—sounding pehaps the death knell of many brave young spirits—aye even those near and dear to us for Father said that

Ashby's cavalry was undoubtedly engaged in the contest and Walter and other cousins were there. I felt as I stood there that I would give anything on earth to know they were safe, and that our cause was victorious. Mrs. M. and E. Hope came running over from home attracted by the firing and wishing to learn from us something of the cause of it. We, of course, could tell them nothing. While standing there talking who should ride up but Dick Bayly. He had "run the blockade" through the Federal line—escaped from Winchester, where he was living comfortably and in comparative safety and come to join the Southern army at this most unpropitious time. How I admire his spirit—and he so young, too. He represents the Yankees as very jubilant over their late successes, but behaving with more moderation than could be expected of them. Had seen Northern papers in which it was confidently asserted that Beauregard was fortifying Island Number Ten and denying the formal report of his death. That's good news at least.

March 19, 1862

The cannonading still continues and everyone believes a sharp conflict is going on—though nothing definite can be learned. Worked steadily until five o'clock when we completed our task and gave it to Dick to carry home with him. He took a final leave of us—expects to join his regiment tomorrow. Poor fellow—how little he realizes the trials and dangers of the service into which he has entered. He seemed so gleeful when he left. Father came in late saying Ashby had received orders to engage the enemy near Woodstock and continue falling back until he decoyed them into the narrow pass in the mountains where Jackson would wait to give them the warmest of receptions. There has been much firing, but "nobody hurt."

> Late in March, the Federals began to concentrate troops around Fortress Monroe at the tip of the peninsula between the York and the James rivers in Virginia. It became evident that McClellan, instead of striking Johnston from the north, was going to utilize the United States navy and advance on Richmond via the peninsula. General McDowell, U.S.A., was to attack from the north. General Banks, U.S.A., was to clear the Shenandoah Valley and join General Fremont moving down from West Virginia and then meet McClellan at Richmond.

March 23, 1862

Muddy and disagreeable, but Father, Nellie and I went to hear Mr. Berry. Ma was with Aunt L. Buck. Immediately upon taking my seat by Emma she inquired what I thought of the "news from Winchester"—was much surprised at my ignorance of any news and proceeded to enlighten me. It seems a soldier had just arrived from Strasburg and he stated that our troops were advancing to that place en route for Winchester which place the Yankees had evacuated—the reason ascribed for their movement was that they were ordered back for the protection of Maryland, where the inhabitants had risen in rebellion against the vandal crew in power there. I laughed incredulously at the rumor—but oh, what a feeling of thanksgiving I experienced when, after church was dismissed, I found that those who were competent to judge credited and corroborated the tale. O, if it be but true! Mr. Berry's sermon was such a good one—the subject, the contest between David and Goliath, in which he so plainly proved the superiority of the physically weak, who rely upon a Higher power, to the might of the strong, who confide entirely in their own strength. It was so comforting.

March 24, 1862

Reading the *Richmond Dispatch*, which, however, contained no items of interest save a very pithy editorial about the bogus neutrality of England. Father told us that Cousins Newton Cloud and Tom Buck had arrived in the neighborhood—had come all the way from Arkansas to enlist and reached the valley by the way of Staunton. How delighted will Emma be!

After night I was sitting alone by the fire thinking of our absentees when Father came in and said that Jackson had been worsted in the conflict yesterday.

> *General Banks' forces had followed Jackson south and thinking that the Confederates were leaving the valley, he began to withdraw to the east. In the battle at Kernstown, March 23, 1862 (Sunday), Jackson was trying to prevent Banks from joining McDowell in the east. Stonewall sent his cavalry leader, Ashby, to strike Shields forces at Winchester while he struck at Kernstown. Kimball's brigade of Shields command repulsed Jackson and the latter retreated up the valley to Mount Jackson.*
>
> *This was the only battle Jackson lost, but it produced the desired results. The troops sent to McDowell were recalled. McDowell was maintained close to Washington for its protection and was prevented from joining McClellan on the peninsula.*

It seemed that he received forged dispatches from Johnston ordering him into Winchester upon the plea that the enemy was evacuating that place to go for the protection of Washington and Maryland. 'Twas a miserable Yankee trick, a trap which they had laid for him, for when our little army of 3000 advanced, it was immediately surrounded by 20,000 of the enemy lying in wait for them. Jackson stood his ground manfully and only retired after killing ten to one of the enemy and losing three pieces of the artillery.

Oh, it is too mean, too contemptible, the petty stratagems to which they must needs have recourse! They cannot meet us in open honorable warfare, cannot subjugate us by force, and so depend upon their Yankee craft and cunning.

March 25, 1862

Had seated myself to teach the children this morning when Cousin Mary and Elizabeth Cloud were announced. Went in to see them and Cousin M. had just commenced telling us the contents of B's letter when Uncle Newton and Aunt Jane entered, and soon after came Emma, Cousin Newt and Cousin Tom, and the latter the same genial affectionate relatives that they ever were. Cousin N. told us he had seen the young Blakemores, not one of whom had fallen at Donelson. Oh, so glad to hear it! After dinner we played and sang a little until Cousins N. and T. took their departure and then Cousin Mary, Emma, Laura and myself went upstairs and had a great time concocting a scheme of mischief and revenge. While thus engaged, Ma hastened in pale and breathless with excitement to say that Uncle Newton had just come in bringing intelligence that the Yankees were over the river at Mr. Richards'. Our company instantly dispersed like a flock of frightened pigeons. Father went up to Strasburg today and Nellie was at Mr. Richards', both in the midst of the Yankees, and we were so anxious to have them safe at home again. I felt utterly astonished at the nonchalance with which I heard of the miscreants being so near us—did not experience the least symptoms of fear. I suppose we have so long been expecting them that their advent has become a matter of course. Father came in about five o'clock under considerable excitement—said he was on the pinnacle of Fort Mountain and witnessed the progress of the Yankees down the valley from that point—was once very near meeting them face to face in a narrow defile of the mountain. Just about sunset when patience had waxed threadbare, we were startled by a loud shout and presently in bounded Nellie and Dick waving scarfs and cheering "Jeff Davis." Forthwith they launched into an animated description of the descent of the Yankees—told how they were very near capturing Dick in his Confederate uniform and how they did take poor Mr. Kendrick away from his little sick children and poor delicate wife, leaving them almost heartbroken. They described them as being "men" but anything else than "gentle" men. They have returned to Winchester—am so delighted that they did not cross the "Rubicon" this time.

March 26, 1862

The morning was so bright and beautiful that we could not resist the temptation of spending it in the open air. Emma, Nellie, Laura and myself with Dick, Orville, Allie, Carey, Woodville Moore, Willie J. and Eddie Myers all boarded a nice little truck on the railroad and were soon flying along as if by steam. We spent a most delightful morning—went down to the old "tank" and found some beautiful little white flowers, the first of the season. It reminded me so much of the excursion which we took about this time last year, and the remainder of the pleasures of the morning were much marred by thinking of the difference, the carelessness of our enjoyment then, and the fitful gleams of clouded sunlight that were cast upon our lives now. But our happiness or misery in this world are so often all comparative, for had I not known the brighter, sweeter joys of the past would I not now feel my usual delight in the present—in the dawning spring, for the sunshine is as golden, the birds and brooks sing as musically, the sky is as blue, the air as invigorating as ever it was when such sweet influences used to thrill my soul with exquisite pleasure. I sometimes wonder if there comes to the denizens of this world one single hour of perfect happiness and content. One hour in which the soul does not yearn for something which it has not and cannot have. If there is, I have never known that hour—at least not since childhood.

> *Lucy, although a Christian since she had trusted in, relied on, and clung to the fact that Jesus Christ had paid the penalty for her sins; perhaps had not at this time in her life learned the Christ-controlled life. That life is one in which a person lives moment by moment, step by step, breath by breath, with an attitude of total dependence on Jesus Christ.*

Commenced reading the *Pilgrims of the Rhine*—am delighted with it. There seems to be so little real happiness that I would like to make for myself an imaginary life in the mimic world created by the author's pen. I like to merge my individuality into that of the imaginary characters, enter into all their joys, share their trials and forget the ugly realities of real life around me. 'Tis wrong I know, enervating to the mind and unfitting one for the part which, however reluctant, we must play in the world and in the end creates for us a deal of unhappiness, but, for the present, it diverts one from sad reflections, and I feel that anything is preferable to thinking and fretting over disappointments entirely unavoidable and irremediable.

II

INVASION AND OCCUPATION

March 27, 1862 - May 22, 1862

March 27, 1862
Had a bad headache this morning—taught the children though and then tried a nap without success. Poor Dick came in late in the afternoon to kiss us good-bye, for he's going in reality this time. I could but look at him so young and small going to engage in such arduous duties and endure hardships such as were never dreamed of in his philosophy—poor fellow! I thought it was a hard school for him to learn in. He told us Mrs. R. had a letter announcing the welfare of the boys, that was all.

Henry Buck is at Clover Hill and Cousin Mount at Cousin Sam's sick. Fear the Federals will get him. While we were chatting before the fire, about five o'clock Laura ran in and announced that "the Yankees were coming" as verily there were about forty cavalrymen gallantly cavorting along into town with as much assurance as if they had a right to do it. I do not think we any of us felt the least sensation of fear—every tremor of timidity seemed swallowed up in one great feeling of anger and indignation. We expected though that they would certainly immediately commence a series of depredations, but they did not remain in town over fifteen minutes. Rode up to the hotel and made some inquiries respecting the political sentiments of the people and received the comforting assurance that they were "Sesch" to a man. One, who proved to be the veritable renegade "Porte Crayon" inquired if the Reverend R. T. Berry were in town.

David Strother was known as "Porte Crayon" from his pen and pencil sketches of Virginia. He was from West Virginia

> *and a Union sympathizer. He was attached to the cavalry service and was stationed at Manassas but had been detached and put on General Banks' staff. Before the close of the war he was commissioned a colonel. He led the first Federal troops into Front Royal.*

Being answered in the affirmative, he and the rest of the company raised their caps and hoping that we might "never have a more unfriendly visit from them" said good-bye and decamped. Cousin Mary went home after the exodus. Must go to bed and try to sleep my headache off.

March 31, 1862

This morning was bright and beautiful as yesterday was gloomy. Was hearing the children recite when someone came in and said that the Yankees were down at the mill. We immediately looked out and saw three of the wretches coming over the hill by the icehouse, crossed the meadow, went down to the little footbridge over the creek and stood there taking a leisurely survey of the premises. On our bridge they stood where we have so often spent such delightful hours sitting on it in the twilight looking at the creek shimmering in the moonlight and gemmed with the stars—stood there with as much assurance and composure as if the place belonged to them. We were so provoked at their coolness. They went on up the mill road to town. After dinner I was in Ma's room rocking the baby in my arms and singing "Maryland" in no suppressed tone and the Yankees came up on the porch step. We were determined not to let them see us—so peeped out of the window and saw two of them sitting on the porch and one leaning against the pillar, looking so insufferably, coolly impudent that I would have liked to have shot them. To think that they should dare come here and pollute with their footsteps the dear old familiar home-spots sacred to the memory of so many dear associations! They requested something to eat, and though we would have rather given them a "stone or a serpent" than the "bread" they asked—yet we were in their power and dare not refuse them—spread for them a very frugal meal for which they had the hypocrisy to thank Father. Doubtless they were overpowered by their debt of gratitude. Mr. Brerwood came in and he and Father subjected them to a regular cross-examination which they endured with commendable fortitude. Certainly their faces do bear more ineffaceably the impress of their characters. I never yet saw the traces of low cunning and beastly ferocity so plainly written on human countenances. They soon departed with many promises of good behavior—of course, they'll keep them (?). After they left, Aunt Bettie came in and Mrs. Moffatt, Julia and Eliza and we had quite a hive of buzzing Secessionists. All left about sunset. Who could have thought that we could thus receive in our midst our deadliest, bitterest enemies without any sensations other than those of rage and curiosity?

April 1, 1862

This month one year ago witnessed the commencement of our horrid war—witnessed the inauguration of all the sorrows we suffer—witnessed our separation from our soldier friends. Will the anniversary of it dawn upon the conclusion of all our troubles—will it restore to us those dear ones in health and safety? Heaven only knows. I had almost said I would wish to lift the pale that shrouds the future and read the record of the coming year, but I would not. "Sufficient unto the day is the evil thereof."

Ma, Laura and I went to town—Nellie preferred remaining to superintend the spring cleaning in the parlor. We went first to Mrs. Roy's—found her still in bed, but full of mischief—she taught me the only prayer I can ever offer for Abraham Lincoln.

Sitting by the window we saw five soldiers ride towards us and at first thought they were Yankees—but so soon as they saw us they raised a shout for "Front Royal and the ladies" and called out "No Yankees here." We sprang to our feet as if electrified and moved to and cheered them most heartily. They seemed like dear friends, those brave Confederates and we watched them with straining eyes and beating hearts as long as they remained in sight. They were perhaps the last of our soldiers we should see and seemed to be a tie between us and our army and absent friends, and when they were gone that tie was severed and we felt more than ever forlorn and abandoned.

When we returned home in the evening after tea, they told us the Yankees had all left the river and were gone to Winchester. Glorious! Found on my arrival at home a card bearing "Porte Crayon's" name—an April fool from Cousin Mary Cloud—will retaliate.

April 2, 1862

Father came in to tea; he explained the cannonading heard yesterday. It seems Ashby's cavalry had been hovering about the advancing columns of the enemy until he—Ashby—reached Woodstock when he rode through the place—planted several pieces in the further end of the street opposite to where the enemy would enter, piled bales of straw and rubbish about him and stood waiting their entrance, the inhabitants having been previously warned to remain indoors. As soon as the advance guard of the Yankee cavalry crowded into the streets, he gave the order to "Fire!" and the shrieking, hissing messengers of death dropped into their very midst, killing and maiming numbers of them. In this confusion Ashby ordered the straw to be ignited and under cover of the thick smoke retired, and by the time they commenced returning his fire, he was, unknown to them, standing on an adjacent hill coolly surveying their operations. Noble and gallant spirit! May he live to reap and enjoy a rich fruitage of success and ample reward for his untiring devotion to our glorious cause.

Wrote a note to "Porte Crayon" and one to Cousin Mary tonight.

April 5, 1862

Willie came up to say that there were "two Baltimore soldiers downstairs, one exactly like brother Irvie." Went down and was introduced to two young gentlemen—a Mr. Barrett and Mr. McCormick of Clarke County, not Baltimore as Willie imagined. They had been at the Virginia Military Institute until within the last week—when reflecting upon the great need the State had for all her soldiers, they took French leave "and came off to join their comrades in the ranks." They had walked all the way from Lexington—spent several days with Jackson's army and were now en route for home where they would remain but a short time before returning to the army. How I glory in such spirits! So young as they are and yet so resolute in discharging what they conceive to be their duty to their country. Mr. McCormick was the prototype of dear Irvie so that I felt that he was like a familiar friend instead of a perfect stranger. The sight of him has troubled the depths of my spirit and created within my heart such a yearning to look again upon the dear absent brother's face. After dinner Nellie and I played and sang for them and they made ready to resume their march promising to call on their return next week. Orville and Cary acted as their guides a short distance. They are apparently nice young fellows and I dislike to see them venture into danger as they are doing in returning to Clarke now

April 9, 1862

Did not wake until late and had quite a scuffle to be ready in time for breakfast. Found the snow eight or ten inches deep on the ground and traveling on foot out of the question. Everything looked lovely—the peach trees were just ready to bloom and each little pink bud was encased in dazzling crystal armor, which produced a beautiful effect where the rays of the sun fell upon them, and the violets, too, looked royally through their gem-like covering. It snowed steadily until in the afternoon. Jule and I went upstairs and had a cozy little chat all to ourselves—a philosophic dialogue—very edifying. After dinner I tried to continue my reading but the girls were leagued against me for a general romp and tried to force me to join them. I was disinclined. They tried to vex me into it, and at last I had to take refuge from them in my room. Threw myself on the lounge and tried to get a nap, but could not succeed. On going down into the parlor again, I found the girls looking very sober. In explanation they said Uncle Mack just returned from town where he heard that Jos. E. Johnston had been ordered to Fredericksburg, where an attack was expected. Uncle Mack was very much distressed and we were all very sad to hear it, but tried to be hopeful and had our usual singing in the evening and sat up until quite late laughing and talking about "old times" with Aunt L. And after going upstairs the girls played a number of pranks that kept us laughing until long after we were in our beds.

April 10, 1862

The sunbeams were abroad early, thus gladdening us all by their enlivening presence. I think I never saw a more beautiful snow scene in my life—the dark pines and evergreens borne down by their fleecy burdens making the woods look like a gigantic encampment with its white tents. And these were mingled with the more delicate and graceful of the sisterhood of trees that looked like cascades of diamonds. 'Twas so beautiful! Some of the girls proposed walking home, but Cousin Mary and I vetoed the wild resolution. Alice and I read steadily all the morning and until three o'clock in the afternoon and finished our book despite the efforts of Nellie and Jule to prevent us. I do not think the work a very profitable one, it's well-written and interesting as giving a very vivid picture of the manners and customs of the people and age and well serves to beguile a weary hour—yet one could be better employed than in reading it. In the afternoon Nellie appeared in the parlor in masquerade and amused us very much by her representation of the invalid North Carolinian just from the "horsepital." This reminded Jule and me that we might costume and we made preparations accordingly, but while sitting at the tea table a servant came in and announced that Rob Roy (*Negro freeman who with his wife Harriet lived in the west end basement*) had brought an open wagon to carry us home in, and said they had sent us word there were two young Baltimoreans at our house. I did not know who to believe they were, but concluded they were some acquaintances. We were a merry party that drove off from the house cheering for "Jeff Davis" and so waving adieux to Aunt L., who stood in the door to see us off. On our way down the mountain we met Uncle Mack who insisted upon our returning to Bellmont with him and wait until daylight for our trip, but we concluded moonlight was preferable and go we would. He told us that news had reached town of a very important victory achieved by Beauregard at Corinth in which he had taken vast numbers of the enemy prisoners and captured eight batteries.

> *Following the Confederate reverses in Kentucky and Tennessee, Gen. Albert Sidney Johnston moved from Murfreesboro, Tennessee, to Corinth, Mississippi.*
>
> *Maj. Gen. Henry W. Halleck, U.S.A. was named a commander in the west. Grant was ordered south on the Tennessee River. Brigadier General Buell's forces in Nashville were ordered to join Grant at Pittsburg Landing in Tennessee.*
>
> *General Johnston, C.S.A. elected to strike Grant at Pittsburg Landing before the reinforcements arrived from Nashville. The Confederates left Corinth April 3, 1862. Rain delayed the march but on April 6, 1862, at Shiloh, the Union army was completely surprised. Gen. Albert Sidney Johnston's forces attacked the Federals on Sunday morning and scored a victory but the Federals received reinforcements from Buell and on the seventh of April held the field. General Johnston*

> was killed on the sixth and General Beauregard assumed command and retreated after the seventh to Corinth.
> U.S.A.... Grant had 42,682 men and reinforced with 20,000 of Buell's men from Nashville; Killed ... 1,754; Wounded ... 8,408; Missing ... 2,885.
> C.S.A....Johnston had 40,335 men; Killed ... 1,723; Wounded ... 8,012; Missing ... 958.

Magnificent, if true! How we shouted and blessed Beauregard! The moon was shining brightly by the time we reached the foot of the first hill and we all commenced singing our tratorous songs, which were ever and anon interrupted by some wild sally or gleeful burst of laughter from one of the party. Everyone seemed intoxicated with the beauty of the night and the pleasure of the ride. We were singing "Maryland" when driving around the hill at Bel Air, and all the family were on the stile to greet us, seemingly as much excited as ourselves. Each one had something to tell, or some question to ask, and such a chatter as we kept up for the ensuing half-hour. There was a saucy letter from Scott to Nellie, enclosing her an excellent parody upon "Maryland." They had heard in camp of the victory at Corinth and were, of course, jubilant. We learned that our Baltimore guests were a young Reed and Coffield—new acquaintances but rebels, who had run the blockade and come over from Maryland to join the celebrated Ashby Regiment. Though very youthful in appearance, the young gentlemen were evidently no novices in the service, having been living a sort of bandit life on the banks of the Potomac for seven months past, and it was most amusing to hear them recount their various escapades while in this guerrilla service—they are shrewd boys, both of them. We gave them "My Maryland" in full chorus and very soon after they departed not daring to remain where they would be so convenient to the Yankees should the latter take a fancy to cross the river at the invitation of some of the traitors in our midst. As they would go to the army early in the morning and offered to mail any letters we wished to send to the Confederate lines, Jule, Nellie and I put on our dressing gowns, drew up a table before the fire, trimmed our "tapers" and commenced writing, although it was near twelve o'clock. Nellie wrote to Scott, Jule to Henry and I to the two "boys." Nellie concluded her incubations half-past twelve, Jule at one o'clock and now, weary and utterly exhausted after writing a long, long letter, I retire at three A.M. 'Tis very doubtful as to our having another opportunity to send letters out.

April 12, 1862
Were all very sober this morning with our reading and sewing. At noon someone came in saying they had seen a gentleman from Jackson's army—he brought news that a dispatch had reached that general from General Johnston, stating that Beauregard had not only achieved a victory,

but a great victory, having taken from 6,000 to 9,000 prisoners, 50,000 stand of small arms with eight batteries. We were perfectly enchanted with the glorious news, which, if true, must prove a great thing for us.

April 13, 1862

Ma and Father came home at eight o'clock. Ma had seen a *Dispatch* in which the late battle of Corinth alias Shiloh was discussed—'twas no defeat on our part. Beauregard did gain a victory and only retired from the battlefield at Shiloh to his entrenchments at Corinth. Good—he may still be victorious!

Walter came in early this morning and told us an Irishman had taken prisoner a Yankee courier down at the "Y" and sent him on to General Jackson. It does me so much good to see Walter. He is so cheerful, so sanguine of success that his very presence inspires me with renewed confidence. He confirmed the news of the victory at Shiloh, which was a very important one though not so great in results as was at first represented. He was busily talking when Jule and Neville entered. They said they must start home immediately as the Yankees were reported only six miles distant and expected in town every hour. Walter laughed very much at the idea of our feeling so anxious about him, saying he defied them to take him if they would only give him a mile's start of them. Walter and Jule both left about eleven o'clock and then, the weather being so tempting, Ma went to town to spend the day. Amused (?) myself renovating my summer wardrobe, as I see no prospect of having it replenished this season. Mr. Berry dined with us and I had to preside at the table. Went in the parlor to practice after finishing my sewing when little black Mary came in with a note from Aunt Bettie begging us to spend the night with her, and as an inducement said that Cousin Sue was there. Found upon reaching there, not only Cousin Sue, but two young soldiers, members of Ashby's cavalry, who had been on very dangerous service and very daring in scouting in the enemy's lines. One of them, Lieutenant O'Ferrall (afterwards governor of Virginia from Jefferson Co.,) I had heard of before through Alice Morehead—the other, Mr. Hunter, I knew nothing about, but they were both very gentlemanly and the best of Southerners. A young friend of theirs, whom they designated "Captain," hurried in at nine o'clock and warned them to leave as the enemy was expected in during the night and would certainly discover and take them. But they were not to be frightened out of comfortable quarters and said that as it was raining they had no fears of unwelcomed visitors—so their advisers departed as they came. Cousin Sue and I jestingly offered to mount guard for them, but they, of course, declined the sacrifice, and after some hours of pleasant conversation they retired. Cousin Sue and I, however, lying awake a long time having an old-fashioned confab.

April 17, 1862

This morning while dressing heard that a cavalry company had been quartered in town during the night and could see their horses picketed in the depot lot. After breakfast they rode by the house en route for Harrellsville. 'Twas such pleasure to wave to and cheer brave Southern boys! Walter soon came in to say that Bowen's were in town—presently a sick soldier came in to rest and recuperate. After the company which passed this morning (Captain Gilmore's of Clarke) returned and quartered in town for the remainder of the day

> *The exploits of Captain (later to become Major) Harry Gilmor rivaled those of Mosby as an independent cavalry leader. Gilmor was captured twice. In 1862–1863 he was imprisoned for five months and upon his release raised a cavalry battalion. In 1864 he headed the advance of General Early into Maryland and raided north of Baltimore. In the latter months of the war he was again captured and held until the end of hostilities.*

Two of them came over to get their dinners and I did enjoy waiting on them at table—for ragged and unpolished though they might be, they were yet our defenders and protectors and perhaps the last Confederate soldiers we should see. The day was one of great excitement—running to the door every few minutes to wave to the scattered detachments of scouts constantly passing to and fro—each time thinking that the next soldier we should see might be a foeman—'twas no wonder that we looked wistfully and sorrowfully for our own men. Walter was over three times during the day, and then about twilight came in, took a hasty supper, spun us some camp yarns and was off again on some mysterious and I knew dangerous expedition. Went in the parlor after he left and played and sung—recalling the anniversary of the night when we first were startled with the intimation that the Virginia troops would be the next day called to gird on their swords for the contest. The sick soldier returned to stay overnight and he amused us much by his account of the Battles of Manassas and Kernstown.

April 18, 1862
Were out early this morning to see the return of our picquets when Walter dashed up to the stile and begged for a bit of breakfast—had been out all night with Gilmore's company—walked six or seven miles through the "Forks" seeking a detachment of Yankees who had been the day before pillaging there—but the birds had flown and their toil and trouble were of no avail. Walter seemed worn out with the fatiguing walk and loss of rest and went to bed and slept until ten o'clock. Uncle Mack came in at noon and said that Jackson was falling back from Mount Jackson because of the insufficiency of his force. Oh, it seems every day that our desertion by our army seems more and more inevitable, but we must trust to Providence and under Him to our generals.

> *Gen. Joseph Johnston and his army of 56,500 men retreated
> from Yorktown to a position to better defend the peninsula.*

Could hear no confirmation of the reported victory gained by Johnston and Magruder at Yorktown. Oh, for a Richmond paper! Was very unwell all day—got cold working in the garden yesterday evening. Sat up as long as I could and crept up into Laura's sanctum where I lay down thinking so much of this day a year and of the changes since then, a sad, sad year it has been to many hearts. This was the day year that so many dearly loved relatives and friends left us in the bloom and glow of high-hearted, fresh-feeling youth and who might never be as they have been to us. Our merry-hearted playmates will be all gone, and in their stead we shall welcome home stern, war-worn soldiers. We shall never any of us be the same as we have been. Do I not know how gradual and yet how such a change this comparatively short season has wrought in me—because not physical, the alteration may be imperceptible to others —but none the less sure and marked. And alas!—'tis not for the better —for I grieve for the loss of a freshness and buoyancy of feeling which the progress of the year has swept from my heart as a rough step brushes the dew off the flowers. The blossoms are apparently unimpaired in their loveliness, but, deprived of the refreshing, cooling drops, that lent them such a charm, they soon wither and fade. I wonder if the boys remember this day.

> *The attic room's plaster ceiling served as an autograph spot
> for the friends and family of the Bel Air household. Many
> valiant soldier signed his name there before going to war.
> These signatures are plainly legible today.*

Was hastened downstairs by hearing Nellie and Laura exclaim "Why, Dick!" in accents of glad surprise and going down found Dick Bayly our youngest soldier seated in Ma's room. So glad to see him—did not tarry longer than to tell us how he was pleased with the service and give some account of his adventures in camp and field. This, too, is an anniversary memorable for the great riot in Baltimore.

> *On April 19, 1861, the Sixth Massachusetts was on its way
> to Washington. Southern sympathizers erected barricades in
> the streets of Baltimore and the troops had to fight their way
> through. At least nine civilians and four soldiers were killed.*

Tried to be well enough to pursue my usual routine of duties, but was soon forced to go to bed where I remained until the afternoon, when feeling better, I went downstairs. Walter rode up in all the hard rain to bid us good-bye, as he intended returning to camp with Gilmore's company when they came back from their picquet duty. He laughed and told us an adventure which he and Lieutenant O'Farral had just had. They heard, it seems, that the Yankees were crossing the river at the mill and they concluded to try and bag a prisoner and started off together. Upon reaching the hill overlooking the ford, they saw four of them on this side of the river, two on horseback and two in the boat just pulled up to the shore. Walter flung his reins into O'Farral's hands and leaping to the ground ran nearer the river and fired—but as he had nothing of longer range than army revolvers the ball fell short of its designation. The Yankees, startled by the report and thinking there were, of course, more than two men among their assailants, made for the river throwing their very guns in the water, so frightened were they and one even left his overcoat on the bank. Walter ran down to the bank and fired again, and this time, although the boat was near the middle of the stream, the ball just whistled by the ear of one of the voyagers. He shouted to them assuring them that they were only rebels, two of them, and entreating them for an opportunity of making a horse by the encounter. They replied by a shower of minnie balls from their long range rifles—five more Yankees having joined the fugitives who had reached the opposite shore. They fired volley after volley, but their balls whizzed harmlessly by our brave boys. By the time five or six Confederates, who had heard of the skirmish, came up, the Yankees were gone. Those who from a distance witnessed the firing said they were firmly convinced that Walter bore a charmed life else he could not have escaped being shot. He did not tell us all this, but we heard from those who saw the whole affair—he did tell us though how mortified and disappointed he was that he did not capture one at least of the miscreants. We were anxious to have him leave immediately before the Yankees (who were daily expected) should come in, but he resisted all our entreaties—said that he could not leave Gilmore in such a predicament as he was in—cut off from every avenue of egress to our lines and a perfect stranger to the mountain by-paths. 'Twould be discourteous and cowardly in him—he must wait for Gilmore at any rate. When he said this, we said never a word more, and I was secretly glad of his decision. Brave, generous fellow! We may well be proud of him.

April 21, 1862
Still raining. Played for Emma and Walter after breakfast until the latter said he would go to the river and make enquiries for "that overcoat the Yankee left" him and be back in a little while. Soon after he left Gilmore and his whole company passed the house, bringing with them some half dozen captured horses and a brace of the Yankee captives themselves. The captain was mounted upon the most superb charger I ever saw—paused at the gate to enquire if we had any commands to be executed in the Confederate lines—then bowing, turned the head of his noble steed and rode on in front of his braves. How enthusiastically we cheered them and waved our Secession scarfs and how they shouted

and cheered in return! They had been 'in eight miles of Winchester and escaped to a man. I suppose Walter has gone with them and we won't see him anymore—it is sad enough to think of indeed.

April 22, 1862

One of Ashby's cavalry—a young Mr. Sowers of Clarke—dined with us today —was talkative and sensible and we spent several hours very pleasantly listening to his recital of the various individual incidents that came under his cognizance. Bade him adieu with regret and watched him as long as he remained in sight, for verily he is the last of our soldiers we shall see. Jackson is moving towards Richmond and the valley is fairly evacuated. Well it is hard, but I suppose we might as well submit with a good grace to the varying fortunes of war.

April 23, 1862

Mrs. Cook came in about nine and sat till near noon—says our latest advices treat of another and more decisive victory on our part at Yorktown. But we did not believe it. Dr. Dorsey dined with us and croaked like a very bird of ill-omen—said Island Number Ten was certainly taken and that we had lost very heavily in the engagement; that the enemy had possession of Fredericksburg, where they had burnt our manufactories.

> *Island Number Ten in the Mississippi River surrendered on April 7, 1862.*
>
> *The surrender was brought about by the combined operation of the Union army under Gen. John Pope and gunboats under Flag Officer Foote. The surrender was on the same date as the Confederate retreat from Shiloh, Tennessee.*

Confusion! Ma and Grandma were already very low-spirited and hearing this they were literally submerged in the "Slough of Despond." As the day was so fine, Nellie and I concluded to go to Mountain View. We took Cary with us and had a delightful walk through the woods, gathering wild flowers and mosses. Found all well and received a hearty welcome. Aunt Bettie came in from Mrs. Wheatley's and took tea with us. Uncle Newton came in from town and told us a great deal about the depredations committed by the Yankees in Fauquier. After tea they were discussing a bill from the Federal Congress for the confiscation of all Secession property in the hands of their troops. If it be passed there's no telling the awful consequences that will flow from it. The ruin and exile of hundreds of families and our own large family of little children. Oh!—it has depressed and troubled me more than anything I have yet heard—my heart feels so sore and heavy with the thought of it.

Mr. Fristoe will run the blockade and go to Richmond tomorrow, so Nellie and Aunt Jane wrote to Charley and sent the letter by him.

April 24, 1862

Found it very cloudy and threatening this morning. Cary left after breakfast and then Cousin Sue took us up to her bookcase and gave us a carte blanche invitation to its contents. Nellie laid violent hands on some periodicals and I took down "Shakespeare" and Tennyson's *Idyls of the King* to read, while Cousin Sue was engaged with the children's lessons. Had been long wishing to read these *Idyls* and never had the opportunity before. How I enjoyed the poems so peculiar in style, so quaint in expression, so much freshness and beauty of thought—altogether so unique and charming. Finished before dinner. Willie went to town this morning and returned with the news that the Yankees had been in town and taken Mr. Fristoe prisoner. So!—the villains will have the pleasure of reading Charley's letters—if they do, they will not be the first who have made good the old adage "Eavesdroppers never hear any good of themselves." They did not tarry long, but went away carrying with them Mr. F. and two horses, which they somehow managed to get from Uncle Fayette.

April 26, 1862

Warm this morning and a prospect of a clear day. Dressed quite early and went out into the porch and sat a long time listening to the birds just beginning their matins as the sun drew aside its cloudy curtains and beamed forth on the world. Everything was very peaceful and lovely—the mountains just beginning to wear that soft, hazy vernal appearance they always present when the forest trees are in blossom and the fields and meadows spread with their first emerald velvety turf. But 'twas not of the present so much as of the past that I thought. The twenty-sixth of last April witnessed the departure of our dear boys and the presentation of the Warren Rifles Flag to the little band, leaving home and loved ones to battle in their defense.

> *Warren Rifles, Company B., Seventeenth Virginia Infantry was organized in Warren County, Virginia. Front Royal is in Warren County.*

What a thrilling address made by Mr. Cook as he placed the standard in their hands—what tears responded to it—what farewell embraces and kisses, what warm, firm grasping of kind, true hands that were clasped perhaps for the last time—the piteous wail that went up from the sorrowing hearts of the multitude, who witnessed the departure of their dearest and best on earth. The tears that coursed down rugged, furrowed cheeks, all unused to such baptismal. The bright drops that bedewed the faces of the young soldiers themselves—drops that were an honor to their manhoods—not weakening their resolve, not unnerving them for duty, but attesting their heart-felt appreciation of the love of kindred and country—the priceless value of the things they were to contend for. All this

I thought of all this day and felt thankful that I could review the campaign upon which they entered with pleasure and pride, for not one of those we loved had proved recreant, not one fallen by the hand of the foeman. It was more than we could have thought or hoped for. Just then the soft notes of a flute floated out on the morning air and mingled with the bird songs so plaintive and sweet the melody that I could not repress a gush of tears. Cousin Sue came out and proposed a promenade down the walk and by the time we had taken a few turns the breakfast bell rang.

April 27, 1862

Fine bright morning. Uncle Mack, Mr. R. and Kattie M. here early. Had our bonnets on to start to church when they said the Yankees were coming—went out on the stile and saw them march in—a file of infantry with their bayonets glistening and arms flashing in the morning sun. But for all their fine accoutrements they were a hard looking party to judge from the specimens we saw straggling up the railroad. We went to church wearing thick brown veils. Passed one of the vermin on the street with his arms about the neck of a strapping "colored gemmun," and his lips in loving proximity to the lips of ebony. In comparing the two together, I confess I thought the Yankee lost by the contrast. Was too angry and excited to profit much by Mr. Berry's sermon. We had vowed not to let a Yankee see our faces, but just after church, while standing in the yard with my veil up, speaking to a friend, a most Satanic looking Yankee passed and looked me right full in the eye. It was too provoking, and we very quickly dropped our veils and turned our backs on him.

We could see them all day straggling about so brutally intoxicated that they could scarcely circumambulate. Picquets were stationed at the entrances to town and relief guards sent regularly out, to prove to us, I suppose, that we were regularly invested—rather infested. Uncle Tom came over in the afternoon and told us about three who had been at his house. They asked for "dinner" immediately after their arrival and alleged as a reason for going there that they wished to see the residence of so noted a "Secesh" as "Col. T. Ashby" (of course this was all a romance—they knew Colonel Ashby did not live there.) They then paid very flattering tribute to his prowess, and hoped that he might never be shot as they wished to capture and keep him for a "show." Then they wanted to know if Uncle Tom justified Ashby's course? He replied in the affirmative and added that he also endorsed his son's. At table they behaved like Goths as they are. After dinner one of them sought more congenial society in the kitchen. Uncle Tom proposed that he should return to the house, as in Virginia gentlemen were not accustomed to occupy the kitchen. He and his comrades soon after that departed, remarking as they left that "they liked this part of Virginia so much they intended locating here." At Uncle Tom's suggestion that they should select farms they replied "they had already done so." They announced that the Virginians "were really nice people," not near so "stuck up" as they had imagined.

Ma and I walked up to Mrs. Hope's this evening. Found them all very "wrathy," but withal amused at the uncivilized conduct of the interlopes. Well, one comfort, they've not been near the house today. Some of them said in town today that the Union could never be reconstructed, and they were tired of fighting. I believe the servants despise their deliverers from the bottom of their hearts. Bah! They're greatly their superiors in good breeding.

Accidently broke the philopena ring which was put on my finger with a wish last year. So sorry! Can it be ominous? I could never bear the idea of breaking a ring. Now the wish will never be realized.

April 28, 1862

There were several visitors this morning; Mrs. Marshall and her daughters and Mrs. Moore. Was miserable—whiled away the time reading the Northern papers. It is exasperating to read their "canards" and their poor attempts at wit at the expense of the Confederacy and Secessionists. I wonder if they suppose we are crushed and discouraged because of a few reverses in the tide of fortune. If they do I hope they'll ere long have optical demonstration of the fallacy of their opinions. Father heard that there had been a complete and decisive victory by our army at Yorktown. Oh, for truth! Was very busy helping Ma twist candle wick this evening when Julia Myers and Cousin Mary Cloud came in. Spent a pleasant evening talking over old times and selecting pictures for Cousin Mary to copy. A verdant young Yankee rode to the gate while they were here and asked to have his canteen filled with milk (I hope it'll choke him) was very garrulous and among other things announced that the "hull" of his regiment would soon be in town, and in consideration of this intelligence Cousin Mary and Julia concluded to return home before sunset less they should encounter them on their way. Heard that forty-two of these creatures dined at Clover Hill on Friday and behaved very rudely. Should like to have seen Jule and Aunt Lizzie—know they were the personification of unmitigated dignity.

April 29, 1862

Raining. Heard a low sullen whistle from a locomotive in the direction of the "Y" this morning, and presently a rumbling sound announced the approach of a train of cars. One might have guessed they were Yankee cars by the slow manner in which they came in. Nellie says the whistle was "under breath"—"suppressed and fearful." Suppose they were afraid some rebel guerrilla would hear them, discover that the railroad was repaired and being used and would take the pains to come and destroy the track again. They were evidently cautious, for it took them one-half hour to run from the "Y" to town where our cars used to accomplish the distance in five minutes. It was so provoking to watch the old green

Pennsylvania passenger car as it passed the house crowded with the "azure imps." Don't know anything that has provoked me more than their using for their own wicked purposes the road which cost our state so much time, trouble and money. They were very quiet though—did not make any kind of demonstration over their grand entry as we expected they would, but we shall have more of this anon, I suppose.

After tea, Ma, Nellie, Laura and myself went up on the housetop, thinking to get a sight of the Yankee camp over on the river hill—but found we could not, and it was no great disappointment. Had a glimpse of a most lovely landscape instead—valley, hill, meadows and mountains all looked so charmingly fresh and verdant in their soft spring vestments, and the little "Happy Creek" was murmuring a vesper in unison with the birds, lending interest to the scene, which would else have been all too still and lifeless. After coming down, Nellie and I were in our room revising a song—a parody on "My Maryland," when we heard strange footsteps on the porch below, and presently Ma came up to say there was a Yankee Q.M., down in the dining room drinking milk. It seems that Father heard in town of his having made considerable exertion to protect Mr. Armstead's property the other day when the cowardly rogues were depredating there, so as the young fellow passed through the yard just now, having missed his way to church, Father and Ma, who were sitting on the porch, saw him, and the former thanked him for his courtesy to a fellow citizen and invited him to partake of a glass of milk, which invitation he gladly accepted. Am half sorry that Father should voluntarily offer one of our enemies refreshment, but I suppose it is well to encourage honesty and humanity whenever it is found among them. The Yankee behaved like a civilized being and departed leaving his card, "Daniel B. Hildt," the name inscribed thereon. He professes to be acquainted with Cousin T. F. Blakemore and avers that he is himself a merchant of Philadelphia. Declared himself as very tired of the war, but did not refer to politics at all.

Have rocked the baby to sleep, practiced on the piano and now "welcome Somnus."

April 30, 1862
Ma and I walked over to town this morning with our thick veils on. Stopped at the store at first, then while Ma went up to Mrs. Roy's, I called at Mrs. Cloud's. Found both the ladies at home—spent two hours most delightfully with them on their snug little breakfast room, discussing books and paintings—examined some very fine engravings of Miss Mary's. Then went out to see the flowers in the yard, some of which were in bloom and looking beautiful. Culled a little bouquet of violets, hearts-ease, cowslips and moss and left. Met Ma and Miss Martha Simpson on the street. They told me a gentleman had gotten in last night from Charlottesville, who brought a letter from a friend, who wrote of his having seen the "Warren Rifles" only one week previous.

They were en route from Yorktown in fine spirits and said they hoped soon to "write a bright page" home to their friends. Heaven bless their brave hearts and nerve their young arms to strike a telling blow, for we are sadly in need of something bright and cheering now! Kattie Samuels has a letter from her husband and he writes from Conrad's store near Harrisonburg. So Jackson has not left the valley as we thought—and oh!—who knows but he may come to release us from bondage soon? God grant it.

> *Jackson established himself at Conrad's store on April 19, 1862, as Banks' army moved slowly up the valley.*

We were sitting in the chamber this afternoon, laughing and talking when a slight tap at the door was followed by the entrance of three great uncouth Yankees. Nellie and I kept our eyes upon our work, and did not vouchsafe so much as a glance at the intruders. Ma was afraid our manner might exasperate them and quickly directed them to the sitting room. They wanted their dinners and Father coming in just then carried them to the dining room, where they devoured the food spread before them, for which they offered to pay—just as if they thought we kept "private entertainment." Father declined their pay and told them that there were hotels in town where persons usually went when they wished to contract a bill for boarding—this was customary in Virginia. He did not know how it might be where they came from. That Southern gentlemen never refused a meal gratis to those who could not afford to pay for it. They had scarcely left the house before two or three more of the roughest looking creatures came to "get" their "suppers." Ma had not given orders for that meal and so they said they would wait until it was prepared. I was angry enough to have given them battle—they, Ma and Grandma, would not let Nellie or I put our heads out the door while the Yankees were here, would not let us leave the room and here we were in "durance vile" until that supper was given out, cooked and dispatched. While waiting for it, they told Father that a movement on McClellan's part had disarranged General Johnston's plans at Yorktown, thereby compelling him to fall back towards Richmond and the final struggle would take place between the two places. They also said New Orleans was in their hands and there's only too much reason to believe their tale.

> *New Orleans was occupied April 29, 1862. Farragut had led the way and Gen. Benjamin Butler commanded the Federal army. Butler became known as "Beast," because of his proclamation to the women of New Orleans.*

Oh me!—the cords seem drawing closer and closer about us. Tomorrow a detachment of Geary's men are expected in town, and then martial law will be proclaimed. And oh what next no one can guess. Have just been reading aloud to Father.

May 1, 1862

A disagreeable, rainy, misty morning—congratulated myself upon what I thought would afford us one day's exemption from the troublesome vampires. Vain hope! Was sitting in Grandma's room when we saw a Yankee wagon drive up to Father's barn, and the soldiers accompanying it commenced appropriating the hay therein. We watched them from the window—presently Father appeared upon the scene, and then the wagon drove off and he with a half dozen of the creatures came towards the house. Among them was Hildt, our quondam visitor. Guards were placed around the house and they went to work examining first the granary and then the smoke house. This time, however, they took nothing there being as Hildt averred "nothing to spare" in the way of meat or corn. They will doubtless be back again and reconsider the matter. Oh it was so provoking to see the sentinels pacing the yard as though they really considered Bel Air a prison and we their lawful captives. Father went to town and when he returned told us three thousand of Geary's men would be in about three o'clock and Front Royal would probably suffer. He had just seen one of their lieutenants, who told him that he had always heard this was a "fast place" and that "if the people did not behave themselves very nicely it would be slower before sundown." The wretch! We have heard the fall of New Orleans confirmed. Ah, woeful day for the South! I don't despair of our final success, but there seems to be such a vast fathomless gulf of misery through which we must wade to attain to it. Oh my heart shrinks with dread at the prospect! If I were only prepared for death how gladly would I yield this troublous existence for one of that "Peace that passeth all understanding."

Geary did not come, neither did his men. One night more of grace allowed us. I am utterly worn down—this existence of passion and excitement is wearing away my strength like a consuming fever. When the day closes, I feel as if it had been lived in a perfect delusion. I agree with Nellie that if this state of things continues, I shall burn up with wrath. Heaven forgive me if I sin in it!

May 2, 1862

Sally Davis came in very soon and told us they were going to administer the oath to every gentleman in the place—unmitigated wretches! About five o'clock a hundred infantrymen marched into town, bearing with them their poor disgraced old "Star Spangled Banner." Made no demonstration upon taking possession of the place. Hildt called in to "buy some eggs" in the evening and told that there had been a skirmish between the Yankees and Ashby's men, and also that there was a battle going on at Yorktown, but did not state the results as thus far developed. Ah me!—truly we have fallen upon evil days.

May 3, 1862

Looked out of the window very early this morning expecting to see the "Stars and Stripes" floating over the courthouse, but was most agreeably surprised to find it "non est." Martial law was proclaimed in poor little Front Royal and sentinels stationed at every avenue from the place. Three of Father's servant men who went into town on business were arrested and detained in town until late. When Father attempted to go over to have them released, he was halted by the sentinel and told that he would not be permitted to return home again if he should go within their lines—so he was forced to beat a retreat. I had not been able to get Ma to confess she was angry until from an upper window she saw Father compelled to submit to dictation and restriction thus upon his own premises. She was exasperated then truly. It was a lovely day and we spent the greater portion of it upstairs at the windows from which with the aid of our spy glass we could witness a great deal of what transpired in town during the day. Could see the citizens as they were every now and then arrested by the patrol and marched off to "headquarters." Could see the tents pitched in the courthouse yard and all the bustle and confusion consequent upon the first forming an encampment. Oh but 'tis galling to see them taking such cool possession of our town and our property and figuratively shaking their fingers at us and threateningly telling us—"Now behave yourselves—we're your masters and if you but so much as breathe rebellion against our authority we will consign you to a corner of "Davy Jones' lockers." And we dare not resist so much as by a glance of defiance! When we know too that if one of Ashby's companies should dash in they could bind every Yankee villain of them hand and foot and carry them away over the mountains—for they have neither their artillery nor gunboats here now, and everyone knows a Yankee can accomplish nothing without these.

All day the creatures were calling in or passing by the house, keeping us in a state of continual ebullition, but the climax of our indignation was not capped until about five o'clock when a cavalry company passed and among them we recognized a mulatto in uniform. This boy a short time since had fled from the best of masters and joined these miserable hypocrites. Yes, there he rode at the head of the detachment as grandly as the first officer among them, and he looked as if he felt a savage satisfaction in thus coming back to his old home and lord where he had once served. Yet I should not blame him near as much as I do his instigators. I am so weary and exhausted with rage that I could scarcely drag myself up to my room tonight. Ma tells me it is so wicked to allow my passions to get such an ascendancy over my better feelings, but I cannot help it—it seems as if I am possessed of an evil spirit as well as surrounded by them.

May 4, 1862

To think that although it was so pleasant this morning we could not go to church because of our Christian-like garrison! Saw from the upper porch their Sunday morning dress parade, which took place in Uncle Tom's front yard at Oakley. Poor Aunt Bettie! How lonely she looked standing out on her portico, for all the world like the prisoner she is! There she stood looking through her spy glass at us and we regarding her so wistfully in the same way. Was sitting in Ma's room about nine o'clock reading when I was attracted to the window by the sound of coarse, rude tones addressing Father—and saw three ragged old "Teutons" gesticulating violent and heard one of them say—"But we've a right to know and we will know." This frightened me, but I at once concluded that they suspected Father of harboring some designs against them. Laura just then ran in saying—"Come Lucie, give your testimony!" Stepped into the passage and saw Ma there with Father and she told me these men had been on guard last night and fancied they saw us displaying signal lights to the "Secesh cavalry" in the mountains. Father told them that the baby had been sick during the night, and that Ma had to have a light in her chamber (which was the case) and then taking them into the front yard explained how it was they had seen the light shining through her windows. They professed themselves perfectly satisfied with the solution of the mystery and begged for a draft of milk —this they disposed of with remarkable gusto. They then warned us against permitting any lights to be seen after nine o'clock, as they had been ordered to fire into them wherever seen—advised us to either extinguish them or have very thick curtains over the windows. They had been ordered to fire at the house last night and would have done so but for the kindly interposition of Mr. Seymour, who told them that what they saw was probably a sick lamp, as our family was a large one and doubtless some member indisposed. Now was ever there such cowardice! Soldiers frightened because of a sick taper in an infant's chamber! Veteran warriors. I presume we are to have a revival of old curfew system, but surely such a state of affairs cannot last always.

After the Dutchmen left, I got Butler's *Analogy* and read aloud to Father. Had just become interested in the book when poor Father was called to see another Yankee. This one, however, a young corporal from Philadelphia seemed to be rather better than the generality of his class, and I was very much amused at his conversation, which I heard without making myself visible. He had come to ascertain whether or not there had been any of the previous night's guard over to see about that light —then explained that the sentinels were intoxicated and they imagined they saw such a pyrotechnic display. He remarked that the matter was a subject of entire indifference to him anyway, as he had not come here to fight or for love of the Union—he had been very desirous of traveling and seeing more of the Southern country and thinking a soldier's life would best permit the indulgence of his fancy he joined the army. Professed to have no sympathy or patience with the Abolitionists and said that if they with the turbulent spirits of the South had been hanged long ago, it would have averted all these troubles. He prophesied that Lincoln was the last Republican president who would occupy the executive chair. Father was much pleased with these sentiments expressed with such naivete and upon the strength of it offered him some tracts, which he took saying he would reciprocate favors the next day by bringing him some papers—gave Father his card "Charles McGetigen" of Philadelphia. Well, he does seem more like what a human being ought to be than anyone of his tribe that I have yet seen.

Much to our surprise and delight Aunt Letitia Buck came in while we were at dinner—she had "run the blockade" to church and then succeeded in getting over here. We were so glad to see her as she was the first of our friends we had been able to see since our imprisonment—then she could give us items from town. Uncle Mack she said had attempted to come to church, but they even threatened to shoot him if they ever saw him on horseback again, because "some Secesh" cavalry in citizen's garb had shot some of their men sometime since. Poor Uncle Mack! What is to become of such an active restless spirit limited and confined thus? 'Twill be terrible to him. Poor Father is writhing in spirit under this galling restraint. I can see though he speaks but little he grows perceptibly older day by day—looks already so bowed. Aunt L. also told us that the "Rangers" were reorganized under Cousin Horace Buck as captain, Mr. Simpson, first lieutenant, Mark Wells, second and dear Walter junior second. So delighted to hear it! Soon after Aunt L. left, Julia Hope and Mrs. Moffatt came up and told us Mr. Fristoe had been released and returned home and his captors did not take either his money or his papers from him. Mirabile dictu!

How delighted we were this evening when we saw the tents struck and the whole of Company E. marched out of town. We at once concluded that the whole garrison had been summoned away to reinforce Banks up the valley. But alas!—we were doomed to disappointment for the other two companies remain. Oh dear!—what an unsabbath like Sabbath we have spent!—and yet how could it be otherwise in such excitement.

May 6, 1862

Another morning we've risen in safety to welcome the bright May sunshine! The boys were engaged with Father, so I did not keep school. Ma and I concluded to sit a couple of hours with Mrs. Hope but nothing would satisfy her until we promised to stay and dine with her, as she wanted us to share her peaches and cream with her, and also a cup of real genuine coffee, something of a novelty to me now, as I left off drinking the rye coffee the first of May, thinking our present supply should be reserved in case of sickness and knowing we shall in future be dependent on the Yankees for our groceries—of course, I do not wish to patronize them.

May 7, 1862

Mr. Richards rode up, and while talking to him we saw a fire near the hospitals and at once concluded the Yankees had from caprice or malice fired the buildings. The wind was very high and would blow the flames towards the surrounding houses and then the whole town would be swept. Oh how frightened we were!—and with what intense breathless anxiety we watched the progress of the conflagration—the light gradually diminished though and after all proved to be nothing but a chimney burning and it was soon extinguished. Mr. Richards told us that Jackson had engaged Banks at McDowell and defeated him, driving him back twelve miles.

> *Maj. Gen. R. S. Ewell's division was sent to reinforce Jackson at Swift Run Gap. Jackson's aggregate force was now approximately 15,000. Leaving Ewell's division to occupy General Banks, Jackson moved his men to Staunton.*
> *On May 7–8, 1862, Stonewall attacked Brig. Gen. R. H. Milroy, U.S.A. of Fremont's army at McDowell. The conflict lasted four hours and Milroy retreated to unite with Fremont.*

That was all very well, but alas!—he tells us our prospects are very gloomy in every other respect and we cannot but credit what he says from everything we hear. Thus the horrors that have hovered over me all day have begun to assume a tangible form. Never before have I allowed myself to dream of subjugation, but now when even Father is despairing, I begin for the first time to realize all the perils and dangers of the stormy sea upon which we are launched—for the first time opened my eyes to the awful consequences of subjugation. God knows what is to become of us all—our bark seems fast hurrying against the breakers—if "he does not interpose a strong arm to arrest our destruction we are indeed lost!" Lost! My own dear brothers!

May 8, 1862
This morning Mrs. Moffatt and Eliza came bounding in whispering—"We've such good news for you!" They then repeated the news we heard yesterday with regard to Jackson's victory over Banks and added that General Johnston had surrounded McClellan in such a manner as to completely cut him off from receiving reinforcements or supplies—that the Yankees in town were looking very dispirited and a number of little incidents she related which served to revive our courage no little. Spent the greater part of the day up at the window, reading, sewing and spying. In the evening after tea we walked with Father down to the old mill where I had not been for an age. It really looked like an old half-forgotten friend with its discolored mossy wheel dripping with the cool bright drops that fell into the water below with the same musical unobtrusive tinkle so like I have heard them hundreds of times long ago. Then the weeping willow—how it had grown!—and how like a cascade

of verdure it looked in the soft May twilight with its graceful flow of verdant branches. We stopped to exchange the compliments of the season with old Uncle Ben and Aunt Bettie. On our return found May in the garden with the flowers and we stood there a long time watching the mountain which was burning—it looked beautiful, reminding me of a volcano so liquid seemed the flame and smoke that shot up and hovered about the peak. We admired the scene until the damp evening air admonished us to return to the house.

What lovely moonlight evenings we have now, but alas cannot venture out to enjoy them for fear of lurking Yankees.

May 9, 1862

The day promised to be so beautiful that Ma and I concluded it would be a moral impossibility to stay at home any longer, so we agreed to spend the day with Aunt Bettie.

Cousin Mary took me up to her room and pointed out the encampment just back of the house and I saw how all hours of the day they were annoyed by having the Yankees passing through the yard for water. They're ruining the lot and have actually torn the lining out of Captain R.'s carriage to use instead of curry combs for their horses. All seemed in good spirits though and followed us to the yard, showing us the beautiful flowers and extracting a promise that we would call there again on our way home. Found Aunt Bettie alone, but Uncle Tom soon came in and we discussed the war—Uncle T., I think, is much more cheerful and hopeful than hitherto. He told us among other things that he had seen Benton Roy's name in a paper mentioned as one among other staff officers uninjured in the late southwestern battle. Staff officer to whom? I wonder. "Capt. J. B. Roy." How funny it sounds. But I've no doubt he enjoys this distinction very much. After spending a most pleasant day we left about five o'clock calling at Mrs. R.'s to tell her of Benton's promotion.

Did not encounter a single Yankee on our way home. As we reached the foot of the hill I thought I had never seen anything looking more beautiful about the dear old home. The lilacs in the front yard were literally overwhelmed—bowed down beneath their sweet burdens of rich plume-like blossoms, while the soft evening air was redolent with their perfume. Nellie was sitting on the stile waiting to tell us the good news; she had heard the victory at Corinth confirmed and flattering news from the peninsula. Am afraid to believe it all though. Played some on the piano this evening for the first time in an age. Have been reading aloud to Ma tonight.

May 12, 1862

We were much amused this morning by the arrival of two couriers and a messenger besides from Major Tyndall, the provost, requesting Father to form one of a committee of citizens who were to convene at his headquarters in the afternoon. Good! Instead of Father having to go and solicit of his "Majesty" he is cordially invited to see him. I like this! Mrs. Brown, the housekeeper from the hotel, came over this morning and recited numerous instances of his petty tyranny exercised over them there. She spoke of how isolated and lonely poor Alice felt, so I arranged a bouquet of my prettiest flowers and sent her in lieu of more substantial society.

Father came home before tea and told us all about the furious meeting at headquarters. All the principal citizens were present, the object of the convention being (as Major Tyndall said) to "consider how best to arrange for the mutual benefit and convenience of citizens and soldiers." He presented them with a paper which they were to sign—by this paper they were to pledge themselves not to do anything which would induce a collision between our men and theirs, whereupon all the Yankees were to be withdrawn from the immediate vicinity of town and not permitted in any way to interfere with the peaceful occupation of the citizens. This, upon consideration they concluded to do particularly as they knew how utterly powerless they were to give aid or information to our army, no matter how much they might wish it. Yet, I am sorry for it—hate to think of my father binding himself in any way to the old Yankee's conditions.

May 13, 1862

We were all sitting on the front steps in the afternoon when Father came up and said he had just heard that seven thousand of Shields' men were on their way through here from Luray en route for Fredericksburg and that the long expected Geary was coming too from the opposite direction. No more reading for us. As I felt very dull and unwell, Ma proposed a walk to the creek thinking it would do me good. We went to see a very beautiful little spring which the children had recently discovered (near Kenrich home) gushing in a bold bright stream from the hillside, clear as crystal, and delightfully cool. Played about in the water for some time until Mr. Richards rode by and told us the Yankees were crossing the river, so we hied back to the house and finding our little nook under the lilacs sat there to make observations. A cavalry company came in, but staying only a few moments returned to Cousin E. Richardson's and picquetted in her field adjoining the yard. A number of baggage wagons and some few straggling squads came in also. Father went over town after tea and the little corporal told him that his company (I) would act as guard for the citizens at night against the incursions of the Michigan cavalry whom he represented as a perfect band of outlaws—and offered to come around about nine o'clock to see if any of them were hovering about Bel Air. We sat on the porch in the beautiful moonlight until late. We were just preparing for bed when we heard Martha whisper to her colleague, Eliza Ann—"Oh there's a whole parcel of Yankees right here by the window." The "whole parcel," however, proved to be only the corporal and his assistant whom Father invited down into the basement to take a glass of milk and bread. He tells us that he will patrol the railroad all night so that in case of any disturbance we will only have to call him when he will settle it all. Thus far, all is quiet enough.

May 14, 1862

An ever memorable day to the inhabitants of Bel Air. Found it raining very hard upon awakening this morning, felt quite unwell and went up to my room to lie down immediately after breakfast. Presently Nellie came bounding up the steps laughing, yet vexed, to tell me about three Yankee Dutchmen who had just come in to demand their breakfast—one proved to be a connoisseur of flowers and had been discoursing eloquently upon my poor little geraniums set out on the pavement for the benefit of the rain. Went downstairs with her and observing an unusual stir at the door, I stepped on the porch to learn the cause. Father came forward with a very grave face to say that General Kimball's brigade would be in immediately to quarter in the meadows in front of the house.

Small Federal forces had frequently been in Front Royal. It was not until May 14, 1862, that a large number of troops entered the town. These forces were under General Shields and were moving from the upper valley to join General McDowell at Fredericksburg. This move was ordered on the grounds that Jackson had left the valley. Banks opposed this depletion of his command.

We were all perfectly thunderstruck and had not time to recover our scattered ideas before we heard the notes of the band and looking over toward the depot, saw the head of the column advancing into the field. On they came, a dark mass of human beings winding through the meadows like a great black serpent until the whole four thousand were in the two fields. They were a sorry looking sight, wet and muddy, with their dripping banner clinging dismally to the staff. Next came the wagon trains and the artillery—eleven pieces besides their caissons, and the horses and wheels cutting up the beautiful green fields terribly. Father's beautiful stone fence, too, had to be leveled to afford them ingress. Then came a regiment of cavalry to the barn where they unceremoniously proceeded to turn their horses upon a fine field of clover, which Father and I had been admiring so much just two days ago. One of General K.'s staff now rode up and announced that General K. would pitch his tent near the house to prevent the troops from molesting us. He remarked moreover that the general being much indisposed, would much prefer being under roof if he could. Knowing that they were to be such close neighbors at any rate, we concluded that it would be best for them to be in the house where their presence would be some protection to us. Father, therefore, told the officer that there was a vacant room in the west wing, which they might occupy if they wished. The proposal was gladly accepted and the other members of the staff having arrived, "headquarters" was duly established at Bel Air. By this time the troops had gone through with their evolutions and the signal given to break ranks when ensued such a scene of destruction as I hope never to see repeated. All Father's beautiful fencing disappeared—melted. I could not tell how. It seemed as if the rails were endowed with a strange vitality so rapidly were they spirited away. They commenced upon the plank-fencing along the railroad and I could compare the quick regular blows of their demolishing hammers and axes to nothing but the gnawing of a monster worm in the wood. It was all endurable until the fence enclosing the field of luxuriant, heavy wheat began to disappear, then when I remembered that our dependence for bread next year was in this very wheat, I could only wring my hands and cry. To the credit of the general (Yankee though he be) I believe he did all he could to prevent unnecessary destruction; sent couriers to all the officers of his regiment expressly forbidding them to permit the demolition of outside enclosures threatening to hold them responsible for the disobedience of his order. The work of desolation was thus gradually arrested, and there were sentinels placed about the house and yard to prevent annoyance from intruders. The meadows soon wore a most stirring military appearance—dotted with white tents and miniature huts of rails and boards from which ascended curls of smoke looking quite comfortable. There were three tents pitched in the back yard ten feet from the door—one for the adjutant and captain of the staff, one for the clerks and orderlies and one for the servants of the staff. If I live a century, I do not think I can ever forget this day—it was all the time dark and cloudy and the rain descending in torrents. All the while they were bringing in news of increased losses—now they had captured the pigs, now the cows had gotten loose and deserted to the thirsty Yankees, and now the mill was broken into and pillaged—comparatively speaking, little things—yet, in our nervous, excited state of minds, most vexatious. Poor Father!—he could only walk the pavement with folded arms and drooping head looking helplessly on the scene of desolation, trying to bear up philosophically under all his troubles and losses for our sakes, but we could see what a mighty effort it required for him to appear unconcerned, how he struggled, how the day was doing the work of years bowing his form and furrowing his brow. This distressed us more than anything else. One incident of the morning impressed us very favorably—standing on the porch noting the arrival of the staff, Charley McGetigen made his way up the hill, but as he passed headquarters was halted by the general, who demanded "why he was there?" Saluting his officer respectfully, he replied, "I have business with Mr. Buck" and hurried to where we stood and grasping Father's hand told him how sorry he felt for him and begged to know how he might serve him—if he should not detail a safety guard. Upon our informing him that the general had appointed one for duty here, he politely bowed and retired. He lingered near, however, and a little while after—seeing Father at the back door, out of the sight of the officers—he tried to come to him through the back gate. But the sentinel stationed there refused him admittance, was deaf to all entreaties and the little corporal with a farewell wave of the hand and a gesture of impatience cried out—"They won't let me see you" and walked slowly off. We did appreciate his evident sympathy and desire to serve us so much, he could have had no sinister motives in this I'm sure—if he is a Yankee I must believe him sincere.

It seemed so strange to have the sentinels pacing the pavement all the day, to see dozens of couriers dashing to and from the doors, to hear the tramp of dragoon boots, the rattle of spurs and clanking of sabres. And then such a busy scene as the camp presented, such washing and cooking, such housekeeping on a small scale! We had dinner for five—General Kimball, a tall, spare, yet muscular man of about forty-five, a grave, firm looking face, acquiline nose, projecting chin, grey eyes, heavy brow and dark brown mustache and hair slightly grizzled; Captain Mason, a small dapper specimen of masculinity, sharp nose and chin, florid complexion, pale blue eyes, vermillion hair, eyebrows and mustache—a disagreeable, sinister expression of countenance; Captain Bunting, a Falstaffian looking mortal—bullet-head, full, chubby face, florid complexion, red hair and blue eyes—a perfect personification of the good-natured, well-fed, well-to-do quarter master; Adjutant Schweiger decidedly the finest looking of the party, tall and straight as a young pine, well proportioned, frank and modest countenance, fresh, healthy, boyish complexion, beautiful brown hair and whiskers and dark blue eyes and withal a very pleasant, quiet demeanor; last but not least Mr. Crippen, the reporter for the brigade—a foreign looking personage—a very frog-eating "Monsieur." Nellie and I concluded not to eat salt with these Yankees and to wait until the second table to avoid an encounter—what was our surprise then upon stepping into the dining room to see the colossal Q.M., sitting tranquilly at the foot of the table—retreat was impossible, for he had observed us immediately and greeted us most politely whereupon we were reluctantly compelled to take our seats at the same board with his Yankeeship. In the afternoon I happened to be looking some hard things at a Yankee out of the window, when I saw a singular, cleric-militaire figure in regimentals crossing the yard. It proved to be one Freeman, the chaplain of the Eighth Ohio Regiment. He established himself in Ma's room, where he "proceeded to dry his feet" and I having occasion to go through there for a restorative to apply to Cary's head was introduced to him and compelled to show some seeming of good breeding. He drew me into conversation and made me so angry that Ma, fearing I should say something to exasperate him, came in and interrupted us. I got up and slammed the door. Old hypocrite!—his very countenance proclaims his insincerity. I was provoked enough with myself for condescending to exchange words with the old "wolf in sheep's clothing." He told me three consecutive falsehoods without any apparent violence to his feelings—seemed determined to convince me that the

South was nearly subjugated and I was actually so excited as to indulge in a hearty cry when I went upstairs, thus losing the benefit of two bands performing in the meadows below the house.

There are some queer specimens of humanity quartered in the back yard, one whom Nellie (from seeing him perform some extraordinary feats) denominates "Breakfast"—another exactly realizes my ideal of that famous nursery bug-bear "Raw-head and bloody bones." Then there were "Wasp," "Freckles," "Redhead," "Mouth," "Nose" and "Mutton" all characters in their way.

Took tea at second table with a red-headed Yankee much to my disgust, though truth to say he did behave very discreetly and I had the opportunity I had all day been looking for of saying something of all I have been thinking about them. After tea, Ma, Laura and I went on the house to see the campfires, which looked beautiful despite the rain. Besides the brigade stationed here, there are two more quartered near Dr. Turner's. There were large fires on every hill surrounding town, and just where the principal encampments lay we could see the twinkling lights like thousands of stars clustered together in every variety of constellation. The camps immediately below the house looked like distant cities, but with rows of gas burners. The sight altogether was beautiful and novel.

Have been reading aloud to Ma until now at bedtime. It seems so strange to be sitting here in Grandma's cozy quiet room and hear the tramp of the sentinel on his beat just under the window—anon rings out on the night air the sound of hoofs as a courier dashes by, or the tattoo's beaten by some distant drum. I shall lay my head on my pillow tonight with a sense of perfect security, for I know the two sentinels before my door are responsible under pain of death for any intrusion or disturbance. Shields is really in town.

> Kimball's brigade of General Shields' army encamped upon the Bel Air farm the fourteenth to sixteenth of May. There were approximately one hundred acres of land owned by Mr. Buck around Bel Air. The Yankees burned half the rails around the field of wheat of fifty acres and the greater part of the plank fencing of heavy locust posts and oak plank around timothy meadow of the twenty-eight acres adjoining town. A portion of the rail fence from a field of thirty-five acres of clover was also destroyed.

May 15, 1862

Was awakened by reveille and found to my chagrin that it was cloudy and rainy, which rendered a departure of the troops today very improbable. Eight Yankees to breakfast. We had real coffee and, not feeling well, I could have enjoyed a cup of it very much if it had not been Yankee coffee. As it was, we did not drink it at all. After breakfast they said some of them were going away and we went up to the dormer window to witness their departure. 'Twas only the artillery corps that left with some few stragglers—still we accepted their removal as a favorable augury of a general exodus tomorrow. The children, although freely declaring their rebellious inclinations, have apparently made themselves great favorites with their new acquaintances. One of them gave Willie the benefit of the butler's establishment today and being introduced to its delights, they have ever since been reveling in the unwonted luxury of oranges, candies, etc. The officers are all men with families and seem glad to be in the midst of little children again. The General in particular generally manages to have some intercourse with them as they pass him in his promenades on the pavement, sometimes catching them in his arms and kissing them. He met Willie yesterday and taking him into his arms inquired his name—upon being answered he clasped him to him and said "God bless you! I've got a little Willie at home too!" at the same time giving him a piece of silver. If he loves his "little Willie" so well he should have remained at home to take care of him.

This half dollar was kept as a souvenir all of Willie's life and passed into the hands of his son, Mason.

Not so many couriers today, but a great clangor of drums, horses and fifes. When I went down to dinner today, Ma leaned over the table and told me the officers said it was rumored in camp that Ashby had been captured and carried off in an "oxcart." I knew then how to account for the shouts that went up from camp a little while before. It was too provoking, and although Burwell, the red-headed Yankee, was at table I could not help expressing my aversion and contempt for people who were never better pleased than when they were circulating and crediting all sorts of palpable falsehoods, and wanted to know why it was that Beauregard, whom they had reported dead eight times had yet survived long enough to give them so much hard work at Shiloh. Ma remarked that the officers only gave the news as a camp rumor, and would not and could not vouch for the truth of it, one and all agreeing that there was not a man in the brigade who would shoot Ashby if they could, so highly was he respected by them—of course not, that's what they all say and yet, I never have heard of their neglecting a single opportunity of having a shot at him. General Kimball said at table that the band would be ordered up in the afternoon to "play for the ladies." Uncles Tom and Mack came in after dinner. We were so glad to see them. Uncle T. says he has four or five very gentlemanly officers, one was General Carroll quartered with him, and thus far had suffered no damage—expected an officer with his wife there tonight. Grandma and Aunt Betsy were still there, apparently very well-contented. Mr. Berry also came over and contradicted the report of Ashby's capture. He says Shields had called a meeting of the citizens and told them that they should be reinstated in their losses. Am afraid the promise is too good to be true. While talking in Ma's room the band, a very fine brass one, had come up on the pavement and struck up an inspiring air, attracting a number of outsiders to the yard. The music was very fine and had the performers been any other than they were, I should have enjoyed it unspeakably. As it was, I liked it until they struck up "Yankee Doodle" and "Dixie"—that would not do any way as Nellie, Laura and I gave them to understand by turning our backs to the window and dropping the curtains. They were requested to play the "Mocking Bird" in memory of Irvie and some other popular airs. They did not know them, but offered to go down to camp, practice the pieces and come back and perform them. They just played their old "Yankee Doodle" with so much gusto because they knew how obnoxious it had become to good Southerners. And as for "Dixie" 'tis the height of impudence in them to appropriate one of our national airs. We were a good deal provoked and I had just gone into Grandma's room to try and regain my temper by reading when another band more magnificent than the first commenced discoursing sweet music more magnificent than the first commenced playing sweet music under the windows. Dear absent brothers!—when they played the "Mocking Bird," "Annie Laurie," "The Dearest Spot on Earth" and "Be Kind to the Loved Ones at Home"—songs so often sung together in our home in so many happier hours—I could not restrain my tears. Just then that hound old crocodile Freeman stepped forward on the porch and called out in an insulting tone—"Boys! boys!—you're no true Yankee soldiers if you could think of omitting to play "Yankee Doodle." Whereupon they commenced vigorously playing the odious Yankee air a second time. Down went the curtains and down they remained until the musicians departed. I do not know when I have been so provoked as at this piece of effrontery—for such it evidently was. Old Freeman has noticed how little pains we some of us— have taken to conceal our disgust for him. How we have tried to avoid him, and this was a species of mean petty revenge for personal contempt. The officers have conducted themselves with as much courtesy and delicate consideration as I ever saw in my life, but this miserable old chaplain carries his character in the hypocritical expression of his face. Suffered all evening from a severe headache in consequence of "Yankee Doodle" and begged Father and Ma to let me go into the parlor and play "Johnston's March to Manassas" as a restorative. They consented provided I would not announce the name, as they thought it unnecessary to aggravate the Yankees, but, of course, I did not care to do so on these terms. They say there's a Virginia regiment in this brigade. For shame!—I hope they'll keep out of sight.

Father and General Kimball while promenading the pavement this afternoon seemed engaged in an earnest conversation—the subject of which I guessed—the result I felt curious to learn. Presently Father came to the steps where Ma and I were seated and remarked that it was very strange what a horror all these officers seemed to entertain of abolitionists—all with whom he had conversed upon the subject denouncing them and General K. just having gone so far as to say if any man wanted to raise a fight all he had to do was to go down to camp and tax one of his men with being an emancipator. It is remarkable though that they still permit contrabands to go with them and harbor all who flee their masters, but I must say although I have endeavored to detect them in some way trying to influence our slaves, that thus far the effort has been vain. Their own servants were perfectly respectful to the family and seemed to have little to do with the others. Our servants conducted themselves even better, or at least more cheerfully than before. I have not discovered the least trace of abolition's cloven hoof unless it be in the black attendants they have with them and these are less numerous than I had supposed. When I went down to tea tonight, I heard Ma and Captain Mason (the other officers had left the table) talking. Captain M. was just saying—"When a minister of the gospel gets up into the pulpit and loses sight of religion in discussing political questions I feel perfectly disgusted with him and am well assured he has no right there." And he proceeded to give his experiences in that line. I liked his views so much and immediately conjectured that the conversation had reference to the chaplain—so I enquired what he had been doing and was perfectly delighted to hear that the old sinner's free expression of opinion at the table had called forth a justly merited rebuke from the general who told him he thought "If ministers of the gospel would content themselves with expounding the scriptures and teaching morality and virtue that politics would come right of themselves." The captain seemed to enjoy the old nuisance's discomforture most hugely, said he knew the general would not slip so good an opportunity of giving him a hing—never did—and he had been expecting it all the evening. After he left the table, Ma told me how shamefully Freeman had talked—he's a black-hearted villain —an Abolitionist. Said he had formerly resided in Louisiana, but had left there with the full determination to do all in his power to "crush the miserable rebellion." Poor old soul!—if it depends upon your exertions —either praying, preaching or fighting—I think the South may rest perfectly easy, secure of achieving her independence.

We went up on the house to see the campfires and as the atmosphere was clear they were seen to a greater advantage than on last night. Just as we stepped out on the roof a band in the meadow below commenced playing—not "Yankee Doodle," but a sweet, plaintive air, one of dear Irvie's favorites—immediately everything was forgotten, my surroundings, the Yankees, and everything, and the tide of thought and feeling flowed far away toward the dear brothers whose sympathies I felt would be so surely ours now could they but know our trials. Poor boys!—how unconscious they are that their home shelters, their hearthstone warms, and their fondest friends are compelled to contribute to the comfort of their bitter deadly enemies—enemies hungering and thirsting for their heart's blood, and the life blood of every true Southerner in the field.

What though these foes wear the guise of gentlemen—the hilt of the dagger may be jeweled and velvet-cased, and yet the blade none the less cruel and keen. What would Alvin and Irving think would they know that their mother and sisters and little brothers were in the centre of a hostile camp dependent upon their oppressors for protection from insult and injury; to know that their father had to stand impotently by and see the toil of years brought to naught in as many hours—had to stand tamely by and have the names he honored, the sentiments he revered cast into his teeth as terms of reproach. Oh!—how long I sat there and "revolved the said vicissitudes of things" until we were forced down from our retreat by the inclemency of the weather. Passing through Ma's room where sat Captain Bunting and the old chaplain telling anecdotes of their early life, I paused at the window to listen until growing weary of the relation I came into Grandma's room to prepare for bed.

May 16, 1862
The reveille was the signal for my uprising this morning. The camp early gave evidences of contemplated removal by the incessant hum and stir of the assembled multitude. I was so glad when the first tent fell that I actually took the trouble of going upstairs to witness preparation for the exodus—'twas so very amusing to watch their "packing up." There was one little Yankee, apparently an attache of the staff—Frank Crippen, who has quite won the hearts of the children by his telling stories and treating them—he did seem so very kind and fond of them and is such a lively, bright looking young fellow that I am reluctantly half inclined to think he's a good-hearted fellow. But no doubt he is an accomplished hypocrite and his suavity assumed to subserve some selfish purpose. We were on the porch when the general and staff took their departure—their adieux were very politely made, the general even promising to do all in his power to have Father reinstated—but, of course, we know the value of their promises. When the troops commenced their march we went up on the roof to see them file past the house and were there all the morning for not only the three brigades, the one stationed here and the two at Dr. Turner's, but one at the river, making in all some twelve or fourteen thousand troops were on the move. I never had seen so many soldiers together before, and I marvelled at the mighty multitude, but thought how the number would sink into insignificance in comparison with the vast hordes now before Richmond.

General Shields division left Front Royal on May 16, 1862, to join McDowell around Fredericksburg.

Looking down on the deserted encampment just as the last column left the field, we saw Father (who had gone down to try to to reclaim some of his "confiscated" plank and timber) joined by the little corporal who grasped him most cordially by the hand. Presently they came to the house and as the young fellow congratulated us upon the removal of the troops, he seemed to feel almost as glad as we were. While they were all talking, Uncle Tom came in and said that Company (I) McGetigen's had just been ordered from town on account of their having just heard that a part of Jackson's command was in pursuit of Shields. Do hope 'tis true. The corporal left very hurriedly upon receipt of this information.

Spent the day cleaning up the house and writing a little. Oh me!—what an intense relief this is!—to be without a houseful of Yankees once more.

May 17, 1862

A company of Yankees came in about four o'clock the band playing "Johnston's March to Manassas." Thieves!—they come to steal our liberty, steal our property, our slaves, and, not satisfied with this robbery, actually steal our national music, which I should think would be the very last thing they would desire to do.

> *After Shields left the valley to join McDowell near Fredericksburg, the First Maryland Federal Regiment went into camp on a hill one mile north of Front Royal. Two companies were detached and stationed in the town as guards for the provost marshal. Outposts were maintained on the roads leading into the village.*

May 18, 1862

'Tis said martial law is more rigidly enforced in town than ever. So much for trusting to Yankee promises! All Major Tyndall has to say in excuse of his perfidy is—"Tis military necessity" and we have to succumb quietly. Dear, dear, dear! Such petty tyranny!

E. Hope came up this morning and amused us very much with funny accounts of the Yankee boarders they've had there.

Nellie and I after tea went out to our old seat under the locust tree—it was a strange, gloomy twilight, the moon was shining, but in fitful, straggling gleams that cast a weird, pallid light over everything, the very faint shadows of the trees on the ground had a ghostly appearance. As we sat there and thought of the future before us so dark, so hopeless, as we thought of the separation from friends by greater barriers than distance, as we turned upon every side for light and comfort and saw nothing but grim, black despair, our hearts sank within us and we felt the still gloom of the night but a fitting type of the still horror of our souls. There is such an oppression on my heart tonight that I can scarcely breathe—such a suffocating sensation in my throat. If I could only cry!—but it seems as if even my tears have been frozen up. There is surely some great evil impending over us—some awful "coming event" that "casts" this dreary "shadow before." God help me now! I feel how "vain must be the help of man."

May 19, 1862

A Southern paper had been smuggled in confirming our victories at Staunton and Corinth, and also stating that we had hurt the enemy severely at Williamsburg.

But alas!—poor Willie Richardson, Giles Cook and Willie Rust were all slightly wounded—the Seventeenth suffered heavily, but none of our immediate friends had fallen thank Heaven! Poor dear wounded boys! What would I not give for the privilege of nursing them carefully, tenderly now?

Cousin Mary Cloud, Mrs. Kiger and Kattie Samuels spent the afternoon with us—a pleasant afternoon it was. Kattie says Belle Boyd is in town en route for Richmond and will carry letters through to be mailed for our friends within our lines—will write the boys by her. Poor boys!

May 20, 1862

Aunt Letitia Blakemore came up from Rose Hill quite early this morning and said they were all very much distressed about poor Willie. But alas!—we know what they do not—having heard today that his left arm has been amputated and he a prisoner in the enemy lines. Poor fellow!—what a mortification, what a misfortune to him! Giles Cook made a very narrow escape, but was only slightly wounded. Willie Rust had two fingers shot off. How thankful I am that they all escaped with their lives though.

I spent the day alone in my room writing a long, long letter to my dear brothers. I could restrain my feelings no longer and the long pent-up agony burst forth with resistless strength, and I wept passionately, wildly, wept as I had never done before in my life. At last relief came from sheer exhaustion—relief from the passionate excitement of sorrow, but not from distress itself, for I felt completely crushed and heartbroken, yearning for the dear brothers whom I might never see more—for the cousins—one sick unto death in the hands of strange friends, one wounded and suffering in the hands of the enemy and others perhaps even now cold and still on the bloody field of death—victims to this horrid war. I felt how hopeless were our prospects for success in this life and death contest, where every advantage save the justice of the cause seemed to weigh in favor of our adversaries. Even Father has given up now.

In the afternoon Dr. Dorsey came in to vaccinate the children for the smallpox, two cases of which were reported in town—they sent for me not knowing how hopelessly all day I had been sunk in the "Slough of Despond" to come down to hear him talk. He was in a perfect flow of spirits; had seen a paper containing an account of another victorious skirmish at Corinth, confirmation of the news from Jackson and Milroy and the battle at Williamsburg, though claimed as a victory by all the Yankees—was nevertheless a victory so dearly bought as to be equivalent to defeat.

After defeating Milroy, Jackson moved from Mount Solon, where he was in camp, to New Market on the nineteenth of May. Ewell began to advance down the Luray Valley. From New Market on May 21, 1862, Jackson moved across the Massanutten Mountain into the Luray Valley to join Ewell. A few of Ashby's cavalry companies were sent to demonstrate in front of Strasburg on the twenty-first.

May 21, 1862

Early finished my letter and Nellie and I took it over to Mrs. Boone's and asked Kattie to go with us to the hotel that we might deliver it in person to Miss Belle Boyd. Found a carriage at the door in which was seated the young lady with a Yankee officer—concluded not to intrust my letter with one who appeared upon such familiar terms with those whom we most dreaded, so crossing the street we went on up to see Cousin Mary and spent the day very pleasantly with her.

Johnston's retreat up the Peninsula left Norfolk in an exposed position. The city was evacuated on May 11, 1826. The crew of the C.S.S. Virginia *(Merrimac) at anchor off Sewell's Point were not aware of this move until its commander, Commodore Josiah Tattrall, noticed the Confederate flag not flying over the shore batteries.*

Two courses of action were open to Commodore Tattrall. Either he must run the blockade and attack the shipping or lighten his ship five feet to allow passage up the James River to assist in the defense of Richmond.

The latter course was selected and by removing everything from within the ship but the ammunition, the ship was lightened three feet. The pilots aboard stopped the proceedings on the ground that with the westerly winds blowing, the tide would be decreased and would not allow passage up the river.

Two feet of the ships hull was exposed below the protective shield. The ship would be an easy target. The only alternative was to destroy the ship. The crew marched twenty-two miles to Suffolk after the C.S.S. Virginia *was sunk. From Suffolk they reached Richmond by train.*

The Union fleet now began to ascend the James River. This action created great alarm because the Southerners had depended on the Virginia *to protect Richmond from a water attack and not a gun had been mounted at this time to protect the city from this route of attack.*

Dreway's Bluff on the James River and the first high ground below the city (seven miles) was hastily fortified. Several small vessels were sunk to obstruct the river.

On May 15, 1862, five Federal warships including the U.S.S.

Galena *and U.S.S.* Monitor *arrived below the bluff. After a four hour action in which the crew of the C.S.S.* Virginia *participated, the Federal ships returned down the river.*

Some of our scouts were said to have been in town last night. Wonder what that means?

Jackson joined Ewell near White House Bridge on the night of the twenty-first of May and on May 22, brought Stonewall's army ten miles from Front Royal. Ashby (Jackson's cavalry chief) and his cavalry crossed the South Fork of the Shenandoah River at McCoy's Ford and headed for Buckton station.

III

LIBERATION

May 23, 1862 - May 29, 1862

May 23, 1862

Was all the morning busily engaged sewing for Father. He came in about twelve o'clock saying he had made a very narrow escape from town—martial law having been so rigidly enforced in town that none of the citizens were allowed to leave the place, and he not being aware of this had gone over and narrowly escaped detention there. He said he feared the citizens would suffer for the necessities of life, for they were not permitted to go out to get either fuel or provisions. I told him I thought this extreme caution rather a favorable augury than otherwise, for I felt convinced that they had good reason to believe that the garrison here was menaced in some way, that I was willing to endure this oppression calmly for a short time if, as I believed, it presaged some change in the existing state of things here. He brought Ma a letter from Mrs. Millar giving an account of the death of her husband.

Although the afternoon was oppressively warm, so anxious and restless were we that Ma and I concluded to go up to Mrs. Hope's to see if they had heard any news. Found them very desponding—had heard no news save that Banks was reported to be moving his stores from Winchester, which proceeding on his part would seem to indicate a threatened attack upon that place, though we could not think what reason he had for fearing such a thing. While sitting there talking, a Yankee obtruded his head in the door and asked if he could "buy some pies and pigs" and scarce had his footsteps grown cold on the threshold when there was heard the quick, sharp report of a rifle and another and another in rapid succession.

On May 23, 1862, Jackson made contact with the Federals about two o'clock in the afternoon.

Going to the door we saw the Yankees scampering over the meadow below our house and were at a loss how to account for such evident excitement on their part until presently Miss B. White rushed in with purple face and dishevelled hair crying—"Oh my God! The Southern army is upon them—the hill above town is black with our boys! Julia Ann, give me water or I shall die!" Of course, Ma and I did not wait to see the result of her case, but started for home in double quick time, all the time hearing the firing exchanged more and more rapidly. Found all excitement upon reaching the house—all the family upstairs at the windows. Nellie, spyglass in hand clapping her hands exclaiming—"Oh!—there they are! I see our dear brave fellows just in the edge of the woods on the hill over the town! There they are, bless them!" I looked in the same direction and saw surely enough some of our cavalry emerge from the little skirt of woods above the courthouse. As long as I live, I think I cannot forget that sight, the first glimpse caught of a grey figure upon horseback seemingly in command, until then I could not believe our deliverers had really come, but seeing was believing and I could only sink on my knees with my face in my hands and sob for joy. Presently someone called out "Only see!—The Yankees run!" Leaning out the back window we saw them, contrabands and Yankees together, tearing wildly by. One obese Dutchman as he ran through the yard sans arms heard cheering from the window likening his speed to the Bull Run race—he looked most malignantly at us over his shoulder, but had not time to give vent to his feelings in words. There had been quick random firing all this time, and now, those of the Yankees who did not run at the first alarm, rallied and formed into line, some climbing into the dome of the courthouse, some into the upper hospital windows, firing from these and making some feint of resistance.

By this time some scattered parties of Confederate infantry came up and charged their ranks, when firing one volley they wheeled about—every man for himself they scampered out of town like a flock of sheep—such an undignified exodus was never witnessed before. John Gilpin's race wasn't a circumstance to it. However, when they reached the hill north of town—opposite to where our men were entering the place, they halted and drew up in line in support of a battery that had been planted there. We all stood on the upper porch and waved and cheered our dear Rebels, who were by this time pouring in eagerly from every direction. The larger body came down the Manor Grade, others down the Chester's Gap road, and others on the F.R. and Luray Turnpike, while there were yet others who eschewed all the regular roads and flocked through the fields and across the hills without regard to order or uniformity. Captain Alexander's company now dashed by the house, returning our salutations and cheering manfully. Two of them, who proved to be dear Walter and the captain himself, cantered up to the door to inquire which way the Yankees had gone. We had been all the afternoon vainly trying to obtain a glimpse of Walter and now that he was really among us, his own cheerful, confident self, we were almost beside ourselves with joy. The children caught and kissed his hand as if he had been a host of deliverers in himself. He turned to Nellie, who stood sobbing near him and exclaimed in his joyous way—"Why Nellie, child! Crying? Cheer up! Now is the time to be laughing. Jackson's army is coming and we're going to drive the Yankees away from you!" We could not speak for joy at his words and just then the enemy opened fire from a battery stationed on a hill north of town and Walter thinking there was work for him elsewhere ordered us all to the basement for protection and then rode calmly away regarding the bullets falling around him less than I should a heavy dew. We descended all of us to the basement where we found some frightened contrabands assembled. The house was exposed to a cross fire and we were all in really much more danger than we were at the time aware of—at any rate I could not bear the idea of being entombed ingloriously in the cellar while our deliverers were gallantly endangering their lives in our defense—it was not to be thought of for an instant—I must witness if not assist in the struggle. So Nellie and I went on the porch with a pitcher of water with the contents of which we refreshed our soldiers as they would ever and anon stop in their chase weary and thirsty. And all the time the cannon on both sides were carrying on a most animated dialogue—one shell whistling over the house and cutting the twigs off the aspen in front of the porch where we stood, another exploding in the barn—a third striking the mill—another falling the meadow below. I did not feel the least fear as the missiles of death screamed and shrieked around—the sound was rather pleasantly exhilarating and I watched the discharges with positive enjoyment—did not one instant doubt our success in driving the varments out.

> *The Confederate cavalry was between the two forks of the river and was fighting between Front Royal and Strasburg. Union troops, realizing they would be cut off if the bridge across the North Fork fell to the Rebels, quickly retreated. In the face of Jackson's infantry Colonel John R. Kenly, Union commander at Front Royal, ordered the bridge to be fired and the Yankees retreated toward Winchester. The bridge was saved and Jackson's forces crossed. Lt. Col. Flournoy leading the Sixth Virginia Cavalry forded the North Fork and attacked Colonel Kenly and succeeded in capturing him and most of his command. The night of May 23, 1862, Jackson camped at Cedarville, approximately two miles north of the North Fork.*
>
> *The Union had one regiment and two companies approximately 1065 infantrymen, 90 cavalrymen and a section of artil-*

lery stationed at Front Royal. Their casualties were: killed... 32; wounded... 122; prisoners... 750. Jackson had 36 casualties, killed and wounded.

Our men soon succeeded in silencing the enemy battery on the hill and drove them across the river, having to encounter, however, a very heavy fire from a well disposed battery on Guard Hill. After some trouble we dislodged and pursued after them as far as Nineveh killing numbers of them. Here a most disgraceful circumstance occurred. Two of our cavalry in a reckless charge fell into the hands of the enemy who called upon them to surrender, whereupon, seeing no possibility of escape, they grounded arms. Their inhuman captors no sooner saw them unarmed than they fired at them piercing them through the breast with rifle balls and killing them immediately. Such is the method taken by our invaders for cementing our affections to the Union. Now the death song of the Union has too long since and too often been sounded in the gasps of mortal agony bursting from the lips of the thousands of murdered brethren—the wail of bereavement going up from our thousands of desolated Southern homes and hearth. Union forsooth.

The skirmishing lasted until about sunset—a good deal of the fighting was done on the Rose Hill farm near the house and knowing how delicate the family was we were anxious to know how they stood it. Presently we saw Uncle Tom coming from there into town and we concluded to go across the street and intercept him to make inquiries. While standing there the main body of the army came in and we had an opportunity of cheering and welcoming in our gallant boys—regiment after regiment filed past all looking pale and haggard, dusty and ragged and yet when we saluted the battle flag when they were going by, their countenances brightened, their step grew elastic and cheer after cheer rent the air as they seemed to forget suffering and danger in their enthusiasm. Cousin ... to where we stood and chatted with us a few moments telling where and how the boys were and adding that some of our friends had a letter from Irving—dated the third saying all were well and in good spirits. Then he went on to rejoin his company and we returned home to tea. Found Mr. Morris—and our afternoon acquaintances there—indeed he remained all night. After tea went out on the pavement to listen to our bands playing as the regiment celebrated and while there we heard the car whistle and in a little while a train of several cars came in. Major Wheat of the New Orleans Battalion had captured the ... telegraph wires had been cut at 11:00 A.M. so that all communication between the two divisions of the enemy was entirely at an end for the present. Almost ... o'clock two officers came in to tea—Colonel Johnson and Adjutant Ward of ... old regiment ... two of the most agreeable gentlemen I have seen in an age.... While presiding at the supper table Ward made some ... and ... then told me that he was the "Cousin Frank" about whom Nannie wrote so much—he had known her in Germantown and although no relation were like brother and sister. Spoke in high terms of them all and begged me to write Nannie and tell her he had thus far passed through the ordeal safely and was on his way to his dear Maryland. With this theme of mutual interest for conversation we soon were quite well acquainted—he gave me some trophies taken only this day—photographs of General "Peerless Beauregard," of the Yankee Commander McClellan, Burnside and Corcoran. He has also a couple of daguerreotypes of some ladies in Baltimore—Dulcineas of some of the Yankee lovers who had thus ingloriously deserted their miniatures. In return Nellie and I sang "Maryland" and the "Bonnie Blue Flag" for them with a great deal of pleasure. They left at about eleven o'clock, but so excited and happy did I feel that I did not close my eyes until one A.M.

This then is the reason why they thought our cavalry hovering near—they have been very near, some of them every night for a week and I can't for my life imagine why it is they were not taken by the Yankees. I never heard of such boldness as they have been displaying of which we had not a suspicion until now. Speaking of boldness reminds me of an exploit attributed to Miss Belle Boyd Wednesday. 'Tis said that she wished some information conveyed to the army about the time of the keenest firing and not being able to get anyone to go for her, she went herself to a most exposed point, where the bullets fell like hailstones about her riddling her dress. I know not what truth there is in the rumor.

Of one thing I am particularly glad—our First Maryland Regiment was the first to charge the Yankee First "Maryland"—drove them out of town, captured and then marched back to town singing "Maryland." They have always wanted to meet and have been justified with a vengeance, on one side at least. Old Colonel Kenley's prisoner too.

Colonel Kenley was the commander of the Federal First Maryland.

What a memorable day this and how often have I thought of my darling brothers wishing they knew all and could rejoice with us. Little did they think when they left old Front Royal, that ere they returned she should have won herself a name in future history. I must write them now, bless them.

A contraband and Yankee who were about—applying the torch to the depot was this evening arrested by our men. The servants are disappointed and furious beyond mere words at the treatment their Yankee friends have received at the hands of "Rebels" who they have been taught to believe were a race entirely extinct with the exception of a few outlaws in the mountains who would be easily taken. They don't say anything but are so sullen. The surprise was evidently very great and very disagreeable.

May 24, 1862

Up bright and early this morning and went downstairs. Ma met me and told me that they had just heard that Colonel Sheetz had been killed in yesterday's engagement.

> Captain Sheetz, one of Ashby's valiant men was killed at Buckton.

I was so shocked and grieved to hear this for truly the South had no truer, braver son than he—and to lose him now, just in the full tide of honorable success. Just as he had been promoted to distinction. It was sad, sad. When General Kimball was here his men spoke of Colonel Sheetz and in terms of highest praise for his valor and bearing. Well the hearts of a grateful country should ever hold sacred the memory of this brave spirit who thus wasted his life in his country's care. We had some thirty soldiers to breakfast among whom were some Tigers, Louisiana troops under Dick Taylor. Just before breakfast who should come in but Mr. Hoblitzell and a young friend of his Mr. Russell a very pleasant little fellow too. Mr. H. told us that Mr. Laird and Dr. Reeves and a number of those who spent last winter here were in town—also told of Mr. Wilson having joined the navy. Was jubilant over the capture of the Yankee First. He begged for "Maryland" and "A Home by the Sea" and we had them both in full chorus. While singing I noticed the arrival of a very ... looking personage, to whom I was afterward introduced as Mr. Moreton, the most polished, refined little fellow I ever met—one of the F F V's—conversed very pleasantly and was singing duets with Nellie and me to my very great satisfaction when Grandma came in and interrupted us by saying that Henry Heater was here wounded in the hand. We went out immediately to see him but found his wrist was only sprained. After dressing his wrist repaired Mr. Moreton's belt for him with a great deal of pleasure. Presently Captain Gardner of the N. O. Battalion came in. He wore the badge of the battalion one of the prettiest imaginable designs—a little silver crescent in the concavity of which revolved a silver star upon a pivot on which was inscribed on one side "The Star Battalion from the Crescent City" in a revolution—on the reverse side "Wheat's New Orleans Battalion." It was a cunning little ornament and I really coveted it. Nellie and I were busy playing the agreeable until eleven o'clock when ... and went down to read some amusing letters captured yesterday. Cousin Mack Bayly, Mr. Merriwether and others came in to dinner—the first mentioned gave an account of a severe skirmish which took place at Buckton yesterday in which his horse and that of little Sandie were shot from under them—I can't conceive how any of them escaped with their lives.

> Ashby's cavalry had struck the Federals at Buckton between Front Royal and Strasburg on May 23, 1862.

> *"Sandy" (Alexander Buck) of Co. E. Seventh Virginia Cavalry was a courier for Colonel Ashby at the Buckton station skirmish.*

Here the gallant and lamented Sheetz died just as he had waved his sword above his head in the act of giving the word of command, fell pierced through the heart, expiring instantly. They think they secured the varlet who committed the act—I sincerely hope they did. Mack was looking very well and seemed in excellent spirits and unusually affectionate. He and Cousin ... both left at evening promising to call again. We shall not see the other boys for they pressed on with their company in expectation of engaging with the enemy.

The N.O. Tigers played a most amusing prank on the Yankees today. It seems that in their hasty flight yesterday they left arms, ammunition and clothing, tents, wagons and a large amount of commissary stores in our possession. The Tigers doffed their uniforms and donned the Yankee blue—then they got on the cars and steamed off to Markham where the news of the fall of Front Royal had not arrived and the Federal troops of course took them to be some of their own men, and coming out of quarters at the invitation of the Tigers a number of them concluded to "take a ride up the road a little ways." The hospitable Rebels not only extended the ride to Front Royal but also gave them lodging and board there au gratis. Prisoners have been pouring into town all day—ship Mitchell going by with five (armed with two revolvers a piece,) all of whom 'tis said he took on his own responsibility and alone. Heavy cannonading in the direction of Winchester—hot work going on in that region I expect. Alec came in this evening saying Jackson was just carrying everything before him like a reaper in the grain.

> *Gen. Joseph Johnston had retreated up the Peninsula toward Richmond in the face of Union General McClellan's army.*

They tell us that we did give the Yankees a prodigious whipping at Williamsburg notwithstanding all their boasts and Jackson also got the better of Milroy at McDowell notwithstanding old Fremont's "Freemans" romancing.

May 25, 1862

Clear and cloudless. Mr. Berry preached today—so Father, Aunt B, Nellie and myself concluded to go first to hear Colonel Sheetz' funeral sermon and then to the Presbyterian Church. We were too late—the brave fellow was consigned to the earth at an early hour with only a short service and no military display whatever owing to the inability of a few poor soldiers left for duty. He sleeps in the cemetery on the hill "Soldiers Rest" in an obscure spot—but if I'm permitted to follow the bent of my inclination it shall be no neglected grave.

> *Capt. George Frederick Sheetz's body was later removed to Winchester and then buried at his home near Romney.*

We had an excellent sermon from Mr. Berry—which to tell the truth I listened to with very divided attention so much confusion was there with the thunder of wagons and artillery as they rolled through the street. Heard from Charlie B. He was almost entirely well and on his way home. So glad. There were some of our wounded men at private houses as well as wounded prisoners—Cousin E. B. has several with her one of whom had his leg amputated and died soon after. So far as I know we lost but four men in the skirmishes of Friday, though I suppose some others must have fallen that we know nothing of.

> *While Lucy was worshipping, Jackson, who never liked to fight on Sunday unless it was God's will, was defeating Union General Banks at Winchester. Jackson had pushed his men all night with but an hour or two of rest in order to be in a position to attack Winchester before the Union troops could man the high ground.*

I am uneasy about my friends—they have been fighting desperately and it seems too much to hope that they are all safe. We have taken Winchester, captured a very great number of prisoners and commissary's stores to the amount of one million dollars and best of all driven old Banks with the remnant of his army to the Potomac and the last heard from him Ashby was in hot pursuit of the fugitives declaring no pains to be spared in arresting their progress. Hope he'll get them.

Major Warinick, a Marylander, with seven young friends dined with us. Uncle Fayette B too. The former was very hopeful, and the latter in better spirits than I have seen him in an age and seemingly glad to be with us again. Indeed it is wonderful what a change has been wrought in the appearance of everybody and everything since the occupation once more by our troops. Every face beams, every eye brightens, every head is erect and men walk with an air of curious freedom refreshing to behold. I wonder where the long-faced croakers—those birds of ill-omen who have been hanging around so long have flown to. Happy riddance!

We had a number of soldiers come in for food—poor fellows! It does my very heart good to administer to their wants. Mrs. M. and E. Hope were also here in most ecstatic mood. Ma spent the day at Rose Hill and returned saying they had heard from Willie indirectly—he was in Washington and having obtained parole would soon be home—the loss of his arm will, I suppose, incapacitate him for further service. Dear boy, I'm so glad for his sake and that of the family.

Three Louisianians came in about dusk to get their suppers, and Father just then returning from town engaged them to act as guards for the night. He then told us there were some thirteen to fifteen hundred prisoners in town confined in an open frame building (or rather buildings—the hospitals) with an inefficient guard of disabled soldiers. In the hurry and confusion supplies could not immediately be had even for our own men and all must suffer some little privation until a requisition could be made and met at the commissary. He feard that the Yankees under the existing state of things would make a desperate rush—take the guards and play the "wilds" generally before assistance could be received. So I retired this night feeling anything else than a sense of security.

May 26, 1862

A bright day. Finished sewing for Father quite early. Little Wilbur Trout and Edgar Jones came in this morning to get milk for the sick soldiers in town, of whom, including all, there were some eighty. I was so glad to think that the ladies were caring for them and resolved to do what I could to assist them. Saw a very large number of prisoners going out of town toward Winchester this morning—it is well they're being sent away—for I believe nothing but the ignorance of our numbers here, has prevented them from doing much mischief here.

Went into the garden where I received a fragrant greeting from innumerable floral pets. The roses were looking so lovely—I had not been able to enjoy the flowers as much all the summer before. Indeed there is an atmosphere of beauty pervading everywhere—making all nature "gladsome as the face of joy"—so different from what it was a week since. Then our spirit was so little reminiscent of brightness that light, fragrance and beauty would have been a sad discord surely—now all is harmless. Oh we have so much for which to be thankful in this episode. I feel that we cannot enough appreciate the blessing of liberty—know not its worth until deprived of it. I have enjoyed the accomplishment of its possession hugely today, though to tell the truth it certainly requires freedom, seems a blessing at times too great to be a reality. After one has a limb tightly bound—for a length of time—he becomes so accustomed to the confinement—that after the ligature is removed—he cannot for a long time realize his freedom from restraint. He still feels the impress of the bonds—still for a time imagines that they are about him and suffers from imagination that which he before endured in reality. At such time he is awakening to a reality that is delightful. So it is with what I now experience. Often when sitting at the door I hear a strange footfall on the pavement and spring up to leave the room as I always did when the Yankees came but I instantly recollect that there are none in the immediate vicinity to "vex or make us afraid" now—often I see figures move to and fro hurriedly and a huge anathema hangs pendant on my lips, and a big wave of indignation rolls over me as I think—"there they go—our tormentors—on demoniacal thoughts intent." Then I bethink me "Oh no—our dear blessed Rebels—our protectors" and then at night upon taking my candle to my room and observing the curtains were not low how I would involuntarily throw my hands up in dismay at my carelessness at allowing lights to shine through the window—the Yankees would see it and think it a signal to the "Secesh" out there—but I recollected then that such an act might be performed with impunity now for the eyes of no other than those we loved and those who loved us were on us now. Oh!—this consciousness of freedom is a glorious thing to have. But it will not last—the Yankees will return when they rally their panic, they will return and we shall suffer much more from them, but surely we can bear a little tyranny now after having enjoyed the privilege of seeing and talking to our precious soldier boys again. Bless them. Commenced a letter to my brother as I thought I might soon have an opportunity of sending it to Dixie.

Ma was in town this evening and when she came back told us that the evening our troops came, Captain Roy was at an upper window waving to them when the Yankees discovered him and fired at him—the balls taking effect in the parlor window—shattering three of the glasses and sinking in the frame. It looks something like war.

May 27, 1862

Jacquie brought this morning a pacquet of letters among which we hoped to find the one written by Irvie to Ma, but no, there was one from him to Walter and another to Cousin Horace and one from Benton to Mrs. Roy which we immediately forwarded by Carey. Irvie wrote in fine script—was still with Beauregard and all was well.

Confederate General Beauregard took command of the Western army after Gen. Albert Sidney Johnston was killed at Shiloh. Beauregard pulled out of Corinth, Mississippi, May 29 and 30, 1862, and headed toward Tupelo, Mississippi, in the face of Union General Halleck's 100,000 troops. Halleck started for Corinth April 29, 1862.

He said in regards to the Battle of Pittsburg Landing that we had whipped them very badly notwithstanding the fibs they have told about it, and if they attack them again we were ready to repeat the dose. He also said that he had written to Ma and forwarded it to Winchester from which place he hopes she will get it. The letters had been sent by private conveyance—Mr. Marshall—from Corinth. We were so delighted to hear from the dear fellow again. Carey soon came in with a letter for me enclosed in Mrs. Roy's. Benton wrote very encouragingly and hopefully—had separated from the other boys so, and instead of being with Beauregard was on Hardee's staff—"Captain Roy"—how queer that would look as the direction on his letters. There was also an enclosure from Dick Blakemore to Dick Bayly—the former is at Corinth too and his brother and cousin Willie and Alex how delightful for them all to be there together. I sat right down and finished the boys' letter and then commenced one to Benton that I might send them all out together by Tom Petty who goes to Richmond tomorrow.

May 28, 1862

I heard a slight bustle downstairs and presently Nannie came running up to say—"Captain Massie's downstairs—his wife too and he's wounded." Ma went downstairs to receive them and I completed reading until hearing voices in the next room I stepped out and saw standing before the dressing glass a round faced, black-eyed, dark haired little girl who Ma introduced to me as Miss Chapman. Her father lived in Luray and they were on their way to Winchester shopping carrying with them a cousin who had been wounded in the service. They could not be accommodated at any of the hotels owing to the number of persons in town and were in a dilemma until meeting with a mutual acquaintance Captain Massie who brought them over here. On going down to the parlor found Captain M. there, but he left soon after. Spent the time until tea was ready very pleasantly laughing and talking. Miss Kate told us that Hattie Gillispie was a very strong anti-Confederate and doing all in her power against our cause, her brother had been in the C.S. Army but was now on the staff of a Yankee general. Chaggie and Fannie Mohler on the contrary were good Secessionists, I'm so glad! Miss Chapman's brothers, three of them, are in the service. One of them is one of Alvin's favorite soldier friends, met him last summer.

> Washington worried about Jackson's victories since the greater part of its army was tied down on the peninsula in Virginia. General Shields was ordered back to the Valley on May 25, 1862. His forces were followed by General McDowell with half of his corps.

There was today a rumor to the effect that Shields is returning to circumvent Jackson's plans.

May 29, 1862

Nellie and I were left guardians of the house as Ma, Grandma, Laura and some of the children spent the day at Oakley. We had Captain Marshall and a brother-in-law of his to dinner today—the latter proved to be the bearer of our dispatches from Corinth, a very clever, agreeable gentleman. He had been with the boys at Corinth and brought cheering news of their condition there. We had our bread baked and sent to the hospital before Ma returned in the afternoon. They say that there is some excitement in town in consequence of the reported advance of Shields. Wonder if it's true—if comes he has been very heavily reinforced, but still I trust we may administer a quietus to him.

IV

SECOND OCCUPATION

May 30, 1862 - August 16, 1862

May 30, 1862
 A baneful day—one to which I shall hereafter refer as one of dark forebodings and uncertainties. It dawned brightly—but still from the beginning it seemed sad. First a house containing the dead bodies of the smallpox patients was burned. Charlie Buck came in very unexpectedly about nine o'clock and was looking thin but remarkably well. Alice Morehead and Dr. Rixie next dropped in, each one bringing in some fresh rumors about the advance of the Federals; it seems there must be great alarm in town. Presently a courier came by today saying the enemy was this side Salem and on the march so Charlie concluded he had better ascertain the truth and be off in time to escape them, knowing that the few invalids here would not be able to offer any resistance to the expected army, but promising to return to see us in case there was no foundation for the report.

> Thus Jackson further accomplished his duty, to hold Banks in the Valley and to now have additional troops sent in while Lee and Joseph Johnston were holding Richmond. Jackson at Charlestown received news that General Shields was returning and was within a day's march of Front Royal.

He had not left many minutes ere Dr. R. who has been in town returned telling Alice they must hasten away as the place would certainly in a little time be occupied by the Feds. It commenced sprinkling rain about the time they mounted their horses but the firing had commenced but

88

they dashed fearlessly and even cheerfully away. All the morning the government wagons had been going toward Winchester, and a little while before Dr. R. came over our troops marched out—they did not go "hurry-scurry" like the Yankees but marched out with becoming dignity. We watched them as if they had been well known and much loved friends each one of them, and it was with a feeling of horror that I reflected upon the probability that our poor sick would fall into their hands. Cruel hands they would prove. The depot containing stores was fired and Father went over to protect the store. Our cavalrymen in squads were dashing out of town just as the Yankees appeared on the hill.

> *The Federals under Shields reentered Front Royal at about noon. The Twelfth Georgia Regiment left to guard the stores and prisoners marched north to Winchester.*
> *The stores valued at $300,000 were destroyed by the Confederates. Colonel Conner, the commander of the Twelfth Georgia was put under arrest by Jackson for not fighting at Front Royal, even in the face of overwhelming odds.*
> *Shields' men had now sealed one of Jackson's two avenues of retreat. The other line of retreat was Strasburg, eleven miles west of Front Royal. General Fremont's army was moving on Strasburg from the west. Jackson was forty miles to the north and ordered a withdrawal up the Valley before his army could be cut off.*

There was some pretty brisk firing for a time, and suddenly a horrid shell came shrieking and whizzing over the house. They had planted a piece on the hill next to the orchard, and as they had threatened to shell the place we concluded that they were fulfilling their threat. All took refuge in the basement, the little children screaming and all confusion and uncertainty. Worse than all Father was still in town and we did not know whether they would permit him to come out or not any more. However, there were only a few shells sent on their errand of death, when the hills seemed to be overcast with dark clouds of the enemy's columns. They poured in from every direction, infantry, artillery and cavalry, through the waving wheat trampling it under foot, over the blooming clover crushing out fragrance and beauty there as remorsely as they would have crushed out life and hope in our bosoms. The horrible beings poured in from all sides looking all the more so since our eyes had grown accustomed to seeing our dear Southerners. When Jackson entered town although the cannonading was of much longer duration and far heavier I rather enjoyed it, but during the firing today I was really sick of heart—every report was an insult—a demoniacal roar of triumph, each boom probably the death knell to many a brave spirit. Until Father came in about two o'clock we felt very unprotected with the ruffianly fellows careening through the yard, but he appeared at that time much to our joy and told us the storehouse and all other buildings save the depot were uninjured—that was of course consumed.

But a little while ago and I boasted of my willingness to abide a little tyranny for a while—now after having had the pleasure of again seeing our own army—but I find the prospect of slavery more revolting than ever before—probably because I know they will strive to render it more abject. General Kimball was among the first to enter and sent a message at three o'clock to the effect that he would wish to occupy his former quarters here and have dinner by the time of his arrival. They came the general, the adjutant—Captains Mason and Bunting—Frank Crippen, Kent, Skin, Bob Burwell—Rawhead and Bloodybones to all of them. I was too angry and outraged to witness their arrival but shut my door and sewed away as fast as I could until it was time to attend to arranging the dinner table—or supper table it was in reality. Nothing could exceed my horror on going down to tea, after the officers were supposed to have retired from the table, to see the horrid old hypocrite Freeman there. A haughty inclination of the head was all I could possibly vouchsafe the old sinner. There was another hoary headed old traitor just leaving the table—one in civilian garb—doubtless acting the officer's pilot to his Yankee friends—him, we did not condescend to notice at all. The climax was capped though when in walked that horrid coarse rawhead and bloodybones and took his seat. No more supper for me—so hastily finishing my glass of milk I retreated upstairs. By this time the whole brigade had marched into the former camp below the house and taken quiet possession there—of quiet did I say? Oh no, for as it was raining they had an excellent excuse for a repetition of their previous destruction and fences were prostrated with as much rapidity as on the former occasions. Nellie and I were standing in the door when they made a rush for the wheat field fence and Rob Roy, standing by sick and weak looked on with dismay saying "Oh look yonder! Mass William just put the last rail to that fence yesterday; just fixed what they tore down before and they are taking every bit again." Nellie darted off to tell Father and General Kimball immediately appeared pistols in hand and marched down to the point of attack and quelled the assailants by the time the panels had all been thrown down the distance of a hundred yards. Martha who was standing at the kitchen window evidently did not have much faith in the general's threat that—"somebody should be shot" for the sake of saving a "Secesh's" rails—for she remarked as he passed her "Law Miss Lucie!—that man ain't going to do anything to his men to save that fence—he knew they were going to take it, so why did he not stop them before they commenced?"—an echo repeated the query—"why?" The creatures were coming to the house till ten o'clock at night begging suppers. Nellie and I had to abdicate our room in favor of Captain Bunting tonight.

I was so sorry when Eliza H and Mrs. M came up this evening to say Mrs. H was thought to be dying and they wanted a little ice for her. Poor thing! 'Tis no wonder she should sink under such a pressure of calamity—those less delicately constituted than herself can scarce bear up under it.

May 31, 1862

Was awakened quite early this morning by Eliza Ann telling me that Ma had been summoned to Mrs. Hope who was thought to be dying and Grandma wanted me downstairs to assist her. Went down and dressed the children, helped to tidy the room, and saw about breakfast. Found it was still raining and disagreeable without and yet there on the cold wet pavement lay stretched at full length the guard of the night sleeping soundly on their hard bed despite muddy blankets and a deal of noise and looking for all the world like a trio of resigned and happy pigs.

I'm so sorry I treated that poor old man rudely last night—for Grandma tells me he is a good Secessionist who was kidnapped by the wretches who destroyed his enclosures, despoiled his little lot, left his family unprotected and forced him on pain of destruction to act as guide promising at the same time however, to send him home after the accomplishment of his mission. She tells me she had just heard him out on the porch talking to some of the Yankees—old Freeman for one—and telling them just what he thought of their meanness and how little sympathy he had with them anyway. Well, never mind, I'm determined to show you some marked courtesy in presence of your tormentors if I possibly can, poor old man!

After breakfast I did! While sitting at the breakfast table in marched Frank, Skin, Burwell, Kent and the poor old Rebel. I did not see any but the latter to whom I bowed a pleasant "good morning" and as there were but few seats prepared at table I motioned him to the most desirable and busied myself assiduously in helping him. The others noticed it I know, though they did not let on. That Frank!—he is apparently a clever sort of fellow and if he only just was not a Yankee I should like him so much; he has the faculty of winning the confidence and affection of children which speaks certainly very well for him. I was a good deal amused, when they all came down to breakfast and found the table was not ready for them, instead of standing with staring eyes and gaping with stupid embarrassment like the others he threw himself into a chair standing near the window and remarked pleasantly that he was "sorry they had intruded so soon but he understood from Mr. Buck that breakfast was waiting for them" and addressed some remarks to Grandma until the seats were arranged for them. That's just the way he does—always seems perfectly respectful, never staring at us when we go to the door and conducts himself like a gentleman if he were not a Yankee!—but he is, and that is enough.

Ma came in from Mr. Hope's—Mrs. H is better and all as well as could be expected. She heard while there that Longstreet was expected to reinforce Jackson and if so I hope they'll give General Shields something to do. Such a horrible noise as they are making all this morning in camp. I try to read but can't hear myself think for the confusion. They are making a slaughter pen of the lot before the house and the sharp reports of firearms, the agonizing shrieks of the poor butchered animals mingled with the savage yells and laughter of the inhuman soldiery—all combined to make the morning hideous. There is some movement on foot—a long train of artillery has just passed, couriers and constantly arriving and departing and a general stir in camp. Perhaps they think Jackson will attack them here. There!—that caps the climax, they have just hoisted a flag on the house—not the hateful "Stars and Stripes" 'tis true, but a flag to denote Kimball's quarters—a Yankee flag and I do not feel as if I could get my breath. What would Alvin and Irving say to see the enemy's flag waving over the time-honored roof of old Bel Air? Poor dear boys! It is no less disagreeable than dangerous, for if our men should come in, they would in all probability mistake this for a traitor's house and shell it or at all events shoot at the flag. Too bad! The brigade has orders to move I know by the motions in camp. The tents droop and now they begin to discharge the old loads from their guns. Oh mercy! That volley must have been fired by a whole regiment at once, and they've got their guns pointed toward the house—actually firing into the hill. No wonder the poor children run screaming to our sides and hide their heads in their hands in our dresses. There it goes again! Well this is too much for human endurance. I'll go out and see if there are none of the officers about who can stop this ... went out on the porch and seeing Frank sitting composedly under the aspen reading *Sparegrass—Papers* I commenced abusing the Yankees to Ma for their inhumanity in shooting toward a house full of women and little children. He instantly sprung up and came forward—they would soon stop now as they were only discharging in order to reload preparatory to marching—that they would not fire so high as to strike the house. Presently they moved off ... all gone with the exception of the general and his staff. The air is bright with sunshine again and we feel free to go in the garden to see the flowers. Such flowers! The rose bushes every one seem deluged with beauty, great clusters of lovely half-blown buds, great glowing red hearted full flowers, heliotrope, honeysuckle, fleur-de-lis, bouquets, not for the Yankees but for the house.

It is raining again this evening, and there is something going on which we can't account for: Kimball's brigade has returned bringing in with it some ambulances and the officers speak of a little skirmishing going on over the river this evening.

> Shields' forces finally moved out toward Strasburg to aid General Fremont's army closing in on Jackson's only route of retreat. After meeting a portion of Southern cavalry and being directed on the wrong road, Shields' men returned to Front Royal and began moving up the Luray Valley in an

attempt to get in front of Jackson.

I wonder if "somebody" has not been hurt. They are evidently apprehensive of an attack—have placed cannon on the hill immediately in range with the house with the mouth pointing the opposite direction. But that does not make any difference, for our men would have of course tried to silence the enemy's battery and so we should be in danger from our own cannon. We are just in a cross fire between three of them—or should be if attacked. Father speaks of sending us off to Belmont till after it is all over, but I think 'twould be very wrong for us to desert Father and the house now. Our flight would leave everything much exposed to pilferers and Father, poor fellow, has his hands and head full now of business. Besides we could take refuge in the basement from the shells and balls. Grandma insists on it—she is nervous and sick, and indeed I believe we're all well-nigh worn out with this constant excitement—I tremble and feel so weak that I can scarcely stand up. Even the little children are as nervous as they can be and I was right much amused at poor little Willie a little while ago. He was lying half asleep when a thunder clap burst overhead sounding precisely like the report of artillery: he did not utter a word but with one bound sprang from the bed into my arms and then he shrieked, quivered as if he were frightened almost to death.

Well, Father has told us to make all preparations for an early start in the morning. Nellie and I want to stay with Father but Ma thinks it would be imprudent, and won't go without us. Oh dear!—this is a glowering night and I'm heartsick. It has been raining and lightening and thundering every night since they came to it, and now it is storming furiously. The guard has not been detailed for the house and Father is afraid to go to bed leaving the house unprotected and surrounded by four thousand desperadoes. He is looking so haggard and worn it makes me sad to see him.

We finished all preparations and as it was almost one o'clock A.M. I must woo "tired nature's sweet restorer." Oh!—the myriad sad hearts that throb tonight!

June 1, 1862

Awoke quite early feeling very little refreshed. Father at first thought it doubtful as to whether we would go to B today owing to want of conveyance, the horses having strayed off in the night. It had ceased raining, and the first sound I heard on going downstairs was a band playing to an advancing regiment—playing "Gay and Happy" in the most unsabbath manner. It was Ord's division going by and while standing there looking they commenced discharging their guns again and the balls actually struck the front of the house a few inches below the window of Father's room. Horrid wretches! As they pass by for sheer amusement they kick the water gate to atoms. While they were passing Frank came out and stood near the door—he remarked to Grandma that General Kimball had detailed him to act as escort should we wish to leave today and now for the first time in my life I entered into conversation with a Yankee soldier. I enquired if it were not dangerous to leave the house for fear it should be plundered—I knew that deserted houses generally suffered from such a proceeding. "Oh no, not at all!" He would promise "it should not be so" and from this we entered into a regular discussion which I really enjoyed for I made him acknowledge the superior generalship displayed by our "Stonewall," made him own up to the "Banks panic" etc. After breakfast we went to work packing and locking up bed clothes and after all were prepared went out on the porch to witness the departure of the officers. All of them looked extremely sad although they spoke confidently of success. When Gen. K. came to make his adieux the little baby was in Laura's arms on the porch and walking up to it he put his arm about it and kissed it several times—thinking probably of his own little ones who might that day be made fatherless. He very cordially shook hands with all save Nellie and myself and in reply to our bow he said—"Farewell daughters." Nellie was so much amused at the idea of being called daughter by a Yankee officer. After they left Frank mounted his horse and taking Rob Roy with him went off in search of our horses. And now such a time as we had, we had no officer on guard (though Gen. K. told Father that Gen. Tyler would be over during the day to quarter here if 'twould not inconvenience him.) The stragglers in the wake of every army now poured in from all sides and annoyed poor Father almost to death. Then the shooting recommenced and was kept up for an hour straight ahead. It seems sometimes as if a whole regiment would sometime discharge their pieces simultaneously until the very heavens seemed to be torn asunder by the reverberation. The bullets whistled and sang a tune among the trees around the house, and the little children crying and sobbing with fright crept to our sides burying their heads in our dresses and begging Father to go out and make them quit. Poor children! Little they knew how limited was Father's power over them and what he was suffering for them. Frank came back after awhile with the horses which after some difficulty he had succeeded in securing, and he made the soldiers point their guns another way and in a little while they stopped altogether and marched out. I had a most refreshing argument with Frank while the wagon was being harnessed. He told me that Stanton had certainly received an official dispatch announcing the fall of Richmond a week before—that the South would soon accept terms of peace, etc., etc. All of which I laughed to scorn. In debating the justice of this, on their side, aggressive war—he made a very feeble attempt to vindicate their justice, but he had so little faith in what he was saying that he ended in a hearty burst of laughter and gave it up, saying he wished it were well over. He told me they expected an attack from Jackson at the river, two miles from here, but that there was no possibility of his escaping being made prisoner—he and his whole army, for he was completely surrounded by General Fremont, Rosecrans, all McDowell's division, Ords, Shields, and the hero Banks himself was advancing from Harper's Ferry on him—making altogether eighty thousand men.

> *While General Ewell and Taylor's men held Union General Fremont west of Strasburg, the remainder of Jackson's army marched into town. Late in the afternoon of June 1, 1862, Winder's brigade came in after a thirty-six mile march in one day. Jackson's foot cavalry had the Massnutten Mountain on its left flank and the trap at Strasburg could now close. Jackson was safe! General Fremont followed Jackson up the main Valley and Shields' forces moved south in the Luray Valley.*

My heart thrilled almost to suffocation at the thought of the danger in which our poor little army was—but I did not allow him to see that I was the least bit discomposed and laughingly assured him that I should never believe they had Jackson till I saw him. Even when Frank went over to town to get Father a guard and came back again a dispatch had been received to the effect that Fremont had taken him in Strasburg, even though Father told us to be prepared for the worst, even though I heard the heavy cannonading, I did not and would not believe Jackson would fall into such hands. I never felt such a pain in my heart as when we told Father good-bye and the wagons filled with every member of the family—we drove from the yard, refugees from our dear home which we might return to and find a heap of smouldering ashes. And Father looked so heartsick and almost wept outright. Frank and Bob both accompanied us as escorts and I never in my life saw more delicate attention from anyone than from the former—we went through an entire brigade and Frank would ride on ahead and clear the path for us even getting down to pull the fence away to give us passage. And when the rude soldiers stared and grinned at the fugitives, he would ride between us and them and apologize for them. It was a most intensely hot day and what with a heavy heart and... blood seething through my veins I felt well-nigh crazed—though I cooled myself sufficiently to give Frank some retorts. When we got to the mountains we found they had a guard —among them a young Bostonian Clapp, a very polite but saucy fellow, when Frank went away I could not forbear giving him my hand and well wishes for his individual safety. After giving him my hand I vented my spleen on little Clapp and talked him quiet—It is so refreshing to abuse someone when you've a heart full of bitterness.

Did not hear anything definite from our army except that Jackson was utterly powerless in their hands. Oh no!

June 7, 1862

Well we are at home again, almost worn out. Walked down from Belmont through a scathing sunshine and reached home to find everything about the house safe but in awful disorder which we immediately set about to rectify and have been hard at work ever since. Poor Father! They've ruined him—have taken all his corn, have broken his mill, stolen his implements, burnt his fencing and destroyed his crop and cut the farm to pieces. General Tyler did not come over as he expected, but one Captain Sanderson of Phil. and Mr. Berry quartered here—the former protecting him as far as he could, but he had a hard time of it indeed. The little boys returned home on Monday. We have spent the week I scarcely know how only that we were so spent with nervous excitement that we slept a great deal of the time. Monday I slept and read all day. Commenced raining Sunday evening and rained all day Monday. Heard Jackson and his whole army were on the point of grounding arms. Never saw anything like the number of baggage trains and troops—was glad to see the troops had pretty much cleared out from around Bel Air. The Yankees were up at Belmont before breakfast; took Uncle Mack's spyglass away from him. However he went down to camp and recovered it. Tuesday... raining: amused ourselves watching the arrival and departure of troops from Front Royal. Today they have Jackson prisoner and his son dead never knew he had one before.

> *Jackson's only child, a daughter named Julia, was born November 23, 1862. He had no children by his first wife who died in childbirth, in 1854, fourteen months after their wedding. His second marriage was to Mary Anna Morrison, July 16, 1857.*

Some bitter cannonading on Monday and some Tuesday but no battle as was expected. Jackson we concluded had retired up the valley—the enemy pursuing. A number of Yankees there for corn—cavalry—very saucy. Read, sewed and slept. Homesick. Wednesday. Thought it was going to clear off but it did not—gathered some beautiful roses. Ashby is dead, today.

> *Ashby, Jackson's cavalry leader, was killed June 6, 1862. A horse had been shot from under him and on foot leading his men forward he was mortally wounded.*

More Yankees and more impudence but the guard kept them at bay till late when some of them stole Uncle Mack's horses and one of ours, but he went to camp and recovered them with great difficulty. No cannonading. Sleeping, reading and a little sewing. Thursday: Raining, still. Jackson and five hundred of his men have escaped. Should not be surprised if his whole army did after a while. Had a paper announcing the evacuation of Corinth and vilifying Beauregard to such an extent that I felt like throttling the editor. It also took complimentary (?) notice of Miss Belle Boyd's heroism on the twenty-third. There were accounts of the battle at Richmond—of course they were victors. Clapp was up this evening but did not see him. More Yankees and more impertinence. Sewed a little—homesick very. Had a note from Father encouragingly written. Friday: Nothing from the army in the valley. It was clear and we had intended going home but it was too muddy for walking and they had taken one of our horses and we had no driver, and Uncle Mack could not send us. Captain Sanderson came up at noon and told us there had been a battle at Richmond in which McClellan's whole army was engaged, and that we had repulsed them with very great loss. G-l-o-r-i-o-u-s! How much better we all felt for the intelligence. He confirms the evacuation of Corinth and thinks Beauregard has gone with reinforcements to Richmond. Oh!—if it be but true that we've shipped them at R! As for Beauregard—whatever he does he has a reason for and we shall soon see if it isn't for the best.

I've noticed for a long time that Friday has been a most unlucky day—to verify my belief yesterday Father had six hundred head of mules turned in upon his little meadows, utterly ruining them.

June 9, 1862

Mr. Berry came in and said there was great commotion in town owing to a report that Jackson and Longstreet were advancing down the valley.

> *Jackson moved his army south up the Valley to Harrisonburg, and the night of June 5, his troops were near Port Republic which he entered on June 6.*
>
> *Shields' advance in the Luray Valley on June 5, was to Big Springs, two miles north of Conrad's Store. On June 8, Jackson struck Fremont, who had followed him up the main Valley, at Cross Keys, and on June 9, Shields' was hit at Port Republic. The Federals were beaten in both battles. The trap had failed again.*
>
> *The first Valley campaign was over. In thirty-five days Jackson, with his small army, had marched approximately 300 miles, fought four battles, plus many smaller ones, and had kept over 60,000 Federals occupied. Jackson was a hero and secretly began to transport his army to aid Lee at Richmond.*

There is a great running to and fro of cars and the baggage trains are very busy carrying off supplies. There is something on foot, that's evident. Wonder where Fremont, Rosecrans, and company are? McDowell is in Washington under arrest. Wonder if they'll decapitate him?

June 10, 1862

Raining and disagreeable. Was summoned to the door by double knock where I found two impudent little Yankees who wanted dinner furnished them! They were sent to the kitchen and presently another one a major from "Der Vaterland." He took lodging for the day and night. He did make me so mad telling how one of our men wounded him and how he shot him for it. He was an intelligent man—had been in the German wars and amused Father very much giving an account of his imprisonment and escape from a Prussian fortress and his final exile to America. I had the toothache terribly and Ma went into the room to get something to put on it. As soon as the major saw her at it he sprung up, went to his portmanteau and took out innumerable little flasks of all kinds of brandies—prune, wild cherry, etc.—some of which he presented to her. Dutchman to the last. One of the little Yankees informed us today that Jackson was well-nigh surrounded as "Fremont had taken him in hand now."

June 11, 1862

Nervie came in to get a little salt for their bread and he told us that they had heard from a reliable source that Jackson had given Shields and Fremont a most complete "Dressing." Laura went up to Mrs. Hopes in the evening and returned bringing a confirmation of the account and addenda in the fact that they had been hauling off the dead and wounded all the night before in the cars besides a large number who were said to be in a house some distance up the creek. They also said it was reported that there had been several of our men seen in the mountains—some were even known to have been in town. Wonder what it all means?

June 13, 1862

Went downstairs this morning before breakfast and made up my first biscuit and helped to get breakfast. Then we girls washed up the dishes and cups and set the table for dinner. Ma, Nellie, and Laura milked and strained it and put it away. Then Nellie and I cleaned up our rooms and went to help Martha iron. Finished ironing by dinner time and after resting awhile went down and folded the clothes. Brought them up and put them away. Dr. Turner came in and told us that there had been 240 wagonloads of wounded brought down from above and that the Yankees themselves acknowledged to the defeat.

> *Tyler's casualties (Shields' army) in the Battle of Port Republic were 1,008 (67 killed; 393 wounded and 553 missing.) Jackson had 800 casualties.*

Oh!—I wish I could see Frank now to ask him where all those men are who were to have surrounded and eaten Jackson's army up bodily. He said he did not know how Shields' men would feel in a retreat, but I guess he knows now. Helped to get supper and my biscuits were a decided success. Dressed myself and went out to gather some sweetbrier roses to put on Father's plate—I always like to see them on the tea and breakfast tables and they are Father's favorite flowers.

June 14, 1862

Two young New Yorkers called to get some milk and making the children's acquaintance one showed them the photographs of his family and his own on which was written his name "Fred Allen"—the boys brought them up and showed them to us. The other one—Johnnie Rokett was a combination of resemblance to Irvie and Dick. He was a school boy and orphan, very tired of the war and homesick. Father was without a guard and learning that their regiment was near acting in that capacity he engaged them as sentinels to protect the house and yard. I do think little Rokett reminds me more of Irvie as he sits out there his face buried in a book—and Alden is not unlike Alvin.

Uncle Tom was over this evening and told us that a Yankee major had given him an account of the battle. Jackson had sent all his wagons ahead of him and the prisoners were sent to Lynchburg long before the Feds came into Winchester. He marched to a certain position, took his wagons to a high point put cannon behind them, unhitched the horses and waited for the Feds who, when they rushed forward to seize the supposed abandoned wagons, were met with a withering fire from the "masked batteries." The slaughter was fearful and the major confessed they were cut to pieces. They fought two days, one in which Shields' was used up and the other Fremont. Oh this is more than our most sanguine hopes could have asked. But I very much fear Colonel Ashby is dead—they all bring the same account of his death. Poor fellow—'tis said—"Whom the Gods love die young" and it seems so in this case truly, for both friend and foe vie in giving him credit for his gallantry as a soldier and his nobility as a man. May God give thy spirit rest, noble son of a worthy mother—valiantly and well hast thou contended for the freedom of our home and thy people. Well hast thou earned a patriot's monument in the hearts of thy brother and sister Southerons, and mayst thou win a crown of glory in that higher destiny that awaits thee—the crown of the Christian soldier. What an irreparable loss to the South! Woe! Woe!

June 15, 1862

Mrs. Moffatt brought us a paper in which was published a dispatch from Walter to poor Colonel Ashby when the former was scouting in the mountains just before Jackson's army came in. It was captured on the cars at Staunton and had W's full signature to it. Father was afraid it would get Uncle Mack into trouble, but I guess 'twould be more apt to make captivity an awkward thing for the writer should he ever be taken. Nellie and I played and sang some tonight. Poor Kattie! Mr. S. was carried off prisoner yesterday. He was sick at the time and I can imagine she must be very distressed and anxious about him.

> *Green Samuels was exchanged. He was again captured in the Battle of Winchester in September, 1864 and was not released until the end of the war.*

June 16, 1862

This morning Orville came over from Uncle Tom's and told us that there were two Confederate prisoners there taken in the battle at Port Republic—they were of Louisiana Seventh which suffered so much and one of these was wounded. There was also a wounded Yankee there. We had been intending to go over to Oakley all the morning and although we heard Shields was to be in about noon—we concluded to go and return before that time. Father could not go himself so he sent Johnnie Rokett to guard us across the fields but I was very sorry he did so when instead of going back then, he walked on through town and up to Uncle Tom's. I never did have any fancy for perambulating with a Yankee—be he never so civilized a specimen, and besides, I know the Fed all took us to be Unionists and that I hated. Found Aunt Betty sitting on the front porch with the "Secesh" and Union boy very amicably shelling peas together. Arthur Wough, our little Confederate, was a trim nice fellow whom I should have taken to be seventeen, if he had not told me he was twenty—he gave us a cordial grasp of the hand such as only a Southerner could give and seemed very glad to see us. I was so glad to see a grey coat again for my eyes have been aching with monotony of blue cloth. 'Twas right amusing to see the captor and captive together. Ma, Nellie and myself went out to help them in their task and when little Secesh saw the Yankee fishing in the basket after the pea pods so awkwardly he would say "Stop Captain, I'll show you how" and he would skillfully shake the basket up for him. Every once in awhile our old Yankee would read something from the paper detrimental to our cause, but little Wough always gave back as good as they sent. After such little ebullitions they were soon as sociable as ever and making arrangements with each other relative to going to Washington their destination. The other prisoner was in his room wounded but I met him once in passing through the hall.

Uncle Tom came in and said a letter had been received from Bailey Jacobs since the battle at Richmond and he wrote that poor Charlie Richardson was wounded—perhaps mortally. Poor, poor Charlie, how often he has jested about going to Richmond to defend it, and how often has he spoken of his willingness to lay down his life for his country and now—but I do hope still that it may all be a mistake. He mentioned no other friends who were hurt. Nothing has been heard from Willie R since he left Williamsburg and we are so uneasy about him. Oh! me ... I do wish this was well over!

We left Uncle Tom's about eleven o'clock—we gave Wough little bouquets of one white and two red rosebuds when we bade him good-bye. He said his captors were very kind to him and he hoped soon to be exchanged, when he would rejoin his regiment. He said poor Ashby was certainly dead, but he confirmed the most flattering accounts we had from Port Republic and moreover said we had just gained a signal victory at Richmond where McClellan had been repulsed thirty miles. Better and better. Carey came home with us. Shields' army did not come in till four o'clock and when they did come such a looking party! Every other one was barefooted, some coatless, some with garments well-nigh torn off them, all dirty and harassed almost to death. Ambulances and wagons with the sick and wounded passed by and the house and kitchen were besieged until late at night by soldiers begging for food—"just a bit of any kind of bread," for they were "almost starved," or else they wanted "a morsel for a sick friend." I had vowed never to cook anything for a Yankee but when a man walked in and begged for a little thickened milk for a sick friend, my humanity overcame my hate and I made him a nice bowl of the coveted refreshment. I even went so far as to make up the biscuit dough—I could do this when they were in retreat, but had the case been otherwise I would not have done it. Colonel Thorborne—acting brigadier general in Carrol's absence engaged quarters here—the brigade camping in the barn-field back of the house. General Kimball had said that in case of a return he would like to stop here, but he did not do so, for reasons I think I can comprehend.

> *General Kimball's brigade was transported to McClellan's army on the Peninsula. On July 16 the brigade was made part of General Sumner's corps, and served with it for the balance of their service.*
>
> *Kimball was wounded at Fredricksburg where his command suffered heavily. Upon recovering he was assigned to the command of a division in the west.*

Kent, Frank and Skin came in quite early to tea, though, and we invited Frank to the first table. He came in like a man who expected to pass a severe ordeal and was resolved to do it gallantly, so when we demurely asked him for Jackson's address that we might call on him and cheer his imprisonment—he commenced deploring "poor Ashby's death." We soon disposed of that though and he acknowledged their defeat, said he would "not sorrow for it as they would get home the sooner by it" but added that if their brigade and Shields had been there in person, they would have had a different tale to tell. I asked why they were not there? Well the men wanted shoes, they could not march without shoes. Why couldn't they march over the same, barefoot as well as Jackson's men had many of them done? Well, he confessed, he was tired of this way and would be glad to be home again. We would not vex him any more after that but Skin and the other boys took their departure soon after expecting to return with the brigade.

After awhile some officers came down to the table to supper and while Ma presided, Nellie and I stood at the side table washing cups and saucers. They commenced talking of their defeat, lauding Jackson and praising their own intrepidity and at last spoke of Ashby's death and what a great loss he would be to the Southern Confederacy, seeming to think it a death blow to Jackson's power. I couldn't hold my tongue any longer, but turning to the spokesman remarked that while Colonel Ashby's death was bitterly deplored by the Southern people, yet Ashby's men, who had done the fighting for him were still alive and able to do them a deal of mischief. The officer replied that he had some of them in camp now who looked very harmless—spoke it so tauntingly that I could not help reminding him that lately it was thought they were considered harmless. Ma came in just now and told me that it was Colonel Shalosse and his staff to whom I was talking. Well I don't care, in fact I'm glad of it for I've been wanting to give vent to my feelings a long time and now that it is done I feel relieved. Oh!—dear me!—dear me!

Frank told me that in the engagement at Port Republic the parties fought even with stones and that in taking a battery a party of Southerners had hold on one end of a cannon and the Northerners tugging at it for dear life.

June 17, 1862

Well, this has been a tiresome day and I believe another such will about finish my little stock of patience. In the first place I discovered that our compulsory guests were Virginians—so called—traitors I consider them and at the second breakfast table Nellie and I had a quarrel with a young lieutenant and clerk—trying to shame them in their treason, but they evidently considered us the heretics and tried to convert us from the error of our way. They succeeded so far as to strengthen yet more our secession opinion. One comfort—the colonel and all his staff at the breakfast table owned that (to use their own expression) they did "skedaddle faster than they ever did in their lives before," and one of them laughed and said he had "left Jackson all his nice clothes." They jested each other a great deal and I enjoyed it under these circumstances. All day long the horrible Yankees were coming in the yard wanting milk, wanting bread, and I think there were not less than one thousand here for water and notwithstanding the wet season we've had, they pumped the well dry—a thing that has not been done before since it was dug sixty years ago. And then the few cherry trees in the yard and garden had a little half ripe fruit on them and they were a constant source of annoyance ... the Yankees through the garden—trampling down the young corn and breaking the palings and ruinously mutilating the trees. They were scared almost to death this morning thinking Jackson was going to attack them; the colonel told Father they were expecting a battle here and Father prepared us for it. But our brave Stonewall did not come.

Oh I'm very tired of oppression!

June 18, 1862

I was angry all the morning, angry with the Yankees for trying to proselyte—angry at them for fibbing and angry with them because they were Yankees. The servants were vexatious too. Rob Roy in whom we had so much confidence even espousing the cause of the Yankee. I never was half so mad in my life. Insinuating wretches!—to come here and tell Father how kind and good they are going to be to us after our subjugation—how they will soothe the pains of submission—trying to win him over to the opinion that the Lincoln government when once established will be very mild and equitable. Gracious heavens! If I thought it were my fate to submit to them I believe it would craze me! No—

> "Better the fire should o'er me roll
> Better the shot, the blade, the bowl
> Than crucifixion of the soul."

An old traitor came into them from the mountains today and his presence served to increase until by supper time I was in a fine mood for abusing. Ma, Nellie and myself did give Lieutenant Mesod a good talking tonight and Captain Stephens too. After supper Father begged us to play and sing, to which move I strenuously objected until they called for Southern music—whereupon I sat down and played "Johnston's March to Manassas," "Bonnie Blue Flag," and "Maryland," in this latter Captain S accompanied me. He then proposed the "Red, White and Blue" which I respectfully declined. Nellie would not even go into the parlor where we were. After playing Captain Stephens dived into politics again and we had quite a quarrel—Lieutenant Morrel wished to take a part but being told that lawyers would distort anything into an appearance of fact he forebore.

June 19, 1862

No sign of movement yet, spent the morning in my room upstairs, about eleven o'clock Jacquie brought us a letter from Irvin, bless him! It was dated May 15 therefore the latest advice we had—sent by flag of truce to the Yankee line where it was mailed to Cousin H. Helen Hieronimous and forwarded by her to Front Royal through a member of the signal corps now at Uncle Mack's. I was so glad to hear that they were all well and in good spirit—he said we must not be uneasy about their welfare as Colonel Jordan would take good care of him. He spoke of enclosing a letter to me which I did not receive—I do wish I could have gotten it for no doubt he wrote more at length in that and more unrestrainedly and probably that is the reason they would not let it come through. Poor boy! I wish I knew where they were now.

I noticed the porch looked very untidy and seeing it vacant, went out to sweep it off. While thus employed Captain Stephens came out from his headquarters and sauntering up asked me if I were acquainted with Miss Hattie Gillespie. When I told him that she had been an acquaintance of mine he proceeded to inform me that she and all her family were at the hotel in town, "having been forced to leave their home on account of Dr. G. having accepted a commission in the Federal army." I wonder how many Southerners have been driven away from their homes by the Yankee forces. The little kid glove captain succeeded in what he had been endeavoring to do for some time—picking a quarrel with me. I tried to retain my equilibrium by reflecting on his insignificance, but his cool assurance was too much for me and by becoming angry and excited gave him decidedly the advantage. The idea of his advocating perfect social equality and affectionate intercouse among parties differing as widely in political opinions as Unionists and Secessionists—giving parties to each other, and, cherishing feelings of bitter, venomous hatred in their hearts, yet clasp hands in apparent friendship—and concealed under a hypocritical mask of bright smiles the scorn we feel. As an argument he cited the example of his own family which was half Union and half Secession, and yet were perfectly harmonious as ever before. I told him that I had no fancy for hypocrisy and as for feeling any desire of coming in contact with any Union acquaintances I did not, as the intercourse would be productive of nothing but ill feelings on both sides. He then fell to depreciating our generals and it seemed to me did everything he could to incense me—and succeeded beyond his expectations. I should not have cared so much if he had been graced in having such a renegade son—and I presently picked myself up and marched off. He's so different from Captain Kephart—the latter is so quiet and well-behaved, not often speaking except to tease the other officers and administer a wholesome rebuke to their vaunting and boasting—he's not a Virginian though. Uncle Tom came over in the evening and told us that Miss Hattie Gillespie and her sister went up to his house to call on the wounded Federal officer there. I think it would have been more proper to have sent their mother as proxy.

That Rouse is a good chap—Nellie and I were sitting in the back door this evening, while the officers were down at the tea table and Rouse coming by sat down on the steps and commenced talking. Said he was "awful tired of this war, tired of marching and counter-marching and he wished if we were going to whip them that we'd make haste about it and vice versa—he wished he could be taken prisoner and paroled or be promoted and resign." Captain Stephens told me this morning that Carrol's brigade had lost but 259 men in the recent conflict; knowing that Rouse was the clerk I asked him the number without making any allusion to what the captain had said, and he told me that he had made out the record and that there were eleven hundred. So much for the Yankee veracity—a plain fib somewhere. While we were talking I noticed in the twilight a light female figure coming from down the Mill Road leaning very confidently on a "blue coat sleeve"—I concluded it was either Belle Boyd or Hattie G. Presently, hearing the gate open, I looked up and saw the figures walk into the yard. "That's Dr. Gillespie's daughter," said Rouse; and without more ado Nellie and I rose simultaneously and glided upstairs telling R that should we be inquired for we were "not at home." She only came to see the officers though and went away in a little while. Captain Stephens was late at supper and on coming in announced that he and Miss Hattie had been taking a walk on the railroad. No one replied to him and he continued asking questions and talking until he concluded his repast. I hope he has learned our sentiments by this time. I did not play the "Red, White and Blue" as he requested me tonight—felt too much disgusted with the whole party to entertain them. I had Adjutant Reid tell the most unfounded falsehood this evening, and indeed indulge more or less in the recreation.

Rouse came down in the dining room on an errand while we were washing up the tea things and commenced talking about his mother and home. I could not help feeling sorry for him, he seemed really homesick. A poor little drummer boy fell out of the cherry tree today and broke his arm. If it had been one of the "fighting" men who had broken his neck I should not have objected much—but this was a very small child, and as I had my arm fractured I can guess how much he will suffer particularly with no gentle nursing—and care. Poor child.

June 20, 1862

We thought they were really going this morning—such a stir as there was in camp, such arriving and departing of couriers, but they did not go. Skin came over about eleven and informed us that the first brigade would move in the evening. After he left Frank came over and dined with us, telling us that Longstreet was coming over the mountains and that men had been sent out to capture his train of wagons—however the news was very unreliable. I never saw anyone so haggard and dispirited as Frank, he said he had been sick (to account thus for not having been over before) and I believed him, he certainly was homesick. He and his brother both said they were heartily tired of the war, they had seen enough in Virginia and if they could but get home now would be content to remain and never come back. It seems to be the universal sentiment and I have not heard one yet who did not wish he could leave the ranks and retire. Frank spoke of one of the regiments being almost in a state of mutiny and said that old Captain Bunting spoke of resigning. I hope 'tis true for I always wanted to like that man, but I felt that I could not, sustaining toward me the relation they did.

Certainly there is some move of importance in contemplation, for the orderlies have been dashing about all day in the most distracting manner with their dispatches. I just wish that I knew what it all means. One of the orderlies told Father that they were trying their best to get away from Jackson who was believed to be approaching. He said for his part he thought it a shame to be playing such a game. "If they intended doing anything, why didn't they push boldly forward instead of killing the men with their marching and counter-marching? The men were getting tired of it he knew." That's the way I like to hear them talk.

Captain Stephens excused himself at the tea table—pleading an engagement with Miss Hattie. The little fellow does not seem to have been in a good humor all day—wonder what has offended his lordship. Ralph says nearly all the officers in the division are sending in their resignation, but there are not many of them accepted. I wish Kephart would resign, for I believe he has a "soul above his buttons"—in other words I believe he is ashamed of playing a part in this most unjust war—indeed I heard that he had expressed his opinion to the effect that this was an unholy war. Be that as it may, I know he loses no opportunity of counteracting the vaunting spirit of the other officers and extolling Jackson. He is much more modest and retiring than the others too, and that speaks well for him. They are certainly going to move tomorrow. So they say.

June 21, 1862
Captain Kephart and Lewis Rouse were at breakfast when I went down to the table. The former, in course of conversation, being asked very demurely by Nellie if they would "burn the town when they left," assured her, with a look of astonishment, that they had no idea of such a thing—that such proceedings were positively forbidden—they might have to burn some stores, but certainly not the town. He was told that some of the Federal officers had censured Jackson very severely for burning stores when he left here—they choosing to denominate it— "wanton destruction." He said it was most singular that an officer should have said any such thing when everyone knew that it was a standing rule with commanders when they could not remove stores to destroy them to prevent the enemy enjoying any benefit from them and that Jackson had as much right to burn them here as Banks had in Winchester. Rouse then told us that we would very soon see our friends in Longstreet's division as they would probably enter town a few hours after their departure, he laughed and said they were retreating from him as hard as they could.

> *Longstreet's division was busy with the rest of the army fighting around Richmond.*

This fellow is the most complete specimen of Yankeedom that I've yet seen. When he first came, we all treated him as we do all of them, with sublime contempt; very soon however by little attention to our convenience and some remarks to his chums in our presence, he produced the impression that he was a good-hearted simple sort of school boy very homesick, and we somewhat relaxed toward him. That he is homesick and very tired of war I surely believe, but as to his simplicity I was never more mistaken in my life. He's as shrewd a Yankee as Yankees generally get to be. I thought we would hurt ourselves laughing at his quizzing one of the soldiers this morning just before they left. The man was quite saucy and inclined to boast, and would speak of the battles he had been in and give a glowing account of Yankee prowess. Lewis would let him go as far as necessary and then say "Well, stop, I happen to know something of that—I was on the ground" and then he would give his version of the current as entirely the reverse of what the other had said and in such a quizzical way that the soldier was finally glad to skulk off. Sometimes he would say something about our army to provoke a retort from us and then he'd drop his head in his hands and laugh heartily. He informed us this morning that Captain Stephens was playing a neat practical joke on Miss Hattie—passing himself off for a single man and pretending to be desperately smitten, while she seemed to be pleased in reality. I was astonished to hear that he was married, but he declared it to be a fact and told him he had been carrying on flirtations with the ladies in Page. I thought when I first saw him, that Captain S lacked in an eminent degree the elements that go to make up a true gentleman but I scarcely believed him capable of such duplicity toward one of his own set. If he had tried to raise expectations in me for the pleasure of disappointing them, I should not have been surprised, for he knows I'm an enemy and he might feel justified in punishing my heresies. But he and Hattie are fellow martyrs in the same cause, they are brother and sister Virginians and one would have thought, if he had possessed much of that chivalry of which he talks so much, he would have constituted himself her champion and resented every injury, warded off everything painful that approached her as a brother would have done instead of making a sport of her womanly feelings and girlish credulity. But I wasted too much time and space upon the insignificant mannkin, one might know that a man who could default to his country might well be recreant to every other duty. Only I'm glad I bluffed him off as I did.

They all left by eleven—the colonel and staff taking lunch and declaring they expected to be taken by Jackson's advance guard. We had a paper containing an account of the "whitehouse" sortie a most gallant dash bravely carried out.

The White House sortie was probably the action of J. E. B. Stuart, June 29, 1862 and seventy-five dismounted cavalrymen. They attacked the Federal gunboat Marblehead *on the Pamunkey River. A single howitzer opened on the gunboat from a position which the warship's guns could not bear. The vessel withdrew her landing party and retreated down the river.*

Previous to this episode, J. E. B. Stuart's cavalry had ridden around the entire Union army on the Peninsula June 12–15,

1862, while on reconnaissance for Lee.

Spent the evening in glorious repose, it seems so pleasant to enjoy a little quiet once more. Of course our men did not come in. I felt a little uneasy this evening when I heard that our cavalry were near town, for Shields' men had declared they were just going over the mountains a little way and when Jackson returned here they would fall back upon him in company with forty or fifty thousand that had come in during the night and were concealed in the woods around. We had every reason to believe the latter part of the information true and for a little while I felt afraid they might decoy our men—but presently I laughed at my fears, for I trust in Jackson and his God. The signal corps on the mountain have been making some demonstration this evening—of course entirely unintelligently to us.

June 22, 1862

Ma told us that Mr. H told her the paper announced the recognition of the S C by France. I have lost all confidence and dependence in such rumors, but I would be glad if it were so. I was at the window this evening after tea and heard Grandma talking to someone, evidently a stranger, out in the yard. Looking out I saw a very youthful, boyish looking personage in the dark blue uniform, standing bucket of water in hand. I stepped out to know the meaning of a paper which he handed Grandma, and learned that it was a girl dressed in Yankee uniform. She said she lived near Edinburgh, she had a stepmother who treated her so unkindly she was obliged to leave her home and went to live with her aunt. Here she and her sister assisted in washing and doing the housework; Fremont's disgraceful band came in, men very rude and they used the unruly member rather too freely for her pleasure, whereupon two of the soldiers led her off prisoner, took her female attire from her and forced her to assume her present garb with the name of "John Smith." They had even cut her hair off. She traveled in the wagons and succeeded in a few hours in giving her captors the slip in the confusion of passing trains, and joined another regiment where her sex was not known. She went on to Washington, not being able to get home, returned to Linden and finally obtained a pass to Front Royal and across the river. But she could not get through the pickets to her home. She was afraid to appeal to any of the higher officers lest they should suspect her of being a spy, afraid of telling her story to anyone for fear they should betray her. She had been away from home just a week living all the time in the wagons; at last she went down to Aunt Black Betty who lives in the mill, told her story and begged for protection and had engaged to bring water and assist her in washing to discharge her board there until she could get home—had just come up now after some water and seeing Grandma had concluded to tell her troubles. Poor thing, what an awful situation to be in—only sixteen years old and thrown thus among strangers in the hands of cruel enemies so far from home. She was evidently a rude, uncouth girl carelessly raised, but I thought I could detect an innate delicacy of feeling in the blush that mounted her cheeks when she looked down at her unusual costume and even the bitter epithets she bestowed upon her savage captors were called forth by a feeling of outraged pride and outraged propriety that I could approve. When she spoke of home and of the probability of her sister sharing the same fate I could see the tears well up into her eyes. We determined to adopt some measures for her relief, and told her in the meantime to go back and retain her present character until our plans were ripe for execution. In these days of treachery and deceit there is no knowing whether there is truth in her story—no knowing but she may be playing the spy—but I don't believe it. I'm convinced that she is a female—her features are delicate, her hands even or rather so for one working as she says she has done; her hair which is rather long will not consent to part on the side as she tries to wear it, but persists in falling asunder in the middle showing a straight, white line—and her voice is clearly that of a girl. And if the remainder of her story be not true she is one of the most consummate actresses I ever saw. I watched her narrowly and could but notice how glad she seemed to be with her own sex once more, how she shrank back when Father, who was passing by, stopped to speak to her. And when she rose to walk, she seemed so much ashamed, said she did not know how to move in those clothes and felt "very mean." She may be quizzing us, but I'd rather err on the side of mercy, than suffer a woman to want for any assistance which I could render at such a time. Poor thing!—we must do something, I scarcely know what, but to be in her situation, would almost kill me I know and no doubt she suffers.

June 24, 1862

Wrote all the morning. About eleven o'clock the provost marshal came over and Father took him down to the mill and laid the case of Nancy Jenkins—alias John Smith before him. He seemed to be very much incensed at the treatment she had received and vowed that the offenders should feel the effect of his wrath, promised to give her a passport home. This evening Father got the pass and we fitted her out with wearing apparel as far as we could but as our dresses were all too small for her we had to send her over to beg one from Aunt Betsy. She came back at sunset looking very happy and deposited some money with us that Aunt Betsy had given her, said she would call by early in the morning to see us as she intended starting immediately. I'm so glad the poor thing has thus far escaped so well and as she's homesick I hope she will soon get back to her friends.

June 25, 1862

Nancy Jenkins came in this morning and having equipped her and given her written directions she set out on her return home. Poor thing she is very ill-bred and rude, but I can't but help feel sorry for her and hope that she may arrive safely at her destination.

June 27, 1862
Ma and Laura took advantage of this beautiful day to walk down to Rose Hill. Allie came over and said they had news of Mr. Hope and I ran up there to hear it. Found them all in great trouble, all the family in the kitchen emptying a bee stand. They told me the Yankees had been out robbing and plundering all the night—had taken every bee stand but that one they were fixing. There had been great running to and fro during the night but they did not know how to account for it all. 'Twas reported that Beauregard was at Charleston and had whipped them all there.

> Beauregard, due to illness, turned over his command to General Bragg in Tupelo, Mississippi, June 20, 1862. Beauregard then went to Mobile to rest. In September he was in charge of the South Carolina-Georgia area.

It was said that Jackson was advancing down the valley in three different directions frightening the Yanks terribly. The news came very directly—I wonder if it is so. Spent a very pleasant day all by ourselves—Grandma and Aunt Betsy being at Uncle Tom's. Two Yankees came in to take a five o'clock dinner and after they left we missed a spoon.

Jule left us at five o'clock said she would go over to Dr. Turner's and if they could get a passport "would go home tomorrow, if not she would come back to see us again."

Ma came home after tea and told us that they had heard from Willie Richardson, that he was in Richmond and comparatively well. Cousin Sue Buck was at Rose Hill and Eltie was quite sick. They must have had a pretty hard time both at Rose Hill and at Mountain View, poor things!

June 28, 1862
This day one year ago dear Irvie had his picture taken in Baltimore for us. Poor fellow! How little he recked as to his whereabouts the anniversary of that day.

June 29, 1862
Uncle Tom came over in the evening and said he thought they saw some of our cavalry on the mountain today. Would be surprised from what I previously heard.

We had singing until bedtime and after that sat up till late talking with Aunt L. This morning early we saw numbers of troops going out of town—cavalry and infantry in three different directions. What does it mean? We all think there will be a battle on the mountain very soon.

I hope much from the result.

June 30, 1862

Mr. F came in to dinner and told us that ... certainly was on the mountain, that he had talked with him and learned from him that poor Ashby was certainly dead. Was standing near him when he fell. It seems that cavalry could not be of service where the engagement took place. Ashby would be in the engagement and took command of an infantry company; his horse was shot from under him, and he then went on foot. Just as he waved his sword above his head calling "Come on, my brave boys!" one of the regiment, accidently discharged his gun and the ball took effect in his wrist passed through his breast and out the back of his shoulder. Poor fellow! He uttered not a word, but, turning and giving one look at his executioner fell to the earth. —Had a fragment of wood from the spot which was covered with blood. How I would like to have possession of such a precious relic.

Also told how Jackson actually rode into the Federal lines and impersonating a Federal officer ordered them to remove a cannon which commanded the bridge "to a more favorable position." He was obeyed, and then immediately turning to his own men, he told them to cross the bridge which they did before the Yankees could recover from their surprise and consternation. He whipped Shields, crossed the bridge, burnt it after him, drove Fremont back, forded the stream below and finished Shields, taking from him all his baggage, artillery, and everything. Shields himself was not there in person, and only a part of his division, but that was badly served up. Four thousand was their loss, one thousand ours in killed, wounded, and missing.

On May 27, 1862, Turner Ashby was promoted to the rank of brigadier general and was given command of all the cavalry in the Shenandoah Valley. The Seventh Virginia Cavalry Regiment, Ashby's original command, was the nucleus of his brigade and was commanded by Colonel Funsten. The Seventh Virginia had grown from ten to twenty-six companies under Ashby. The Second Virginia, commanded by Col. T. T. Munford and the Sixth Virginia, commanded by Colonel Flournay, were added to Ashby's brigade.

Ashby was killed on June 6, 1862 and Colonel Munford became temporarily the commander of the Ashby Brigade. After Ashby's death the original ten companies of the Seventh Virginia were placed under the command of Colonel W. E. Jones. Gen. George Robertson soon became commander of the brigade. Ten companies of the original seventh were organized to become the Twelfth Virginia Cavalry under command of Colonel A. W. Harmon. The additional six companies were organized into the Seventeenth Virginia Battallion under

Major Patrick. The Eleventh Virginia was formed with L. L. Lomax as it's leader.

Thus the Ashby Brigade which was reorganized under General Robertson operated in the Valley until the campaigns of the Second Manassas when it joined J. E. B. Stuart.

Had gone back to the army. I pray he may be safe. We spent a most delightful day and were about returning home about sunset when the Yankee cavalry entered town preceded by two ambulances. We sat on the porch waiting for them to pass, Nellie had on a white dress and a hat trimmed with red, white, and red. Some of the creatures turned around waving their hands and calling out—"little Secesh in white dress!" and a great deal more which we did not hear.

It is thought they only went out on picket duty, had a brush with our pickets and returned bringing their ambulances.

Heard that poor Eltie Richardson was very ill today. Oh, I hope she may be spared! 'Twould be a fatal blow to the family—her death.

Father commenced harvesting this morning.

July 1, 1862

Mr. Allen told us this morning that three of our prisoners were brought into town last night among whom was Captain Martin. Mr. Berry confirmed our victory at Charleston. Just before he left we heard volleys of musketry from several points back of the woods and towards the mountain road and very soon after a report very like an artillery discharge and another and another until we were quite sure "Jackson was coming." But this illusion was dispelled upon going on top of the porch and seeing squads of the enemy sauntering leisurely about the street and a regiment marching in preceded by a fine band discoursing elegantly of the "Red, White, and Blue" etc. Old Mr. Marshall calling by soon after explained the event by telling us 'twas the regiment of scouts who had gone out on Sunday and were just returning and the firing was from the different returning bodies of pickets who were I suppose thus celebrating their safe arrival in town. That which we took for artillery was one simultaneous discharge of heavy musketry. Mr. M did not think his son was prisoner because he had made inquiry for him and could hear nothing of him in town. He brought some very bad news, if true but I don't believe it. An officer just from Winchester brought news of the capture of Richmond and the loss of General McClellan and thirty thousand of their men—he stated that General Banks had just received an official dispatch to that effect. This news was first brought to Rose Hill and thence spread through town. I did not believe it because had it been true there certainly would have been more rejoicing among them when they came in today, yet I could not help but feel uneasy and sad. Nellie and I concluded to go up to Mrs. Hope's to try and get something more definite if possible. They did not believe it at all and seemed in pretty good spirits. We spent a very pleasant hour and had a real treat in real cake—something which I thought had become obsolete in Virginia, or at least this portion of it. It has been quite a warm day and the hands of the harvest field seem to feel it very much. Poor Father, I'm afraid he's harvesting his wheat only for the Yankees to take it from him afterwards.

July 2, 1862

A rainy, disagreeable day. —Felt sad and unwell. No news. Mr. Berry came over at dusk and really cheered us so much that I retired to bed with quite a light heart. He stated that they had been fighting for several days at R but that so far from their having the place he believed the fight was still in progress and that we were giving them quite a distasteful experience in battle. He argues very hopefully from disorder prevailing in every division of the Federal army which had occupied the valley—Shields had resigned, Fremont been superseded and would do so and a probability of the removal of Banks—besides there were inferior officers innumerable who were tendering resignations and every kind of petty jealousy existing between the privates of the various commands.

Shields was not heard from again during the war.

I have noticed the same thing myself and believe with him that these dissentions may prove a very fruitful cause of their final defeat. Oh!—dear, would that it were already consummated!

July 3, 1862

Very unwell, was not down to breakfast. Mr. Allen brought very cheering news from town. Said they had been fighting at Richmond since Wednesday before the last and that we had given the enemy a severe repulse there, but that the battle still raged.

> *Lee, after the arrival of Jackson, crossed the Chickahominy River on June 26 to turn McClellan's right flank. The Battle of Mechanicsville became the first of the Seven Day's Battle. This was followed by Gaines' Mill or first Cold Harbor. On the twenty-seventh, McClellan retreated south to the James River. On the twenty-ninth of June, after crossing White Oak Swamp, the Southerners came near victory at Savage Station. On the thirtieth, the Battle of White Oak Swamp was fought and McClellan's forces retreated to Malvern Hill and was assaulted by Lee's army July 1. On July 2, McClellan moved down the James River to Harrison's Landing. Richmond was saved!*

U.S.A.	C.S.A.
Effectives 91,169	Effectives 85,000
Killed 1,734	Killed 3,478
Wounded 8,062	Wounded 16,261
Missing 6,053	Missing 875

I was nearly asleep when about ten o'clock Laura rushed upstairs exclaiming "Come girls, and hear the good news Mrs. Moffatt brings!" It was indeed glorious. We had turned the enemies flank, chased them over the Chickahominy—taking quantities of ammunition and a hundred pieces of artillery beside a large number of prisoners and there killed and wounded ever so many. Thank heaven!—and yet how do I know but in this horrid butchery I may not have lost some of my dear friends and relatives. Ah!—"There is truly nothing sadder than a victory except a defeat." I was so surprised to hear that Jackson the dear "Old Stonewall" had worked his way around and reached Richmond in time for the fight. I hope he met Shields' division again.

Miss Mary Cloud and a Mr. Jeffries of Mississippi—a young Confederate who had been sick, taken prisoner and paroled and now her guest came over after tea and sat till dusk. Mr. J was quite young—a mere undeveloped school boy but a very welcomed visitor because a staunch Southerner. Miss Mary was as friendly and agreeable as ever.

There was a skirmish up the river this evening and a Yankee (perhaps a half a dozen) killed.

July 4, 1862

The Yankees tried to celebrate today but the only demonstrations made toward the object was the constant firing of cannon from the heights frightening Negroes and children. We could distinctly see the bombs as they ascended and then fell again and the reports sometimes were really very heavy.

July 5, 1862

Dr. Rixey called by in the afternoon from Salem en route to his sister's. He says he had seen a Richmond paper giving an account of affairs at the seat of war. We have taken thirteen thousand prisoners, thirty large siege guns, and one hundred and twenty small pieces and "lots" of ammunition. The success on our side is for the present very decided. He also said he had met a man from Price's army who stated that Beauregard with a portion of his command was certainly in Richmond —Price also was there. Their Mayland *News Sheet* which he brought confirmed the news and also confirmed the news which he brought of the recognition of the Confederacy by France and her determination officially announced at Washington, of putting a speedy conclusion to this war. Oh!—this is all so encouraging it seems too much for us ever to have hoped for so soon. I don't believe a word about Jackson and Longstreet being dead and Magruder and Early and Stuart prisoners—no doubt the belief with them is offspring of the wish that it might be so. My dear brothers then are most probably on Virginia soil once more and feel as if they were almost home. Dear fellows, I feel so impatient to hear from and see them now that they are so near. But, wait, I will. For I believe this struggle will not continue many months longer.

(Later) Alice Stewart took tea with us. She is a sweet girl and I would like to have her visit us oftener. Belle Boyd and Mr. Jeffries came over and sat awhile after tea and little as I felt like playing I exerted myself and undertook a piece when just then Grandma came in and asked if I had heard from poor Willie Richardson and then told me he was dead.

> *William Millar Richardson was wounded in the Battle of Williamsburg, Virginia, May 6, 1862, and died May 29, 1862, at the age of twenty-one.*
>
> *Sue Buck, daughter of Dr. I. N. Buck, (Uncle Newton) of Mountain View, was the fiance of Willie Richardson. She moved from her home to Rose Hill and lived with Willie's sisters and widowed mother. To his memory she remained faithful throughout her life.*

Mr. Pettie had just come over to say that a letter had been received from a Dr. Ambler at whose house he had died announcing the fact. Poor dear, dear boy. I had felt uneasy and anxious a long time about him and had sometime almost feared something of the kind, and yet when the announcement came I was never more shocked in my life. It seems so hard to think of losing him thus—he so noble, so young and yet so brave and manly. I did not know how much I loved him before, and if I thought we were distressed, what a death blow it would be to his poor sick mother and sisters—poor Eltie ill even now. Oh it's all right! God knows what's best for us all, but it does seem hard for us to understand how so much useless and injurious lives are spared while those so much needed, the dearest and best are taken away. Poor Willie, he was kindly and tenderly cared for in his last hours. He was taken to Dr. Ambler's near Richmond where he lay sick until the twenty-ninth of May, when he died of hectic fever—produced no doubt in a great measure by his anxiety about his family. He was conscious until within a few days until his death and they had prayers for him until he grew so ill they thought best to desist, but he by his meek look requested them to continue the exercises. They buried him just as they had supposed his friends would have had him at home and "his grave was filled with flowers." I think these little details indicated delicate consideration and appreciation on the part of his stranger friends that soothed while it touches us deeply. Dear fellow—no one was ever more deserving of them and none more apt to receive them at home, and though stranger forms supplied the place of loved ones in the dread hour and stranger hands closed his eyes, yet their ministerings were so kindly that they comforted his death bed. He "wasted his life for his country's care, laying it down with a patriot's prayer," and I firmly believe that dear Willie has gone to a happy rest, that anxiety and pain will be his nevermore.

July 6, 1862

Banks' army came in today and a brigade encamping in the back field we again had the officers here—Colonel Schlaudecker and his staff—the former acting brigadier general.

General Banks' army halted in Front Royal several days in his march to join Pope east of the Blue Ridge Mountains.

Our experience was but a repetition of our previous experience with the Union soldiers, raids on the garden and cherry trees, dairy and kitchen and entreaties for a meal as they professed to be starved and almost worn out. It has been a miserable day, very warm and such an incessant noise with the wagons and bands and shouting and running to the well for water. General Banks came over in the evening but I had not the heart to see him. Poor Cousin Elizabeth, and Cousin Sue and Eltie! I've been thinking of them all day and how agonizing all this confusion would be to them. Uncle Tom was sick and could not go to them, but wrote them by Uncle Newton who disclosed the sad intelligence first to Cousin E who fainted. No wonder poor thing!—for he was her last stay, her last hope and comfort and indeed in Willie seemed to center the affections of the whole family, and they all depended on him entire for he was strong and matured beyond his years. And now he was gone—the last male member of his race gone just when he seemed to become almost necessary to their existence. They dared not tell Eltie, she was too ill, and yet I don't know how they can conceal it from her. Poor Cousin Sue Buck is with them and that will be a great comfort to all of them. I have remembered today so many of Willie's little gentle, kindly acts in days gone by. I remember too how eager he was to be in the service, how desperately he struggled between duty to his mother and sisters and duty to his country, and how much it cost him to stay at home for some months while his friends had all gone to the army. And then when he left again for the war how earnestly and affectionately he begged Nellie and me to visit his sisters and cheer them. I remember how rigidly and zealously he discharged his duty as soldier as well as son. And then I remembered the last time I saw him—last November how well he looked and how bright and happy he seemed as he dashed off on his pet Tom (handsome black horse, "Tom Telegraph.") Poor Willie, there are not many such as he was.

July 7, 1862

Nellie was right unwell—we had a repetition of our former experience in Yankee officers—a continual tramping of man and beast through the yard and an incessant worry. 'Twas a very warm day and we spent it mostly upstairs growling at the hard Yankees. Old General Cooper came over in the afternoon—a very well-behaved old fellow apparently.

> *General James Cooper was in command of Maryland Volunteers in 1861, and at this time was in Banks' army.*

The soldiers after the rain this evening amused themselves with carrying off Father's wheat which he had already cut and shocked. Indeed the Q. M. came over today and formally announced to Father the "military necessity" he was under of cutting and appropriating the remainder of the wheat standing in the field. I thought it quite a crude proceeding.

July 8, 1862

Was aroused about four A.M. by a great hurrying to and fro and flashing of lights. Looking out the window I saw the encampment all ablaze that flickered about wildly and a busy hum proceeded therefrom. Presently the back door opened and Father and Colonel Schlaudecker came out talking and then I heard boots hurrying down into the dining room and then the rattling of cups and saucers. I slipped down into Ma's room where was a light and seeing Martha standing there asked where Ma was. She confirmed my suspicions by saying the brigade had received marching orders four hours before and that Ma was down in the dining room giving the officers their breakfast. That's gratifying at all events. Colonel Van Buren remained behind on the invalid list. There are a great many sick among them here. We were in a perfect furor all the morning trying to keep invaders from the wheat field and garden.

About nine o'clock an ambulance drove up and the attendants lifted therefrom a poor emaciated young man and bore him into the "quarters." He was Colonel Van Buren's clerk—his servant too was sick—young Ambrose and lots of the other soldiers besides.

The surgeon came in the afternoon to see his patients and Nellie's throat being very much swollen Father called him in to prescribe for it which he did much to her discomforture for we teased her not a little about being attended by a Yankee doctor. He told Ma he would bring her a supply of medicine. Wonder if he will? Captain Fisher was here today—a great little humbug and professedly quite a traveler.

Colonel Van Buren showed us photographs of his family today—beautiful pictures they were. After night it was too warm to remain indoors and we occupied the porch and pavement. The colonel gave us a description of his travels in Europe—had visited England, Germany, Switzerland and Italy, explored the ruins of Pompeii and Herculaneum and peeped into the crater of Vesuvius; admired the antiquities of Rome and reveled in the gayeties of Paris. 'Twas entertaining to listen to his accounts and we were thus engaged until bedtime.

July 9, 1862

Had a paper this morning in which was the name of Captain Simpson mentioned among the prisoners taken at Richmond.

The day promised to be a fine one and Ma and I determined to go down to Rose Hill. Uncle Tom had been over the day previous and made an engagement to go down with me. He brought with him the letter which he had written in reply to the one received from Dr. Ambler announcing dear Willie's death. It was a beautifully written and very touching letter indeed, just such a one as it should be under the circumstances.

I felt sick before starting to walk but hoped the exercise would prove beneficial. Found Cousin E's darkened and silent as a grave, but upon entering we saw her black-clad figure at the bedside with her face buried in the pillows weeping. She bears her bereavement more heroically than I would have thought for, poor thing. Eltie she said was a little better. I could but notice what a deathlike quiet pervaded the house, broken only by the rolling and rattling of the army wagons that were every minute passing and repassing. Cousin E. was called from the room on some errand and Ma and I took our seats at the front window and looked out. Such a change as had taken place in that beautiful yard—since I had been there a short time before. The turf which was always so soft and freshly green was trampled and withered and brown and the shrubbery all utterly destroyed. The luxuriant myrtles that in rich masses covered the hill were all torn and sered. I thought how it would have grieved poor Willie to have known all this and when Belle came in and told me some of the insults and annoyances to which they had been subjected I felt glad that he had never known anything about it all. Poor Cousin Sue!—her heart seemed almost broken. She had grieved until she was faint and sick and when I asked her to take something to strengthen and refresh her said it was not worthwhile for she did not want to live now. We started up to see Eltie but I grew suddenly so deathly sick that I could not walk so I lay on the lounge by poor Cousin S and she told me all about Willie—talked all the time about him and it seemed really to relieve her to have someone to unburden her heart to. We were none of us except Ma and Belle well enough to eat dinner. Cousin Sue Buck did not come down at all until after dinner and then looked so pale and sad that I could not bear to see her. Went up into Eltie's room and sat with her awhile. She looked badly but rather better than I expected to see her. I do not think she suspects anything of Willie's death—and they've been afraid to hint anything to her. They are cheerful as possible before her and yet it is strange they can keep the deception up so well. I was miserably sick all day and could scarcely manage to drag myself home in the late evening. Retired directly I got there.

July 10, 1862

One of General Siegel's regiments (Blenker's division) encamped south end of wheat field and destroyed the third rail fence within sixty days from that end of the field, trampling and destroying the wheat and using much of it from the shocks for bedding these men, the Indiana cavalry and mule teamsters—took off about sixty shocks.

July 12, 1862

Sick, sick, sick! Oh me. Read all day when I could. In the late evening Belle Boyd, Alice Stewart and Mr. Jeffries came in. Belle told them all soon after she got here that she and Dr. Bogardus had traced up their relationship and found that they were cousins and when he came in they were evidently very well acquainted from the way they conducted themselves. This I learned from Nellie—I was fortunately confined to my bed.

This doctor seems from accounts to be rather better than the generality of Yankees we have seen, he seems so mortified at the way the soldiers act and does not seem to have much confidence in the cause of his Northern colleagues. He has been very thoughtful and even kind in many instances.

July 13, 1862

Father and Uncle Tom were in to see me this morning, the latter very cheerful and hopeful. Father said he wished Dr. B. to see me and prescribe for me as he thought I needed a regular renovation of my system. So I reclined on the lounge in my wrapper and received the son of Asculapius in state. It seemed very inconsistent in me to permit the attendance of a sworn enemy in a professional capacity, but I felt desperate enough to try almost anything in hope of regaining health and strength. He seemed gentlemanly enough too and taking Father downstairs with him wrote out a lengthy prescription as to my diet, habits and exercise promising if I would obey his instructions to make me a strong healthy girl. Well I'm willing to try almost anything that will effect so desirable results for I'm weary, weary of feeling always weak and sick and unequal to any exertion.

No news!

July 15, 1862

Too unwell to venture downstairs today. Ah me! What a great comfort it is to have kind good friends to attend you when sick, kind friends to prepare tempting dainties for a weak appetite, to administer the nauseous potion with a refreshing draught, to bring cool fruits and fair sweet flowers to cheer your solitude—above all friends with ready sincere sympathy in your suffering. Oh surely I'm greatly blessed in this respect and I thank Heaven for it.

July 16, 1862

Went downstairs today. Felt quite weak but nursed the baby a good deal notwithstanding. Very worn—made a nice pitcher of iced lemonade which we all enjoyed very much. Commenced bathing by the Dr.'s direction in peppered water today.

July 17, 1862

Ma came in at night saying they had many rumors in town, but it had been satisfactorily ascertained that few of the "rifles" were injured in the battle before Richmond and they none of our immediate friends. Captain Simpson, John Steele, J. T. Pettie and others were captured—Scott R and Smith T were very nearly taken but escaped in safety. Oh!—I'm so glad 'tis no worse! This is more than we could have hoped for. Our men are certainly near here some of them and 'tis generally thought Jackson is advancing on Winchester.

They have given Eltie Richardson some intimation of Willie's death and she says she has seen and suspected something amiss ever since the family first heard it and she also said she believes if it were true it would kill her. Poor thing how I feel for her, she little knows how true it is.

The report of our secretary of war has been seen and we're astounded to learn that eight thousand would cover the whole loss of the Confederate army killed, wounded and missing during those dreadful battles. We had thought it must have been at least twice that amount.

July 18, 1862

This is an anniversary—this day one year ago we struck our first fair blow for the freedom of the Old Dominion and I have thought of it all day, have remembered how dear Irvie and I walked down from the mountain and I commenced making his uniforms. I remembered how in the evening Nannie, Clara Taylor and Fannie Stewart came over and how we sang and played on the piano and by moonlight in the yard and after they left the vigil we kept waiting for the cars and my writing a letter at one o'clock A.M. and everything connected with it. Poor Irvie, where is he now I wonder.

July 21, 1862

Father told us not to start to Dr. T's until he came back from town and we thought it would have rained and spoiled our plans before he returned, but this was all forgotten when he came back with his hand full of letters—one from Cousin Kate B to Cousin Sue, one from Irvie to Cousin Horace Buck and from the dear boy to me—a great long nice letter dated from Tupelo, Miss., June 18. They had received my lengthy letter written soon after Jackson's besom had swept the valley and seemed heartily to sympathize with and rejoice in our freedom. Said the climate agreed remarkably with them all—none of them having been sick of any consequence. Alvin had a few days before coming on to Richmond as bearer of dispatches and would not return before the first of July—but I suppose he did not return at all as Beauregard went soon after to Richmond himself. That was a most welcome message if it didn't hail from R.

July 23, 1862
Grandma and Aunt B came home bringing news of a dash made by sixty of our cavalry near Middletown in which the baggage wagons of the enemy containing supplies for the regiment here were cut off and captured and considerable consternation was occasioned in town thereby. A regiment of infantry with cavalry and artillery went out from town this evening in pursuit. Guess they won't get them.

July 24, 1862
General Augurs' bodyguard took possession of the premises, barn, stables and all and broke into the granary. The Dr. told us that he heard in town today that they had recaptured the most of them. Don't believe him though. Sat out on the porch in the evening, writing. Miss Belle Boyd and the Dr. have quarreled, he thinks it "does not pay" to visit her.

July 25, 1862
Heard this morning that a number of our citizens had been arrested near Nineveh and brought to town and lodged in jail—among them Mr. D. McKay, Mr. Bartlett and several others. The cause of their arrest was simply that they had found some barrels of groceries left on the roadside apparently unclaimed and had carried them to their homes for preservation—said barrels proved to be a portion of the plunder our men had captured from the enemy and been unable to remove for want of transportation. Therefore the poor fellows were accused of seizing and appropriating "government property." I knew it was false about their having retaken those stores and am confirmed in my suspicions. We took two sutler's establishments, some wagons, about thirty horses and all the teamsters and accompaniments of the train. All that they recaptured were some old wagons that were too dilapidated to travel with speed and the stores they contained which were left behind and these were partly consumed. So there now! Monsieur Le Yank! Just to think they have issued a proclamation to the effect that for every Federal soldier shot by bushwhackers they will arrest the citizen nearest the spot when it occurred. And moreover that soldiers were to fire into groups of citizens collected at the corners for conversation "because it annoyed the soldiers who saw them." A beautiful state of affairs when men are prohibited the sidewalks of their native town. We had a newspaper of date of twenty-eighth containing some very caustic articles from London papers and also containing Lincoln's villainous order for the troops to rob the Secesh and subsist off them. Oh I'm so tired of tyranny!

July 26, 1862

Nellie and I concluded to walk over and spend some hours with Cousin Mary. Nellie had on her white dress and her hat trimmed with red, white and blue and as we passed off the porch she stopped to pluck a pink oleander to put with a white rose bud on her bosom. I laughingly asked Father if he did not think those dangerous colors under which to make our entree into town? He jestingly referred us to Dr. who stood in the door of his room—his advice very gravely given was that she should doff them but she resolutely declined to "haul down," whereupon he continued the jest by offering to act as guard and protector over to town. Of course his offer was not accepted. Found Cousin Mary enjoying a siesta—spent a pleasant time in her room and then went down to tell Mrs. R. good-bye, she took us out into the yard and showed us her flowers—some rare ones that I had never seen before—she gave me some plants and roots to raise for myself. As we returned home I stopped to inquire of Miss Sallie Kendrick how Mrs. Jackson was and after answering my question she told me that an order from General Pope had just reached town commanding that the oath be administered to each citizen upon pain of their banishment from town and the confiscation of all their property. This is what I have all the time been dreading and now it had come in a more hideous shape than I had ever anticipated.

> General Pope was the first of the Union officers to order his troops to subsist off the country and to hold the citizens responsible for damage by guerillas. He also ordered the arrest of every citizen within the limits of his lines, to administer the oath of allegiance to the Union, and to expel from their homes all who refused to take it.

We met Mr. Hope and Mr. Hainie and the former had been weeping and seemed to be utterly bewildered by the shock. Oh how intensely I did hate the whole race of Yankees. Dr. B met us hurriedly just as we reached the bridge and we were not able even to return his salutation. Orville and Laura came down the hill and told us that Ambrose (aide or clerk to General Kimball) had just died. Poor fellow! I knew that he was very ill before we left but could not help being startled upon hearing that he was gone. Tea was over and the family was assembled on the porch and such shocked faces were when I told them of the order. We were all eager to give up everything and go within our lines but Father soon proved the impracticability of this by telling how such a rush as would be made toward the most accessible points within our lines must necessarily impoverish the places, not only the inhabitants but the army which is worse, and the result of a horrible famine. He said if it were not for his dependent family he would know quite well what to do—be shot first. As it was we must await the issue of events. Wait! Oh how possessed my soul with patience when such a disgraceful fate seemed waiting us—when men whose whole lives had been unblemished, whose lips had been blameless to be thus forced to perjure themselves in thier old age—to be compelled to swear to support a government which their very souls abhorred, to seem to advocate principles from which their souls revolt in horror. Oh it does seem so hard, if our men would but come to our delivery. There is one consolation in believing that desperate diseases require desperate remedies and I think they must see that their cause is waning that they thus resort to warring against defenseless women and children. Poor Amborse, if I were prepared I should envy him his repose.

July 27, 1862

Dr. Bogardis came home about eight o'clock and said that poor Eltie was not so well—he feared she was taking diptheria again. I'm so sorry to hear it. They buried Ambrose today. Poor fellow—they did not give his remains that attention they should have done and I'm glad his mother won't know how he was laid in his rough coffin without sheet or shroud. It was all the fault of those rough men who came to take him away—the Dr. at Rose Hill and knew nothing about it. Harmer says A. was such a good boy, so gentle and honest and indeed he seemed to be very polite and well-behaved all the time he was here. I hope poor boy that it is well with him now. Dr. B. and H. have received their marching orders and leave tomorrow. Father had a conversation with the former regarding that order of Pope's and he pronounced it both iniquitous and impolitic.

We were all sitting on the porch tonight and Father noticing that Harmer seemed very forlorn sitting in his door alone called out and invited him over. He came and I felt not a little amused to listen to his conversation. He is a real Yankee with Yankee ideas and Yankee pronunciation and accent and Yankee in his holy horror of running and fighting.

July 28, 1862

Ma is quite indisposed this morning, Carey is little better, both Evred and the baby complaining. Eltie still suffering from her throat. Our boarders left immediately after dinner in ambulance provided for the purpose. One of the Dr.'s last acts was to hunt for some lemons and fresh beef for Eltie and prescribed for Ma. When making his adieu he went down into the basement to look for Evred and then called for the baby. Nellie, Ma and I were in Grandma's room—I tying up a lunch for him when he coolly walked in and bidding us take care of ourselves and wishing we might soon be relieved of our present troubles shook each of us by the hands in adieu. Harmer too showed some thought. I must confess I liked the Dr. better than any specimen of his race that I met with except Frank—he is so respectful and kind to the sick—has been so attentive to poor Eltie and begged Father to write him and keep him informed of her situation saying he felt so sorry for the family. Then he was so thoughtful with poor Ambrose too. Father will miss him too for he was here always as protector when he was in town.

July 29, 1862

Ma and the baby both quite sick and I quite weak, we all stayed upstairs during the morning. Aurt Betty came in and sat a few hours with us. She heard that Eltie was very ill and said Uncle Tom had gone down to see her. Orville came over from Oakley after dinner and said that Uncle Tom had just come home and told them that dear Eltie was dead. Poor dear Eltie, gone from a troublous world, her brief span of life has been all sorrow and now she is happy. She expressed her resignation, her perfect trust; took leave of all her family, requested that they would not sorrow for her when she would be so happy and begged they would not reflect on themselves for anything they had ever said or done to her and left messages to each and all and made bequests. Then telling Uncle T. that there was much she would like to say to him expired today two months after Willie died. Two more dearly loved schoolmates gone making a happy exchange and I left to envy them their happiness. I do feel such sympathy for the family, 'twill be almost a death blow to them and I grieve more for them than for her though I know how sadly we shall miss her here and she has done a great deal towards contributing to my pleasure, still I would be selfish enough to wish for her back. Cousin Mary Cloud came over this evening and remained over night. She said she had received a letter from Cousin Mount announcing that their regiment was ordered to Gordonsville where they were expecting a heavy battle in a few days. They had heard directly from Scott who had certainly been captured but had escaped. Poor John Steele is certainly dead, fell before Richmond riddled with balls.

> *Jackson's army was ordered from the Richmond area to Gordonsville July 13. They arrived the nineteenth of July to protect the Virginia Central Railroad from attack by the Union General John Pope.*

July 30, 1862

Grandma brought Ma a letter from Aunt Cattie Larue which had been sent up by Grussie B. some days since. She represented affairs in a more pleasing condition there than I had imagined, were harvesting and had been comparatively unmolested though they did not know how long this would continue. The poor little baby is very sick tonight and I must help Nellie nurse him. Belle Boyd was taken prisoner and sent off in a carriage with an escort of fifty cavalrymen today. I hoped they are going to put her within our lines and keep her there.

July 31, 1862

We heard this evening that there had been a great battle at Gordonsville and another at Warrenton Junction in which we were victorious. Oh if I only dared believe it! They have certainly moved a battalion from town to the river and commenced throwing up breastworks and planting cannon which looks like preparation for protecting a retreat. Oh I do want to hear some news so much!

A most ludicrous scene occurred here today. Some Yankees bargained with Mahala for some bread, but upon handing her the money gave her notes which she refused to receive, whereupon snatching up the loaves he swore he would have them anyway and scampered off up the steps but she grasped him by the coat and stayed his flight, but he was not thus to be foiled of his prey, and tossing, the bread up the steps to his companion called for him to make off with the prize. Mahala followed him out into the yard abusing him and charitably wishing he might have a cold bullet through him before he had a chance to repeat the act. The lieutenant and Father happened to witness the scene and the former commanded the fellow to restore the stolen viands, but he only threw her a portion of what he had taken and while she was securing that made off with the remainder. How I would like to send the boys a sketch portraying this scene.

August 1, 1862

Heard through a letter received from Newt. Petty that only three of the "Warren Rifles" were killed before Richmond, none of whom were our immediate friends. He said they were very badly off with supplies and almost starving but as he is something of an epicure I hope this is an exaggeration. He also said he had seen dear Alvin in R. a few days before with dispatches from Beauregard and that he was well and had left his friends in good health. Oh sometimes I do grow so impatient to hear from the boys directly. To think that A was there a month ago and we've not received a letter from him yet.

August 2, 1862

After tea E. and J. Hope came running up breathless to say they had received a later paper in which it was stated that ten of our iron-clad vessels had entered at Mobile and two more were on their way hither so that that port was now opened to the commerce of the world. And told us many more encouraging things. Oh!—this, if true, will prove a great thing for us. Dr. M. has come to board here.

August 6, 1862

Dr. Marshall came in at the tea table. He said that it was reported that Winchester had been burnt and gave other items of disaster to our army with such cool assurance that I could have choked him. Of course, we did not credit the rumors but I was infinitely provoked at his manner of reporting it.

August 10, 1862

Dr. M. offered to stand on guard at home while Father went to church today, so we all went for the first time since the twenty-fifth of May and were fully repaid by hearing an excellent sermon from Dr. Hough. Saw so many relatives and friends at church among whom were Aunt Lizzie and Mrs. Hall. It was a very sultry day. Cousin Bet and Mr. R. dined with us. Spent a very pleasant evening listening to Dr. M's description of geological specimens he had seen. That odious Lieutenant Elliot up here again.

Aunt Lizzie called for us in the evening and took us home with her. Had a delightful ride and enjoyed all the more because it was such a novelty. Reached the river about six o'clock in a dash of rain, but succeeded in getting to the house dry. Dear old Clover Hill! My thoughts and desires have been pilgrims to this Mecca a long time, and now to be there in person! 'Twas so pleasant. The house I found very much changed by late repairs, but the inmates were the same dear warm-hearted friends that erst they were and welcomed us so cordially.

August 11, 1862

Was up bright and early this morning after a refreshing night's rest. Went down into the garden and by the time the bell rung for prayers had a sweet little cluster of rosebuds glittering with dew for Aunt Lizzie. After breakfast we went out to look at the improvements and admired the quantities of beautiful flowers that ornamented the yard. How perfectly delightful it was to stand on the broad portico with the fresh dewy breeze of early morning laving my brow and bearing to me the grateful incense of a thousand flowers and reveled in the beautiful scene before me. The green hills sloping down gradually to the meadows that lay stretched along the bank of the river; the river flashing and dimpling in the sunbeams and reflecting back the beauty of the towering cliffs and wooded heights beyond. Then the picturesque old bridge with the white house by it and the cleft in the mountain side down which leaped the laughing cascade and the soft blue tint of the distant mountains just where it met the clear brilliant sky. All at one glance I took in and might have stood admiring it for an indefinite time had not Aunt Lizzie broken the spell by bidding us come and pick over some berries she was having dried for Ma. While thus employed Aunt Harriett rushed in and cried out that "our men were dashing down the road" and on going out we indeed saw horsemen moving rapidly on the other side of the river but could not at the distance distinguish them. Emma presently came in to see us and said she had met them, that they were our men and that they were going to Front Royal. Not long after, while playing and singing in the parlor we heard the children calling out that our men were coming and the Yankees in hot pursuit. And it was really the case. We saw our men plunge into the river and dash across laughing and shouting. On they came toward the house and just as they got opposite the house the Yankees came in sight on the other side of the river. We all ran out and the gallant fellows galloped up the stile and shouted—"ladies we've been to Front Royal, taken two provosts and a captain and other prisoners—don't be alarmed for us, we have every advantage and apprehend no danger, go into the house please ladies, the Yankees will fire and shoot you." But we remained there long enough to give them some apples and hear that they had seen Henry Buck who was well. Then they rode up the lane to the barn and pausing there defied their pursuers and then disappeared behind the hill. The Yankees did not attempt to cross the river but moving about the river bank cautiously for a while returned to town. It was the most daring feat to be sure, twenty-one men to venture to Front Royal where was an encampment of men sufficient to have taken the whole party without using guns at all. Only seven went into town, went into the provost's office, took his excellency, took Dr. Marshall, went a quarter mile out of town for another prisoner and starting with the officers and thirty other prisoners left town just as the Yankee cavalry were preparing to pursue them. Owing to their haste they were compelled to abandon the thirty infantry prisoners and taking the officers on horseback made good their return. Dr. Marshall came back but 'tis a mooted question whether, as he said, he escaped, or being a surgeon, was released by our men. Three of the Confederates with prisoners went on up a little railroad while the remaining (one of them was I believe captured) proceeded more slowly and crossed the river in view of the enemy, thus leading them to believe that the whole party, prisoners and all, were in the "Forks" and diverting pursuit after the prisoners who had gone on. It is said that the officer in command of the expedition frequently rallied his men on their retreat and turning back fired on the pursuers and behaved altogether in a most gallant and daring manner. The Yankees say they had the "audacity of the devil himself." I feel very proud of our brave boys, but am afraid the citizens will suffer in consequence of their temerity.

> *This daring raid was made by twenty-five men of Company B, Twelfth Virginia Cavalry (The Baylor Light Horse.) It was led by Lt. George Baylor.*
>
> *Front Royal was guarded by the Third Delaware Regiment, over eight hundred strong, four hundred cavalry, and a battery of artillery.*
>
> *Lieutenant Baylor captured fifteen horses, three hundred prisoners and among them, a major and two captains. A mile south of Front Royal, the Federal cavalry appeared. The Confederates mounted fifteen of the prisoners and succeeded in bringing these out safely, while the Federal cavalry released the foot prisoners.*

Nev. came back today from Brown's Cove. Saw Cousin Mack whose wound is so much better as to admit of his hobbling about with a crutch.

They all visited Weyer's Cave and Nev. is delighted.

August 12, 1862

Heard they had arrested all the citizens in Front Royal in retaliation of that dash of yesterday. Feel very uneasy. Know if they have Father that Ma is in great trouble and I ought to be at home with her. Do not think they will injure the citizens themselves at all beyond keeping them under arrest.

August 13, 1862

Went down to Flint Run in the evening and after rambling along its banks for a time Nel, Julie and I, at Mrs. Hall's instigation doffed shoes and stockings and waded the stream—a very undignified but not less delightful proceeding on our part.

August 16, 1862

Jule came in to my room with a glass of sangaree in her hand to strengthen me for the trying scenes which she said were about to ensue. Pointing out the window she showed me about seventeen Yankee cavalry just crossing the river toward the house; and Nellie came hurriedly in bidding me conceal my diary and letters as they certainly make a search. But they did no such thing, only rode up to the house and made enquiry as to the number and movement of the "Secesh cavalry" that had gone over into the "Fork." The servants and children assured them that there were hundreds of the most ferocious kinds of bushwhackers over there which intimidated them so much that they would penetrate no further than to the barn-field. When wheeling their horses they dashed back to the house, some of them coming in to get bread and milk, some searching the outhouses and some trying to capture two little ponies feeding in the meadow. They presently fell into line and rode a half mile down the river whence they soon returned bringing a reinforcement of some dozen more with horses which they had stolen from Mr. King. They halted below the house holding a consultation of war which ended in nearly all dismounting and coming back to the house to ask for "something to eat." Uncle Fayette was absent and Aunt Lizzie had to meet them. She promised to give them a luncheon provided they would not molest her ponies. They assured her they would not and thereupon fell to discussing the edibles placed before them. One of them broke into the cellar and stole the milk there after having disposed of what had been given him, and oh if Aunt L. did not give him a lecture then I never heard one, and he certainly behaved better under her scolding than could have been expected. They assured us however before they left that they had "given old Jackson an awful thrashing at Gordonsville and driven him back to Richmond." I did not believe a word of it though. They rode back to Front Royal very quietly but minus the "guerrilas" they had come after and which they declared with an oath "thunder itself could not find them in such a country as this!"

The girls walked over to our old "Sunset Cliff" this evening but I did not feel well enough to go with them and so stayed with Aunt Lizzie going around with her and talking to her while she watered the flowers. Then went on the upper porch to wave to the party on the cliff across the river, and drink in the loveliness of that river scene which was even more to be appreciated in the mellow subdued tints of the evening than when radiant with the light of the early sun. Dear old Clover Hill! How quiet and what an atmosphere of tranquility and peace hovers ever around here and how often during the turmoil and confusion of the last months have I thought of this almost paradise on earth. Ah me!—I must tomorrow go back to the oppression of Yankeedom.

V

FIRST INVASION OF NORTH

August 17, 1862 - December 31, 1862

August 17, 1862

Nev. rode down to Mr. King's before breakfast this morning to ascertain whether or not we could get into town and returned saying the enemy had evacuated the place. Glorious!—immediately after breakfast the light carriage was harnessed and Julia, Nellie, Neville and myself set out.

> *A regiment of infantry and two cavalry companies were encamped in Front Royal as guards for the provost marshal. This force now left to join General Pope east of the Blue Ridge. From this time to the end of the war neither side used the village as a permanent encampment. However, due to the location at the entrance of the Shenandoah Valley, the town became an avenue for both armies.*

What a delightful ride we had along the cool shaded banks of the river laughing and talking merrily and anon relapsing by tacit consent into silence enjoying the beauty of the day and scenery. But in the midst of our fully blown pleasure we were suddenly disconcerted by the breakage of one of the shafts and as it was impossible to repair damages then and there nothing was left for us but to "foot it" to town the distance of two miles. Found no pickets at any of the posts and when we came in sight of the place we knew the Yankees had left. Such unbroken deathlike stillness as reigned around was never known while their hated influence extended. We walked through the streets without encountering a soul until nearly out of town when we met Uncle Tom who told us all the Rose Hill family—Cousin Sue B. included, were very sick; he had just come from there. So sorry. He gave us the particulars of the dash and it was even a more daring achievement than we had first thought for only seven of our men came into town and three of them rode right down to the Yankee camp and were fired on. One went into the hotel and broke up the rests there, another went a half mile up the creek and yet all escaped. "'Twas gloriously done."

We have whipped Banks again at Culpeper and the 102d New York Regiment which had been here, was cut to pieces.

Jackson on August ninth, defeated Banks at Cedar or Slaughter Mountain south of Culpeper.

August 19, 1862

Father proposed a ramble to the river this morning to see the formidable fortifications there. We had a pleasant walk and a hearty laugh at the abortive attempts at defense made by the Yankees. To think of a mud embankment and rifle pits at the foot of the hill, protected by an abatice of saplings about as impregnable as a box-hedge which commanded nothing but Mr. Weston's garden. Such a farce! While carrying out these explorations we heard a cry of Yankees!—and looking up the road saw a cavalry company approach, plunge in and cross the river and then six or eight wagons. We went over to the Forneys and waited to see the finale of this movement and feeling very anxious for the Confederate soldiers whom we had left in town, some eight or ten of them. On our way home we met a rather nice looking young man in citizen's clothes and feeling convinced he was a Yankee Father halted him and asked an explanation of the entrance of the troops. He told all he knew, then smiling gladly enquired if we thought he could "run the blockade undetected," and then remarked that he was a native of Stafford County, Va., had been living with a brother in Del., was at a party when they drugged his wine, and the next thing he knew he was in camp and "in for it." He had tried to desert three times before but had hitherto been unsuccessful. Now he had obtained his clothes from a kind lady in town and hoped to escape.

Father came in the evening bringing a letter which he said Miss Carrie Brown handed him. It was from Benton to me—dated Tupelo (Miss.) June twenty-second containing however, no news.

August 20, 1862

Heard Scott's letter giving an account of his escape from the Yankees which must have been very cleverly managed by his playing Yankee too. He writes that Benton did not, that the latter had been promoted to his majority. Heard today Cousin F. Blakemore was a regular sanguinary red republican. For shame!

August 21, 1862

Willie still so very sick and Uncle Newton to see him. The latter told us he had heard from Charlie and that he had been accidently shot in the foot and that the foot had to be amputated in consequence. Poor Charlie!—a cripple for life, how distressing it will be to him. We have a paper giving an account of Morgan's expedition in the West—his triumphal march, capture of cities, stores, etc., etc. and the pranks played upon Yankee telegraphic operators.

> *Gen. John Hunt Morgan, C.S.A., raided into Kentucky and Tennessee July 4, to July 28, 1862. One of Morgan's favorite tricks was to cut the telegraphic wires and send messages to the Yankees. In this manner he played many tricks by announcing his approach and alarming the population and then attacking another area. He was known as "Marion" because of his "Swamp Fox" activity.*

It was gloriously done and our "Marion" is surely second to none but our beloved Stonewall. Uncles Newton and Tom to see us today. Willie, poor fellow, is ill. Stayed with Ma tonight to help nurse the children.

August 23, 1862

Felt brighter today, busily engaged sewing all day. Heard that Captain Simpson had been exchanged and was in town. Brought cheering news from all our friends. Aunt L. Buck called by this evening on her way from up the river, and told us that Walter had started to see us but been persuaded not to come by some officious friend. He sent some saucy messages to Nellie and me. Aunt L. says he was in the most hilarious spirits imaginable. Dear fellow! How I should like to have seen him. Through Uncle Newton we learned that Capt. S. had seen Cousin Alex Blakemore in Rd. and Uncle John too. Cousin brought news from our boys—he had just left them at Chattanooga, Tenn.

> *After Bragg had taken over from the ailing Beauregard, he moved his army to Chattanooga, Tennessee, and from there invaded Kentucky in August, 1862. Bragg was stopped at Perryville, Kentucky on October 8 and headed back south.*

U.S.A.		C.S.A.	
Effectives	36,940	Effectives	16,000
Killed	845	Killed	510
Wounded	2,851	Wounded	2,635
Missing	515	Missing	251

They were with Colonel Jordan under General Bragg who intended retaining them in his employ come what would. All were well. Beauregard had neither lost his life nor been deranged but was on leave of absence at some spring to recoup his health. We were so delighted to hear it. Capt. S. was to leave for Gordonsville in the morning and would carry out letters if I had any to send the boys. I thereupon sat down and indited what dear Irvie terms one of my "four story" epistles to the boys and dispatched it by Allie. Uncle Tom came over and told us that glorious "back down" of old Pope. After issuing the most infamous proclamation tending to the inhalations of the Secessionists he comes out in a recantation—prohibits the administration of the oath under compulsion and expressly provides for the protection of Secession property and all just because he was afraid of our dear old president. Well, it is too good.

> *The Confederate government retaliated by declaring Pope and his officers were not entitled to be considered soldiers. If captured they were to be imprisoned as long as their orders remained unrepealed and, in the event of any unarmed citizen being tried and shot, an equal number of Federal prisoners were to be hanged. This ended Pope's proclamation.*

Kattie Samuels went to Strasburg this evening to see her husband who has been exchanged and is there.

August 24, 1862

Father, Nellie and I went to church and just as we entered the churchyard I noticed quite a distinguished looking stranger sauntering slowly toward us in whom I presently recognized the redoubtable Captain Simpson who came forward and spoke to us quite cordially though he as well as ourselves were constrained. While Father was talking with him we went into the house. Dr. Hough preached poor John Steele's funeral sermon and I think there were few dry eyes in the house. The text was—"I will patiently bear the indignation of the Lord for I have sinned against Him and He will deliver me"—and "Rejoice not over me, oh mine enemy. Though I am fallen yet shall I rise again, though I sit in darkness yet shall He show me His marvelous light."

Found on coming out the church that the cannonading was more distinct and heavier. On passing down the street learned from a soldier who professed just to have left the scene—that Jackson had beaten the enemy back from Culpeper and that they were in retreat for Washington—our men hotly pursuing. Went up on the house when we reached home and could clearly distinguish cannonading from two directions and the heaviest I ever heard. It seemed singular that we should feel so calm with the thunder of artillery shaking the very ground and knowing as we did that the fate of the valley, if not of the capital itself depended on the issue of the conflict.

August 25, 1862

Was awakened about twelve o'clock last night by hurrying to and fro and opening and shutting doors. Feeling uneasy I glided downstairs and met Father at the foot of the steps who called out to me not to be afraid that Uncle John, Alex and Horace had just come home from Warrenton. I asked when they left and how went the day. He replied that all was well. At the breakfast table this morning we met all together and Uncle John confirmed all we had heard through Captain Simpson concerning the boys and told Ma over in what high estimation they were held by their superior officers. It is so gratifying to hear it and General Jordan says he'll not give them up under a commission. Uncle John was looking so well and in such a state of delight at being home again. He had a great many anecdotes to tell us—knew about all our friends and confirmed what we had heard of the position of the armies. He told us that poor Major Henry Lane was certainly dead. He saw him after he was mortally wounded at Slaughter Mountain, conversed with him, and remained with him until nearly the last. Another victim, poor fellow, to this unnatural strife. After breakfast went on down to Rose Hill. I dreaded this visit so much—dreaded so much to go where the footsteps that were wont first to meet me and the voice that ever was present in welcoming were now still and silent in the grave. They all looked so sick and so sad—four dark-robed, wan figures all that were left of the once large and happy family. Cousin Sue and poor little Belle were both in black. I started home. I could not but be amused this morning, while giving the baby his breakfast in the dining room Horace and Alex spied me and in they marched to shake my hand cordially and receive my congratulations on their safe return and prosperous appearance. They evidently considered themselves heroes in their fatigue uniforms but they were very respectful though cordial and replied to my questions very proudly. Alex assured me he had assisted in lifting General Ashby into the ambulance after his death and Horace dwelling on the great battles they had witnessed. I was right glad to see them.

Horace and Alex were servants.

Was lying down upstairs in the afternoon when I heard a bustle below as of arrivals and soon distinguished Cousin Betty R.'s voice and Mr. R.'s, then presently Uncle Mack and Uncle John, then Uncle Fayette, Aunt Betty's, Uncle Tom's, Uncle Newton's, and little Bell Richardson's. Dressed and went down where they were all sitting at the door looking so happy and chatting away so merrily congratulating themselves upon this pleasant reunion and regretting that Uncle John must leave during the night. Suddenly in the midst of it all came a cry—"the Yankees!" We sprung to our feet and looked out in time to see in truth a company of about thirty horsemen dashing gallantly into town. Immediately all was confusion, we knew they had come for our soldiers, some few of whom with Capt. S. were with their families in town, and we were for getting Uncle J. out of their clutches. So thrusting some of his things into his carpetsack we started him on foot across the field sending his horse around to meet him and telling him to strike for the pine thickets. As soon as he was off the remainder of the party dispersed like a flock of frightened partridges. Some of us went up to the dormer window on the roof to watch the proceeding of the Yankees. Saw them go out to Mrs. Simpson's and return minus the Confed. Capt. Then saw them go into the private houses we knew for the purpose of searching them and expected a squad of detectives over here every moment but they did not come—and about dusk they left without having taken a single prisoner. The last man of them had scarcely disappeared over the hill. Here we saw Horace (who had gone with Uncle John) returning through the orchard and presently Uncle John himself came riding down the hill looking for all the world like Sancho Panza the second. Just as he came up the yard on one side, Aunt Betty and Uncle Tom approached from the other and such greetings and congratulations and chattering as ensued. I gave Uncle J. his supper, prepared him a lunch to take with him and then we all adjourned to the parlor where we spent a most delightful evening. Horace and Alex seemed so adverse to returning to their military duties that Father permitted them to remain at home.

'Tis said Captain Simpson was concealed in the cornfield near town today while they were looking for him and that he ruined a very handsome uniform presented him while a prisoner by a lady of Boston.

August 26, 1862

Was in the parlor practicing this evening when hearing Nellie exclaim "Oh they'll get our cavalry!" I went to the door and she pointed out the same company of Yankees riding swiftly into town pursuing two of our cavalry—men who had started out to the river a short time before. We watched them until they were concealed by the houses. We afterward saw them galloping up the Luray Road, but presently they returned and some of them again went out to Mrs. Simpson's while the remainder engaged in their favorite amusement of searching houses. We were not honored this time either. The Yankees did not get our men and really looked mean when they went out of town a second time foiled of their prey. There is clearly a traitor among us, else how did they know any of our men were in town.

August 27, 1862

Laura brought me from Ellen Brown a song that I had long coveted—"We Sleep But We Are Not Dead"—Alvin's song. Heard today that Jackson was at Salem.

Jackson passed through Salem, (Marshall) Virginia, on August 25, during his famous march from the Rappahannock

River, via Orlean, Salem, Throughfare Gap to Bristoe Station to attack the rear of Pope's army. This action developed into the Second Manassas or Second Bull Run.

General Longstreet was at the Rappahannock River near Warrenton. Lucy's information was quite correct.

Longstreet holding the Yankee army at check at Warrenton. We took one of Pope's couriers and a dispatch found upon him gives rather an unfavorable account of the condition of the Federal army. It is also reported that ten of the brave boys who made that dash into F. Royal and took the trains of cars in Jefferson with thirty horses were captured today. Sincerely trust it is false.

August 28, 1862
Heard a confirmation of the capture of the brave "Baylorians." Jackson is said to be in or near Manassas and to have completely surrounded the Feds.

> Jackson arrived at Bristoe Station August 27, 1862, and from there moved to Manassas to capture Pope's stores the same night.

August 29, 1862
The children came in to say a company of our cavalry was coming in town. We saw them—goodly sight. Three of the number came over to dinner—one of them was the veritable Coffield who with his friend Reid stopped here last spring en route from Baltimore to join the army. He had with him his brother and another friend. They did not give any clue as to their mission here but confirmed our preconceived conception that Jackson intended taking Arlington Heights. They left immediately after dinner. That rumor of the capture of our cavalry at Newtown was a mistake—it was a band of horse thieves instead and as good riddance to us as the Yankees themselves. It is also said we have taken the robber Means and his band from Loudoun and if that be true we will have use for some executioners.

> The Loudoun Rangers were organized by Union men west and north of Catoctin Mountains in Loudoun County, Virginia. Their leader was Capt. Samuel C. Means and in August, 1862, their headquarters were in Waterford, Loudoun County.
>
> White's batallion was organized by Confederates in the same county and their captain (later colonel) was Elijah Viers White. White's battalion surprised Means' men in August of 1862 at Waterford and captured several not including Captain Means. One of Means' men was wanted for murder. Upon capture he was tried and hanged.

White's battalion became the 35th Virginia Cavalry and in January 1863 it became part of Jones' brigade. White later became commander of this brigade (Laurel Brigade) and disbanded it at Lynchburg after Appomattox.

August 30, 1862

Father came home to dinner and told us he had seen a Balto. Sun which spoke of an irruption of some of the Indian tribes upon some of the northwestern states and 'twas feared they were backed by the Mormons. So Uncle Sam will have an occasion for the use of some of his surplus soldiers—volunteers. The paper also contained a rumor that Sturgis' command (which had been sent to quell the Rebels who made the raid upon Bristoe Station) was taken by those very Rebels. Then the news from England was not at all comfortable. So glad!

On December 26, 1862, thirty-eight Indians were hanged at Mankato, Minnesota for participating in the Sioux uprising. In the Sioux uprising in 1862 from 1000–1500 persons were killed and property to the value of over half a million dollars was destroyed by the Indians.

August 31, 1862

Father came in and said he had just seen a reliable German up the street who was just from the scene of action and he told him that Jackson had repulsed Pope's whole army at Manassas with great carnage, had taken a great many prisoners and vast amounts of army stores—enough to supply our men during the coming four months. But we had lost much too, the "Stonewall Brigade" was terribly cut up and Ewell had been wounded and had his leg amputated and many, many a noble Southern sleeps silently on that sanguinary battlefield.

Pope turned North hoping to destroy Stonewall before Longstreet and Lee arrived on the field. With the arrival of these generals and their armies on August 29, Jackson was saved. The Second Manassas or Second Bull Run was fought on the twenty-ninth and thirtieth. On the thirty-first, Jackson was sent by Lee toward Fairfax C. H. via Pleasant Valley to try to hit behind the retreating Federals. A battle was fought in the rain September 1, 1862, at Chantilly. The Second Battle of Manassas ended here with the death of two Union generals, Maj. Gen. Philip Kearny and Brig. Gen. I. I. Stevens.

U.S.A.

Effectives 75,696
Killed 1,724

C.S.A.

Effectives 48,527
Killed 1,481

Wounded 8,372   Wounded 7,627
Missing 5,958   Missing 89

Lucy's information about Ewell and the Stonewall Brigade was correct. Since Lee had taken over three months previously, the Army of Northern Virginia had relieved its own capital and was now just outside Washington, but McClellan's army was moving into Washington from the Peninsula.

It was a glorious victory though over the enemy and we felt very very hopeful and cheerful for our cause. To think how it has all changed since six months ago. Then, we saw nothing but disaster and destruction before us. We had lost our stronghold and permitted the enemy to penetrate to the vitals of the country with his desolating armies, laying waste the land with fire and sword. Then his ironclad gunboats were swarming on our coast and port after port, city after city were occupied by his ruffian horde and the whole South was being drained of its substance. So that there was nothing but starvation and ruin for the inhabitants. Our capital was menaced by a vast army of exultant and victory flushed foes. Our army seemed to have melted away or were within the coils of a mighty serpent that must soon crush them—oh it was all disheartening enough!—and I have wondered how we ever struggled through such depths of gloom. But the day I trust has gone on our midnight, how it has all so changed I can't understand, but surely God has been with us. 'Tis He that arrested the tide of Union successes and nerved and inspired our men to such deeds of daring heroism. Oh!—may we never forget to whom we owe it all and weakly give to erring impotent man the need of thanksgiving and praise that belongs but to the Maker!

September 1, 1862
"The summer is past, the harvest is ended," and today beholds the dawn of the autumn. I wonder how the summer has gone by I can scarcely tell I'm sure. It has seemed such a short one, and even with all our troubles and annoyances it has not been a joyless season; for those few pleasures we had were all the more keenly appreciated for their rarity. But I fear I have planted few seeds of improvement in the meantime and that this autumn will prove very barren of the fruits of high resolve, self-conquest or anything of good. I believe though that I have learned to be more useful to myself and to others for which I'm thankful.

September 2, 1862
Father came over from town this morning and told us that Scott Roy had come home the night before—was wounded in the forehead and the blow would probably have proved fatal had he not happened to have his face averted at the time. He brought news that poor John Simpson was killed, Sam missing and Robt. badly wounded. Saml. Spangler was

thought to be mortally wounded. Tom Santmyers has his finger shot off. None of our immediate friends were injured. Scott's wound was a mere scratch—only a passing compliment from a saucy bullet. How I would like to see him and hear him spin some of his "camp yarns."

Nellie and I spent a very pleasant day at Oakley. A Confederate soldier dined there and he told us that Stuart's cavalry were at the chain bridge near Georgetown, D. C. He seemed to think Jackson determined to push on to Maryland.

> *Lee knew it would be impossible to capture Washington, because McClellan's army from the Peninsula was again in the Union capital. The commander of the Army of Northern Virginia felt an invasion of the North was necessary. Lee sought provisions in Maryland for his battered army. He also invaded for political reasons, to stir up the peace party in the North, and also to receive into the Confederate army Southern sympathizers from the state of Maryland.*

'Tis said the enemy have blown up their magazines and destroyed quantities of ammunition in the department of the Potomac.

Saw the prisoners marched out this morning—200 of them. Poor creatures, I could not help but feel sorry for them as they trudged so wearily along with their knapsacks on their backs.

September 3, 1862

Father remarked at breakfast this morning that he had heard a very singular noise during the night and on looking out saw in the direction of Winchester a brilliant light. We were at first apprehensive of a general conflagration of the town, but afterwards heard that it was the explosion caused by the enemy destroying his magazines there. They had evacuated the place at two o'clock this morning. Good! I hope the valley is clean now!

Scott left this evening without calling. Unsociable fellow!

September 5, 1862

Cousin Mary C. and Mrs. H. Miller came over this morning—the former to spend the day with me, the latter to get some of the Capon linen.

> *Capon linen was from the hotel at Capon Springs where pure linen was used in all rooms.*

A dear familiar voice was heard exclaiming "How are you all!" and in a moment Dick was in our midst giving and receiving embraces and kisses. We were so glad to see him and spent such a delightful day with the dear fellow who has improved and looks wonderfully well. He with a friend of his Lieutenant Timmerman are recruiting for the regiment and will be with us probably some time. Father was at the mountain all day so we had Dick's conversation all to ourselves and he told us so much about the army that we had never heard before. I'm sure I had no idea the Battle of Williamsburg and Seven Pines were such important conflicts till hearing his accounts of them. I never till today noticed the striking resemblance between our dear Irvie and Dick in manner and conversation and it has if possible endeared him all the more to me—indeed several times today I've been cheated into addressing him as "Irvie."

We expected they would bring young Spangler here tonight, as they are on their way home with him. He did not come though and I'm afraid poor fellow, he never will reach his home.

Charlie Richardson and Captain Simpson I hear are both at home. Sam Simpson is uninjured. No reliable news.

September 6, 1862

Such a fatiguing day as it has been! Father did not think when he brought that lot of Capon linen here what a bother it would prove to him but now the neighbors have all found it out and are begging to be accommodated and if he lets one have he must not exclude another from the same privilege, so I expect nothing else but that he will have to open the whole supply and dispose of them by retail instead of as by wholesale as he had expected to. He will not only lose by the latter mode but it will be an insufferable bother. Oh me!

I could almost have cried when I saw Charlie. At first I did not know him, for with his wan sad face and fever worn figure he looked but the wreck of the saucy Charlie of yore. He carried his arm in a sling—said it had improved very much in the while he had been at home but it knitted very sorrowfully he fears less he be maimed for life. Poor boy—I hope not indeed. He was more sociable and talkative than I have ever known him and amused us very much with his account of the battles and the tough "camp yarns" he spun us.

Uncle Tom came over and brought us good news if true. He had seen a gentleman just from "over the ridge" who told him that a portion of our army some thirty thousand strong was certainly in Md. Oh if that long looked for opportunity have indeed arrived! But we're afraid to believe it just yet.

Young Spangler came last night to the hotel and 'tis thought he must die, poor boy.

September 7, 1862

Estie says Mr. Spangler died last night. The second brother who has died in the hospital during this horrible war.

Mr. Hope came up to see us this morning to impart the news which he had brought directly from the army the night before. He had seen some of our friends and all in the army were well. He also saw Jackson's army cross the Potomac.

Jackson crossed the Potomac September 6, 1862, at White's Ford. In midstream he took off his hat and a band played "Maryland, My Maryland." The men gave Rebel yells and sang with the band.

The old general had outwitted the enemy most completely as he always does. By marching a portion of his forces toward Arlington and making a great ado with his artillery he induced the Yankees to believe he intended making an attack there while all the time our troops were wading the river at Edwards Ferry above Leesburg. What must have been the feeling of those men particularly the Marylanders themselves when they first set foot upon the Maryland shores—the long-wished for goal of their fondest hopes. I think they must have saluted ground with almost the same reverence that Columbus did when he landed in the new world. As the men gained the opposite banks they struck up "My Maryland" accompanied by the bands. Then I think the sternest heart must have throbbed in sympathy and the most unimpressible of Maryland's exiled sons must have wept like children. Oh it was such a scene as one witnesses but once in a life time and I would have given much to have seen it. And we certainly are there to help her "burst the tyrant's chains" and rescue one other bright star of the Southern constellation from the gloom of tyrannical oppression.... Oh I sympathize with those who welcome the freedom which our army brings them, with them I've tasted the bitterness of slavery, with them I've welcomed deliverance which only we could appreciate.

September 9, 1862
Well, its all over thank goodness! I never want to sell another sheet, pillow slip, towel, tablecloth, or napkin as long as I live. Cousins Ed and Will left directly after breakfast and then commenced the excitement which lasted till noon; I believe every family in town had a representative here—some two or three, and among them people I have never before seen. I have to leave my post as saleswoman and go assist Father in clerking, making off my first bills, and a vexatious time I had of it. How I should dislike to trade in this way. I think it must be in very ill accordance with the generous instinct of one's nature. Oh dear!—well they've taken everything away now but the "spreads" and tablecloths and I hope we won't have much more trouble with them.

September 10, 1862
The Winchester people are apprehending an advance from Harpers Ferry and that there is quite a formidable force at the latter point and also at Edwards Ferry which will cut off our communication with our

army. However, I believe our generals will soon remove this inconvenience—at least I trust so. I've noticed a number of army wagons passing through town today and numbers of soldiers en route for Winchester.

> On this date Jackson headed toward Harpers Ferry "to remove the inconvenience." Many Federal troops were left in the vicinity of Harpers Ferry when Lee invaded Maryland. It had been assumed that these troops would evacuate their position and join McClellan in Washington. When they did not, Lee elected to split his army and moved west, sending Jackson via Martinsburg to attack Harpers Ferry. McClellan found an order of Lee's to General D. H. Hill, and realizing Lee's army was divided, moved fast to destroy the Confederates before they were reunited.
>
> The Federals were held at South Mountain and after Harpers Ferry was captured by Jackson on September 15, 1862, Lee moved his army behind the Antietam Creek at Sharpsburg, Maryland.

September 12, 1862

Father saw Cousin Tom Buck today—was just from Maryland but brought no news of particular interest except that the Marylanders were receiving Confederate money and were glad to see them.

There are so many broken-down soldiers passing through town en route for Winchester.

> When Lee crossed into Maryland he directed the stragglers be sent to Winchester to be regrouped into an active unit.

We had some seven or eight to supper and two of them stayed here tonight—one a very handsome little captain—a Georgian and his lieutenant. D. H. Hill has command at Winchester and 'tis said has cut off the supplies for the Yankees at Harpers Ferry.

September 13, 1862

Had a number of soldiers to breakfast this morning and after breakfast at Father's request Nellie and I sang and played for them and for a wonder they seemed to enjoy it very much. One of them sat as near as he conveniently could to the piano and Father says he scarcely moved all the time. I could but notice how much more like gentlemen they behaved than did the Yankees. Loyal blood will show itself in any guise.

September 14, 1862

Uncle Mack came over and said it was rumored that Wirt had surrendered Harpers Ferry and we had taken a quantity of arms and "contrabands."

> *Brig. Gen. Julies White arranged for surrender. Col. C. S. Miles was the commanding officer.*
>
> *Jackson captured at Harpers Ferry 11,000 prisoners and 13,000 small arms, 73 cannons, and 200 wagons, plus many stores filled with needed supplies.*
>
> *By 1 o'clock* A.M. *of the sixteenth, Jackson's foot cavalry was headed to Sharpsburg to aid Lee.*

September 16, 1862

Father topped those old locusts in the back yard: was so sorry to see them thus mutilated. J. T. Petty, A's familiar friend, called by this morning on his way to Winchester. We had heard of his having received a letter from Alvin and sent to know about it. He told us he had not had a letter from him in a long time but expressed the greatest affection and esteem for him. I had never before met with the gentleman and was agreeably surprised by his easy graceful manner and fluent conversation. He told us Scott Roy was in town again, being unable to march for his sore foot.

We had unpleasant news from Maryland this evening. General Garland's command being on Saturday engaged with a vastly superior force was defeated, and he, killed. It has made us feel very gloomy. Ma brought no news from town, plenty of rumors but nothing authentic.

> *Brig. Gen. Samuel Garland, whose engagement for marriage was about to be announced in Richmond, was killed on September 14, 1862. He received his mortal wound while holding back the Federals at Turner's Gap, a pass in the South Mountains.*

September 18, 1862

A pleasant morning. Neville came in about ten o'clock with a wagon load of supplies for the soldiers. Kind Aunt Lizzie! I knew she would do all she could toward feeding the poor things. This was Thanksgiving day and we went to hear a Thanksgiving sermon. On our way to church saw Scott at the gate. Dr. Hough delivered a most excellent discourse from the text ... "Vengeance is mine, I will repay saith the Lord." I liked his views with regard to retaliation so much.

September 19, 1862

Were busily engaged sewing this morning when Scott came in to bring Nellie some later periodicals which he promised her yesterday. He behaved so strangely—sat some ten minutes and then suddenly rising bowed himself out of the room. Wonder if he is hurt at anything.

Commenced making my Lovars jacket this evening. Uncle Mack came in about dusk and told us there had been a most terrific battle at Sharpsburg, Maryland in which we had nearly been defeated but had succeeded in driving the enemy from the field and then slowly fell back ourselves.

> The Yankees attacked at Sharpsburg on September 17, 1862, the day after Jackson joined Lee. Lee's army was minus General McLaws and General A. P. Hill, who were still at Harpers Ferry. These troops arrived just in time to save Lee's right flank. This was one of the fiercest battles of the war and when the day ended Lee's army had held and had driven back the Union forces. On the eighteenth Lee waited for the next blows, but they never came. Instead came a flag of truce to pick up the wounded and to bury the dead. That night Lee recrossed the Potomac.

U.S.A.		C.S.A.	
Effectives	87,164	Effectives	51,844
Killed	2,108	Killed	2,700
Wounded	9,549	Wounded	9,024
Missing	753	Missing	2,000

It is represented as a most disastrous battle to both parties in loss of men and very little advantage to either... got the best of it. Our forces are said to be recrossing the river.

September 20, 1862
The reports concerning the Sharpsburg battle are confirmed—Kattie Samuels told us her father was an eye witness of the affair and he says our army are certainly recrossing the river. It looks rather gloomy for our prospects in Md. and I cannot possibly understand it all.
Heard cannonading and went on the house after tea to listen to it. Sounds very distinct and from the direction of Harpers Ferry.

September 22, 1862
Nellie and I must go down and help Cousin Bet wait on the soldiers. It was very sad at Rose Hill, but not quiet for all day there was a continual stream of soldiers coming for a meal. In the afternoon, too we had such a scene with poor Eliza who had heard that her husband Jim was among the contrabands taken at Harpers Ferry and that Dr. D. his master intended selling him.
Had to cross the ferry with a boatload of soldiers; reached Riverside just in time for tea and receiving a hearty welcome. After tea we adjourned to the parlor where were Miss Lacey and Riley a young soldier Mr. Taliaferro. Music and singing all the evening. I should like to know how

many soldiers took tea here tonight.

September 23, 1862
Soldiers coming in from the time we were up, till this time. Such numbers of wounded as have been passing. I would not live here for the world to see all the poor wounded fellows dragging themselves wearily along. Nellie dressed the wounds of a poor Alabaman today and did it bravely while I turned faint and sick while merely holding the basin for her. In the afternoon a portion of the old Maryland Regiment went by and we waved to and cheered them.

September 25, 1862
My birthday! Twenty years old! Oh how long a time I have lived in this world for the good I've done. Older than wise and wiser than good what a record I have to confront me today! What a summing up of a life of twenty years! And I'm a woman, repel the unwelcome thought as I will, close my eyes to the fact—say passionately—"I will be a child careless and free!"—the truth made apparent—I am a woman in feelings as well as years. A woman by this sensitive apprehension of my own unworthiness, of my deficiencies in every respect, in my loneliness, awkwardness and temper. I can't bear to think or write about it.

September 29, 1862
News came in this morning to the effect that Longstreet's corps was to cross the river at Confluence (Riverton) and marched through town en route for Warrenton. We were so glad to hear it and concluded we should see some of the Rifles. The troops commenced passing through in the afternoon and in the late evening some officers—Captain Luckadoo and some others took supper with us. 'Tis said General Lee passed through town today but he came so quietly and unobtrusively that scarcely anyone knew it but he till he had gone. Longstreet too is reported to have gone by us incog. It's too bad to think I've missed seeing these two brave chiefs. The Rifles are in town but have only leave of absence till ten o'clock tonight so we shall not see Scott or any of the boys. It's right provoking.

October 31, 1862
Troops pouring in all day. About noon a courier dashed up and enquired for General Longstreet, seemed very much surprised when told he was not here. Then the general's bodyguard came in and encamped near the barn. We had not expected General Longstreet till tomorrow but now concluded he could not be far off and about four o'clock they all rode up Capt. L. among them.

The Army of Northern Virginia under Lee was divided into two corps after the Battle of Antietam or Sharpsburg. Jackson commanded the second corps, Longstreet the first corps. Both were elevated to lieutenant generals. This was not formally announced until November 6, 1862, but the troops were assigned. On October 28, 1862, Longstreet was ordered south to Culpeper and Jackson was ordered to move toward Winchester.

Mrs. Moffat was here and just before she left we concluded to make the best of the pleasant evening by a walk to "Point of Rocks;" as we were standing under the aspen trees when Capt. L. came out and commenced a conversation by enquiring how I liked Gen. L. This led to a discussion of the comparative merits of our generals when upon my enthusiastic admiration of Jackson he thought I detracted from Longstreet's fame and he was greatly picqued. I was so much surprised that such a quiet self-possessed individual should have been startled out of his usual equanimity thus. Had a pleasant walk and returned to tea. The staff consist of Capts. Latrobe and Young and Gore; Majors Sorrell and Waldon the number being composed apparently of the most perfect gentlemen. The general retired early and Capt. L. then requested Nellie and myself to play and sing "There's Life in the Old Land Yet" for him. We went in and found Capt. Young there—sat down and played and sang until we were tired and then entered into a sociable conversation. I did enjoy it so much—I never have met with two such refined polished gentlemen, they exactly realize my ideal of the chivalrous knights of yore, so courteous and delicate in their manner. I do wish the world were composed one half of such men. Did not retire till quite late.

November 1, 1862
Was up bright and early this morning. Started upstairs to get something out of Father's room knowing he had come down, but upon opening the door saw a pair of spurred boots on the floor and concluding the owner was not far distant I beat a hasty retreat. I was startled truly. Wonder what Capt. L. would have thought of such an early call had he seen me. Just before breakfast Cousins Mary and E. Cloud came in to see the general and very soon after Captain Simpson, though I fancy the object of his visit was quite a different one than theirs. I was amused at the conversation which ensued at the breakfast table. Neither Cousins M. or E. was there nor yet Capt. S. Father, Capt. L. and myself discussed natural scenery and the old general spoke never a word save to keep up a desultory fire of inquiries concerning Capt. S. and when he arose from the table he remarked briefly in reply to some information given him—"Then 'tis time he was promoted." What a very quiet, dignified old gentleman he is—very fine looking though and with a countenance full of benevolence. He is fond of children too, another trait which I admire. A courier arrived from Jackson about midnight last night which seems to hasten their movements for they announced bright and early

that they must be off immediately and off they did go about nine o'clock. Capt. L. remarked when he left that he would certainly return to the valley if it ever were in his power to do so. They one and all expressed themselves as delighted with this part of the country.

When hearing that Stuart's cavalry were about entering town we ran across the field to see if the Rangers were among them. Waited about half an hour when finding nothing but infantry likely to be in for some time Nellie and I concluded to return home. Sat in the yard some time watching the troops pouring in as they have been doing for the last four days and listening to "Mocking Bird" being played so sweetly by the passing bands. I have a peculiar fancy for hearing that air performed by the band, not so much because of its plaintive notes as that it is dear Irvie's favorite and reminds me of that ninth of July at Manassas.

November 3, 1862

I concluded to spend today at Mrs. Cloud's. Received a warm welcome and found Mr. Daniel Cloud there. While chatting cozily up in Mrs. C.'s room we heard an unusual stir in the street and upon looking out we saw a train of army wagons dashing through at a furious rate and the street which had all the morning been thronged with soldiers were soon without the appearance of any military personage whatever. We could not learn anything definite however—only wild rumors of the enemy's advance, the evacuation of the town, etc. After dinner we noticed the troops were filling the roads leaving the town in different directions and looking over toward Bel Air we noticed horsemen hurrying in and out the gate and a general appearance of confusion. Had just taken my seat at the piano to sing a Southern song for Mr. Cloud when the door opened and Nellie walked in. She told us there were batteries on the hills back of the house and at one time during the afternoon our men were in battle array in expectation of the enemy. The persons we had seen riding about the yard at home were sundry officers who had called for various purposes. The streets about this time were crowded with soldiers, infantry, artillery and cavalry with a long baggage train all passing at once. As soon as these had dispersed a little we concluded to return home and upon reaching there found Uncle John. He explained the movements of our army by saying our troops were falling back and that the valley would probably be evacuated ere long. Such a damper to our spirits as it was to hear this! He seemed in pretty good spirits though and told us that only D. H. Hill's division was near here now but that all Jackson's army would probably pass through soon when we would have an opportunity of seeing our friends in his corps—Willie Kennon among them. He said he had seen Irvie's former friend and employer Mr. Pearce—that he had left Balto., joined the Southern army and would probably call to see us soon.

November 4, 1862

Father came in and brought us a letter from each of the boys. Dear, dear boys! They wrote so cheerfully and hopefully. He also told us that they were expecting an attack here and that Dr. T. had warning to leave home lest their house should stand a chance of being shelled and their lives endangered. He wished to know what we should do as there was probably as much danger in our remaining as there was in Dr. T.'s family. All was turmoil and confusion in the midst of which I sat down to indite a letter to the boys which letter I suppose would be the last we should be able to send them as the mail communications would necessarily cease; it was, I'm afraid a most erratic composition and if the boys do not feel too much for our troubles they'll have a good laugh over it. In the midst of our perplexity the dinnerbell sounded and Mr. Berry came in looking so placid and tranquil that his very presence acted as oil in stilling our troubled spirits—he brought later advices from town of a more specific nature than Father's and assured us there was no need of excitement or alarm. So we concluded by settling ourselves quietly down and Father sent Mr. Berry in person to answer a most touching note he had just received from poor Cousin Sue Buck. I do feel so sorry for them at Rose Hill—they've no one to look to for advice or comfort in these hours of trouble that try the staunchest nerves—even Uncle Tom was away now and they, as well as Aunt Betty, are without anyone to depend on.

A gentleman rapped at the door about eight o'clock tonight and Father ushering him in, introduced to us Dr. Clarkson of S. C. an officer in D. H. Hill's division. He had come at General Hill's bidding to request Father to go down to camp and give some description of the topography of the country—his headquarters were near the old Lehew place and Father was to ride the doctor's horse and the doctor await his return here. Found our guest a clever little fellow with the slightest symptom of the South Carolina boasting propensity—but intelligent and well-bred. He has been in Rd.; knew Nanny Taylor quite well by reputation and personally acquainted with Santy Conrad who I was surprised to hear was a surgeon in the C.S.A. Father returned after ten o'clock delighted with General Hill whom he pronounced a thorough gentleman. His information was of considerable importance according to the general. Dr. C. returned to camp immediately. Yankees said to be near town. Such numbers of soldiers as we have had to supply with meals today! Poor creatures, I do pity them so and I wish I had a great big larder at their disposal.

November 5, 1862
Father came in and in a tone of intense excitement told us that the pickets were coming in and falling into line of battle above Rose Hill, that the officers said there would certainly soon be a fight here and some of them advised him to remove his family as they could not answer for what mischief the enemy shells might do the house, as it would be within

range. So he advised us to put on our bonnets and as soon as he could he would have the wagon at the door to convey us to Clover Hill. Even while he spoke we heard the booming of a cannon but a few miles distant coming from the direction from which the enemy were to advance. Nellie and I did not believe there was as much danger as they all thought for and begged to be left with Father to take care of the house, promising to hide in the basement when the shelling commenced, but they would not hear of such a proposal and bade us make ready as speedily as possible for an onward move. Father then came in while we were dressing the children and told us not to wait for the wagon but put on our bonnets and hurry over to Oakley where he would order it to call for us. We hastily threw a few garments and necessaries for the children into a sheet, did not wait even to tie the corners, but Father taking Aunt C. on his arm led the way. I followed with the dear little baby in my arms, then Orville and Carey, Nellie, Laura and Evered and Grandma and Ma while Martha and Eliza Ann brought up the rear with the baggage. Poor Father how it hurt me to take leave of him when he returned home. He is not often so much moved and when I see tears in his eyes as then I know his spirit is deeply troubled. It did seem so selfish to leave him alone although it was his own wish. We hurried through town with the cannon booming loudly and hearing as we passed all sorts of wild rumors. The cavalry were dashing through the streets and a long line of infantry pickets were being marched to their position on the hill. Aunt Betty, bless her big warm heart, received us with open arms and a cheerful face, not in the least frightened.

    The cannonading ceased soon after our arrival here and now everything seems comparatively quiet. The wagon was detailed until very late and we concluded not to go to Clover Hill at least tonight. Father has just written a note for the boys to go home for tonight; he says there is an attack expected very early in the morning when we can start in time to be out of danger. Nellie and I have determined to remain here with Aunt Betty that we may be near enough to Father to hear from him if anything should happen and see him. Oh dear I'm so tired of this running from home—'tis very well for Ma and Grandma to take the children away for I believe the little things would be frightened almost to death during the bombardment, but Nellie and I are older and have reason to understand that it would be better to stand by our old house as long as we have one. Dear old Bel Air! I looked at it after leaving there and wondered if I should ever again recross its threshold or stand by the old hearthstone. It would almost break my heart to lose the old place of mine nativity, the place hallowed by the recollection that the sweetest, most precious hours that I ever knew or will know were spent within its precinct, that the dearest ties of our lives have been formed there, the best loved friends grew with me there. Dear, dear old home! But hark there is some excitement, they say there is a large fire seen in the direction of our encampment across the river, a signal light I suppose.

An officer has just come in and says 'tis reported our army is retiring across the river.... Since writing the above Willie Buck has come in from Strasburg and confirms the report—he saw the army crossing the river and now I hear the shouting and tramping of a passing brigade which has been stationed just beyond the house here—they are, I suppose, the rear guard of the division and are falling back with it. Ah me what a thrill the sound of those passing footsteps sends through my heart, like the heavy lingering thread of departing hosts, for surely after they leave our day of grace will have ended and we be delivered up to the Phillistines again. Heaven protect us! But we won't despair yet, we may be going to give them battle on the other side of the river in a more advantageous position. I hope so, for a desperate conflict were preferable to desertion by our army just now. I can't help but think "Longheaded" Jackson is prime mover in these affairs and I've confidence that he will make it tell in some ways. Meantime I'll eat an apple with the circle about the fire and woo "tired nature's sweet restorer" that I may be fresh and strong for the enactment of tomorrow's tragedy or comedy as the case may be.

November 6, 1862

'Twas cloudy and bitter cold as I peeped out of my window early this morning, but all was quiet. The wagon came before breakfast but as there was no sign of a battle they concluded to await the issue of events. Nellie and I concluded to go home, the others would wait at Oakley until they could with entire safety return home.

I thought I would have frozen almost in my walk home, found the boys at the woodpile and Father at the barn. The house did wear a most deserted aspect but I was so glad to get back. E. Hope came in to say they had letters from George and that all were well. Had a big fire kindled in Ma's room and everything very cozy by the time Father and the boys came in. They seemed glad to see us indeed. Father told us we had better remove the things from the storeroom into the basement, the Yankees were said to be entering town. Went to work and soon had everything moved and then put some dried fruit on to stew. Martha came in just as it commenced snowing, saying Ma had sent her over to take care of us and to insure our returning to Oakley in the evening. It snowed so hard that Father was weatherbound to the house and we had a cozy time of it—Nellie read one of Charles Lewis' novels—*A Day's Ride or a Life's Romance* aloud to us while I made gloves for the boys. They were down at the mill where they were butchering pork. I could not help but be astonished at ourselves when I thought that there we were sitting placidly before the fire reading a novel while every moment we were expecting the advent of our bitter foes and not knowing but they would burn the very roof over our head. Thus fortunately we learned to accommodate ourselves to circumstances. There were startling rumors all day. Sometimes the Yankees were said to be in town, sometimes near; our troops have fallen back some miles in back of the river. Fancied we saw a cavalry picket in the lane beyond the house. I should like to see one more Confed soldier indeed.

November 10, 1862
A beautifully bright morning. Started on our walk. Arrived at the river and found the boat on the other side and the ferryman non est. Some soldiers soon crossed over in it though and they were so polite as to assist us in, arrange the seats and carry us over—it was well they did too for had it not been for the helping hands of one of the gallant souls I should have been most indubitably precipitated into the river. As it was we had a merry but somewhat hazardous ride, the soldiers not understanding the management of the boat very well, but we arrived on the other shore safely and enjoyed a good laugh at the discomfiture of some of the poor fellows who were in recrossing incontinently jarred into the water, only however receiving a slight wetting. Received a hearty welcome from Cousin B. and Aunt L. and then from Miss Sallie Kendrick who is boarding with them. Nellie soon commenced one of her confidential strains and kept them all convulsed with laughter of her account of Father's maneuvers for her and myself. Mack came in after awhile—his camp is only a few miles distant and he is frequently at home. He brought with him a young friend Lt. Eyster possessor of the prettiest pair of eyes that I ever saw in a man's head. He was from Wheeling and professed to know the Yankee officers Morrow and Stephens.

Found a number of young officers in the parlor when we adjourned thither from the tea table—Lieutenant McAffee and a pretty little Mrs. Ward among them. They begged for music and we played and sung for them until they left.

The railroad was torn up and burnt tonight—'twas right painful to witness this destruction knowing as we did that 'twas but the forerunner of an abandonment to the enemy.

Jackson ordered the railroad destroyed behind him as he headed up the Valley.

November 11, 1862
Colonel Walker genl comm'dg Mack's brigade came to the house and sat awhile—seems to be a pleasant gentleman. Two officers, Majors Wilson and Howard—the latter a genial kind of being and I thought bearing a strong resemblance to Captain L. I was talking to Mack and spoke of the latter in admiring terms, when turning quietly to Major H., who sat quite near, he enquired "if he were not acquainted with the captain." He seemed to enjoy my astonishment upon his replying in the affirmative, and upon my asking where he had known him told me that they were old friends together in Balto. Another time I shall be more cautious how I discuss my acquaintances before strangers. I liked Major H. very

much—he seems so friendly and merry. Major Bryant took tea with us tonight and requested—"There's Life in the Old Land Yet." Was not much prepossessed in Lieutenant M. from a rather saucy message which he left me the night before, but after entering into conversation with him and finding him a very intelligent fellow, I could not help but like him and then in the amusing games which we played he was so quick with his replies and repartees reminding me so much of Scott. He's a peculiar looking person—such a wild, deepset eye and expressive countenance as he has. He's an Alabaman and a true Southerner too.

November 21, 1862

Cold, disagreeable day. We were all sitting reading and sewing in Ma's room when the door opened and a young officer presented himself—Captain Boswell, chief engineer in General Jackson's corps—a handsome little fellow. He had come to borrow the spyglass for the use of the signal corps on the Fort Mt.—and left immediately after getting it—gave us no news from the army.

Poor Uncle Ben died last night and was buried this evening. He has been a great sufferer but I hope it is all over now—a faithful good old servant he has proved. They say Aunt Betty is very much distressed at his death.

November 23, 1862

Two soldiers came in one of them bringing the spyglass with a polite note of thanks from Captain Boswell. Went to hear Dr. Hough today and a most excellent sermon it was. Heard today that all our forces had left Winchester with exception of Hill's division which will be left there as rear guard. Jackson is reported to be up the valley somewhere near New Market.

> *Jackson moved into Winchester November 18, 1862. By November 23, 1862, he was almost to Mount Jackson. On November twenty-fourth he passed New Market, crossed over the Massanutten Mountain and stopped at Hawksville on the road to Madison Courthouse.*

November 25, 1862

The Stewarts have sold out and are going to the country to live. Alice sent a message to Nellie and myself asking us to call and see her before she left. So we concluded to make our visit this morning. Found everything at sixes and sevens there and the room into which little Nettie ushered us seemed to have served the purpose of dining room, chamber, parlor, pantry, laundry and lumberroom.

Alice came down after a time apologizing for her own appearance and also for the disorder of the room—said they were preparing to sell out their household effects—that Fannie had gone over to the farm to prepare for the reception of the family and that she herself—was suffering from the toothache.

News from Fredericksburg reports a threatening aspect of affairs in that region.

> *Union General Burnside, now in command of the Army of the Potomac, arrived at Falmouth, opposite Fredericksburg, Virginia, on November 19, 1862. Longstreet's first corps moved into position at Fredericksburg. Burnside was ready to drive on Richmond.*

November 27, 1862

Father handed me a pacquet today which upon unsealing proved to be a letter—six pages of foolscap from dear Irvie giving me an amusing account of his moving experiences since he left us—I never was more amused in my life and could scarcely read it for laughing. Bless his dear life! I must answer very soon for it has been already written a month.

December 4, 1862

A beautiful morning. When first dressed this morning little black Mary came up to my room to say Carey was below and wished to see me. Went down and he handed me three letters—one from Irvie to me, another to Ma and the third from Nannie T. to myself. I dropped down on the carpet in the breakfast room and read and reread my treasures almost entirely ignoring my breakfast. Sat down and wrote a lengthy p.s. to my letter which I had not finished. Had another letter from Irvie this evening—one which was due some weeks ago. Saucy boy!

December 8, 1862

Had a quiet day today. Ma came home late in the evening and said Uncle T. had just arrived from Richmond after meeting with no success whatever in his efforts to obtain our supply of salt. I don't know what in the world we are to do for salt when 'tis sixty and ninety dollars per bushel. Old Governor Letcher ought to be starved awhile himself and then perhaps he may be less chary of making promises that he will not fulfill—for he did promise Uncle T. most faithfully that this should be one of the first counties supplied and now after decoying him into making several bootless trips to Richmond he comes boldly out and declares that we can "learn to wait as well as other counties." Unmitigated old quizz that he is.

> *Uncle Tom Ashby was a city official.*

Uncle T. brought me a tiny letter from Nannie dear. Says all are very cheerful in Richmond. No movements of the armies on the Rappahannock.

December 12, 1862

Walter and Dick came in. At night we banished the noisy children to the basement where they consoled themselves with blind man's buff, and Ma, Walter, Dick, Nellie and myself had the cheerful fireside in Ma's room all to ourselves till nine o'clock. Dick went over to the office and brought us the papers by tonight's mail and Walter edified us by reading aloud Lincoln's last message. Truly 'tis a most sublimely ridiculous composition—so exquisitely nonsensical—so different from the messages of our own Davis—surely men must see and contrast the two men and—taking the presidents for a type of the people—contrast the ... conclusions.

> Lincoln had waited for a northern victory to issue his Emmancipation Proclamation. This probably appeared ridiculous to Lucy because the proclamation freed all slaves in enemy territory, but not in friendly or Northern states.

Heard that Cousin Tom Buck was captured by a scouting party of the enemy near Winchester yesterday. Hope it is not true.

December 15, 1862

Rumors of a battle at Fredericksburg and a glorious victory indefinite and doubtful.

> On December 11 and 12, General Burnside, sent pontoons and boats across the Rappahannock River at Fredericksburg. On the thirteenth he assaulted Lee's two corps (Jackson and Longstreet.) Charge after charge were sent against Lee's strong defensives only to be slaughtered. Burnside withdrew across the Rappahannock River on the night of the thirteenth.

U.S.A.		C.S.A.	
Effectives	106,007	Effectives	72,497
Killed	1,284	Killed	595
Wounded	9,600	Wounded	6,061
Missing	1,769	Missing	653

December 17, 1862

A quiet day. Walter came in the afternoon and about dusk Mr. Berry came. Then while sitting about the candle discussing our recent victory at F. who should walk in but Cousin Will Cloud. Walter did make me behave too rudely but I could not help laughing when he sat right by my side and kept up a running fire of sotto voce comments upon everything that was said. I know Mr. Berry must have been shocked at my ill-manners.

The Battle of F. must be of much greater importance than we had at first imagined—we had thought only a skirmish on a large scale but if as I hear the Yankees admit a loss of twenty thousand men it must have been a terrible conflict. And oh how many of our own gallant spirits may have shed their life's blood in the struggle. Fredericksburg is said to be burnt too. Poor inhabitants!

December 18, 1862

Heard that the Seventeenth Regiment was not in the late battle—so glad! Poor Generals Cobb and Gregg both fell in the engagement though. Weighed today—111 lbs.

> *General Thomas Cobb, of Georgia, was in McLaw's division of Longstreet's corps.*
> *General Maxcy Gregg, of South Carolina, of Jackson's corps was shot from his horse and died after the battle.*

December 19, 1862

Was up to my elbows in flour this afternoon when I heard a well-known footstep and a cheery voice and Walter was in our midst jesting and caressing in a breath. Put my bread to bake, washed my hands and brushed my hair, settled myself down to enjoy his society—Uncle Tom came in and we had a most pleasant time of it. It was late when they left and Walter promised to call by as he leaves tomorrow. Had papers today giving an account of the three days battle at F. Ah it must have been horrible—and then the shelling of the town and the suffering of its exiled inhabitants. Something must be done for them if possible.

December 21, 1862

Mr. M. left early—attended Mr. Berry's church—he made a touching appeal in behalf of the suffering soldiers and the exiles from poor ill-fated Fredericksburg. Aunt Betty and I are going to raise a subscription for their relief. Was introduced on my way from church to a Dr. Williams from Maryland. We were to dine at Oakley and he walked up there with us. Very soon Captain O'Ferrall, whom I met there last spring, came in and cousin of Mr. Brerwood's from Maryland—Mr. Stewart, and a Mr. McCormick from Washington City came in. All were sprightly, intelligent men but presented quite a contrast to each other. Captain O'Ferrall seemed very much after the order of Charlie O'Malley a gallant soldier dashing and daring but not without a degree of dignity and refinement with it all. McCormick seemed rather reserved and taciturn at first but a refined and well-educated young fellow. Stewart was a devil-may-care sort of personage—with a quick mind ever on the alert and as ready for evil as good—an uncouth nonchalant manner without actual rudeness and a high appreciation of his own merit.

But Dr. Williams was to my mind the finest specimen of manhood of the quartet—a counterpart of Captain Latrobe both in manner and expression—so dignified and gentle, so courteous and refined in his manner. I did like him.

December 22, 1862

We were all in Aunt Betty's room—Nellie and Walter "billing and cooing" and I copying advertisements for Uncle Tom when Dick Bayly and soon after Alfred McKay came hurriedly in and told Walter he had better hasten away with them to Luray as the enemy were said to be near the river. But Walter was not to be thus easily moved and they concluded to go out toward the river and see for themselves while Walter would await their return and leave with them in an hour's time. So he coaxed me to write him an introduction to Kate Chapman and proceeded to copy a song for Nellie when the two boys with Mack Wells and young McKay returned saying the Yankees had crossed at McCoy's Ford just above and if they did not "fall back" very speedily they would be cut off from the army. Walter quietly took his pipe from his mouth—proceeded to twist Nellie's curls about his fingers and finally was induced to don his overcoat. We buckled his pistol and saber about him, brought him his gauntlets, tossed him his cap, filled his pockets with apples and bidding us good-bye too vaulted into his saddle and they were off cheering and waving their caps as they went. Poor fellows! We watched them as far as we could see them and then went to reading a *History of the Mexican War*.

December 23, 1862

Father remarked at the breakfast table this morning that Mr. Richards had arrived with his goods. He had gone a week ago to a store in Loudon kept by the Quakers who had obtained from the Yankees every sort of supply and were selling them out at very reasonable prices. Father had loaned Mr. R. a horse and carriage and sent an order by him. Directly after breakfast Ma and I went over to look at the goods. He had only opened a few of them but those were quite at reasonable prices. I got a pair of lasting kits for two dollars quite a miracle such a chance these items. To our great delight Father managed to get a half bushel of salt for $1.10, thirty-two lbs. loaf sugar for 20 cents per lb. pepper for 20 cents, soda for 37½ cents, indigo 12½ cents, etc., etc. Since May last I have eschewed coffee except ... occasionally a cup of that beverage minus the sugar. Indeed for two months the whole family have been drinking their coffee unsweetened, for sugar has been from a dollar twenty-five to a dollar fifty per lb. and almost impossible to secure at that. Coffee has been proportionable dear and so for pepper, soda, indigo, etc. We were nearly out of them all and knew not where the next were to come from. Ma got from him a supply of sewing materials too, just as she had almost used the last she had. Sewing silk is ninety dollars per lb.—spool cotton fifty cents per spool, needles fifty cents per paper, pins fabulous in cost but she got it all for much less. He sold calicos for fifty and seventy-five cents when it has been selling here for a dollar fifty and two dollars. Oh it's a great thing for the community and they're disposed to avail themselves of the advantage.

December 24, 1862
Laura did not go today—had a letter from Jule stating that they would go down Friday or Saturday next. Was busy all day baking cakes for the children out of sorghum molasses and honey and making pies—they were very nice too when done. Father told us that a Yankee paper had brought to town the intelligence of Burnside's removal, Seward's resignation and a quarrel between Chase and Staunton.

Union General Burnside was replaced by Gen. Joseph Hooker from the west, January 25, 1863.

Glorious! With division in their councils—disorganization of their army and dissatisfaction among the people I think their prospects of subjugating us a very poor one.

Poor Kattie has heard of her husband's death and is almost brokenhearted. Oh I do pity her from my very soul.

It is very late—the children's stockings are all "hung by the chimney with care in hopes that Saint Nicholas would soon be there." And he has been here, in the person of Laura who has filled them with cakes and some candy and toys which Uncle Tom brought from R.

December 25, 1862
Was awakened at two o'clock this morning by "Christmas Gift!" being shouted in my ear by Carey and Orville who had stolen in my room unheard. Then at four o'clock they were at it again. Orville, Carey, Annie, Willie and Evered and such chattering and shouting and running about as there was. They were perfectly delighted with the contents of their stockings.

Ma and I walked over to Oakley at eleven o'clock—met the Misses Marshall in the meadow and they walked nearly there. Found Aunt Betty entirely alone and apparently very glad to see us. The weather was so pleasant that we soon quitted the house for the porch. 'Twas a glorious day. There was pervading everything a soft, peaceful Sabbath-like influence so soothing and delightful—even the sunshine so beautifully bright had a chastened, subdued brilliancy. I did so enjoy sitting there listening to the notes of an enterprising bird perched on a neighboring tree and thinking, thinking so much of the past with its mingled web of events. I employed myself meanwhile with sketching Bel Air on a bit of cardboard making a picture just large enough to send in a letter to the boys.

The boys were exploding bombshells in the field when we came home and we witnessed the bursting of one or two. Sat down and wrote a long letter to the boys when I got home. The news from the Washington

Cabinet has been confirmed.

Mrs. Boone came home last night—does not believe the news of Mr. S.'s death. Kattie went to Woodstock today.

December 27, 1862

Brought a subscription for the Warren Rifles. 'Twas a pleasant evening and Nellie and I went down into the meadow after sundown and perching ourselves in the branches of the old fallen sycamore tree had a delightful swing. A right proper amusement for the dignified Miss Lucy Buck. 'Tis said our army has fallen back to New Market. Kattie Samuels sent down a letter from Mr. S. so he's not dead at all—I'm so glad.

December 31, 1862

Baked some cake and pies for the children in the morning. Father told us at dinner that there were news of Stuart's presence in the Valley and tonight told us that there was a report of a victory achieved by Morgan in East Tennessee. Grant was at Holly Springs, Mississippi retreating down the Mississippi—that General Johnston was about investing Nashville and etc., etc. Oh it is so much good news if only it were true.

> Gen. John Hunt Morgan was raiding into Kentucky as far as Elizabethtown on December 27, 1862.
>
> General Grant was busy trying to open the Mississippi River. He sent Sherman to attack Vicksburg from Chickasaw Bayou and Haines Bluff on December 27-29, 1862. He failed.
>
> Bragg, who had retreated from Perryville, Kentucky, was at Murfreesboro, Tennessee along Stone River near Nashville. On January 2, 1863, Bragg struck the Union army and was successful in driving them back and winning a victory, but the next day he withdrew to Tullahoma, Tennessee.

U.S.A.		C.S.A.	
Effectives	41,400	Effectives	34,732
Killed	1,667	Killed	1,294
Wounded	7,543	Wounded	7,945
Missing	3,686	Missing	2,500

We were sitting by the candle stand in Grandma's room tonight when Father came from the office bringing a paper and two letters—one from Nannie Taylor to me—one from Irvie to Nellie. I was almost beside myself with joy at their arrival particularly when upon reading Irvie's we learned that he had been promoted to the rank of captain and AAG on General Cleburne's staff in General Hardee's corps. He had richly earned his position and I'm glad his efforts have met with approval and reward. Dear boy! I hate the idea of his being exposed to the dangers consequent upon active service and am so sorry he and Alvin will be separated, but he has one kind Protector as Omnipotent to save on the field of battle as in the quiet of home, and as Alvin has gone on to Bragg's army strongly recommended by Generals Beauregard and Jordan for a like position and I sincerely hope he may succeed for he richly deserves it too, I'm sure. "Capt. Irving A. Buck" how ridiculously it does sound.

Am determined to sit up tonight and "watch in" the New Year. Laura will keep me company in my vigils. Will answer Irvie's letter tonight and send by tomorrow's mail.

VI

CHANCELLORSVILLE AND SECOND INVASION OF NORTH

January 1, 1863 - July 13, 1863

January 1, 1863

    Glorious dawn of the year which is destined to form an epic in the future history of our young nation. All hail to thee sixty-three radiant in thy youthful hours, bright with an atmosphere all sunshine and beauty, clear in the light of thy declouded sky; melodious with the minstrelsy of thy rippling waters; glad in the joyous harmony of nature! May the radiance of thy dawning hours be an earnest of the full fruition of the glory of light that shall grace thy crowning days. May thy suns never behold the scenes of bloodshed and darkness that have shamed the earth in the past season of strife and conflict. Ere thy days shall have sunk into the ocean of eternity may the noontide of peace be abroad over our land—may our nation worship under it's own vine and fig tree with none to vex or make them afraid—and peace and tranquility reign where now riot and confusion hold high revel.

    Last night after the children were in bed Grandma, Aunt Laura, Nellie and myself had a petite supree—apples, nuts, cakes, pies, bread and butter, and the rose leaf to the feast was a cup of coffee concocted by Laura and myself. It was my first attempt at distilling the beverage and I had quite a time in accomplishing my task, and when I did it was so strong that it intoxicated me fairly and I was like something wild for the rest of the night. Wrote dear Irvie a long letter and commenced one to Nannie Taylor. Our vigils were not gloomy but still I often cast many a retrospective glance into the far past—the past of trials and suffering. There were woven with my reflections visions of two dear faces that had faded from our midsts, of two lives blotted from existence—one blighted in her youthful being by the poisonous breath of disease and the sickening anguish of bereavement and distrell—one in the young bloom and vigor of manhood in the noontide of his usefulness smitten on the red field of the fight at his post of duty toiling for the maintenance of honor and right—battling in defense of country, home and loved ones—

> "Wasting his life in his country's care,
> Laying it down with a patriot's prayer."

I saw a vision of two fresh-made graves and a vision of their bereaved and desolate homes a living tomb almost. They were two of the brightest links in our chain of dear associations and I felt that they never could be replaced. Yet their memory was a bittersweet, for I knew how infinitely our loss was their gain—how it "has not entered into the heart of man to conceive" of the blissful exchange. —Then the thoughts of the many, many noble and precious lives that had been offered up on the altar of their country in propitiation for a nation's sins—of the torrents of blood that had been poured out a priceless oblation to liberty. I thought of the passionate sorrows, the weary heart struggles, the trials, the hardship, the suffering, the sacrifices that were mingled like gall and wormwood in our cup during the past years. And yet I remembered the sweet drops of comfort and hope that had been wrung into the bitter draught—the comfort of knowing that our trials were perhaps sent as a test of our faith, that as we had come out unscathed from them we might hope for fruition of our trust. That we had learned—

> "How sublime a thing it is
> To suffer and grow strong"

we knew of our powers of endurance—our own strength, our own weaknesses—knew whom to trust, whom to fear. We had the hope in the future that our country would profit by the severe lessons she had conned —that our liberty when achieved would be the more deeply cherished because of difficulties overcome in its establishment. I remembered how much we had to be thankful for in the successes with which God had blessed our efforts so universally. I remember the beginning of last year—how fearfully I tried to scan the blank page of the coming twelve months to learn the lesson therein contained—I remember questioning the future . . . of events—tried to prepare myself for meeting and defeating its difficulties ere they were upon me. How little I knew of its bringings, how little guessed the fiery ordeal stretched before us, how little we guessed of the depths of the troubled sea through which our barques were to steer, how oftentimes we were well-nigh wrecked on the breakers or swallowed in the storm. But thank God that our strength was equal to our day—that we have come forth from the fire with, I hope, our garments the whiter for the burn—that our barques are floating in calmer seas and that the sun will shine through the mist around our path. And now a new page is spread before us in which the ensuing year will write its record—the little page is open and 1863 inscribed thereon in characters of radiant sunshine and gladness—oh may no unsightly blurs of darkness, no tale of crime or shame, no deeds of guilt be registered thereon when time shall stamp his seal of the past upon it!

We retired after two o'clock but owing to my unusual dissipation it was a long, long time before I slept. The children were up quite early and I followed their example—dressed and fixed Irvie's letter for the mail. After breakfast wrote a note to Rose Hill and then finished writing in my diary.

Such a beautiful day I felt ought not to be spent indoors so, gathering the children together, Nellie and I went down to the old sycamore tree and had a merry time swinging. Father invited us to walk with him—so we set off—Carey with his gun and had a tramp through the old fields and spicy pines the distance of two miles. I have often heard of profound silence and audible quiet but I never before realized it. The afternoon was clear and cloudless and delightfully soft—we paused upon an imminence in an old field covered with dry, rusty grass, before us lay the tiny valley through which wound the little brook like a bright erratic fairy, there was the little village nestled so lovingly at the foot of the great, brown mountain, over it brooded the light haze of smoke wreath and the smile of the sunlight. Beyond was a chain of blue mountains like great walls shutting us out from the turmoil of the great busy world. We stopped to enjoy the pleasing tranquility of the scene—not a sound was to be heard—the brook was too distant for its murmur to reach us, not a breeze rustled the coarse dry grass, not the chirp of an insect, not the note of a bird disturbed the deep quiet. The silence so unnatural grew absolutely oppressive till suddenly a deep, booming sound reverberated through the mountains followed by the rush of air. 'Twas a cannon—the spell was broken thus rudely—we descended from the hill and turned our faces homeward. Nellie had a fancy to be weighed and we threw our shawls about our heads and ran up to Mr. Hope's mill where she was informed that there was just ninety-nine pounds of humanity comprised by her frame.

The servants had a surprise party tonight and we witnessed some of their terpsichorean performances from the window—they did enjoy themselves so much and it was amusing to note how faithfully they aped the manners of the "white gentry." Retired quite early feeling completely worn out.

January 5, 1863

A charming morning. Went early over to Aunt Betty's and we started out on our expedition. Went first to Mrs. J. W. Mc.'s found her busily engaged making socks for the "Rifles"—she very readily promised us five dollars and seemed to be pleased at our having called. We next went to Mrs. C.'s and sitting there an hour discussing the current topics made known the object of our visit and received hearty cooperation in a fifteen dollar note. Went then to Mr. C.'s—Mrs. C. was absent but Mr. C. was busily engaged teaching his little daughters. He expressed himself pleased at our efforts to aid the poor destitute citizens of F. and gave us five dollars. Walked out to Dr. T.'s—he and Mrs. T. were not at home but found Cousin Mary C. making one of her pleasant circles and spent a pleasant hour receiving from Miss C. five dollars. Went over to Mrs. R. T.'s but she had already contributed through another. On our return called at Mr. F.'s—had never been there and felt very much like I was venturing into a lion's den but soon felt quite relieved at the peaceful aspect of the interior of the house—was ushered by a tiny colored portress into a cozy room where upon a comfortable sofa before the blazing fireplace reclined the mistress of the house in her neat wrapper and at her feet on the rug slumbered a great white cat. It all seemed the most perfect embodiment of quite comfort. Mrs. F. received us very graciously and to my very great surprise we left with a promise of another $V. Went to Col. J.'s found the small family of four persons sitting at the dinner table spread with the luxuries of the season, but they had not a farthing of all their plenty to bestow upon destitute misery. "Blessed are the merciful for they shall obtain mercy." Went next to Mrs. Jones—and after sitting a space made known our mission which was cordially approved and testified by another $V. I was so much pleased with Mrs. Jones—she is so quiet, so dignified and ladylike and so different from the mass of persons with whom one comes in contact. Proceeded to Dr. Brown's—met the family in full conclave assembled—had a merry chat and soon had the Dr.'s name subscribed for $5.00. Went to Mr. Jackson's—found Roxie there and Mr. Hill. Mr. J. of course willingly aided us with five dollars. Next dropped in at Mr. Weaver's where were a number of gentlemen. Weaver thrust his hands into his pockets, set his teeth firmly together and declared himself unable to contribute "Charity begins at home, etc." Mr. F. thought his wife "had given enough for both." Dr. D. leaning carelessly on his gun with his game in a net at his side drew out a five dollar note and wished he could do more for our object. Poor old Mr. J. Trout was standing near but knowing his losses and the many claims upon his charity we refrained from making any demands on him but he nevertheless slipped two dollars into our hands with regrets for the insignificance of the sum and his good wishes for the success of our enterprise. Good old man! I valued the donation much more for the spirit which prompted it than for the value of the sum itself. Mrs. Mck's was our next point—did not go into the house but Miss M. and Mrs. T. met us at the door and promised us something. To Mrs. Stimpson's next we declared and here found Mr. S. transacting business with his hands full of banknotes but as soon as we mentioned our purpose he declared himself an object of charity and fled the room, but we aroused Mrs. S.'s sympathies and she handed us two dollars. 'Twas nearly sundown and having fasted since breakfast Aunt B. and I concluded to adjourn our proceedings till tomorrow morning. Met Mr. L. on the street and he gave me five dollars. Returned home and found twenty dollars there just sent me from Clover Hill. Sat up quite late writing to Mack Bayly—feel quite tired. News tonight of a great battle at Murfreesboro—the contest not decided but advantages decidedly in our favor.

See December 31, 1862.

No letters—so sorry. The Yankees have been all day expected in town but up to this hour "all's well." Thus has closed my first day at begging contributions.

January 8, 1863
Father told me at the breakfast table that news had been received the night before of the repulse of the Federal army at Murfreesboro.

See December 31, 1862.

But the battle was still raging.

January 9, 1863
Scott came in about twilight to say good-bye for he leaves tomorrow. Scott said he heard this evening that Bragg's army had fallen back to Shelbyville. Just as we had commenced singing and playing and were a little sociable, one of the servants came in to say "a messenger wished to see Mr. Roy." Scott presently came in looking very important and bidding us "guess the news." He then informed us that he had been summoned home for the Yankees were at the river and momentarily expected in town. He did not seem to attach much consequence to the report but concluded to go over and see for himself and bade us a final farewell. I was so provoked and annoyed at this sudden interruption to our enjoyment and felt as savage as possible. When Father came home he brought a confirmation of the news from Murfreesboro but it was not fairly a retreat of our army—we had a large number of prisoners and 'twas not deemed advisable to remain when the enemy was constantly receiving reenforcements, but we had till the time of our falling back repulsed the enemy in all his attempts. There was, he said, a rumor of the presence of the Yankees a few miles distant but he did not seem to apprehend much from their advance.

I feel a little cross tonight but I'm glad at all events that we've gotten the full amount of our Fredericksburg fund $259.00 to send by Scott tomorrow.

The citizens of Fredericksburg, Virginia, had been driven

from their homes by the shellings and fighting in December.

I'm glad to think our citizens out of the little they have left are yet willing to do their part toward relieving those more destitute than themselves. Still no letters from the boys. Miseracordia.

January 10, 1863

Just before dinner two soldiers rode up—one Mr. Pendelton and his friend Mr. Lacy. Mr. P. had succeeded in getting through to his home and was on his return to his regiment. Both left directly after dinner being afraid to remain where they were in hourly danger of capture from any of the enemy who might be daring enough to dash in. The more I see of young P. the more I do like him.

Wrote tonight. Heard that seven of Buck's company were captured two days since—hope 'tis not true.

January 12, 1863

Ma and I concluded to spend the day at Mrs. Cloud's—ran over quite early and had a cool yet pleasant walk for the day though frosty was clear. We had but just taken our seats when there was a rushing sound like a hurricane and the ground shook with heavy tramping. Miss Matty R. sprung to her feet with a startled look and exclamation of surprise and we followed her to the window and looking out saw a cavalryman dash around the corner, another and another. We at the first moment imagined they were our own men but a second glance showed them to be a body of Yankees cavalry, twenty-five in number. They divided into three squads, one dashing each way up the street and the third drew up before Weaver's store and proceeded to take possession. They looked like demons as they galloped through the streets every man with sabre brandished above his head or his pistol pointed at the windows by which they passed—many of them were bareheaded and with their harsh laughter they seemed like nothing human. I cannot think any town was ever so taken by surprise and had it not been serious 'twould have been quite amusing to see into what a consternation the whole town was thrown by their entrance. The groups of citizens scattered like chaff before the wind—the soldiers all escaped excepting Newt Petty who was captured before he left Weaver's store. When they entered the store it was with a perfect rush and presently we saw them pour forth with their hands, arms, hats and handkerchiefs full of cakes and candy. It seems that Weaver had a supply of both these scarcities which his exhorbitant prices prevented being sold and it was so vexatious to see these brutes wasting and enjoying these luxuries that many a poor little child had regarded with longing eye and vainly desired. They packed their knapsacks, fed some to their horses, threw some away and finally one of them called all the schoolboys around him in the street and threw handfuls at them having a regular scramble. From that time until dusk it was a perfect harvest of sweets for the little fellows and they made good their opportunity. The Yankees took everything they could lay their hands on—tobacco, blacking brushes, boxes of little fancy notions and finally the mail bags. Oh it was provoking to see them pulling out letters and papers reading them and then tearing them into fragments and scattering them over the muddy street and at this very time too when we were expecting a letter from dear Irvie with his photograph. I was so excited and vexed I could scarcely restrain myself. They captured both the Culpeper and Luray mail carriers just as they were entering town and must have been led in by some traitor who knew of their expected arrival—indeed we saw one of their guides as he entered with them dressed in Confederate uniform. Villain that he is! We saw them capture some of the citizens and their horses. Uncle Mack and Jacquie were there and their steeds were immediately seized upon and they actually made Uncle Mack take the very spurs off his foot and give it to them. Ma and I kept waiting, thinking they would leave town immediately, but presently Allie Ashby called by and said they had taken their horses to the hotel and seemed to be applying for a night's lodging. As it was dusk we concluded we had best leave at all hazards and seeing Carey on the outside the street called him to accompany us home. We left Mr. Hall at Mrs. Cloud's all anxiety for a fine horse which he had ridden to town and which was in Mrs. B.'s stable. Just as we had crossed the street an officer called by calling out to one of his men "They're coming!" and a servant boy passing just then told us that "a whole regiment of infantry with artillery were coming up the street"—and true enough through the gathering twilight we could descry the dark mass just entering the street and only managed to get out of town at exactly the right moment to avoid them and as we crossed the field we saw the "Star-Spangled Banner" borne aloft through the town. Carey on our way home told us that Mack Erwin and Jule had spent the day at our house and just started home. When we reached home, however, we found them at the door, the pickets having refused them egress they were obliged to remain within their lines. Mack was very much afraid his pet "Skylark" would be taken but fortunately just then one of our disabled soldiers who had fled from town stopped to make some enquiries of Father whereupon he told him to ride Skylark to a certain place in the pine hills where they could both be secure from interruption. Presently Jacquie came in and said he could not get out of town tonight but that his father's horse and his own had been restored to them and that his father had gone home. He was indebted for this good fortune to the kindly offices of one of the privates who not only had his horse returned but walked with him nearly to the house as a protector. Jacquie described this man as very different from his companions for he had not participated with them in their plundering and had done all he could to reinstate Mr. Weaver—expressing great dissatisfaction at their conduct. It is so refreshing to meet with some evidences of humanity among these almost universally inhuman people.

Found at home tonight a letter from Alvin of December 8 so of course, it contained no news. Oh!—dear I wonder what tomorrow will bring forth.

January 13, 1863

A cool bright morning. We were up quite early. Jacquie went over to town and returned bringing with him young Blodget (his Yankee acquaintance of the night before) to breakfast. He was late though and we did not meet him at table nor until we were standing all of us in the front yard watching the boys skating. He had a wound on his forehead which he said was inflicted by his lieutenant, in a moment of rage because of his protecting some Secession property. He did not remain very long but before leaving expressed very great dissatisfaction at the conduct of his men. Neville went over to town to see if there was any probability of the Yankees leaving and presently returned saying there was none and that he had just heard an order issued by an officer commanding a vigorous search of all the houses, and advising us to conceal what we could as they were also ordered to seize upon everything contraband—letters, papers, etc. We immediately went to work and sugar, coffee and sweetmeats, letters, papers, money, etc. were secured. The turkeys were put in the dark cellar next to Harriet's room and the bacon in a packing box under the boy's bed. The horses had already been spirited away by Father's directions.

> *The horses were sent to the mountains until the Yankees would leave. In later years "Carey" told that often the animals would have eaten all the bark off the trees as high as they could reach by the time he was allowed to retrieve them.*

The morning passed in expectation then but it was not until four o'clock that Father came in and told us that a file of the Yankees was approaching from Mr. Hope's. We went to the window and looked at them as they stood there on the pavement with their guns on their shoulders. I had my hand on the doorknob to unclose it when it suddenly opened from the outside and I was astounded to find my face a few inches from the great, rough phiz of one of the soldiers who was swearing of a great big oath in reply to a remark from Father declaring that he "never went anywhere without his gun." Father assured them that there was only a house full of little children and some ladies and that they would surely not harm them. Presently they came in—a portion of them remaining as guards about the doors. They looked into presses, cupboards, trunks, pantires, closets, cubbies, drawers, wardrobes, lofts, boxes and baskets and at Nellie's earnest solicitation they even peeped into our bandboxes and Ma's dress pockets. They even crawled under the bed and found the bacon which they however did not disturb. They went down into the basement and searched the servant's things and found a blanket which had belonged to Ambrose and which, after his death, Dr. Bogardus gave Martha as a reward for her attentions to him. This they took and also tried to hook a watch belonging to Horace which attempt he detected and frustrated in time. In passing to Harriet's room they found the turkeys and grew quite facetious over their discovery but did not seem to take a fancy to them. Once I had occasion to pass out the front door and around the "west end" where Ma was alone and I wanted to be with her. Upon opening the passage door I found it full of soldiers standing idly by their guns whistling, singing, and spitting amber all over the floor; they had formed a file on the porch on either side the door with their guns crossed. I doubted whether they would permit me egress—so called Mack Erwin to escort me through them. He stepped before me and bade the men move aside and let me pass—this they obeyed so far as to shuffle themselves into a better position for looking and stared and shuffled as rudely as possible while I had literally to walk over their feet and I know in my progress they must have been made acquainted with the huge pocket of valuables which I wore on either side of my skirt. Oh!—but I was angry. They went to the smokehouse, the granary, the carriage house, the barn and the mill and finally departed with two old worm-eaten haversacks, which the little boys had found on the deserted campfield, an old shotgun of Mr. Hope's which was here, and a musket which the boys had also picked up on the field—together with a shot pouch of Father's which was presented him by a friend a long time ago and which Irvie would want to use in his hunting excursions. I felt as if I could shoot the man who carried it off myself. I don't think they will repay for the trouble of their search here unless the knowledge they gained of the extent of our possessions and wearing apparel availed them something. A pitiful business, thus brutally investigating ladies wardrobes and dressing bureaus—I've no doubt they would have made their visit a more profitable one had they not been so strictly watched. As it was they were accompanied by a crowd of children as well as by others wherever they went. I hope they did not go to Rose Hill and alarm them there. They promised Father not to do so but their pledges are good for naught.

After they left this evening we had quite a time relating individual observations of all that had occurred. We fared much better though than some of our neighbors who were robbed of meat, etc., etc. They quartered in all the unoccupied houses in town and that accounts for our not seeing their campfires—we did see where the artillery is encamped though. We went into the parlor this evening and had a cotillion and after tea Jule, Nellie, Mack, myself, Neville, Laura, Orville and Carey went into the basement and had a regular old-fashioned game of "Blind man's buff" and "Tap the rabbit"—then some of them proposed a game of cards which I declined participating in. We enjoyed ourselves so much I feel quite worn down with the unusual excitement and exertion. I'm uneasy about "Skylark"—Father sent Alex to find him this morning but he was not at the place designated. I hope, however, that the boy only carried him to another of greater security. 'Twould be a great pity to lose so fine an animal and such a pet too as he is of Mack's.

January 14, 1863

The first thing I heard upon awakening this morning was Father calling out—"The Yankees are gone!"—and looking out saw the last of the cowardly crew disappearing over the hill. Oh such a sense of relief as we experienced at their departure!

Such a time as we had discussing the events of the last few days—it seems that they were more rigorous in their search of Captain Roy's than here. She told us that they had taken old Isaac Overall and his beautiful little Canadian pony "Roderick Dhu." They also took Mr. Hall's fine $6 horse. They left town with some nine or ten horses and some four or five prisoners. I certainly should not think that all they got would begin to repay them for the trouble of their coming. Mack heard of Skylark and went in search of her. Nannie and Bob Buck and Neville dined with us. He and Jule determined to go home and begged me to accompany them—concluded to accept their invitation. Had quite a cold drive and reached Clover Hill about sunset.

The Yankees went to the Academy and broke the school children's desks and tore up their books—and yet they're the pioneers of civilization and enlightenment and religion. A meek act for such reformers.

January 15, 1863

Bright pleasant morning. Commenced reading *Charms and Counter-Charms*. Was deeply interested in the book when the sitting room door opened and "Lieutenant Baylor" ushered in—the same individual who led that daring charge into Front Royal last summer. He referred to it very pleasantly and then said his battalion was on its way now upon a similar expedition into Clarke and would presently pass down the road. Mr. Lovel and Charlie Buck came in—they had been hiding in the "Forks" and hearing of the exodus of the Yankees were on their way home. Very soon they said the battalion was coming and while we were standing on the porch watching it the gentlemen bade us adieu and departed.

January 17, 1863

Bitter cold but bright. Slipped downstairs this morning before breakfast and placed a liberal supply of salt in the glass of milk intended for Mack. The plan succeeded admirably—consideration for the feeling of the host and hostess prevented any allusion to the peculiarity of the naseous draught for a long time, but when the fact became bruited he attempted retaliation by making me take the remainder of the glass full. Cousin Sam acted my champion, defeating his purpose and finally restoring peace. It created quite a laugh among us.

We spent the day coqueting with some light sewing and pleasant books and in pleasant conversation and jesting.

In the afternoon we, by general persuasion, induced Emma to accompany us to Clover Hill. The stars were shining cold and bright when we reached there, and who should come out to assist us off our horses but Walter. Dear fellow, I was so glad to see him—he had been to Front Royal on business and was now returning to his regiment. There was a brother of Lieutenant Baylor there too—wounded in his arm but very animated and loquacious despite his misfortune. When we adjourned to the parlor after ten Walter told me he had been to Bel Air and left all well.

January 18, 1863

Intensely cold and bright. Walter and Mr. B. left early and then I proposed going home and Mack was to drive me in his rockaway. Neville went with us and we had a pleasant ride discussing persons and places. We were told by groups of cavalrymen whom we met coming from town that the Yankees were crossing the river and when we were within two miles of town a dragoon dashed by telling us they had already entered the place. We concluded we would be in danger of participating in a skirmish by proceeding further and concluded to retreat in good order to Clover Hill while we could. They were surprised to see us return and thrown into consternation by the news. Emma instantly fled home and Aunt L. made preparations for enduring a search. But the evening waned and they did not come.

January 19, 1863

Clear as a crystal. The boys informed us at breakfast that the ice on the river was fit for skating on and insisted on our accompanying them across to witness their performance. I felt so low-spirited that I was disinclined to any movement but knowing Jule wished to go I consented to the arrangement and went. The bracing air invigorated body and spirit, and I felt a great deal better when once skimming about over the glassy ice looking through the clear water beneath to where great shoals of fish were gliding and darting about as though skating too. Climbed up on the high cliffs towering over the river and sat there under the pines and looking down on the river murmuring and flashing along between its ice-bound shores I wished oh!—so earnestly, that my life were such a sunlit softly flowing stream. There was all the time hanging over me some presentiment that it would never be thus that even then some gloomy "event was casting its shadow before." We went home about twelve o'clock and I sat down to write the boys a letter which Jule would forward by some passing scout.

Court had to convene out in the courtyard today and they had to station pickets upon the surrounding hills. Very primitive proceedings!

January 23, 1863

Cleared off cool. Father came in this evening bringing a letter from dear Irvie dated from.... Poor fellow, he was in the late dreadful battle—how glad I am that we were unconscious of it till it was all over. He writes very despondingly and seems almost to wish himself back at Charleston with Alvin whom he says has returned thither. He says our friends all escaped unhurt and almost as if by a miracle. The battle must have been much more deadly than we had thought for. Must write to him soon. Ma wrote to Alvin tonight.

January 26, 1863
I heard Carey shouting from the porch—"Two letters! Two letters." I presently found myself on the porch contending with him for two pacquets which he held tantalizingly above his head. I succeeded in capturing them and saw my own name written by two hands dearest in the world. I immediately commenced a succession of ecstatic gyrations which were suddenly put to a dead stop by an assault made upon my treasures by Ma, Laura and Nellie combined. We compromised by settling ourselves down on the front step—Father, Ma, Grandma, Laura, Nellie, myself, Carey, Orville, Nannie, Willie, Evered and Frank—Ma read while we listened with absorbing attention. The first was Irvie's dated from Tullahoma and giving us some account of himself since his last letter—this was dated the thirteenth. Seemed better reconciled—said he was working very hard but is pleased with his brother officers which is a great thing. Dear fellow, he writes so cheerfully and affectionately, I'm so glad to see it. 'Tis a pity there's so much dissatisfaction against Bragg—I hope it may be removed however. Irvie sent me the promised photograph so like his own dear self and yet so unlike with that grey, earnest face and that officer's uniform. We have been looking at it through a magnifying glass and every eye I believe looks on it through a glaze of tears. Alvin, dear brother as he is, wrote me such a long, long letter—five pages of foolscap—such a good one, such a one as only a great, warm heart and comprehensive judgment could have dictate. 'Twas written from Charleston where he had just arrived from Tennessee. After witnessing that battle which from his description must have been most appalling and deadly. To think too how near he was participating in its horrors and we did not know it! He writes in such good spirits and is very sanguine of receiving an appointment. I think I was somewhat intoxicated with the delight these letters afforded me. I might have stood one but both together were more than my weak head could bear and I scarcely knew whether to laugh or cry and so compromised by doing a little of both. Wrote an addenda to Irvie's letters thanking him for his letter and photograph—will write to Alvin too, in a few days.

February 3, 1863
Father butchered his hogs today and just as each swineship had been executed news came to town that the Yankees were crossing into town.

Knowing that they appropriate or destroy the pork if they chanced upon it he had the bodies removed to the house and upon going down into the dining room I was forcibly reminded of the Old Revolutionary times when I saw the porkers stretched at full length upon the floor.

Mr. Berry brings cheerful news of the confidence and good spirits of the troops around Richmond. In the Yankee army General Burnside is deposed and superseded by "Fighting Joe Hooker."

"Fighting Joe" took over from Burnside on January 25, 1863.

February 4, 1863

When Father came from town this morning he brought news that the blockading squadron at Charleston had been sunk or driven away by some of our "ironclads." Oh!—I do hope 'tis true—what a great advantage it would be to us if we can only keep the port open for sixty days as they say we will be able to do according to maritime law.

On January 31, 1863, off Charleston, South Carolina, the C.S.N. gunboats Palmetto State *and* Chicora *raided the Union fleet. Union losses were thirty killed and wounded.*

Oh for a letter from Alvin now!

February 5, 1863

Henry told us that Harry McDonald had just come out of Winchester on business for his mother and brought dreadful tidings of the state of affairs there. Milroy had issued a proclamation to the effect that no citizens should be allowed a pound of flour unless upon condition of his taking the oath of allegiance. Mrs. McDonald's family had been living on bread and water for weeks. It was truly pitiful to hear the account he gave.

February 6, 1863

In the afternoon Father came in bringing a letter from Irvie to himself giving a more minute and interesting account of the battle. He writes in good spirits but nevertheless thoughtfully. He enclosed two letters from George Wms. to himself—both very "spicy" and one containing quite a compliment to Irvie.

Gus Tyler came in tonight with Henry and gave a most interesting account of the battle of F. and related a variety of anecdotes. Among other things told us of a mock battle which our soldiers fought with snowballs during the late snows. It was conducted according to strict military rules—the officers playing a prominent part in it. One of the colonels was standing on a stump trying to rally his men when Scott Roy struck him in his mouth with a snowball. It must have been rare sport—and as usual the Seventeenth distinguished itself. He also spoke of an instance of their cruelty. An old Negro in the Yankee camp had the smallpox and the miserable miscreants put the poor creature into the river to swim across to our camp that the disease might be introduced there. But he was drowned in attempting the passage. The very men who were guilty of this inhumanity were themselves drowned the next day in crossing in a boat to exchange papers. Righteous judgment.

Wrote a long letter to dear Alvin tonight.

February 12, 1863

Read the president's message today for the first time. Surely it is a masterpiece of composition worthy the source from which it emanated. If "Neutral Europe" does not feel ashamed after the perusal of this document I do not know what is to prevent them.

February 13, 1863

The Cincinnati Times edited by Mr. Crippin—Frank's father had expressed such decidedly Secession views that they would not permit the mails to bring it into Missouri. Glad of that.

Nellie received a quiz or valentine this evening. 'Twas a letter purporting to emanate from Giles Cook requesting the privilege of corresponding with her, but it was too evidently Scott's handwriting and style for it to be mistaken. Saucy boy!

February 14, 1863

Was busy all the morning manufacturing valentines (at Horace's request) and sewing on my wrapper. Commenced reading the life of Patrick Henry aloud to Father. Laura summoned me to Grandma's room where I found Ma and Nellie curiously investigating the superscription upon the outside of a huge fancy envelope bearing my name. Opened and found it to contain a very pretty valentine embellished with some sweet little verses. The handwriting and style of composition would indicate Scott as the donor, though 'twas postmarked in F. R.

February 23, 1863

Cloudy and snow falling. Cleared off in the afternoon. Father found among the papers sent by Uncle John an *Examiner* giving an account of the Battle of Murfreesboro in which mention was made of the different generals engaged and their staff. Among the officers upon General Cleburne's was mentioned "Captain I. A. Buck" as having behaved with others with great bravery and done good service. It was such a surprise and pleasure to see it. Ma and I went up to the dormer window in the attic and sat a long time looking out on the beautiful snow scene. Were immeasurably happy, all. Felt entirely well—did not feel a single pain. And that of itself was delicious novelty.

February 25, 1863

This was one of King Winter's gala mornings—such as he sometimes vouches us as though to reconcile us to his harsh and generally unlovely aspect. He had exhausted the contents of his jewel casket to give brilliancy to the scene—his mantle of ermine was sewn with rubies, amethysts, and diamonds, every tree was encrusted with rich seed pearls and every branch, every twig seemed a constellation of tiny star gems that glittered and flashed in a blaze of regal splendor in the bright clear rays of the morning sun. In the distance the trees looked white as with myriads of blossoms lending an appearance of enchantment to the fairylike scene.

Was busy all the morning writing and sewing.

We all went to the mill to be weighed. I counted the same as upon a former occasion—111 lbs. Mr. Hope conducted us through the mill and took a great deal of pains to explain the whole mechanism. I was very much surprised to find it so very complicated and to see how much velocity might be involved in a simple grist mill.

March 9, 1863

About four o'clock Scott came in. He is so kind and thoughtful—went in the parlor to hear the "Officer's Funeral" which he says he learned for me—'tis a sweet, sad thing and reminds me so much of Willie R. Scott says he has ten days to remain at home—so glad! He saw the Taylors when in Richmond—seems to like them much. Told us some very pleasant anecdotes and then left.

March 17, 1863

Laura came over bringing a little microscopic collection of our generals' and statesmen's photographs—Davis, Lee, Beauregard, Jackson, Hill, Morgan, Price, Bragg, and Semmes—all composed in the space of a large sized pinhead. The collection belongs to a refugee Marylander, Mr. Winchester, who is staying in town.

Ma came home in the evening—had called by Mrs. Roy's—saw an account in the papers of the marriage of General Hardee to Miss Alice Ready of Murfreesboro. Wonder if it can be so. Wish we could get a letter from the boys to hear the particulars.

March 19, 1863

Received tonight a *Southern Illustrated News* from dear Irvie—not a very interesting number though. Was sitting up till late tonight reading the *Lamplighter*. Heard that Scott was going tomorrow. Do wonder if he will go off without coming to tell us good-bye.

March 20, 1863

Father came home and told us that Scott did not go today. He also said it was rumored in town that all of Jones brigade would be through town tomorrow—destination unknown.

> *Brig. Gen. W. E. Jones was assigned Commander of the Valley District on December 29, 1862. He replaced Brig. Gen. Beverly Robertson as commander of Ashby's old brigade.*

There had been firing heard in the direction of Middletown yesterday. Many thought there was skirmishing going on there. Walter stayed last night at Rose Hill so there's some movement on foot beyond a doubt—wish I had some idea as to its object. 'Tis said there was a fight near Culpeper a day or two ago.

Stuart with one brigade driving back five of the enemy. Don't know how true it is though.

Scott came over tonight and has just left after eleven o'clock—he's such a social, good fellow. We had music and singing and a discussion of "old times," very pleasant it was. At parting he promised me the photograph which I asked him for last spring. He thinks he'll never come back, poor fellow.

March 22, 1863

Scott was not at church but I sent him his book and a card through Cousin E. Cloud. Mr. Maury the Episcopal Chaplain, Captain Marshall, and Mr. Berry dined with us. All the gentlemen went to church about three o'clock Mr. Maury preaching. All the young cavalrymen came in directly they were gone. All had succeeded in getting through to their homes excepting Mr. Pendleton—poor fellow! He looked so disappointed I really pitied him. They only remained long enough to collect some baggage they left here yesterday and then, thanking us for the care of their things rode away. Was lying down on the bed by Ma when some one ran in to say Scott was coming—was surprised to hear it as Cousin E. told me he would leave this evening. He immediately proposed going up on the housetop—'twas a lovely evening and everything looked so beautifully springlike. He gave me a little verse, a waif he had culled somewhere—a sweet, plaintive little poem—and then sitting down talked a long time so much more kindly and unreservedly than he had ever done before. Bless his great warm heart! He's a dear good boy. I'm so sorry he's going away so soon now that I know him so much better than ever before. He left about sundown and does not expect to be back for a long, long time, poor fellow.

The different regiments have been passing by all day today—the Seventh is in camp only about a mile and a half from town and all the others scattered around. I'm so glad to see our soldiers about now instead of the Yankees whom we had feared would have been here ere now.

March 27, 1863

The day appointed by our president for humiliation and prayer. We observed it strictly so far as fasting and attending divine service was concerned. Just before the church bell was rung Henry B. and Charlie

R. called. They both behave very singularly—don't know what to think of them. Henry told us that Cousin R. Helms' wife had just arrived at Rose Hill—had been forced to flee from home by the threats made by a Negro servant formerly belonging to her. Her husband is with his regiment near town and I suppose will be gratified at her arrival. He also said Cousin Tom Buck had been heard from directly. Was in Camp Michigan, in Illinois, quite sick—and his sister Lucy was making preparations to visit him there—poor fellow! No one knows how rudely he is cared for.

March 30, 1863

Uncle John came in upon us very unexpectedly and under great excitement—had just received orders to return to Staunton for some supplies for the soldiers. Nellie and I must accompany him in a walk to the mill where we were much amused at his analysis of some new specimens of mechanism. We were going to Mr. Hope's and walked along by the side of his horse while he talked to us while Nellie and I "quizzed him" nicely with regard to some matters in which he seemed to take the deepest interest.

Heard Ellen sing "Lorena" for the first time. 'Tis reported that the Warren Rifles or rather the Seventeenth are ordered to N. Carolina—am afraid 'tis true. Practiced till tea time.

April 1, 1863

Father told me he had a letter from Irvie with one enclosed to me but would not let me have it till after all had finished eating. Of course, I have not much appetite for the repast and of course I hastened upstairs to read them. To me he writes very softly, very amusingly—to Father thoughtfully and seriously. His letters were dated the.... So Father did write him about Captain Latrobe really. It's right funny! Opened and added a postscript to my long letter which I must mail tomorrow. Ma writes to Alvin too. While sitting about the stand writing, who should walk in but Walter. So glad to see him. We sat up till eleven o'clock talking. He is so cheerful and confident that I almost wonder at my allowing myself to grow depressed this afternoon. Truly Captain Mosby is making to himself a name and bids fair to rival Ashby.

On March 9, 1863, Union Brig. Gen. Edwin H. Stoughton was captured while in bed at Fairfax Courthouse by Captain, later Colonel, Mosby and his men.

John S. Mosby began his independent career in January, 1863, with nine men. His command grew and was named the 43rd Battalion. Before the end of the war it consisted of eight companies. Mosby's immediate superior was J. E. B. Stuart. His men lived at homes of friends and relatives within the enemy lines in Fauquier, Loudoun and surrounding counties of Virginia. They would assemble for missions at designated locations.

Poor fellow. 'Tis said all of Aunt Cattie's servants have left her—poor thing I wonder what she will do, for she is more dependent for their services than almost anyone I know of.

April 3, 1863
Such a lovely morning such as we've not had in a long time. Nellie and I were seized with a violent desire to take a ramble to the river and made angling the ostensible object of our expedition. Nellie went up and got E. Hope to accompany us, with Orville for guide we stepped forth—(Carey was sick and could not venture.) We struck a new path through the fields and climbed the high hill directly opposite town from which we had a charming view of the little valley that intervened between us and the mountains stretching away in smooth meadows that were just changing their russet winter garb for the soft velvety green of early spring. The little creek dancing amusingly along seemed brimming with sunshine, and the woods wore a soft, hazy appearance, the state between leafless branches and full foliage. The mountains had drawn about them a transparent azure veil—all save one a far distant peak that reared itself in sharp outline against the clear sky glittering and white with ice and snow, lending an agreeable diversity to the scene. We crossed one field which had been last summer the site of a Yankee encampment and where we still saw half-hidden under the brown, crisp grass traces of their presence in the fragments of boxes, old canteens, tin cups, broken bottles, bits of rope, odd shoes, dismanteled huts and all the etcetera of one of their lairs. Once we paused upon a breezy hill just above the river and sat down to rest. I felt as if I could have spent the day there in the tall dry grass with the warm balmy sunshine falling goldenly like a shower of loving smiles around me: with the river flowing near murmuring its soothing lulling lullaby; with the sunny hillslopes forest-bound looking rich and green with their beautiful mingling of evergreens. Ever and anon the soft, plaintive cooing of a solitary dove came to our ears. Sounding so sadly weird—for from my earliest childhood has been associated in my mind something unearthly, something unreal in their sweet notes—a something that awed by its very sweetness. I was sorry when my eager companions proposed the descent to the river bank that they might begin their arts of blandishment on the finny tribe. We succeeded in getting our tackle in order and flung into the stream when the bait dropped off one hook, another line became hopelessly entangled in a snapp under the water and one of the party caught herself on her own hook, so we finally gave up the sport more especially as we found we had come upon a nest of loafers who were shipping the stream with their fishing lines and were enough of themselves to disgust any of the enterprising fishes that might be inclined to nibble the bait. After a long consultation we

concluded to return home by way of the railroad thinking we might possibly find some early spring flowers. When we reached the old "tank" we commenced climbing the steep wooded height, and such a time as we had! Pushing through tangled undergrowth, drawing ourselves up the steep mossy rocks by the overhanging boughs, pausing now on some grassy slopes to draw our breaths, now diving into a mossy crevice for the wee, waxen white and azure blossoms that grew in the sylvan spot; and ever and anon stepping on the moist stones over some little rivulet that trickled down the hillside. Even in this secluded spot were traces of the Yankee pollution, for in stooping to pick up a white pebble or a bit of moss or tufts of flowers one would find a bayonet or bullet, or the remnants of some of their castoff instruments.

It became oppressively warm and we were hungry, tired and footsore upon reaching home about two o'clock P.M. Bathed our faces, rearranged our disordered dresses, ate our dinners and then I lay down and was on the bed nearly the whole afternoon so weary and stupid. Was preparing to disrobe tonight when they came in to announce that Messrs. Yates, Alexander and Crane were in the sitting room. Johnnie Yates was one of the principal actors in that raid into Front Royal last summer and I was anxious to see the redoubtable young soldier. Great was my surprise therefore upon being introduced to a delicate youth scarce as tall as myself, with a round child-face and a hand that looked much better suited for playing on the guitar than wielding a saber. And yet this boy soldier had been engaged in some of the most daring feats imaginable—had been captured and imprisoned in Fort McHenry for five weeks—the idea of confining such a child in a military prison—it seemed too cruel—he is the same who captured our provost in town last summer. The other gentlemen, Mr. Alexander, a tall handsome youth with a pair of fine dark eyes and nice little moustache and Mr. Crane, apparently a perfect "rough and ready" in his way were completely thrown into the shade by the little hero. They had come with the intention of remaining overnight, but Mr. Crane, the latest arrival, told them their party (who in Rutherford Clark would leave tonight so as to have advantage of the beautiful moonlight for travel)—and they all soon took their departure by foot. Oh so sleepy!

April 4, 1863

I was sitting in Grandma's room reading when a tap at the door was followed by the entrance of Walter. He was very much hurried and would remain long enough to go down to the second table and dine with me. He was very serious and taciturn and at leaving he gave Nellie his saber and pet merschaum to take care of till his return. We knew he was bound on some dangerous enterprise, but knowing equally well that he did not wish to reveal his object we made no enquiries concerning his movements. I hope poor fellow his intrepidity will not lead him into needless peril.

April 5, 1863

Dick Bayly called in the afternoon and confirmed the reports we have been hearing from the servants during the day of firing of musketry over the river. A body of Yankees had come down the river and had been shooting across from Guard Hill with their long-range guns at our pickets at this side. Cousin Horace Buck, who was staying at Mr. Richard's started to come over in the boat when one of the scoundrels fired a bullet so close to him that it almost grazed him.

April 10, 1863

Cousin Mount hurriedly entered. We were asking him something about Walter when a loud shout startled us and one of the children rushed in to say "Cousin Walter's coming at last!" In he came laughing and jesting, just took time to tell us that he's been to Clarke, had seen Uncle Larue who told him that only four of his servant men had left him. He said he had been all day dodging the Yankees, running out of the back door when they came in the front one. He had been to see Josey Grantham and as the Yankee picquet post was just at the house he had great time hiding from them once even getting in the bed—and the scamps had pursued him as far as the island ford and then fired at him after he crossed the river. He seemed in a great hurry for he soon called Cousin Mount out. They held a whispered consultation and then mounted their horses and rode off in great glee; W. telling us he would be back sometime tonight to take his supper. But 'tis eleven o'clock now and thus far he did not eat. I've no doubt they went to camp to try and get reenforcements to go and capture the pursuing party at the ford.

We were surely disappointed when Father came in tonight and told us the mail had brought neither letters nor papers. It's very plain that Scott has forgotten to keep his promise. Uncle N. left me some nauseous powders to take tonight. Ugh!

April 11, 1863

Walter came in a little before nine o'clock to say good-bye—it seems they have changed their program after leaving here last evening and didn't after all go after the Yankees. He gave us a more minute account of his trip into the Yankee lines and then with many injunctions to us "keep brave hearts" he vaulted into his saddle and galloped away—he with all the rest of the troops will return himself to Luray tonight. Squads of cavalry were continually passing this morning and we cast after them many a wistful glance for each company that passed seemed like a funeral cortege carrying away the dead body of another and another bright hope. We are wholly deserted.

Tonight while we were sitting at the supper table it seemed so pleasant to have no one but our own immediate family together—such a thing had not occurred before in a year. Father remarked as he arose from the table that he thought some one of the family would be apt to receive a letter tonight saying which he proceeded to draw from his pocket two missives, one, at least, of which I felt sure was for me—either a letter from Irvie or the package from Scott—but no, both were addressed to Nellie one in Dick's handwriting—the other in that of Giles—both were in good spirits and dated their letters from near the Blackwater. I was so disappointed, but my chagrin was some removed by the news contained in the papers—we have gained a glorious victory at Charleston and completely repulsed the enemy. Thank God! And next to Him, blessings be to our blessed Beauregard for I'm convinced 'tis greatly to his energy and ability under Heaven that we owe this glorious success. Oh for a letter from Alvin now!

April 13, 1863

Heard early this morning that poor Mrs. Turner died last night about the time Father passed there—poor little Robbie! Poor Miss Tensia! I felt so much for them and Dr. T. too. About eleven o'clock was surprised at a call from Fannie Stewart and Miss Emma Johnson. They had ridden up from home escorted only by a little servant boy—were on a shopping expedition—quite a quixotic errand these days. Went to town after doffing their riding habits, promising to return to dinner. They did come in late, and from that time forth Miss Emma just kept up one continuous fire of anecdote and jest until they had mounted their horses and departed a little after three o'clock. What an inexhaustible stock of animal spirit she possesses to be sure. Dick Bayly here this morning.

Ma, Father, Nellie and I walked up to Dr. Turner's about four o'clock to attend the funeral service there. Poor Tensia, how sorry I felt for her—she seems perfectly crushed—an orphan, just lost a brother by a cruel death and now an only sister—almost like a twin—both within so short a time of each other. And Dr. Turner too—how lonely his life will be now! I hear little Robbie upstairs laughing and singing merrily, all unconscious poor little thing of the great loss she had sustained. They laid Mrs. Turner to rest in one corner of the garden, and I thought as they bore her body through the walks and arbors how much pleasure and interest she had taken in superintending the cultivation and decoration of it and now that she was no more, everything would go on as usual, the flowers spring and bloom as brightly as if the hands that had planted and nurtured them were not mouldering into native dust again, the sunshine visited every nook and corner of the place just as freely and goldenly as if the shadow of death had not been there. And the hearts too that now were so full of breaking would ere many months throb as quietly as if they had never leaped up in gladness to the sound of the voice that was hushed, the light of the smile that was fled forever. Oh!—'tis a humiliating thought that when our visible persons fade from the earth the traces, the influences we leave behind us are so soon erased, so soon forgotten. I did not see the corpse at all. It is I think so painful to carry in one's mind the memory of the pale distorted features seen after death instead of the life face we were wont to look upon. Mr. Berry read a chapter of the Testament and made some comment, drawing very comforting assurances from the sacred text. Aunt Lizzie and Julia were there and Katie Samuels too, and Mack Erwin and Harry.

Mack Erwin drove Ma home in the carriage and Nellie and I walked through town with Aunt Betty—found the mail had just arrived and Nellie and I concluded to wait on the depot corner till Allie got the contents out for us. While standing there Henry and Willie and Bob came over and entertained us with accounts of Cousin Tom Buck's return. Henry had seen him and heard him tell of the long trip he had taken—how he had been confined in a half dozen different camps and forts etc., etc. He says Confederate money is selling in Chicago for fifty cents in a dollar. Good! Old Major Lewis was so dilatory in opening the mail that we were warned by the gathering shades of evening to return home. Tea was over when we arrived. Dick held up a letter and bade me guess who 'twas for. Nellie and I made a simultaneous rush for it and gaining possession of it found was addressed to "Miss Sallie Kendrick"—we commenced revenging ourselves for the disappointment when he drew forth two others which were really for us, one from Benton to me and one from Irvie to Ma—the latter I heard read while preparing tea for Emma and Dick, the former I just found time to read at eleven o'clock after all were asleep. Irvie writes no news but gives quite an amusing description of the manners and customs of the natives of the Tennessee barrens. Benton mentioned the probability of our army again entering Kentucky. Oh dear!

April 14, 1863

Nellie, Dick and myself called at Oakley and then at their earnest solicitations I consented to call in at Captain Roy's to see something Cousin E. had promised Nellie. Found Mrs. Dr. Hough there and we all had a merry time over looking Cousin E's daguerreotypes—and I saw Scott's miniature—the very best I ever saw and so handsome. Oh!—I was more than ever provoked at his noncompliance with his promise. It's too bad of him! Cousin E. does act very strangely—I wonder where was the use of her making that display of her letter in Mrs. H.'s presence.

Feel very tired tonight and cross too—think I'm a much injured individual and the injury inflicted by hands from which I had little expected it.

April 18, 1863

Toujours le meme.

A bright beautiful morning. Cut out a pair of gloves to make for myself. Father proposed that I should "press" Jacquie's idle horse into service and take a ride. Willie rode with me as escort and a delightful canter we had of it all over the high hills east of town from which we had such a charming view of the mountains—arms stretched embracingly around our little valley, looking so soft and blue in contrast with the mellow richness of the sunset sky; of the little glimpse of river scenery the bits of water looking like truant lakes hiding behind the intervening wooded heights; of the little quiet "dulce-far-niente" looking stinging brooks leaping and flashing over their brows. A calm, sweet prospect it was over which the very genius of silence seemed to have woven its spell.

Aunt Betty told me a great deal of good news too, only I'm afraid 'tis not true, about Longstreet having surrounded sixteen thousand Yankees in Suffolk forcing them to surrender, of our having achieved quite a little victory at Kelley's Ford, of a second success at Charleston and of Stuart's having been promoted and assigned the command of the Valley—but this, the most cheering piece of intelligence to us seems to bear the stamp of authenticity—oh if it be but true.

> *Longstreet was detached from the Army of Northern Virginia in late February 1862 and placed in command of the Department of Virginia and North Carolina. His main objective was to draw supplies from North Carolina for Lee's army. These supplies were being threatened by Union forces at Suffolk, Virginia.*
>
> *On the thirtieth of April Longstreet was ordered to rejoin Lee, the latter having been struck by the enemy along the Rappahannock River.*

How I wish it may be! Called by Mrs. Hope's and then reached home just as the bell rang for tea. Felt positively happy—too much so to talk, so stealing off into the parlor I sat down to think with my piano—memory and fingers talked to the keys of bygone hours until Nellie came in to tell me of her evening at Mrs. H.'s—she soon went out though leaving me to the twilight and the society of my own thoughts. I was thinking of this ever to be remembered anniversary—playing half unconsciously the "Farewell to Mary Queen of Scots" when just then Ma called me in a quick eager voice. Closing the piano I hastened to her room—she and Father were sitting by the candlestand inspecting the contents of the mail just brought in. She held up to me a letter—one glance sufficed. Snatching it eagerly I ran off into Grandma's room to open it and was there ever anything so like another as that miniature like Scott?—the same candid, manly face, kind in expression and to my eye handsome too. And his letter so frank, so mischievous, so characteristic withal—I almost cried in my excess of delighted surprise and scarcely know yet how to behave myself. The day's pleasure has quite turned my head and I shall have to hasten to bed that sleep the "kind restorer" may set me all right again. Ah me!

April 25, 1863

News of a battle at Suffolk in which both Giles and poor Scott were wounded though only slightly. Poor fellows! I do hope they'll come home now until fit for duty again. Could hear no particulars of the battle at all.

April 29, 1863

A shower this morning. After it cleared off I went into the garden and was weeding the flowers when hearing the children shout a welcome, looked up and saw Walter riding in at the yard gate. We were as much delighted as surprised to see him and to hear that he had been again to Clarke. Remained long enough to give a very stirring description of the late affair at Fishers Hill in which he was engaged and to tell how near he was being shot (his horse was killed) and then left.

April 30, 1863

Tonight Ma, Father, Cousin E., Nellie and I went into the parlor and had a private concert—a very pleasant one till bedtime. Just as we were going upstairs Ma whispered to me that Father heard in town of a battle in which the Seventh Regiment had been engaged losing very heavily but she bade me say nothing about it to Cousin E. lest she should be alarmed about her boys. Since coming down we have been discussing the matter and are seriously afraid some of our friends and relations must have fallen in the fight, but nothing definite can be learned of it.

May 2, 1863

The report of Willie Jackson's death reached town. He was mortally wounded in Jones' late engagement, charging at the very head of the regiment and being ridden over by the rushing cavalry charge. Poor boy!—so young, so brave to be doomed to such an early and horrible death. I trust the news is without foundation. To think he should fall in his first engagement while so many of his comrades have passed unscathed through the shock of many battles.

It is generally believed that the Seventh was not as much injured as we had feared at first. How well I remember this day, year—the anniversary of our investment by the Yankees.

May 6, 1863

Alex came in from home bringing a note from Ma and letter from Irvie received yesterday afternoon. The letter was evidently written in the greatest haste and he poor fellow perfectly absorbed in the gayeties in which he had been participating. Reading the letter struck a chill to my heart for I thought how soon he might be summoned from the festive hall to the deadly conflict and how poor a preparation he was making for the change.

Uncle Tom came in and told us there had been a terrible battle at Fredericksburg in which we had repulsed the enemy both sides losing very heavily.

General Hooker's army crossed the Rappahannock River and started its drive for Richmond around Lee's left flank. Lee, minus Longstreet's corps, sent Jackson toward Chancellorsville to flank Hooker. On May 2, 1863, Jackson struck Hooker's right flank in a surprise attack. The fight continued into the night during which Jackson was wounded by his own men while returning from reconnaissance. He was wounded in his left hand, left forearm and the third wound was three inches below his left shoulder. General A. P. Hill took command of the Second Corps but he was also wounded. The battle continued and on the fourth of May Hooker ordered a retreat. On May 6, 1863, the Army of the Potomac was back near Fredericksburg. Its march to Richmond was over.

U.S.A.	C.S.A.
Effectives 97,382	Effectives 57,352
Killed 1,575	Killed 1,665
Wounded 9,594	Wounded 9,081
Missing 5,676	Missing 2,018

Jackson's arm was amputated in the early morning of May 3, 1863, and the operation was a success. His wounds had begun to heal when he was struck with pneumonia May 7, 1863. He died May 10, 1863. Before Jackson's death, Lee asked Chaplain Lacy to carry him a message, "give my affectionate regards and tell him to make haste and get well and come back to me as soon as he can. He has lost his left arm, but I have lost my right arm."
General Franklin P. Paxton was also killed.
General Heth was wounded as were Generals Ramseur, Pender, Hoke, McGowan and Nicholls.

Generals Jackson, Hill, Heth and Paxton were said to be wounded I trust only slightly though. Oh how thankful we should feel for having been once more able to repulse the enemy in mortal conflict.

May 9, 1863
A most delicious day, so warm and so bright. Taught the children, sewed some and read some. In the afternoon Father invited us to walk down to the old "tank" with him. We went, he, Orville and Carey went on down to the river to fish while Laura, Willie and I returned through the meadows home. Stopped on the rugged wooded hill below Clifton

and gathered some new violets and dug for "Crowfoot" for Ma. Had a pleasant walk home, sat and chatted awhile with Ma then read in *Alone* and finally went with her out on the old stile about sunset where we sat cracking nuts and watching them fixing the footbridge swept away by the high waters of the last few days. The boys came back exhibiting a little string of fish of which they seemed to be extremely proud. Mr. Berry came in before we had left the tea table—brings only a confirmation of what we had already heard of the late affair at F. Had seen General Lee's report—did not learn the list of casualties. Jackson, it is thought, is but slightly wounded.

May 13, 1863

Carey carried our letters to the office this morning and came back telling us that intelligence of Jackson's death had reached town—we did not credit it at all though. But alas!—Emma and Nellie came with sad faces and told us that it was but too true, a Richmond paper all heavily in mourning had been received in town announcing the melancholy event —though giving none of the particulars. Oh what a blow is this—our bravest and best, the most devoted and earnest in the cause in which we all have staked so much—the truest and noblest, our Christian patriot. Gone! Everyone seemed stunned by the news—and it has been a mournful day with us—nature seemed even to partake of the general gloom, for the sun although shining in a cloudless sky seemed sickly and wan. During the morning Willie Buck came over to tell us good-bye preparatory to going into the army and the Mack Erwin called and they both left together.

I can't realize that dreadful story of General Jackson's death—perhaps it may be after all a mistake. I hope so.

May 15, 1863

The papers bring additional particulars of Jackson's death. I never fully believed it before, but I've read it now.

May 16, 1863

Was aroused from a sweet dream by Nellie's voice in the early dawn crying out—"get up girls! I've bad news for you—the town is full of Yankees!" Not crediting the tale I turned my head to a more comfortable position on the pillow intent on resuming the thread of my dream, but she finally succeeded in convincing me that it was my duty to believe and obey her. Had not completed my toilette when I heard a knock at the front door and then the clanking of sabres as the owners were admitted. They inquired for Father and were directed to the stables, where he had gone to send the horses off to a place of concealment. The household was wide awake and stirring though not excited, Emma, Nellie, Laura and I sat down by the window to finish *Alone* and were at an interesting crisis of the fascinating narrative when the door flew back and in came two Yankees with Father. They had come to search for "Rebel soldiers" and upon being told their trouble would be fruitless they said there certainly had been some in Front Royal last night. They did not prosecute their investigation quite as rigorously as their predecessors though, only peeping under the beds and making Father unpack the large box of table and bed linen in the upper passage—provoking wretches!—to give so much trouble. The gallant officer in command was dressed in full Confederate uniform. There was a box of bed and table linens in the hall which they insisted upon overhauling for "contraband goods"—they had their troubles for their pains as there was nothing suspicious contained therein save a piece of cotton which had been bought before the war and this they did not take. There were only two of the sinners who came in the house the captain and a young, well-dressed seemingly mortified sort of Yankee boy whose office seemed to be to watch the expression of our countenances to ascertain our opinion of their proceedings—he was gratified and edified I know at the curled lips and contemptuous smiles of some of his spectators. They behaved very well for Yankees, only one of them was drunk and indulged in very free use of oaths to his companions while relating to them how he would have burned Mr. Hope's house to the ground but for the sick woman in it. They were members of the famous "Jessie Scouts" of Fremont notoriety.

> *"Jessie Scouts" were a company of scouts famed at spying and often donned the Confederate gray. They first served under General Fremont in Missouri, later in Tennessee under Grant, McClernand and others. Still later the company served in Virginia under Fremont and Milroy.*

About eight o'clock we were dismayed at seeing a body of infantry—from one to two hundred marching in preceded by their baggage wagons. After they came in the cavalry went across the mountain on some secret embassy. We spent a very quiet day—not another Yankee appearing on the premises the whole day. They did not form an encampment but bivouacked in the public square in town.

May 17, 1863

Our first inquiry—"have the Yankees gone?" was answered negatively. Of course, Sunday School was not to be thought of or church either for that matter. We wandered listlessly about all the early morning, first in the parlor playing and singing hymns, then in the garden gathering flowers and awakening the lazy bees, next upstairs, then on the porch until we finally settled down in something like the following order: Father went to town to get the news, Ma, Nellie and Emma committed themselves to napping and I had resource to reading and writing. Father returned after awhile accompanied by Miss June Cramwell and her little brother. He brought no news except the reported capture of the Yankee cavalry—the soldiers in town are evidently laboring under some such apprehension—there is no other way of accounting for their unprecedented good behavior.

Was sitting on the porch reading aloud to Father about three o'clock this afternoon when looking out we saw the Yankee infantry marching quietly out of town—minus their cavalry escort. We soon learned that they had heard of the loss of their troops and that fear had hurried their departure. Mr. Berry came over soon after they left. Very soon after their exodus a body of the officers came galloping back and scattered over the suburbs of town as if in quest of something but soon collecting they took a final departure. They had returned vainly hoping to capture some of our men who might have crept from their hiding places but in this they were disappointed although there were several in concealment there.

Father says they injured his store somewhat having taken the drawers out to feed their horses in and burst some of them besides scattering some of Father's old receipts about in the upper store room. They took, in the post office, yesterday a letter from Scott Roy which had been overlooked in the distribution of mail matter on Friday—don't know to whom it was written but they read it publicly in the street and threatened to publish it.

The Yankees only took off with them some three or four old horses, three or four old worthless contrabands and four citizens captive—Joe Miller among them.

May 18, 1863

All busy with spring cleaning today. That was all a mistake about the Yankee cavalry having been captured. This is the summary of their proceedings. Our cavalry—fifty in number went down to Charlestown a few nights since and captured some sixty Yankees and with their prisoners were returning by the Piedmont Route via Delaplane. The Yankees in Winchester hearing of this feat vowed vengeance and retaliation and sent forth this detachment to intercept them. They surprised our men in a very disadvantageous position—a skirmish ensued in which they retook all the prisoners and four of the Confederates but not the arms which we had taken from the prisoners and with which we made our escape. 'Twas a miracle that all our boys were not captured—poor Charlie Richardson was among the number taken. The Yankee cavalry in returning to Winchester did not come through here but took the "Island Ford" Route—which accounts for their being here when the infantry evacuated the place.

May 21, 1863

All the hands busy planting corn and as Father seems so anxious to get well through with the job the house servants were also engaged in it. So Nellie and I had the children to attend to. Grandma went up to the Hope's in the afternoon and while she was there Eliza came in and sat some time with us. Nellie and I went in the garden in the evening to help Carey water the plants. The flowers are beginning to bloom beautifully and there is such charming weather with so much of beauty around the very fact of existence itself almost seems a pleasure.

May 25, 1863

Had commenced writing this morning when quite early Aunt B. came in to fulfill her engagement with Ma and begged me to make one of the party. 'Twas chill and disagreeable without—misty and grey and I had a suspicion of the neuralgia—but Ma, Grandma, Nellie and Aunt B. were bent on it and go I must. We were to walk until we met our conveyance which Father had sent for from Mr. McDaniel's where it had been concealed from the Yankees. Father went with us—we met the wagon only after we had, as we thought, arrived nearly at our place of destination and we decided to continue our way on foot. Father put us into the wrong road though and we had a pleasant but a very long weary walk. I found some strange wild flowers in the woods through which we passed and some pretty leaves. When we arrived at "Happy Creek" ('twas my first visit there though living in sight of the place twenty years) a little urchin directed us around to the front entrance. I could but be struck with the air of dilapidation and desolation that reigned over everything despite the natural beauties of the place. The whole appearance of house and grounds reminded me of descriptions of the old "Halls" of some of the impoverished English gentlemen. The porters lodges looked but the shadow of what they were intended for, there was no gate—scarcely any enclosure about the lawn, the hedges were beautiful in their wild luxuriance but unclipped and ragged, the grass tall and rank growing even in the walks and drives. There were flowers and blossoming shoots though that gave a pleasing contrast in their neat arrangement to the general neglect visible everywhere. Old Mr. M. was standing on the stone steps of the great hall door to receive us and give us a cordial welcome. We were ushered into an immense hall and thence into the sitting room where Miss Mary soon made her appearance apologizing for the temporary absence of her sisters and inviting us to her room where we laid aside our bonnets and shawls and rearranged our toilettes before going down to see old Aunt L. who has been sick so long. She was apparently very glad to see us, and sitting up in bed talked a great deal. I never saw such a looking object as she is—almost a skeleton, her livid brown skin falling in loose wrinkles over the projecting bones—her mouth all drawn—lips thin and eyes bleared with age yet quick and restless and yet there she sat and talked as clearly and distinctly of her situation—spoke so calmly and happily of her removal to the "Happy Mansions" as if 'twas a journey to her native land and early friends on which she was going—even chiding herself for her impatience to be off. How I envy her quiet happy confidence!

Misses H. and M. had returned home in the meantime and after going back to the house we were invited in to luncheon and then shown into the parlor. There we spent the morning talking, admiring the pictures, listening to a long letter from the Rebel brother in Wheeling. Then we went into the great old garden and out among the flowers.

While at dinner the boys—Orville, Carey, and Allie came in with our spring wagon in which we were to return home. They having left no one at home "on guard" in case the Yankees should come in, Father had to hurry home. Old Mr. M. is a hospitable courtly old gentleman in his house and took more pains to amuse me than I deserved—even bringing a volume from the library—*Froissart's Chronicles* for me to look at to compare the "art in its infancy with its present state of perfection." They were grotesque, stiff, droll-looking figures on the yellow parchment very unlife-like and very insipid. In course of conversation today *The Antiquary* was spoken of and learning from me that I had never read it she promised to loan me it as soon as she could find it and just as we were leaving putting on our bonnets in the chamber, I took up a couple of books laying on the bed—*Dyneron Terrace* by the author of *The Heir of Radcliffe* and Miss Mary noticing me with it remarked that was interesting and if I had never read it I should take it home with me. I accepted the offer delightedly promising to send her an exchange in the shape of my *Messengers*. We had spent a very pleasant day notwithstanding my aversion to going and I discovered to my surprise that Miss M. instead of being the sour, silent being she appeared in public was a most talkative merry creature imaginable, Miss Hattie not near so uncouth as one might imagine but a notable, kindly, intelligent housekeeper and Miss Ann Maria—the quiet bird-like pet of the household. It won't do to judge from appearances and I am glad my many false opinions of this family have been rectified by this day's visit.

May 30, 1863
The papers came tonight and my June *Messenger*. The papers confirmed the welcome tidings we have just received of the late Confederate victory at Vicksburg.

Grant had now ringed Vicksburg and assaulted the city May 19–22 but the attack failed.

Thank heaven!—'tis more than we could have hoped for.

June 1, 1863
Was lying half asleep on the bed when Laura rushed in with two huge envelopes saying something about Alvin and Richmond—I sprung to my feet and snatched one from her—"Miss Lucie R. Buck" in Scott's familiar handwriting and the postmark "Richmond"—was a little disappointed but 'twas the next best thing to being from Alvin himself. The other

pacquet was for Nellie containing a note and a piece of music—"Her Bright Smile Haunts Me Still"—mine also a note and "Rock Me to Sleep, Mother"—which no longer than yesterday I had been longing for. Bless his life!—'twas so kind of him to think of it. He has rejoined his regiment and is doing well.

June 5, 1863

They say one of our independent companies are to picquet in town —Captain Stevenson's. They are said to be brave and I hope will keep our enemies at bay for a time. One of the number—a young Faulkerson stopped in tonight to get his duffle and gave us some interesting descriptions of the different actions in which they have been engaged.

June 6, 1863

An amusing incident occurred tonight. Just as we were preparing for bed there came a knock at the door—we were all in our night clothes and every one made a simultaneous rush for the little room. I had fortunately presence of mind to open the door a few inches and peeping out inquired "Who's there?" The answer came—"Nobody." 'Twas very indefinite so the question was repeated and then came—"No Yankee nor nothing of that sort." That was all sufficient and E. Ann was dispatched to admit him. 'Twas a member of Captain McNeil's company and we could hear him through the door giving Father an account of a skirmish in which they were engaged yesterday near Winchester—they must be a brave band.

June 8, 1863

After retiring at ten o'clock Alex came in and told us that a company of Yankees had come into town. Uncle John immediately got up and dressed and went away and Alex took his horse and some baggage after him. They all seemed a good deal excited but I did not believe the story Alex told at all. This morning, however, 'twas confirmed. There were some four or five hundred—they came in from below, got in the rear of our picquets, captured them and left unmolested. They did not know even that our men under Captain Stevenson were encamped near town —and they did not know that the Yankees were here.

June 9, 1863

Awoke about five o'clock this morning and came in Grandma's room to dress. There was no fire made, no water brought, no movement whatever below stairs. Just then I heard Father enter Ma's room and exclaim—"All gone horses and all." Throwing on my shawl I stepped in and inquired what was the matter when Ma told me that the servants had all left in the night and carried our three horses with them. We every one of us made a dash for our clothes, hauled them on, kindled a fire, brought water and Laura and I went to milk the cows while Ma,

Nellie and Grandma cleaned the house, got the breakfast and dressed the children. Old Uncle Gilbert came and declared his ignorance of the exodus—and to do him justice I don't believe he did. Immediately after breakfast Mrs. Moffatt came in and then Uncle Tom and Uncle Mack and Allie and Elliott and Aunt Bettie and Mr. Kiger—poor Mr. Kiger's servants went too. When they all came to us they kissed and cried over us but we laughed and told them 'twas more than we had done for ourselves as yet. Indeed 'tis surprising with what calmness one learns to bear all such sudden shocks—now my sensations when first becoming cognizant to their flight were a mixture of wonder at their dexterity in baffling so successfully all suspicion of their movements and indignation at their ingratitude in taking the horses when they knew they were our main dependence of support. The first thing we did after cleaning the breakfast things was to clear the trumpery from their various rooms and truly Hercules' labor in the Augean stables was the only thing it could be compared to. Mrs. Moffatt very kindly sent us Matilda and Miss P. Haynie, Caroline and Aunt Bettie contributed Lucy and we fell to work in good earnest, never thinking of such a thing as sitting down to rest during the day. The servants took apparently nothing with them but their finest clothing and in the midst of trumpery left we had an opportunity of discovering various articles hitherto counted among the missing. Father and Mr. Beecher started about twelve o'clock to Winchester to attempt the recovery of their horses—poor Father his loss is the heaviest of all, amounting, it is thought, to some sixteen thousand dollars.

It has been stated that less than twenty percent of the slaves left their masters during the Civil War. Most remained loyal to their owners and even aided in protecting property. Others followed their masters into the army and served them there.

Wonder where Father is—wonder if the servants don't some of them feel a little homesick. Poor creatures! They little know the fate in store for them. 'Tis said Belle Boyd is in town tonight. What next? My biscuits were pronounced faultless tonight.

June 10, 1863
Mr. Kiger came in to breakfast—said he had been patrolling the premises all night. One of his servants, the mother of the family, didn't go with the others—remained behind to sell out and wind up business intending to follow after them. Eliza came up from Rose Hill this morning and milked and made the fires for us and cleaned up the kitchen, put on meat for dinner and everything we couldn't do for ourselves. She's such a good, able servant—if we only had such!
'Tis our wash day. Mrs. Normal took the clothes to the mill to wash them—we think of hiring her to come and do the work next week. Old Uncle Gilbert looked sorely distressed and lonely. I feel sorry for

him—particularly as he has been making himself so useful since they all left.

Mr. Berry came over again tonight. Just as we arose from prayer some one called out—"Father's come!" and to our great surprise he was in Grandma's room, having just gotten home—bringing with him his two horses. We were so glad to see him and hear him give an account of his interview with old Milroy who consented to his receiving his two horses, upon condition that the third should be given the servants as their "lawful (?)" hire since the first of January. Father saw the servants—all save Horace and Marshall—they were all together in a crowded, close shanty with not a single convenience of life. Miserable creatures—there's no doubt but they wish themselves back in their comfortable home many times ere this. They tried to brave the matter off very bravely when they met Father—told them they had had no idea of leaving until about noon that day before, when Martha said she had overheard Grandma tell Mrs. Hope that all the servants ought to be sent South (which was probably false) and that they took the alarm—knowing Mr. Kiger had bought a wagon to take his servants there and concluded to start right off. They sent for Allfair (named by Laura from a character in a favorite fairy tale) that night upon the plea that her sister was dying—so she went with them and all of the twelve (including Rob Roy) went on the three horses and carried their baggage—how they ever managed it I can't conceive, and they did not start either until just about dawn. They said they would like to have all their plunder if they could get it but Rob Roy confessed he was almost afraid to return on this side of the river for it. They asked no questions whatever but told that they were en route for Alexandria where they expected to meet their mother. To think that Mahalla even went off without taking John Henry, her pet child—he being not quite so convenient as Allfair but I suppose she thought he could come on at any time with old Aunt Hester. Poor miserable creatures! I do pity them rushing so blindly to a fate that they little foresee. We are so thankful that Father made all the trip without taking any pledge or any way compromising his principles—truly 'tis more than we could have reasonably expected.

June 11, 1863

Cloudy and damp this morning. Aunt Eliza milked the cows for us and very soon Aunt Evelyne came down from the mountain to iron for us and Armanda saying Mrs. Roy had told her to come over and do what she could for us. We concluded, however, that was better not to have all our assistance at one time and then at another to be entirely without any, and as Aunt E. had come such a distance we retained her and sent Armanda home with a note to Mrs. R. explaining our reasons. We girls assisted in ironing and getting dinner too. Quite early Miss Betty White came in to bring butter (the idea of such a thing!) and regaled us with a dash of gossip. Then Uncle Newton and Aunt Jane and Mr.

Kiger were to dine with us. Laura made a valise dumpling which elicited general commendation. Aunt J. assisted in washing up the dinner service and while cleaning the dining room we were summoned to the top of the house to see a long wagon train of pontoons that were being brought into town. We instantly conjectured the purpose for which they were intended, and as it had cleared off Ma and Father rode down the river to see them thrown across.

'Tis generally believed in town that a portion at least of Lee's army is advancing on Winchester through this way.

June 12, 1863

This has been a most glorious day, weary and footsore as we are. Armanda came over quite early though Eliza milked and made the fire in the kitchen before she came. Mrs. Normal also came to finish the ironing. Aunt Eliza went home after breakfast and Armanda proceeded to scouring and cleaning. One of the little boys having gone to town in the morning returned with news of the near approach of the expected army. About half past ten o'clock we heard music and looking out saw the vanguard of Jackson's old corps entering the place—in advance of old General Ewell in his carriage surrounded by his escort.

> *Ewell, who marched into Front Royal with Jackson on May 23, 1862, had taken over the command of the II Corps after Jackson's death. Ewell had been wounded in the Second Battle of Manassas and had lost his leg, but now he was back with the army. He could mount a horse by himself, but on long trips he traveled in a carriage.*
>
> *After Jackson's death, Lee divided his army into three corps. The I Corps was still under Longstreet. Ewell had Jackson's II Corps, and A. P. Hill was in command of the newly formed III Corps.*
>
> *On June 3, the Confederate Army of Northern Virginia began to move North again. Lee was hoping to subsist his forces on the rich abundance of Pennsylvania for the summer rather than the battle-weary Virginia soil. This northern invasion was also designated to relieve the pressure in the west. By winning a victory on Northern soil it was hoped that the peace party in the North might be strengthened and a peace could be obtained. Such a Southern victory might bring recognition from the European powers.*
>
> *Ewell's corps led the way down the Valley. It was followed by Longstreet's corps and A. P. Hill's corps was left to guard Richmond. When Hooker turned north to follow Lee, A. P. Hill followed the other corps down the Valley. J. E. B. Stuart's cavalry guarded the army's flanks east of the Blue Ridge mountains.*

Oh how the gallant boys cheered and shouted—Ma and I went up on the house and when they saw us they waved and hurrahed us. Oh!—it was glorious! Column after column filed past with glistening bayonets, flying colors and rolling artillery, while the strains of martial music and their soul-burning shouts mingled in one unbroken, soul-thrilling volume of sound. I felt almost frantic with excitement and delight. The soldiers commenced stopping in for milk. Presently a servant came with "Major Roger's compliments to the ladies" and a request that they would send him "a lunch." I arranged a beautiful bouquet of roses and Nellie made up a box of bread, butter and chipped beef and honey and milk and sent him. His reply to the courtesy was an assurance that he was "everlastingly obliged" and would "never get done loving." While getting dinner a messenger came over from Mr. Cook's to inform Father that the Reverend Mr. Lacy was there and would be glad to see him.

Probably this was Reverend B. Tucker Lacy, Stonewall Jackson's close friend and chaplain of the II Corps.

He returned about an hour before dinner accompanied by Mr. Moreton, the gentleman who breakfasted here the morning after the Battle of Front Royal. Making arrangements for my dinner I gave Armanda directions accordingly and left it in her hands and dressed myself and went into the parlor to welcome our guests. He was most cordial in his greeting and seemed really glad to see us again—said he had been some time anticipating a movement in this direction and resolved in his own mind that he would call on us again. He was so cheerful, so hopeful and so agreeable with all. Charlie Richardson soon came in and after him Young Sheppard. It was amusing at the dinner table to notice the efforts the gentlemen made to wait on themselves and how they disliked being recipients of our attention. Nellie and I enjoyed it—particularly as our exertions received so much unmerited praise. Cousin Mount came in directly after dinner and we all went up on the house to watch the troops coming in and waved to them. Mr. Moreton and I were discussing books and I mentioned *Tannhouser*— he had never seen it. When he came downstairs I handed him the volume and told him he should glance over the contents while at camp that night. (His brigade was in Cousin R.'s field.) He begged for some music and he, Cousin Mount and I sang and played till the latter left with Charlie. Nellie being dairy maid was much engaged in giving the soldiers milk. Mr. Moreton left about four o'clock promising to come up again from camp this evening "should his brigade remain where it was" and bring to hear some music a young Dr. Cannon from S. C.—a gentleman whom he represented as illustrating in an eminent degree the "chivalry" of the Palmetto State without its "bombast." He professed to be very anxious to procure for his friends a young Va. wife and wondered if we would not one of us "take him in."

Lucie came over from Uncle Tom's to help us get supper—while Armanda assisted Nellie to clean the churn. Mr. Moreton returned just before supper to say his brigade had moved off and he would but just have time to bid us good-bye. We persuaded him to remain to tea to eat some of my biscuits and all the time at table he kept us in a roar of laughter with his rich, spicy anecdotes. Upon leaving he expressed his gratitude for what he termed our goodness to him and begged to know in what way he could serve us—offering to do all in his power toward restoring to us our property. He likes *Tannhouser* very much—reviewed it this evening. I do think he is one of the noblest specimens of manhood I ever saw—so earnest yet unaffectedly pious, so intelligent and refined in nature. It is a treat to meet with such a being.

Had a hard time milking tonight—Armanda and I were both inexperienced hands and "Criser" (black and white cow) was most refractory. We've gotten through our day's work at last though and now are quite welcome "Tired Nature's Restorer." The troops are still passing through and have been in an uninterrupted stream since this morning. Their shouts and cheers are making heartful music to our ears as they ring out in the stillness of the night air and their watch fires gleaming from every hill are so many beacons of hope to our anxious eyes. God bless the dear, brave ones and make us thankful for His enduring mercies.

June 13, 1863
Aunt Eliza came up again this morning, but not before Ma had made the fires and we commenced milking. She finished this and then Armanda came in and she left. Finished ironing, got dinner and did some cleaning up. In the afternoon there were pies to make for tomorrow, salt rising to bake, and supper to get besides milking, and washing the children. Oh such a weary time as we had of it—the children were sleepy and fretful, the stove wouldn't get hot, the bread would not bake and the cows would run. Uncle Tom and Aunt Bettie and E. Hope came in in the midst of all the confusion until I felt almost crazed. Just as supper was put on the table Father came in bringing with him two letters from both Alvin and Irvie. Bless their hearts. How affectionately and cheerfully they do write—'tis as cordial to our drooping spirits to have such pleasant tidings from afar. Could not eat a bit of supper—indeed I've not eaten two full meals since our labors began. After much tribulation we succeeded in getting the children washed and put to bed—then we brought in wood and water for the night for Armanda had left after supper—cleaned up the kitchen and arranged to have a nice bath. The kitchen floor being partly brick we moved in buckets and tubs, filled them with tepid water and proceeded with our ablutions—Ma, Nellie, Laura and myself. Feel greatly refreshed by the operation but am still very, very footsore and weary. The soldiers all left for Winchester this morning save a few broken-down ones and the sick in the hospital here.

> *Ewell reached the vicinity of Winchester on the thirteenth of June and most of the Federals in the city were captured on the fourteenth–(3,358 prisoners). General Milroy, U.S.A., with 200 to 300 cavalry escaped. Ewell's corps received 269 casualties.*
> *The II Corps crossed into Maryland on June 15, and entered Pennsylvania on the twenty-second.*
> *Ewell's main objective was to gain commissaries.*

'Tis said cannonading was heard up the valley today—no news from Winchester though or from any other place. Oh me!

June 14, 1863

Went in the garden to get a bouquet, and was dressing myself when they came in to say Uncle John has come. So he had and with him a young Captain Armstrong of Maryland, an acquaintance of Irvie's. They remained but a short time, Uncle John doing a great deal of talking though, asking questions, condoling with us, prophesying brighter times and telling us the news. 'Tis only within the last few days that we've heard of the cavalry fight over the Ridge in which there was more cavalry engaged than has ever been on this continent before.

> *J. E. B. Stuart with his entire cavalry command; 9,536 officers and men; at Brandy Station was surprised by the enemy on June 9, 1863. The Confederate cavalry had been on parade before Lee and all the young ladies in the Piedmont area on June 5 and 6. Stuart succeeded in driving the enemy back but no great victory had been won.*
> *Col. B. F. Davis, leader of the Federal cavalry in the raid, was killed by Lt. R. O. Allen and Pvt. Gilbert Larue assisted, both of Co. D., Sixth Virginia Cavalry. Private Larue is frequently mentioned in Lucy's diary.*

Uncle John tells us Cousin Sam's son Willie was quite severly wounded, poor fellow—thought dangerously so. Father went to town immediately after breakfast and did not return until after Sunday School and then went back to church and dinner out. I betook myself to the kitchen where I quietly spent the morning writing till about ten o'clock, and Belle, E. Hope, and Nannie Buck and Allie came in. All save the latter and Belle soon went to church though and we were engaged in getting dinner—we were all cooks, Ma made bread and fried meat, Grandma prepared onions and lettuce, I dressed the latter, brought water and arranged table, Nellie and Belle brought milk, cream and butter and Laura warmed the pies. We did enjoy it so too—it seemed so sweet after working so hard for it. While eating Aunt Eliza came-in and then before we had cleared the table Charlie Buck, Orville, Carey and Allie came. Aunt

Betsie spent the day at Mrs. Glasscock's. Charlie is a great boy—remained down in the dining room after dinner and helped Nellie to wash the service and clear off the table—all the while talking so cheerily. There has been the heaviest cannonading heard in the direction of Winchester. I never have heard such a succession of rapid and heavy firing in my life—we all went out to listen and felt very anxious to ascertain the cause of it. 'Twas the day reported by some that Milroy had made good his escape—by others that he had been captured, etc., etc.

Our company was all gone and we were sitting at the back door listening to the cannons which were still booming more loudly than ever when the gate opened and Uncle Mack rode in. He had just returned from Winchester—told us that Ewell had succeeded in completely surprising Milroy, had surrounded, cut off his reinforcements and supplies, and driven him with his ten thousand troops within their entrenchments beyond the town from which we were endeavoring to shell them. Their fortifications seemed almost impregnable but there was no doubt of our being able to oust them very soon as we had already seventy huge pieces pointed on the fort and were mounting some immense "parrotts." Uncle M. seems very confident that all of our servants will be retaken for they had not left W., when he was there. Oh!—it was glorious, glorious, beyond measure—never was presence of men more welcome, never tidings so rejoicing. Thank God! Father had been in the mountains with the spyglass to endeavor if possible to discover the locality and exact position of the battle and had only just returned to hear from us the grand news. The cannonading still continues without intermission.

June 15, 1863
Father came in to dinner with news of the fall of Winchester. We had heard cannonading early this morning and when it suddenly ceased were convinced that they had surrendered, and so they had. Milroy and all his minions—not a man escaped and we took supplies, three thousand horses, ammunition, arms, etc. Delightful. Nothing could be more charming than this capture of Milroy—may his deeds be visited on his own head now. I guess they find that although our Jackson is ascended his mantle has fallen on a man most worthy to be his successor.

The report came to town about sunset that Milroy and three thousand of his troops escaped from the fort early this morning before it surrendered, but we did not credit it at all. While sitting in the back door after dark we heard a step on the pavement and looking out saw Father pass with a cavalryman who proved to be Charlie Richardson. He had just returned from Winchester bringing Horace with him. He confirms the report of Milroy's flight but states the number of those escaped to be much less than was at first supposed. It is too vexatious to think that cowardly old villain has outwitted us thus and how pitiful of him to go off and leave his remaining men alone in such a perilous situation—never mind, Providence permitting we'll get him yet. Charlie says Horace and Alec were in attendance upon Yankee officers, which accounts for the capture of the former. The latter left, it is supposed, with the fugitives who accompanied Milroy. Of the other servants we could learn nothing but that they had left Winchester for Martinsburg a few days after Father saw them and are probably by this time beyond the arm of justice. Horace had been put in jail but Father and Charlie soon went over and brought him home. He looked humble enough when he stopped at the door to get a candle, but no one knows whether he will not make another attempt very soon to follow his kith. Father has determined to keep him at home if he will remain and behave himself.

June 16, 1863

Nancy came in to work this morning and we had Aunt Eliza too, so things were soon put into shape. There were soldiers in quite early for milk. Charlie showed us the beautiful horse which he yesterday captured from the Yankees—'tis a spirited, beautiful animal, truly, but has some star artillery gaits. C. tells me he captured some writing paper for me. Glad of it—very!

> *The original diary of Lucy Buck was written on a great assortment of paper in very fine handwriting to allow as much as possible on each page. Some sheets were written on twice in different directions.*

Aunt Bettie, Nannie, Mollie and Miss S. Thorpe came in and told us Longstreet's corps was expected through town either during the evening or early in the morning and they had brought us a basketful of beautiful bouquets to throw them. While they were telling us this some cavalrymen rode up to the gate for milk and they told us 'twas a mistake as their corps would certainly cross below at Berry's Ferry. Oh, it was provoking to have them coming in every five minutes with contradictory reports —sometimes we were wild with delight at the assurance that he certainly would come—then disappointed beyond measures by the assurance that 'twas altogether impoltic for him to do so. To provide against contingencies, however, we went into the garden and arranged a dozen more bouquets—while thus engaged two soldiers approached to inquire if they could get their suppers here. We knew it was impossible to accomodate them and told them so but invited them to seat themselves. One of them—a long Alabamian produced a most unfavorable impression from his resemblance to the Yankee adjutant Reed. The other was a nice fellow and while we were singing and playing for them he would say almost with tears—"Oh, it reminds me of my home." They all left quite early and we had a good resting space after tea. Armanda says she's going to bring us some roses for the soldiers tomorrow.

June 17, 1863

Was at the dairy extremely early and yet there were already numerous applicants for milk. While filling canteens a courier rode up and inquired for Father and when he came informed him that he had dispatches from Ewell to Longstreet desiring the troops of the latter to form a junction with his own at an early date and to accomplish this they should take the lower route and the courier wished to intercept them at Berry's Ferry and called to obtain directions as to his way. We knew then that our boys would not come through town and oh!—we're so disappointed. After we had finished breakfast there were six or eight applicants for a meal so the dining room was not ready for dinner till late. The gentlemen begged for music and Nellie and I played and sang for them some time. There were three of them, really nice fellows, a good portly fatherly gentleman, jolly and kindly, and a thin visaged, quite yet sociable personage, and finally the little Doctor Hardaway, one of the most gentlemanly pleasant of men. Just as they were leaving Charlie Richardson came in and sat a little while—brought me my Yankee paper—'tis such a prize. After he left went into the garden and gathered peas for dinner. Ever since daybreak a portion of Longstreet's wagons had been passing till about nine o'clock when the artillery followed in their wake. Passing as the soldiers did, right by the house, we of course had a continuous stream of the weary, dusty, travel-worn fellows calling for milk, bread, water—everything that could be imagined in the way of refreshments. We sent buckets of water down to the road from which the children supplied the thirsty, and those who came to the house were furnished with every drop of milk that could be spared—and indeed more than could conveniently be spared from the family rations. It was a pleasure to see their faces lighten when we would answer in reply to the invariable question "What do I owe you for this?"—"Nothing"—or "You are paying what you owe us every day you are in the army." They continued to come in so rapidly at last that we had to take food out of the stove which was being prepared for dinner and give them. So constant was the excitement—so fatiguing our work, (for Nancie having the washing at the mill, Grandma, Ma and I got dinner) so warm the day that I could not eat a morsel. They were all at dinner and I was in the kitchen cooking, attending to my "salt rising" when two soldiers called at the door and begged for something to eat. Without thinking what I did, I invited them to take a seat in the kitchen while I went into the dining room to ascertain if there was anything that could be gotten for them. While setting their dinners for them I saw they were perfect gentlemen to all appearances and presently when Ma came in they told her they were members of the Washington Artillery which was just going by. The spokesman was a delicate featured, slight and graceful youth and conversed fluently and elegantly. He remarked that he was acquainted with some Bucks, one of whom, Doctor Horace had married a cousin of his, Miss Herbert. We told him a cousin Horace of Mississippi who married a lady of that name and he said 'twas the same, then traced up a connection with another of the name. His own name was Herbert and he seemed to feel almost as if he had met with friends and commenced telling of a young brother of his who died in Warrenton a year ago and I'm almost sure 'tis the same young Herbert of whom we before had heard. He was tenderly nursed by a lady after receiving his wound and when he found himself dying he called her to him saying—"You have done for me all that my mother could have done save one thing—you've not kissed me for her, will you do so now?" She bent over him and pressed her lips to his while his arms closed about her neck—then sinking back on his pillow he said contentedly "I'm ready now" and soon died. 'Twas so sad and sweet. In taking leave of us the young man very cordially invited us to visit them should we ever go south. Was busily engaged in making up a batch of bread about three o'clock this afternoon when Nellie came bounding in with "Lucie, Mr. Macauley is here and has asked for you!" 'Twas such a surprise, for we had well-nigh forgotten the little Fourth Alabamian who called to get his breakfast that first morning when Longstreet passed through last autumn. I was busily engaged making up a batch of bread when he came and could not appear but after having inquired for me once or twice I sent an invitation for him to come in and see my excuse for not being visible. Into the kitchen he came laughing and expressing his plesure at returning to Front Royal again. He watched the process of bread-making with great apparent interest and when all was ready helped me prepare the oven, draw out the fire, etc. etc. very much as he might have helped me furl my parasol or tie my overshoe two years ago. Invited him back to the parlor, came up into the house, arranged my dress and went into the parlor myself where were two nice looking soldiers who were introduced as Messrs. Baker from N. O. members of the Washington Artillery and acquaintances of Cousin Cornelia Buck's. They were fine young fellows, intelligent, well-bred and agreeable, having evidently seen a good deal of fashionable life. The elder sings very well and we had quite a concert—then followed a discussion of music and poetry and novels.

> Major Page Baker after the war was owner and editor of the New Orleans Times Democrat. Carey visited him in New Orleans during the later years of his life. Major Baker was visiting Dr. Robert Carey Buck in Virginia when he was stricken with the illness that resulted in his death.

That Mr. Baker was thorough with all standard publications of these classics, I felt convinced but was somewhat surprised to find that Macauley appeared equally well-informed. He's a singular compound anyway. My own impression is that he's a spoiled boy—the son of an easy Southern planter who has been allowed the alternative of study or amusement and has preferred the latter in the shape of lying on his back in the woods and reading romances, or hunting game in flood and forest. How surprised Mr. Baker seemed when I expressed my admiration of Tennyson—he says he is one of his favorite poets but can never get anyone to agree with him and in leaving remarked that he sould remember me as the young lady with whom he could express the merits of his much maligned favorite. He gave us his autograph as did his brother and Mr. Macauley. When Mr. McC. heard that Irvie was in such constant communication with his place of residence, Huntsville, Alabama, he begged that we would write him and insist upon his visiting his home averring that his family would be glad of the opportunity for showing kindness to one whose friends had extended the rites of hospitality to their absent "romping Bob" as he says they dubbed him. He seems really grateful and in a degree attached to the family just because of the two meals furnished him when hungry and tired. The long "Reed-like Alabamian" who was here yesterday and the little half-demented Creole who got his luncheon here were both of them hanging around the house today. Don't know what to make of their singular movements. The Q.M. who was here this morning left a quart of spirit which he told Father to use until he send an order for him. We are so glad—'twill be a perfect treasure—there was also a mule left upon the same terms but 'twas so unmanageable that they could not get it into the field. Armanda was over again this evening. We begin to think there is a powerful magnet in the kitchen here now in the person of our returned fugitive. This fugitive I'm afraid is not a willing captive restored. There is an air of discontent and unrest about him that is very suspicious—it may, however, be only the effect of mortification and loneliness—time will prove.

June 19, 1863

The morning bade fair to be a quiet one but about ten o'clock we were surprised by a visit from Jimmie Blakemore and his cousin Captain McWillie. Jimmie has grown and fattened wonderfully—is otherwise pretty much what one would have prophesied three years ago when I last saw him. His cousin, the captain did not strike me as particularly fascinating—a man who immediately after introduction announces himself in a magniloquent manner a governor's or ex-governor's son seems rather to base his claims to consideration upon that fact more than his own personal merits. Did not have much conversation with him, though, for Jimmie soon rode away with Charlie Buck who was also here.

We've learned from Jimmie that A. P. Hill's corps would pass through town during the day and Anderson's brigade was hourly expected. About eleven o'clock the broken-down poor fellows commenced dropping in and they came in a perfect avalanche until about one when there was a cessation with only an occasional caller. Captain Grey and Captain Spann of S. C. dined here. A gentlemanly old bachelor he is. Had a hard time cooking supper this evening. Soldiers still coming in—while I write their shouts are ringing in the air.

June 20, 1863

At ten o'clock A. P. Hill's corps commenced marching through town and there was an immense sensation.

> Longstreet's I Corps and A. P. Hill's III Corps followed Ewell's II Corps across the Potomac into Maryland. Ewell sent his divisions (Early, Rodes, "Maryland," Stuart, and Edward Johnson) via different routes as he headed northward and east. Early's division entered Gettysburg on June 27 and passed on to York, Pennsylvania. Ewell entered Carlisle, Pennsylvania, and on June 29 was shelling Federal works on the Susquehanna River when he received orders to proceed south toward Gettysburg; Lee was beginning to concentrate his forces.

Children all went over to see troops—bad to worse. Commenced letter to Irvie. Miss Betsy White here to dinner. Mr. Berry over early in the afternoon. No news. Our army is in Maryland and Pennsylvania now though. Was working up in salt rising in the evening when a drunken soldier came into the kitchen from out in the rain—represented himself as one Captain Carey of the Madison artillery—commenced swearing, was frightened and sent for Father who came and settled him. ... here—very lavish in presents and money to children. Armanda came over to help milk, and wash the children. Got through earlier than usual.

June 21, 1863

Pender's division passing through—bands playing and colors flying. We were on the house a long time watching them.

Ma did not get home until late—two soldiers to supper and had to go into the dairy after dark to skim milk for the sick at the hospital. There's a rumor of a battle at Upperville today. Scarce believe it though.

> J. E. B. Stuart's cavalry on the eastern side of Blue Ridge Mountains was, as stated, protecting the army's right flank. At Upperville on June 21, 1863, a fierce battle was fought. After the battle at Upperville, Stuart started on another of his famous rides behind and around the enemy's army. He cut between Hooker's army and Washington and came within sight of the city on his way to join Ewell.

June 22, 1863

Soldiers in to breakfast early. Father walked in looking pale and excited. At table he and Ma both looked much disturbed and in reply to my question as to the news from the army he said the news of the Battle of Upperville had been confirmed and that 'twas reported that Jones brigade had suffered severely in the action. After dinner Ma called me out and told me that dear Walter was said to have fallen. Oh!—such a shock!—it seems as if my heart had stopped deating and my limbs stiff and cold—still I did not credit the report—first news was always so exaggerated. Cousin Mary went home as soon as she heard it and we were all alone with our sorrow and suspense. In the afternoon cavalrymen coming directly from the scene of action confirmed all we had heard till there was left no room for hope. Father had written for Uncle Mack to come down as soon as he heard it and about three o'clock he and Jacquie rode up to the gate. Father told him all—he did not come to the house at all, but sending Jacquie with a message to Aunt L. he started immediately for Upperville to learn what he could with regard to the fight and tried to recover his body. This is what causes us such grief, to know that the dear fellow was shot and instantly killed was bad enough but to have no assurance that he might not have been mortally wounded and left in the enemy's hands to die a cruel death and then his dear form cast a mangled and disfigured heap under a pile of their own unhallowed slain—'twas distressing beyond measure. Ma and Nellie went on immediately to the mountain to stay with Aunt Letitia during Uncle M.'s absence. I do feel so much for her, poor thing!

A letter has just been brought in by a cavalryman from Cousin Horace Buck announcing poor Walter's death and tendering sympathy to his parents but giving no particulars as he had not been able to learn any himself. This destroys the very last vestige of hope. Oh!—I'm so sick!—so sad at heart!

June 23, 1863

Early after breakfast this morning they told me Uncle Mack had come. Presently Father came in and said he had recovered the poor boy's remains, which would be here in a few moments. How like a knell those words sounded!—till then I had not altogether resigned a hope that the evil tidings might be groundless or exaggerated. Now the sad truth was established beyond a doubt. And yet with this great sorrow mingled a feeling of earnest gratitude—he should have accorded us the sacred privilege of performing for him the last sad duty—his dear form should not rest in an unknown and unwept grave, but we should lay it with kindred dust where we could plant over it flowers and tend it with the loving care that we delighted to bestow upon him while he lived. I went out and gathered some beautiful jessamines, lilies, and roses and some ivy for a wreath and while twining these for his bier, Nellie came in. In a very little while the house was thronged, ladies bringing baskets of wreaths and flowers and all with sad, tearful faces. They brought dear Walter in about ten o'clock, Cousin William Cloud coming with him. I saw the black great wagon drawn slowly along and thought how often we had watched for his coming as for a ray of sunshine and had seen him dash up to the house so fearlessly looking so handsome and graceful, so noble—and now to think of his being brought so sadly, so unconsciously back to his second home which he entered for the first time in his life without a tender greeting. Ma soon came home and after awhile they called us into the parlor to see the dear boy once more. Never shall I forget the sight—there lay the still white figure under the southern window, the attitude one of such perfect, majestic repose as seems to quiet and subdue my grief. The face that lay there among the wreaths and masses of lilies and jessamines was the most beautifully placid one that I have ever seen and so natural, so free from the usual ghastly terrors of death that I could almost have imagined that the dead was breathing as the wind stealing through the window just lifted the hair from the pillow. There was something almost holy in the expression of that loved countenance—the hair was brushed back from the broad smooth brow, the lids just closed as in gentle sleep while about the mouth hovered an expression of high resolve just softened into a peaceful smile. Never have I so realized the beauty of Bryant's words—

"Approach thy grave as one who wraps the drapery of his couch about him and lies down to pleasant dreams."—

as when looking upon this very embodiment of the sentiment. Dear Walter!—how I looked on those mute lips and thought of the gentle, kindly voice that should cheer us no more, on the closed eyes and remembered that never again should they look with their warm light upon us and those footsteps forever still with their familiar music. Oh!—it was hard, hard to think of giving him up in his glorious full flush of youth, in the full tide of honorable fame—hard to give him up who had been so true and dear a brother in the absence of those who had hitherto been all this to us. I know he died as he often expressed a wish to—the pang of death was short—his transition from time to eternity a quick one, and his summons found him at his post of duty gallantly defending the soil of his dearly loved state—nobly vindicating the cause to which he has devoted his every energy for the last two years. And in his death we have nothing painful to remember of his unworthiness and yet, oh! yet—all cannot reconcile us to giving him up so suddenly, so unexpectedly just as we had begun to believe that he bore a charmed life—that he was destined to the glorious making of being one of the deliverers of his country, of rescuing—name from oblivion. Dear boy!—how gratifying it was to see the universal respect and attention shown him—unaffected regret expressed by everyone at his loss—he was regarded by the mountain people as a kind of Sir William Wallace—his adventures and associations with them last summer when scouting endeared him to them so much—as indeed it did to everyone. There were persons present today who could have appeared upon almost any other occasion and, looking out of the windows I saw an old hoary bearded man sobbing like a very child as he stood under the trees in the yard. There were those present whom I suppose were never known to attend funerals before scarcely. Uncle

Mack, Jacquie, Mary and Eltie came down just before Mr. Berry arrived. Poor Aunt L. could not bear to see her poor dead boy and remained with Gussie at home. Mr. Berry read the 90th Psalm, sang and offered up a petition that strength might be granted the afflicted to bear up under the great sorrow. Then we went in to take our last leave, to press unheeded kisses upon the dear familiar features. I led little Mary by the hand and after she had kissed her poor brother took a spray of jessamines and rosebuds and gave her to keep as a memento—poor little thing!—she little comprehended all the great loss she had sustained. Cousin Sue Buck told me there would be a seat in the Rose Hill carriage for one of us if we wished to attend the dear boy to his last home. I persuaded Nellie to go knowing as I did that could he have had a wish upon the subject he would have said—"Let Pa, Jacquie, Uncle William, Nellie and Cousin Sue be there." —And it was just as he would have had it for very few others could go for want of conveyances. The coffin when carried out seemed to cast a shadow over the house which is lying there still—it seemed so lonely and sad when one knew he had crossed the threshold never to recross it again. Tonight I went into the parlor where the moonlight was lying on the floor just where he had been laid this morning and it seemed almost as if his gentle spirit had stolen back to brighten the old home with its presence.

Cousin Mary, Ed, William, Evred stayed with us today—the latter is here tonight—he gave us the full particulars of dear Walter's death.

> Lt. Walter Buck was in Company E., Seventh Virginia Cavalry Regiment, of the renowned Laurel Brigade, Colonel Ashby's old command. C. T. O'Ferrall, who is mentioned in the diary with Walter in Front Royal on scouting parties, was with him when he was killed. O'Ferrall became governor of Virginia and wrote a book Forty Years of Active Service in which he wrote, "On the march Lt. Walter Buck, of the Seventh Regiment, who had been delegated to gather forage for his regiment, joined and rode with me ... as we rode along chatting, we both expressed a desire to see home folks, but we concluded there was no chance unless we could get a wounded furlough, and we both expressed a willingness to receive a little wound so that we could see our loved ones. ... he wanted his in the leg so his arm would be free to embrace the girls who would greet him. –I decided to take mine in the arm, so that I would have my legs to get away on, in the event it became necessary in the Union country in which my home was located. All the time we could hear firing in front ... neither of us ever dreamed what terrible fortune to both was just ahead.
>
> "When we made the charge he was by my side in the front of the squadron. He was a tall, handsome young fellow, near

my age; he was well-mounted, and was a typical Southern cavalryman; he had been trained by Ashby the first year of the war, and had won his lieutenant's spurs by his chivalry and daring.

"I do not remember seeing him at the stone fence, but he was there, as attested by his dead body. I was told he saw me fall and started to me, when he was struck by a ball and instantly killed. So, as I have said, we both received wounds ... 'furlough wounds'; his wound furloughed him forever, mine for months; and almost eternally. His body was recovered and buried at home in Warren County, and on no mound should grass grow greener or roses bloom sweeter than upon his grave. He added a leaf to the laurel wreath of the Bucks, whose members of the Confederate army were many, everyone of whom was entitled to a medal of honor. It was most truly a family of fighters."

It seems that when the colonel became aware that a desperate struggle was intended feared for Walter's daring, impetuous spirit and detailed him to act upon some duty relating to the Q.M. department, thinking thus to detain him from the battlefield. But he could ill brook inglorious ease at such a time so he quickly transacted his business and took his place in the foremost rank. The enemy were overwhelming us with superior numbers—our men wavered and seemed upon the point of falling back —Walter cried out—"Boys, don't let them do so! Let's charge them back!" They swept on and just as they reached a yard belonging to the house of a Mr. Thomas, our poor boy fell pierced through the throat with a ball. He exclaimed when first struck—I'm a dead man!" His companions saw his horse give a few bounds and he reeled from his saddle just as they were forced to retreat before an overpowering number of the foe. His horse was found riderless after the fight all bloodstained but no trace could be discovered of Walter. At last the Yankees abandoned the battlefield and Monday evening while Cousin Will was looking for him he made inquiries at Mr. Thomas' and the ladies of the house told him a young Confederate lieutenant had been shot in their yard—that the Yankees said he was on General Stuart's staff but they thought his name was Buck. They had begged for his body but the Yankees refused their request and had buried him in the yard. Cousin W. opened the grave, recognized the body then covered it again and went away to procure a conveyance for it. He met Uncle Mack who had just gotten into Paris—informed him of the recovery and having procured a wagon returned to the place and proceeded to disinter the remains. The inhuman Yankees had robbed him of everything—Porte, Monnaic, papers, boots, clothing, arms, the little ring which he had worn until it seemed almost a part of himself, and even cut the buttons from his coat, after doing this they wrapped a blanket about him, scooped out a little hollow and covered him over. Dear, dear boy!—to think of his being subject to such indignities from such hands. And yet, he was unconscious of it all for he could not have lived many minutes after receiving the fatal wound and I'm glad he was spared the knowledge. There was a cut on his head but 'tis thought was inflicted by his falling on the sharp rock and not a saber cut. Oh, what would I not give to know what his last thoughts were when he knew that eternity with all its mysteries lay before his gaze, that the next hour all would be revealed to him, how I would like to know whether he had time for a thought for us all, whether he realized the fate which was his! But this is vain, vain!—he cannot come to us "Let us strive to go to him," and together decipher the mysteries that have so perplexed us here. Oh, if he could only have been happier here!—but he suffered as only such sensitive, passionate natures do. Suffered like the Spartan boy while the wolf gnawed at his vitals beneath his cloak. Dear boy, how often he has said that life was a valueless gift, how often has he asked "Lucie, what have I worth living for?" ... He had an insatiable yearning for tenderness and affection such as few men ever experience and with it a firm conviction of his own inability to win it that was touching to see.

But he is quaffing now, I humbly trust, the pure water from the fountain of Love, his restless, troubled spirit like the sea has grown quiet, tranquil in the smile of the Peace and Love and his repose is one of unbroken blessedness. We all can remember his having expressed his unshaken trust in a merciful God, his resignation of his will—and this more than anything on earth has consoled us in our great sorrow—'tis a blessed, blessed knowledge.

Nellie and Father did not return till late—Jule met them at the burying grounds. Cousin Will with us and a Mr. Carter, a wounded soldier.

Dear Walter—a lonely slumber will be your's tonight—all with the silent dead, but you will not heed—'twould be all the same to you were it the snowdrifts instead of this soft moonlight that mantles your grave. Your head does not ache as mine does now and you have not dreary, heavy sorrow at your heart. Poor Aunt Letitia!—what a sad, sad night for her. And Dick, poor boy—I cannot bear to think of the blow that must soon fall upon him in this sad knowledge.

June 24, 1863

Nellie and I spent the morning gathering up and putting carefully away all our little mementos of the little lost brother—the letters, locks of hair, and flowers, and trying to recall his every look and gesture in his last visits to us. It seems so very lonely now, as if a greater part of the family was gone. Ah me!—I scarcely feel an interest in any news from the army now at all, with Walter's death has died my interest for his branch of the service to a great degree.

Wrote Irvie an account of poor Walter's death—poor fellow!—how it will distress him to hear it.

June 25, 1863

Was in the garden entwining white roses and thinking that I never should see one of a lily or jessamine without thinking of that flower-strewn bier, when Laura handed me a letter from Nannie Taylor. It had just arrived by mail. Dear Nannie!—how sadly she writes. My heart aches for her in her sore distress and we are indeed sisters in affliction. There was also a letter from Irving. Poor fellow! He writes so gleefully, little dreaming of the shadow that has fallen over us all.

How much I've been thinking of that lonely grave of poor Walter's lying out in all this dreary rain and cold—just as if he were conscious of it, dear boy.

June 30, 1863

Writing. Uncle Tom returned from Richmond yesterday and came over quite early. Says he saw poor Dick at Hanover Junction and told him all—that he was deeply grieved and said he would willingly have laid down his life for Walter—poor dear fellow! Oh, if he could just come home now! Says he wants to do so but does not think he will be able to get off. The boys are reported all well but badly off for clothing.

Poor Walter, buried but one short week and yet seemingly absent a long, long year.

July 3, 1863

Father told us at breakfast this morning that he had heard through a cavalryman from a part of our servants—Mahala and her children had been captured—he was ordered to guard them with some thirty others as far as Green Castle, Penn. She recognized in him a young man who had lived in town, made herself known to him—said she wished she was back in her home, that 'twas a good one and that now she had spent all her money and was without food and had no one to provide for her. The children next she said—crying and in great distress. Poor things! I feel sorry for them because they are the innocent sufferers by their mother's folly and I'm afraid this will only be the commencement of their suffering. The men had all been sent to Richmond to work on fortifications.... nothing was known of Harriet and her clique.

Father was riding to the Mountain and invited me to accompany him. Did not care to go but he seemed to wish it and I accompanied him with Ma. My horse was a delightful one and the ride was charming. Ascending the mountain through a wild, solitary road dark and cool in the shadows of the overarching trees I for the first time in my life heard the wood robin—there was something almost supernaturally sweet in the liquid, flute like notes that seemed to ripple down from the hills upon us. It was perfect to be out in the woods once more, careless whether or not the fire was burning in the kitchen—riding along on a freely ambling pony, breathing the fragrant, spicy breath of the woods, listening to the soft murmuring flow of the brooks way down the mountain side and to the rustling leaves and the many birds. We went to Mrs. Fox's—dismounted at the old spring under the cherry trees and quaffed the clear, ice-cold water that bubbled up from their roots. Mrs. F. came down and invited us up to the house—found everything looking cool, clean and sweet about it. Presently Father proposed that we should go about fifty yards from the door to gather raspberries from a mass of bushes that grew by the fence—we went but 'twas so intensely warm, and the place presented such a tempting rendezvous for serpents that we were afraid to venture where the ripest fruits were to be found. Father, with two soldiers—boarding at Mrs. F.'s sat under the shade at the spring all day, and Ma and I in the parlor. I was thinking so much all the time of dear Walter for here was the scene of his adventures last summer. Every foot of ground passed over in the morning, every rock and shrub and tree seemed in some way associated with him—indeed there's scarcely one of them that were not intimately known to him I'm sure, dear boy. We left about three o'clock and rode on down to Uncle Mack's—Walter's route again—where we dismounted—found all well as usual but sad, Aunt L. looked so badly, poor thing. Gussie immediately after my arrival took me into her Ma's room to show me her precious mementoes of "Dear brother Walter"—his account book, little bosom pin, lock of hair, tiny fiddle and keys, checquer board, etc., etc. Poor little thing! I never saw a child so deeply grieved in my life—there's nothing noise or obtrusive about it but she just sits or stands with averted head while the tears flowed silently down her cheeks and she could scarcely speak for the tears. I won her into the yard to show me the flowers and still he was her theme—"Poor brother Walter admired this so much"—"Brother Walter tied this up" and "The last time I saw dear brother Walter here" etc., etc., poor child. The clouds were so threatening that we were forced to return home earlier than we had intended. Reached home to tea. No news—no mail.

July 5, 1863
Jacquie came in the evening on his return from Grafton, brought with him the daguerreotypes of Richard and poor Walter which Eve had in her possession. Poor dear Walter!—how natural was the picture representing him in full military equipment looking so spirited, so careless and grateful just as I've seen him times innumerable.

Jacquie tells me Cousin S. Buck will go to W. in a few days to have a copy taken of it and I've requested her through him to get one for me. It will be such a treasure. Dick's also is good but not so spirited as Walter's. Hope some times to have both.

July 6, 1863
Uncle Mack called in about dusk to take a luncheon and told us of a battle fought at Gettysburg, Pennsylvania—a desperate conflict not at all decisive but resulting in heavy losses on both sides—feel very anxious

as to the particulars of the struggle.

On July 1, 1863, General Heth's division of A. P. Hill's corps started for Gettysburg to obtain shoes for his men. Lee had heard that the Federals were north of the Potomac but he was not sure of their exact location. His "Eyes," the cavalry under Stuart, had not been heard from since the start of the ride around the enemy. Lee had begun to concentrate his forces but felt he should avoid a major battle before his entire army was up into position. Heth met strong opposition on July 1, 1863, but the III Corps with aid from Ewell's approaching corps, drove the enemy back and captured Gettysburg. The routed Federals retreated to the higher ground south of the town. The Confederates did not press their victory.

Gen. J. E. B. Stuart made contact with Lee on July 1. The enemy had already been located, the battle was on. Longstreet's corps arrived that night and on July 2 and July 3 of 1863, the high ground was stormed and the Confederate attacks were repulsed. On July 4, 1863, the Confederates prepared for an attack by Meade, U.S.A., who had taken over the Army of the Potomac from Hooker. The attack never came. Lee was stopped but his ground gained on the first day was his. July 5, 1863, found Lee's army in retreat bound for Virginia.

U.S.A.	C.S.A.
Effectives 88,289	Effectives 75,000
Killed 3,155	Killed 3,903
Wounded 14,529	Wounded 18,735
Missing 5,365	Missing 5,425

The greatest battle ever fought in America was over.

Six Confederate generals were killed or mortally wounded, three captured, and eight wounded. Armistead, Barksdall, Dale, Garnett, Pender, Pettigrew, and Semmes were the generals killed or mortally wounded. These men and the others that had already fallen were hard to replace. The South was running out of trained military leaders.

Ma and the children came in late. Mr. Berry just before ten o'clock brought confirmation of Uncle Mack's news and the additional intelligence of Corse's brigade having been ordered into Maryland. Heaven forbid it!—for Pickett's division is said to have suffered severely in this last battle.

July 8, 1863

The Warren Rifles was Company B of the Seventh Virginia Infantry Regiment of Corse's Brigade, Pickett's Division.

Corse's brigade left Gordonsville, on July 8, 1863 and began its march to and down the Valley to join the rest of Lee's army. The march took them via Madison's Courthouse and on the tenth of July they began the ascent of the Blue Ridge. The brigade left Luray on the eleventh and bivouacked on the night of July 11, 1863, at McCoy's Ford above Front Royal. Many of Lucy's friends in the Warren Rifles were permitted to visit home, but by the thirteenth the brigade was at Middletown. The march ended at Winchester where the particulars of the Battle of Gettysburg were learned. The brigade remained in Winchester until July 20 when they moved south toward Front Royal. On July 21 the brigade became engaged in the defense of Manassas Gap where it fought gallantly and helped to push back the Federal regulars.

Very pleasant. Grandma and Aunt B. spent the day in town. Looked all day for Father but he did not come. All sitting on the porch after tea when Uncle Mack came in to say Victor and Charlie Brown were at home and brought news that the Warren Rifles would all be in tomorrow en route to rejoin their division in Pennsylvania. Our joy was too deep for words mingled though it was with sadness with the thought of meeting poor Dick again. Feel so nervous and excited at the thought of their coming.

July 9, 1863

Uncle Tom came over in the afternoon and brought some papers and a letter for me from Benton—written some time since, though—on the eighteenth—had been sick. Irvie was well. No news excepting that he had been promoted to the colonelcy. We were sitting in the door after tea when Dick rode through the gate. Poor fellow!—how he struggled to be calm and how thin and pale and sad he looked. After sitting a few moments on the porch where his pa had just come, he got up and went into Grandma's room and we followed him. Then he commenced talking over his great loss and wept so sorrowfully. Lifting up his head he said "Well, I would have given my life a willing sacrifice for his!" It seemed a relief to talk . . . tragically and he continued with us till sometime after his father left—so 'twas nearly dark when he left promising to return tomorrow. We watched him ride off from the stile as we had seen him do hundreds of times before but missed that other familiar form that was wont to accompany him. Had a note from Father by an old gentleman—a traveler in search of his nephew killed in battle. Father will be home tomorrow. Says Uncle Larue has been very ill. Dick says Scott's in town. Wonder if we shall see him. All have furloughed till Sunday morning.

Anniversary of our trip to Camp Pickens at Manassas—two years ago.

July 10, 1863

Worked very hard this warm morning. Was almost exhausted when about four o'clock in the afternoon they sent me word that Scott was in the parlor. Made a hasty toilette and went down to see him. He looks thin and pale, poor fellow!—could only remain a few moments as they had just secured orders to report at the McCoy's Ford about six miles distant this evening. It really distressed me his visit so short and unsatisfactory and I almost wished he had not come at all—pleasure though it was to see him again. How disconnectedly he talked and how fitful his manner—no wonder though when he was so hurried.

While discussing the unpleasant news of the fall of Vicksburg (which by the way, we didn't believe) Father came in quite tired and with headache.

> Vicksburg fell to Grant July 4, 1863, after many weeks of siege. The Mississippi River was now in Northern hands, and the South was split in half. Grant's large army could be released to other areas.

Told us he had seen Uncle John—heard nothing from servants and went no further than Berryville—heard Cousin Tom and Sandy Buck were dangerously wounded and John Johnson, Rush Lacy and Charlie Henry were killed. Poor fellows! Poor fellows! Oh we are but just beginning to realize the terrors of this rain of anarchy much as we have hitherto suffered. The boys on leaving promised to see us tomorrow before starting. Gave Father his tea and then while he was unpacking his saddle pockets Mr. Berry came in but remained only a short time. Uncle John has sent me a new calico dress, a perfect beauty—so neat and clean—'tis very kind of him. Laura and I attended by Lucie took a bath in the creek tonight down under the willow trees. Ah, me! I'm so distressed about the boys.

July 11, 1863

Finished my work quite early this morning so as to be ready for dear Dick when he should come. Uncle Mack was soon here but we waited some time for Dick. Meantime Uncle Mack gave me a letter to read—one from Colonel Marshall to him giving him an account of poor Walter's death and paying such a tribute to his excellence as a patriot, and Christian boy. Oh, it gives me such pleasure to know that others besides ourselves, who, though they did not know him as we did, yet appreciated his sterling worth and loved him. Poor Dick struggled bravely with his feelings and strove while with us to talk and appear cheerful. He was with us about an hour and then bade us farewell with brimming eyes and husky voice. Dear, dear boy, it seemed like giving him up as we had never done before. We went on the house to watch for them as far as we could see them. Ma and Father went to church. Nellie and I stood on the house watching Dick, Jacquie, Uncle Mack, Scott, Smith and Gus Tyler as they rode out ot town—it seemed exactly as it did the morning the Warren Rifles left the first time for the seat of war—more like it than at any time before.

July 12, 1863
Raining. Busy all the morning—had a note from Cousin E. Cloud making a request relative to dear Walter's uniform—answered it and complied with her wish—we've three buttons and the two shoulder straps as mementoes of our dear soldier's services to his country.

Reading a *Harper* of sixty-three which Father brought home with him—quite a novelty these times and interesting from that very fact. Never saw it rain harder than it has done all day. Wonder what will be the effect upon Lee's army should the streams rise—Father is evidently uneasy about it and we are all perfectly miserable tonight with thinking of our poor boys sent off like sheep to the slaughter—going with such sad hearts, thinking of our gallant army perhaps hemmed in by high waters in the enemy's country subject to such tremendous disadvantages—of the confirmed news of the fall of Vicksburg which Mr. Berry brought this evening, and the rumor that Grant successful in that quarter, was advancing on Richmond.

> *Lee's army braced for attack by Meade north of the Potomac. The river was high because of the recent rains. The Federals failed to attack in strength and the Confederate army returned to Virginia July 13 and 14.*

Everything seems dark and threatening, yet I will not despair but commit our cause to His hand who "out of chaos" brings forth order.

July 13, 1863
Old Governor Smith called by this evening to see Father on business —was just from Md. and stated that the army was in status quo and did not seem to apprehend any dangers from the rise of the waters at all. So glad! Repaired Father's stock.

VII

RETREAT

July 16, 1863 - June 19, 1864

July 17, 1863
Rumors of our army falling back this side the Potomac. Don't believe it though.

July 18, 1863
Anniversary of the Battle of Bull Run. Working very hard cleaning up etc., etc. Many soldiers here in the afternoon for milk. Can't help but feel a little anxious as to Lee's army. What can it have crossed the Potomac for? Perhaps 'tis a feint.

July 19, 1863
Our army is certainly all on this side the Potomac. What can be the cause of it I wonder—so sorry. And we'll not have Baltimore after all. Wonder when Mr. Morton will get to Boston. Willie Buck's come home.

Father came in in the afternoon and told us Corse's brigade would be through town either this evening or tomorrow morning—the pontoons were already over the river. Delightful rumors in town to the effect that the Yankees are at Chester's Gap and will certainly be in town ere long. Don't credit a word of the report.

Heard of the grand anti-conscription riot in New York. Nemesis is awakening.

> Three hundred to five hundred people died in New York City in antidraft riots on July 13 and 14. Negroes were beaten to death and buildings set on fire. Troops from Gettysburg

were rushed to the area.

July 21, 1863

Anniversary of the great Manassas Battle. Corse's brigade commenced arriving quite early—about half past nine o'clock. I went over with the children to shop to see the Seventeenth. Met there with Willie Buck. The Seventeenth was next to the rear regiment in the brigade and as they filed by us I felt as if they were somehow dearer to us than those who had preceded them albeit I saw not a familiar face in the regiment—not one save the "Warren Rifles" and but one or two there—poor worn, dirty fellows. While trying to distinguish some familiar countenance I heard a "Hello, Lu! Where's Nell?" Turning about who should I see but dear Dick, dusty and bronzed with the sun. My hand was again grasped and this time 'twas Smith Turner whom I've not seen for a year. They were so hurried that they could only exchange greetings with us and say they hoped to remain near and see us again after a little and then off they went. I never shall forget how disappointed I felt when they ran on to rejoin their regiment and I saw their receding figures gradually lose themselves in the throng of martial forms. I looked after the regiment as long as it could be seen through tears and then we turned and retraced our steps homeward. All the forenoon there came rumors of the advance of the Yankees into town. Father came in about noon and told us the Seventeenth had engaged the enemy near Mr. Armistead's and 'twas reported they were surrounded and would be captured unless Pickett's division, which was expected, should arrive in time to relieve them. We were quite anxious and restless listening for the discharge of musketry which was ever and anon heard and wishing so much we could only know our poor boys were safe.

The division came in about four o'clock and we soon ascertained 'twas as well with our friends in the Seventeenth that they had succeeded in repulsing a body much larger than their own, of dismounted cavalry—old U. S. regulars. Huzzah!—bless our glorious Seventeenth!—how they have longed ever since the war for a brush with the foe in the Valley and near their homes and now that wish has been gratified they've whipped them bravely and well and now they no doubt feel more exultant than they've ever yet felt after a miniature battle. 'Twas said General Longstreet passed through town and about five o'clock one of his aides, Colonel Sorrell called to inquire if the general had stopped here—said he had expected he would have done so. A little later Major Latrobe's groom came in with the major's horses to be stabled for the night but still too—shall I say it?—my disappointment ... they didn't come. We had scores of soldiers though begging for milk, bread and every imaginable article of food—poor fellows—I wish our ability to serve them only equalled our will. Had quite a laugh at Nellie's excuse for her inquiries for Mr. Macauley. Certainly induced some of his comrades who were here, to believe that he was a very near and dear friend. Poor fellow!—we learned that he is badly wounded and in the enemy's hands. I think of his impressive farewell to us and wonder if it were ominous. Just as we were washing the last cup and saucer after tea who should walk in but old Major Moses, General Longstreet's "aide" who was here last fall. What a cordial, jolly old soul he is—how warmly he greeted us and recalled every little incident of his short sojourn here. Have just been sitting in the porch watching the cordon of campfires blazing on the brow of the hill and listening to his account of the incidents of the Gettysburg affair. He explained to us the probable object of this rapid falling back of all our Army of the Potomac. Says he thinks the Valley will be deserted by our troops but does not think we will suffer any from the incursions of the enemy. Says that the desire of both the Confederate and Federal army seems to be to reach the line of railroads between here and Richmond—that the two armies are running a race, that Meade has sent a detachment of Union troops to hold these mountain passes just long enough to detain our men till he shall have accomplished his object, but as we have the advantage of the shortest routes and have possession of one of the passes—"Chester's Gap"—he thinks we will be before them. It does grieve me so to think that we are to be left unprotected again so soon just as we had begun to feel secure once more too—however, if General Lee so orders it, of course 'tis all right and we've nothing to do but await results.

It is now nine o'clock at night and I'm almost broken down with running to and fro waiting on the soldiers. Poor fellows, I don't mind this though as long as we've anything for them. The last squad of applicants have just departed and I must confess one of them provoked me not a little when I told him we had just given away the last bits of bread and would not be able to get them supper as we had but little help—our servants being all gone and he thereupon replied—"Ah, well—that's always the case, we can't expect you ladies to trouble yourselves in providing for us. Were your servants here I should insist upon having my supper gotten at any rate." That too after I've been doing my very utmost to minister to their wants! Well I suppose there are some unreasonable ones in every army.

Dear Walter! This day one month ago—how I've thought of it.

July 22, 1863

Was awakened by hearing Nellie called up to supply the soldiers with milk this morning, but what chagrin was ours when as we were dressing Father came in and told us the dairy had been broken into and robbed of everything except the jars and little Britania cream pitcher. Here was a predicament, a large family with guests in the house and not a drop of cream for coffee or ounce of butter for breakfast. Laura thought some could be procured of Aunt Bettie and started off upon a foraging expedition while we proceeded to clean up and get breakfast. Just before the meal was ready she returned with dress draggled in dew and laughing heartily—said she had passed through a whole brigade, infantry, artillery, baggage wagons and cattle in going to town, and coming back had discovered a soldier in the middle of the field below the house paying his respects to our large cream jar, which lay there half empty. She demanded it as her property—he yielded very meekly saying he had found it there not knowing where it came from, and she hid it well; we could send for it. Uncle Gilbert, too, soon came in bringing a missing crock and plate. We had a number of soldiers to breakfast; Mr. Moore, a courier of General Longstreet's—old acquaintance of Dick Buck's and a young artillery man from Richmond—an invalid. I was quite sick all the morning and 'twas with great difficulty I succeeded in getting through my work. Had to go to bed finally. Meantime Mr. Berry and Captain Marshall came in—the latter having just made a narrow escape through the deception practiced by the Yankees upon his children. Was feeling a little better when Nellie rushed up to my room bidding me "Get right up" for a servant of General Longstreet's had just come in and said the general and staff were to be here in a little while. This information was a powerful tonic and restorative. I dressed myself and then Ma came to tell me Mr. Herbert, my kitchen acquaintance, was here and had a surprise for me. Going down we found him with a friend Mr. Stone. They sat a couple of hours chatting most pleasantly, telling us anecdotes of their sojourn in Yankeedom. They are my ideal of the genial frank Southron—are well educated, refined and polished in their manners—don't know when I've seen two more agreeable gentlemen. By the way, O what a beautiful face Mr. Herbert has!—eyes like liquid violet and sunshine. They heard cannonading and thinking was perhaps their batteries they took a cordial leave and departed. We were sitting waiting for a summons to dinner when Dick dashed up the stile—he disclaimed against dismounting declaring he had but two hours leave and must go immediately home for his clothes. Poor fellow!—what joy it was to welcome him back from the battlefield and hear him tell the news from the fight. He says Scott Roy is prisoner—can't say I regret it, for he is at least safe and it may be the cause of preventing his being in a more dangerous engagement and perhaps shot. The Seventeenth acquitted itself gloriously being for the greater part of the fight unsupported and opposed to thrice its number. Dick was soon off again and we went to dinner—still no General Longstreet.

A little after four o'clock the boys went over to town to see General Lee who was expected in and Father down to the river to see the pontoon bridges. Presently one of the little children ran in to say Father was returning with General Longstreet. It proved, however, to be General Lee with his staff. They dismounted, some of them walked out under the shade of the aspens, some went to look at little Frank asleep in his wagon under the trees and the general with his chief and one or two others took his seat on the porch. Father stepped to the door and called Nellie and me and introduced us to him. The old gentleman greeted us heartily with such a warm, fatherly manner and then turning introduced us to his staff one by one. He then said to me—"Won't you sit down, my daughter and let us talk some?" I laid my hand on a chair standing near in compliance but he made room for me on the seat by him and said "No, not there, but here close by me." When I was seated I told him how much pleasure it gave me to see our defender—the Father of our State—he replied—"Oh, no! my daughter. I only wish he were more worthy of being seen. There! Look at those young Rebels (pointing to his staff) they're a great deal better worth your looking at—gallant young beaux that they are." They asked for a Rebel song and Nellie and I played and sang for the first time since dear Walter's death—the excitement and embarrassment caused a great difference in our singing, I knew. General L. wished to know if we were not afraid to let those treasonable songs resound beneath our roof such as the "War Chant of Defiance." They remained but a short time and just as they were leaving the old gentleman hoped we might not be troubled much more by our enemies and bade Nellie and me by all means not to "let any of those fine young Yankee officers carry us off." We replied that we depended upon him to prevent such a possibility. Before leaving he enriched Nellie's autograph book and mine with his name at the same time protesting that he knew we would much prefer having our sweethearts' there rather than his. Dear old General!—how I've always admired and loved him, but what a filial reverence mingles with that feeling now and how much more the father than the general he seems. How his hair is silvered and his brow marked with thought and care, yet what a noble, benevolent spirit looks forth from his brown eyes. What an air of dignity about his every movement. General Chilton was with him looking very natural.

> *After the war General Robert E. Lee wrote Lucy in answer to a letter and sent her a button from his uniform. These items are now on display in the museum in Front Royal.*

He told us that Major Peyton had gone by another route which accounted for his not being with them.

Indeed I've had my feeling so wrought upon today that I've almost wished I had no heart. To see the poor fellows coming in worn and weary and with tears in their eyes begging for something to eat. We had tried to provide for such demands, but where hundreds were coming in, 'twas impossible. Even now they are still coming late as it is.

We've a guard for the garden tonight. General Lee says we've good news from Charleston—he having received a dispatch from General Beauregard stating the repulse of the enemy at that point.

No General Longstreet. Well, never mind—who cares? A. P. Hill's corps came in today—Ewell's tomorrow—wonder if we'll see any of our friends.

July 23, 1863

Received two long letters—one from Irvie to Ma and one from Cousin Mack to Nellie and me. They were at Chattanooga whither Bragg had retreated. Irvie writes in bad spirits, attributable to some very hard traveling through rain, some unpleasant indefinite skirmishing and a deprivation of his accustomed creature comforts—and the society of his lady friend. These letters were dated the seventh but Mrs. Roy sent one of the fifteenth and one of the sixteenth from Benton in which he stated—that they were "just ordered to Jackson, Miss."—so there's no knowing where they are now. Scott Roy passed the road early this morning leading a horse which he had just captured. Father saw and talked with him and learned that last night while they were encamped near Linden he rolled himself through his guards, found a horse worth $1,000 and decamped but the owner of the horse awoke just as he was leaving and he quietly left the horse and went on till he found another horse near the outposts which he possessed himself of—taking a route directly opposite to the one he intended pursuing, traveled all night and had just arrived. Oh, I'm so glad!

> *Scott Roy was a member of the Warren Rifles, Company B, Seventeenth Virginia Infantry Regiment. He was captured during the action at Chester's Gap and escaped on July 22. This same account of Scott's escape is described in* History of the Seventeenth Virginia Infanty, C.S.A. *by George Wise.*

We had numbers of cavalrymen to dinner—among them young Holman who was here last spring.

Early this afternoon we heard heavy musket firing in the direction of "Green Hill"—we had heard that Scott Roy had brought from the army some important information with regards to the Yankees and that General Stuart had gone up to see him about it. Scott had sent over for a saddle to accompany Gen. S. on a reconnaissance. So we at once concluded that Gen. S. had gone with the detachment of his command and attempted to surround and capture the part of Yankees at Linden. The firing continued pretty regularly all the afternoon. We went upon the house after tea to see an artillery and cavalry encampment in the field above Johnston Lakes. While Ma and the children were still up there the position of the troops was shifted and a piece opened fire on the left below where they had been previously. They all scampered downstairs thinking this but the opening of the ball but presently a couple of General Wright's staff officers came and we all went upon the house together. There we could distinctly see the flash of the cannon, see the smoke, and see the shell when it exploded—could see the troops moving about the pieces. We at once concluded the Yankees were forcing a passage through the Gap there and that our forces would oppose it to the bitter end, that we would have a general engagement during the next twenty-four hours.

We saw General Johnston's division marching in that direction and a battalion of artillery went by the house toward the scene of action. But toward dusk the firing gradually ceased and now all is calm—the calm that precedes the storm, I'm thinking. Broken-down soldiers are still coming in although it is now nine o'clock at night—some just from the fight. Poor fellows, poor fellows!—my heart aches for them. Father, I'm afraid will not sleep much tonight for we have just heard that General Johnston's division will pass us and unless there is someone to keep watch the garden will be destroyed. Poor fellows! I wouldn't blame them much for it because they've marched from Bunker Hill this far without anything at all to eat. I verily believe though we fed two Yankee spies who came in character of Confederate soldiers—they were in citizens dress and professed to have "run the blockade from Maryland and just come to join our army." Don't believe a word of it though. Well, Ewell's corps has come in—the last one, so I suppose we've no troops north of us now but Jones' brigade which is said to be at the river. Mr. Morton did not call either—I thought he would have done so particularly as Johnston's division is so near.

July 24, 1863

We were awakened several times in the night by soldiers passing through the yard some inquiring directions, some begging refreshments. General Johnston himself was down in the hill and he and Father rode out to select a site for an encampment. There was firing too about 11 o'clock at night. We expected to be awakened by cannonading this morning but nothing unusual occurred so soon. From the constant rolling of wagons last night and the scarcity of troops this morning we were inclined to believe there was some important movement on hand. There were soldiers in for breakfast before we were dressed and from that time forth. Just as we had gathered up the breakfast things to wash they came to say Scott was here. We went on the porch where he was sitting, found him looking very well and just his own kind, cheerful self. He gave quite an amusing account of his capture, how the officers in command treated him so well taking him into their tent and giving him the most delicate bits for his breakfast. How he told Major Hazeltein that he was going to escape and invited him to call at his father's when they came to Front Royal. What a boy he is to be sure!—to think of his having taken leave of his fellow captives and guard not long before he left and then having come out scatheless. I really did enjoy the hour he spent with us—there are some persons whose mere presence exhilirates us as mine is said to do—and 'tis very seldom the case that I do not feel happier and better from his visits unless 'tis the regret at his departure mars it. He spoke something of leaving for Luray this evening but as his going seemed doubtful we expected to see him again before he left. He had been gone but a little while when old Mr. Marshall came in and while the old gentleman was sitting on the porch talking, our men were thrown into line of battle on the hill just south of town, skirmishers thrown out, videttes stationed and in a little while the irregular discharge of musketry was heard on the hill near Dr. Turner's which was quickly followed by the opening of a battery upon the hill south of the place. It was very exciting, very exhilirating, too much so to permit of our remaining in the basement where Ma and Grandma carried the children and even they remained there but a short time. Some of the bullets and shells passed near enough to whisper some confidential messages to us. The firing continued about three quarters of an hour, then gradually ceased. Then some of the cavalrymen who had been stationed in our orchard, came in. Next we saw the line of infantry on the hill move off and the cavalry from the surrounding hills gallop off toward the river and a few moments after—while our videttes were yet on the hill by Rose Hill the Yankee cavalry dashed into town. A few shots were exchanged without any effect on either side. They only pursued our men a short distance. Captured but two of them while we took three of their's. There was a brigade of infantry in town all day—Yankee General Jones' brigade was on the opposite side of the river and there our cavalry retired—the remainder of our army went on up to Luray. There were but two of the Yankee wretches on the premises and they were infantry who called at the pump to get water. There were nondescripts in the yard this afternoon—professing to be Confederates who were cut off from their regiments and dressed partly in Confederate uniforms—but I never should believe they were anything but Yankee spies—they carried the mark of Cain in their faces. Very soon Uncle Tom came in and told us they had committed few, if any, depredations in town. Had taken Colonel Jacob's meat, searched a few houses, etc., etc. But they went into Mr. Cook's, saw Giles at the dinner table, learned he was a soldier, yet never attempted to molest him. They went to the hospital, and though they cursed the poor wounded and sick who were unable to move, they didn't take one prisoner nor parole one of them. They went to Rose Hill though by a traitor, who had been there the day General Wright stopped there and professed to be one of his men. They took off her only two horses, leaving one sore-footed one in their stead at the instance of a former acquaintance of the family who happened to be with them. Took all her meat excepting four pieces, searched the house and behaved most insultingly. They went to Dr. Dorsey's, near which place the fight occurred and stripped him of everything—all his horses, save one which happened to be in town, all the cows, sheep, hogs, poultry, destroyed his garden, stole everything they could lay hands on and even went to the basket of newly washed clothes and took Ginnie Jones' nightdress which they put on and told Mrs. D. they intended tearing them up for towels. There was one of our wounded soldiers there whom they dragged into the yard and threatened to kill before her eyes, but she cried and begged them not and they at length desisted. There was a poor man living near there—Kenney by name, who had a number of children—they went to his house, cut up the furniture, tore every stitch of clothing save what they had on at the time, destroyed all his garden, leaving him nothing but the roof and walls of his house. This was their mode of proceeding wherever their steps led, we would all in town no doubt have shared the same fate had they not been in a great haste and fear all the time. Mr. B. says we lost about 150 killed and wounded Thursday evening and the Yankees from three to five hundred. One of their captured officers declared that one of our shells exploding in their midst killed thirteen and wounded fifty of their men at one time.

'Tis such a lovely quiet moonlit night and very difficult to realize that our fiendish foes are couched in their lairs a few hundred yards distant ready at the first signal to spring upon their prey. Oh, dear! Such vicissitude! One day in the very heart of our army the next abandoned in the hands of the Yankees. Would like to understand the movement of the troops today. Scott made his escape, but lost his horse by one of our own men.

July 25, 1863

All quiet, Yankees non est. Two soldiers came in this morning in Confederate uniforms—we at first suspected them but they showed us their credentials till we were convinced they were the genuine Simon Pures—members of the Fourth Georgia Regiment cut off from their commands. One of them wrote a letter to his mother while here and left if with Father to mail. This is one of the most unpleasant phases of our present situation, we cannot distinguish friend from foe and ten chances to one if you aid a poor distressed looking soldier today tomorrow he will return at the head of a band of ruffians to murder and plunder you. This evening just before tea a little Yankee strolled into the yard—gun in hand took his seat by the pump where Father was and commenced a stupid conversation. He was left behind by his comrades yesterday—so he says—I believe he's a "decoy" nothing more nor less. Father gave him no encouragement and finally succeeded in ridding himself of so unwelcome a guest. Wonder which it will be next—Yankee or Confederate or a mixture of both. Rained hard this evening.

July 26, 1863

Pleasant. Father carried some milk over to the hospital and brought back a favorable report concerning the patients there. He learned too from conversation something of the purport of the fight on Friday. It seems that Meade's whole army was just below the Ridge and he had thrown them forward to intercept Ewell, cut him off from the main body of our army, compelled him to fight here under great disadvantages and after defeating him going on and whipping our army in details—the vanguard of his army was the portion that advanced on Friday to capture our pontoons and baggage trains—but they were moved on Thursday night which accounts for all that stir and rolling of wagons which we heard. Had Meade been one day earlier, had Ewell been a day later, had our generals been less prompt and energetic, our gallant Stonewall Corps must have been compelled to fight ten to one and defeated and cut off, our baggage trains lost, our pontoons captured and our little valley and village the seat of a deadly struggle and destructive conflict. Thank Heaven for so miraculous an escape. Our men accomplished on Friday all they intended. They held those mountain passes and kept the enemy at bay till our army was safely distant—and then made good their own escape. 'Twas a masterly movement—that escape—executed in a very Jackson-like manner.

Father dined at Oakley—spent a quiet pleasant evening, had passed over the battlefield of Thursday, saw numbers of our poor dead yet unburied, says the track of the battle can be traced for several miles by the earth plowed up by shot and shell, dead horses, broken guns and equipages of every description.

Jones' brigade crossed at McKay's ford yesterday and has gone to join the army at Luray. So we shall see none of the boys.

July 29, 1863

Last night we were awakened by the arrival of Sallie, our new cook, with her two little children. Like her appearance very much, she seems accommodating and pleasant. Experienced quite a sense of relief in view of this assistance. Mrs. Marshall and Miss Betty in about noon to borrow the spyglass. No news. Rained this evening.

August 1, 1863

Concluded to go to Clover Hill this morning as nothing could be learned of Estie excepting that he was very sick. Borrowed Mr. Hope's horse, took Carey as escort and set forth. Met Henry Buck who told us the Yankees were coming into town. He was on his way to Linden to rejoin his company. Arrived about 11 o'clock after a warm but pleasant ride—received a hearty welcome and was surprised to find them all in such good spirits until they told me how much better was Estie. Went up to see him. He looked sadly emaciated and bore marks of suffering but was better than could have been expected. Miss Julia, Jane, Robbie, and Annie Ford were there and Cousin Sam Buck came in to dinner. Spent the day almost entirely in Estie's room, keeping off the flies and talking, poor little fellow!—he held my hand when I was bidding him good-bye and said "Oh, Cousin Lucie, don't go, I thought you'd come to stay a long while with us." They urged me most earnestly to remain but I left just an hour before sunset. Felt a little nervous about riding the five miles all alone save with Carey as protector and so many soldiers passing and repassing. However, we met with no untoward accident and reached town just at dusk. Cousin Mary was standing at Captain Roy's gate and called me to tell me that Mrs. Roy expected to break up housekeeping and going to make refuge within our lines—and that they would have to leave too—but I hope they'll take boarding somewhere else for I should miss her so much.

August 9, 1863

Very sultry tonight. Took Evred and Frank down to the creek this evening and let them have a play in the water, they looked like little cupids—so white and plump they looked under the shade of the trees. They've been talking so much about robbers and mad dogs tonight—from all accounts both are very rife. These same robbers may prove very formidable annoyances. I'm afraid there is quite a number of them—deserters from both armies, armed to the teeth, who have taken up an asylum in the mountain fastnesses from whence they descend upon unprotected farm houses, plunging the wilds. Several of them were captured the other day among whom was the leader and a young female in masculine apparel. This captain represents himself as a Mississippian—our men have opened negotiations with the lawless band proposing that they shall give themselves up to justice in order to save their chief from death—otherwise he will suffer the extreme penalty of the law. Of course, though, they will never have the generosity to do that. Wonder what will be the next phase which this state of society will assume.

August 10, 1863

At the creek put Evered in to "swim" and then all walked up to the house where we had a merry game of "puss-in-the-corner" with the children in the front yard, then a song in the parlor and then it was dark enough and Armanda had come over we all adjourned to the creek where we would have had a delicious bath but the timidity of Julia and Eliza who were frightened almost to death at the lightning, the shooting stars and a mysterious noise heard among the sticks on the bank. Laura, Lucie, and I escorted them a part of the way home and have but just returned in a fine glow.

August 20, 1863

Mack went to sleep in his chair in the front porch and Jule and I tied him fast with our handkerchiefs. Had quite a hairdressing experience in the evening—Mack officiating as "coiffureur"—had music till tea time and after tea we strolled through the shrubbery in the front yard, Mack and I having quite a philosophical discussion. Such a walk as we had home over the hill literally wading through the tall, tangled grass and weeds! I think I satisfied Mack that he has found his brown-eyed beautiful ideal. He has had us playing and singing for him since the first moment we came into the house—is trying to learn to sing bass. Beautiful moonlight night.

August 21, 1863

Day appointed by our president for national fasting and humiliation. We all decided to observe it.

August 25, 1863

Was lying on the bed about dark trying to get some relief from my miserable toothache when a hard rap at the door was followed by Father's entering to announce the arrival of a gentleman and lady with their two children to stay all night. I sprang to my feet picturing in my imagination some weary, desolate refugees, homeless and friendless on such a night, and I thought to do my utmost to make them comfortable and easy, but my ardor was considerably abated upon learning that they were persons of wealth—traveling in easy style with their three servants on a ... tour—'twas right provoking to have them come in with such easy assurance—such calm indifference and have all the household thrown into a state of unutterable confusion—supper to get at such a time of night, bed linen to be changed and a thousand and one inconveniences and annoyances to be suffered and all because Mr. and Mrs. Pegram are fond of traveling. And then the insufferable assurance of that lady nurse of theirs! I do hate to be made a piece of convenience of! Oh, me! How my tooth aches and how I wish I might go to bed, 'tis nearly eleven o'clock and yet I can hear that woman's laugh ringing as loudly through the house and her talk as uninterrupted in its flow as it was an hour ago.

August 26, 1863

Up early—tooth better—cleaned up—helped dress children and made my own breakfast toilette. The Pegrams left directly after breakfast with cool acknowledgment of our hospitality—so glad to have them go for I'm so sick of confusion and noise. Mr. Armistead has sent over the girl, Lucie, whom we intend hiring. The other girl, we will send home.

August 28, 1863

Mrs. Armistead's girl Lucy has come to live with us and the Clover Hill Lucie went home yesterday. They tell me the present arrangement is quite an improvement upon the old one. Glad to hear it very.

September 10, 1863

In the afternoon we were sitting in the door reading aloud to each other when a stranger rode up to the stile and Dick introduced him as "Dr. Menafee" whereupon the gentleman proceded to inform me that he had come to examine Miss Buck's tooth. It directly occurred to me that Father was going to have my offending masticators extracted. Father was absent and Ma spending the afternoon at Mrs. Turner's. I nerved myself to the trial and just as he was in the act of having the first one drawn Father came in and so quietly was it done that he knew nothing of the operation till it was over. But the second attempt was more trying and I thought it would almost kill me. It was an immense relief to have these annoyances gone.

September 12, 1863
This morning after breakfast Dick beckoned Nellie and me out and carried us to see poor dear Walter's horse—"Belle"—it seemed almost like looking at a part of himself so often had I seen him mounted on her looking so proud and bright and to see Dick caressing her so sadly. Then he shewed his saddle and all bloodstained. Poor dear, dear boy.

September 13, 1863
Dick sat in our little room and we entertained him showing all our little mementoes and treasures and talking over days of lang syne till dinner time. Just as we were going down to the basement he slipped a fragment of paper in my hand and bade me read it when I left the table. Father and Uncle John dined at Oakley. When I opened the paper it proved to be a little poem clipped from the paper—"The Empty Saddle" and had it been written for Dick and Walter it could not have been more appropriate, so sadly sweet, so touching. I copied it to send Irvie. I don't know when I've enjoyed anyone's society as I have Dick's this evening. He seems not changed one iota since the first day he enlisted save that he's more subdued and affectionate as a general thing. We gave him melons, pears and peaches just to enjoy seeing him eat them as he used to so long ago. He seemed loath to leave and lingered at the stile as late as possible till five o'clock.

September 15, 1863
Uncle M. is uneasy about Dick as he is gone to Fauquier and will probably meet with the Yankees' reconnoitering parties—Oh, I hope not. There's a report of a battle at Culpepper and that our forces have fallen back from there.

September 16, 1863
Nellie and I upstairs busily sewing when an alarm came that the Yankees were approaching town—did not believe it until nearly thrown off my equilibrium by hearing that they were at the barn. We all made a simultaneous pitch to get our letters and treasures out of the way, but it all proved to be a company of our own men—Baylors—they had gone to Clarke—had a skirmish with three times their number of Yankees and were returning unscathed with four prisoners who were mistaken for a whole Yankee regiment.

Uncle John came home tonight. Nellie and I played for him in the parlor and then we had a chat together. He confirms the news of the fight at Culpepper with no additional particulars, though.

September 17, 1863

Bright and beautiful day. Uncle John left about nine o'clock for the mountain.

September 20, 1863
Mrs. Kiger was at church, she told me she had tidings from Missouri and that "Angie Smith was married to a gentleman from near Plattsburg—a Mr. Lincoln." Poor Angie, to think of her going through life encumbered with such a name.

September 21, 1863
Mack Erwin and Mr. Luke came in to tea—just from Clarke. Bring the news that all are well and the additional good news of a victory by Bragg over Rosecrans in Tennessee.

> *General Rosecrans, U.S.A., moved his army through the mountain passes south of Chattanooga. General Bragg, C.S.A., was forced to evacuate Chattanooga September 8, 1863, to prevent being cut off from his supply lines. Bragg saw a chance to turn the Yankees' left flank and moved his troops across the Chickamauga Creek September 19, 1863.*
>
> *Longstreet, with his I Corps, arrived from the Army of Northern Virginia on the night of September 19, 1863. The Confederate attack on the twentieth got off to a late start and General Thomas, U.S.A., held on the Union left, but he needed assistance. General T. J. Wood's division was sent to his aid from the Union center. Longstreet on the Confederate left, noted the gap in the Union lines, and struck driving the Federals back into Chattanooga.*

U.S.A.		C.S.A.	
Effectives	58,222	Effectives	66,326
Killed	1,657	Killed	2,301
Wounded	9,756	Wounded	14,674
Missing	4,757	Missing	1,468

> *Thomas held long enough on the Union left to save the army, but as it retreated into Chattanooga it was beaten and surrounded. Bragg, much to the dissatisfaction of all his generals, elected to lay siege to the city.*

Oh! I pray it may be true. Played and sang for Mack till he left, then came upstairs and sat at the window writing.

September 22, 1863
Was sitting at my window trying to write by the poor light when Ma

came in bidding me guess who had come and ended by saying Mr. Bowman from Charleston and he brings news that Alvin is well and getting on finely and that he has had no letters from home for three months. Father went to see Mr. Bowman to try and learn some particulars of the siege at Charleston.

> *After months of siege, 413 marines and sailors from the U.S. fleet attacked Fort Sumter in Charleston Harbor. They were repulsed with the loss of 124 casualties.*

September 23, 1863
The news from Tennessee is not so flattering as at first account—yet we've whipped the enemy in an engagement there. Nellie and I practiced, "All's Quiet on the Potomac."

September 25, 1863
My birthday—twenty-one years old today—free, white and twenty-one! Heigh-ho!
Father told us at the tea table that General Bragg's official report was received in town and that the battle in the West had been a great though not decisive victory on our side but that we have lost largely in officers among whom General Hood was killed and General Cleburne wounded—poor Irvie!

> *Hood was first reported killed but in fact received a leg wound necessitating amputation.*

Tonight while Nellie and Sue were on the house talking, I have been sitting at the window not looking at the beautiful moonlight silvering the aspens but living in those thirty minutes the past fifteen years of my life marshalling all the brightly tinted pictures on memory's wall and basking in their light, turning over the leaves of the past to read what of me was there recorded and alas! humiliated at the sad array of wasted hours against me—standing like accusing spirits with glowing pictures of the "might-have-been" confronting the dreary prospect of the present. The hour was not spent without many resolutions of amendment and yet alas! those resolves are often but ropes of cobweb to constrain the habits of a lifetime. Twenty-one and free! Free indeed, why 'tis reversing the order of things when every year since I was a little child the shackles of care and anxiety have more and more closely clasped about me confining and restraining even the natural impulses of my heart. Free forsooth! I could laugh the idea to scorn were it not such a sad—such a mournful burlesque.

> *Rosecrans, U.S.A., needed help, so Hooker, was sent from the Army of the Potomac with the Union XI and XII Corps*

on September 24, 1863. This force arrived at Brown's Ferry below Chattanooga on the twenty-eighth of October.
Sherman, from Grant's army in Mississippi, was ordered to Chattanooga. Bragg still waited.

September 26, 1863
Father brought no letters from the office; this evening but a paper containing brief accounts of the battle in North Georgia. General Cleburne is certainly wounded and we are all so uneasy about poor Irvie. Received a note and bundle from Cousin E. Cloud tonight.

September 30, 1863
We had been feeling so sad about dear Irvie for Father heard in town that in the late Battle of Chickamauga our loss in officers was very heavy and have no reason to suppose we are to be exempted from bereavements which others better than we are enduring. God grant our fears prove groundless yet I feel very, very sad.

October 1, 1863
Went over to spend the afternoon with Mrs. Wheatley. On our way passed near the old graveyard and Cousin Mary wished to visit her father's grave. It was a sad, sad scene!—the sky covered with drifting gray clouds through which ever and anon burst fitful gleams of sunlight, the long, sere grass rustling and the trees shivering in the wind that sighed low and mournfully through them. The enclosure of the graveyard was all dilapidated and gray and moss-grown. The tumble down gate half off the hinges and grating harshly as we tried to open it, then the graves themselves overgrown and almost concealed by the tall rank grass and briers, the walks between full of goldenrod, blackberry bushes and sumac shrubs—such a desolate, desolate place as it was—the white tombstones looked ghastly and the crickets made a sad weird sound in the leaves. I shall never forget the appearance of the neglected resting place of those loved and gone before.

October 6, 1863
Was up by five o'clock to make up my rolls and helped dress Father's foot which gets no better. Aunt Eliza up early to milk for us. Horace and Uncle Gilbert went up to the mountain to dig out potatoes. Nellie's day to cook but we helped her and I helped to churn and twist yarn too. Upset the churn and inundated the kitchen with sour cream.
When Horace and Uncle Gilbert came home tonight they told us that of the twenty bushels we planted only ten were realized, the robbers and deserters in the mountains having dug the remainder of the crop. There goes our dependence for next winter. Thus it is "unmerciful disaster follows fast and follows faster ...."

October 7, 1863

Ma says a letter has been received in town from Scott Roy but that the Warren Rifles are certainly in Tennessee having taken part in the late battle there. Only a few of them were hurt, thank Heaven.

October 13, 1863

Dick Bayly over in the afternoon—is at home on a furlough. Got the music of "Stonewall Jackson's Way" and Nellie and I learned it. Sue and Dick Bayly over in the afternoon, on the house again to see more cavalry. Both Sue and Dick left before tea. Heard that Lt. Thomas Marshall was killed in the fight at Culpepper on Sunday last—hope 'tis not true.

> *Confederate lookouts reported on September 24 the removal of a large Federal encampment east of Culpeper Courthouse and three days later scouts confirmed that Meade's XI and XII Corps under General Joseph Hooker had left for Chattanooga.*
>
> *Lee, weakened by sending Longstreet to Chattanooga, decided to advance on an equally weakened foe. On October 9, Confederates began to move north around Meade's right flank. Meade retreated to Centreville. General A. P. Hill's III Corps caught the rear of the Union army on the south bank of Broad Run and attacked hastily with the cost of heavy casualties. Lee returned to the Rappahannock River. No great victory had been gained.*

Had a message from Mrs. Roy to the effect that Miss Mary Simpson had a letter from George Williams in which he stated that I. was safe but with a bullet through his cap. Thank Heaven that 'twas not an inch nearer the head. Oh!—it has made me so happy to know that our dear one is safe and well.

October 19, 1863

Cousin Sam was summoned away not long after breakfast and Emma and I had the house to ourselves for some time—roasted and ate chestnuts and sewed a little and read and wrote. In the afternoon Cousin Sam proposed that we should go chestnutting. We set out—found two trees and oh 'twas glorious to hear the rich brown nuts showering down through the leaves to our feet. We soon had a basketful and started on our return home. I shall never forget the evening—the most glorious type of autumn splendor I ever saw. It reminded me of Bryant's description of "those calm mild days," only this had more of life and glowing beauty and not the melancholy sadness of his autumn days. Returned home about sunset and had just a little while to write before dark.

October 25, 1863

Nellie and I went over to hear Dr. Hough. Had a good sermon from Corinthians 13. Saw everybody at church. Reading to Father a short time in the afternoon, then commenced writing some when Charlie Buck came in. Very soon Em. came in with a pacquet of letters from George Williams to Benton which Mrs. Roy had received and kindly sent over for us to read. They were very interesting and gave the most minute accounts of the battle we have yet received. Also a letter from General Cleburne to General Hardee in which the former denied having been wounded. How much pain a slight mistake may cause one! Think how we have suffered in believing that if Gen. C. were wounded Irvie must have sustained injury too. I went down into Grandma's room, got Frank to sleep and read in my Bible. Every one in bed, I the only being in the house astir.

October 27, 1863

After breakfast this morning we were sitting quietly at work when they ran in to say the Yankees were coming—sure enough there were parts of two regiments of cavalry. Laura went in a great hurry off to Mrs. Hope's to tell Mr. Moffatt and while she was gone one of the scamps dashed up to the door where Father, Sue, Nellie and I were standing and, without a word of greeting demanded "Where that man was that came up here." Father told him that there was no one here to the best of his knowledge. He in the most insolent manner said he knew there was and he would find him in this house before he was done. Father then turned to us and inquired if we had seen any man here—Nellie replied with a mocking laugh that "he was the only man she had seen come." He turned with a most fiendish look and said—"I 'spose then the nigger lied—he's here and I going to find him." With that he commenced blustering around with his hand on his pistol and marched into the garden where sure enough he stumbled over a Confederate soldier lying under the syringa bushes near the gate—'twas John Taylor who had taken refuge there unknown to one member of the family. The Yankee brought him triumphantly forth and went off with him to town. They all very soon after turned and left town in a violent hurry—stopping as they went at Rose Hill! We heard after they left they had taken Uncle Tom's last horse, Charlie Buck's pony and five of Mr. Richards besides twelve barrels of corn and all Cousin Bet's turkeys.

October 29, 1863

Up and had breakfast very early. Confusion and trouble. Sat upstairs reading in my Bible, then came down and wrote in my diary. All the whole family from Mrs. Childs and Grandma down to Frank and Lucie went down to the mill to see the process of molasses making. Aunt and I had the house to ourselves and I improved the delighted quiet by writing. They did not return till dinner time and then Nellie came bounding in with face full of excitement to say George Hope was home. My first thought was "Oh! why could not it have been Alvin?" but I checked it remembering how poor Mrs. Hope seemed to desire a prolongation of life only for the sake of seeing him and now this was perhaps for the last time. George Hope and Mrs. Moffatt called about four o'clock in the afternoon—found George looking thin and pale though improved in manner and conversation—but George Hope still. He could give us but little information respecting Alvin as he had been in Augusta, Georgia for over a month. He laughingly told us though that Alvin cared all the world for a little Tennessee damsel and that delighted me, for I feared he might have forgotten her to a certain extent. I love him so much better for being so true. George tells us Alvin can have a furlough if he wishes it and he will either come home or go to Kentucky as he prefers.

November 4, 1863

About eleven o'clock we were startled by the sound of a drum and running upon the house saw ten regiments of infantry marching through town, ... their bayonets glittering in the bright morning sun. Troops supposed to be en route for Imboden's command sent up for the purpose of protecting the "valley."

November 7, 1863

Lieutenant Baylor left about ten o'clock though not before he received warnings from Uncle Mack that the Yankees were in camp in the McKay neighborhood last night. Ma, Grandma, and Aunt Betsie went over to Oakley to prayer meeting. Sue heard from home—was very low-spirited. About twelve o'clock Father came in to say the Yankees were coming and there were four hundred cavalrymen. Such a time as we had putting away things! Laura ran off to Mrs. Hope's to warn George and came back almost dead with the fatigue. They passed the home repeatedly but not one was in the yard. Mrs. Marshall called in to rest and told us they had taken Mack Bayly, who had gotten home the night before, and John Boone and John Sumption. They remained till a little after three o'clock and then left town whooping and singing like demons. Ma came home after they were gone and told us they behaved unusually well—searched Mrs. Hope's house for George but did nothing brutal. They invited themselves to dine with the citizens—took as much as they wanted of hay and corn for their horses and got the Luray mail—this was the "most unkindest cut of all."

November 11, 1863

Pleasant. Reading—crocheting—repairing Father's old hat. Uncle Tom came over in the morning. Laura and I suddenly concluded we would try and walk to Clover Hill—wrote Wythe Cook inviting him to go with us. Mary came over to bring his answer. Got ready directly and left immediately after dinner. Met Wythe at Miss Bettie White's door—met Aunt Bettie there too. 'Twas a delightful evening for walking just cool enough to be pleasant—did not feel half as much fatigued as I anticipated. Wythe made himself very agreeable. Mack Erwin was on the river bank on the opposite side and seemed overwhelmed with astonishment—brought the boat over for us though and seemed glad to see us—told us that Sue and Miss Tencia Tyler, who came up yesterday, had gone with Aunt Lizzie, Annie, Lilie, and Belle over to Mrs. Grimeley's. Uncle Fayette, Estie, Fettie and Nevie were there though and Laura and I made ourselves at home till they arrived just about dusk. Then we were a merry party about the fire. After tea adjourned to the parlor and had a series of amusing games till time for prayers and then we girls retired to our rooms where we had a merry time relating our experiences during the war. 'Tis very late the girls in bed—just begin to feel the fatigue.

November 12, 1863

Felt sore and stiff this morning—did not get down to prayers. After breakfast Miss Sue sang and played for us and then all save Miss Tencia and I went to take a walk—I was too tired to venture. Gilbert Larue came from Clarke bringing a letter from Jule. Miss T. and I left the parlor and took our sewing to Aunt Lizzie's room where we sat chatting till I became so stupid and felt so badly that I went in the parlor and taking my book lay on the sofa attempting to muse myself to sleep. Had not succeeded when they all returned. After dinner we went to our rooms copied songs, laughed, talked and lounged about till time to walk when we determined to revenge ourselves upon Gilbert Larue for his evident avoidance of our presences by forcing him into service as escort. A hint to Mack was all that was necessary—he proposed to him that he should help him take care of the ladies and he could not in conscience refuse—still our plans were in part frustrated for he did not walk with Miss Susie as we intended to maneuver him into doing, that she might make him talk in self defense, but he quickly stepped to Miss Tencia's side and offered himself as her cavalier—Wythe went with Miss Susie, Mack with me and Laura and Annie and the other children promiscously. There were two boatloads of us—Sue, Miss Tencia, Wythe, Cornel, Gilbert and Esten went over first and just as they left shore we fired a salute by throwing rocks into the water causing a great splashing. They vowed they'd return the compliment so we took on a cargo of rocks for ammunition and just before we reached the opposite shore where they stood we received a perfect broadside which we vigorously returned and quite a naval skirmish ensued but we succeeded in effecting a landing and had a charming walk to "Diamond Falls"—gathered ferns to deck the boys' bed and after having a great deal of fun returned toward home. Our party were the most rapid walkers and reached the boat first thereby escaping a sprinkling. We waited on the banks for the return passengers but after coming in range of our batteries they tacked and floated off down stream to land below the "fort." Dispatching Mack to defend the lower landing Annie, Lilie, Laura and I went up to the house and coaxed Tell into sewing up the sleeves of the girls' night dresses, hiding their toothbrushes and so etc., etc. They all soon came in in great excitement telling how Captains Mack and Gilbert had fought and the result was a drawn battle. Presently Charlie Buck came in and not long after a carriage and cart drove up to the stile and a gentleman came up saying a bridal party—Mr. and Mrs. Newton, Miss Newton and himself—Colonel Mayo wished to get lodgings for the night—of course, the house was crowded but still they could not be refused accommodations and were welcomed to the hospital roof. There were thirteen visitors and two tables full at tea—Mack, Annie and I were planning to wait till the second table but Aunt Lizzie would not permit it so we went down and were introduced at the table. The bride was a little rosebud of a thing with a very sweet face and most engaging manners and an old acquaintance of Miss Sue Tyler's. Miss Newton, a tall dark-eyed girl not pretty but pleasant, the groom a wounded man having lost one limb at Chestersville and scarcely able to walk even with the aid of crutches—a pair of piercing black eyes, black hair and moustache and whiskers, firm looking mouth and rather a moody, stern expression of countenance. Colonel Mayo—quiet, stars and gold lace in abundance—gentlemanly. Remained till the second table and had a chat with Gilbert—seems a nice sort of fellow. We all helped clear the tea table that we might have the basement for a game of Blind Man's Buff. Had a glorious round of games—consequences, Lamger, House-top and everything. We found that Gilbert had not only a tongue but confidence too when once brought to the test. Annie Ford is the greatest scamp! Miss Newton had to be accommodated in our room and although the poor girl is I know tired she has not been able to get to sleep for the noise we've kept laughing at her—Annie's nonsense—oh well!—tomorrow will soon be here and our merry party will be scattered so we'll e'en enjoy ourselves while we can.

November 13, 1863

Bright, balmy and beautiful morning. Up, all of us quite early and Miss Sue and I coaxed Mack out to the "pit" that we might cull a bouquet of flowers for the bride—got some pink roses, white chrysanthemums, geraniums, citronellos, and myrtle. They left soon after breakfast. We saw them off and then betook ourselves to the parlor where we had music till after ten o'clock when Wythe, Laura and I started home. They all went with us to the river, crossed in the boat and then clambered over the hills with us a half mile. Mack piloted us to the road and then we waved adieux and parted. 'Twas extremely warm still we walked fast, stopping only three times, once to rest, once to watch some cattle fording the river and once to drink from the big spring. Was almost broken down upon reaching home.

November 14, 1863

Gussie came down about four o'clock bringing with her a letter from Dick in which he stated that poor Scott had been captured while scouting near Norfolk on the second of this month. Poor fellow! To think how we have been looking forward with so much pleasure to his visit to us in December and now he's in the hands of the enemy and there's no exchange for prisoners either. Vile wretches!—these Yankees I wish—but no matter, that won't give poor Scott his liberty. What was the use of my learning the song, I just don't believe any of the boys are coming home and oh! me I've got the blues.

November 22, 1863

Grandma and Aunt Betsie to church. Aunt L. Buck returned with them from church but only sat a short time—she and Sue had a letter from Dick brought from the regiment by Major Simpson. He spoke of Scott's escape from the Yankees—then they told me they had heard how he effected this. It seems there was a blockade runner in the same apartment with him and he told in the course of conversation that he had a little skiff not far distant which, if he could reach it would enable him to run the blockade free of his captors. Scott asked for a sketch of his plans which the man readily placed with his pencil on a bit of paper. The captain of the guard had reason to suspect Scott of having designs of escape and had him up before the provost marshal who tried to convince Scott that 'twould be very dishonorable to attempt any such thing, but Scott very properly told him that he was not on his parole of honor and that 'twas perfect fair for him to go if he could—that were the provost in his place he would do the same thing. The officer then ordered that he should be more securely confined, but the order from some cause was not put into effect that night and Scott persuaded the young man who accompanied him to try to give them the slip. They climbed out of a window over a beam projecting from it, from there they descended to the roof below them, from the roof they slipped down by means of the lightning rods to the ground—made good their way to the place designated by the "Blockade Runner" as the harbor for his little skiff, found the boat, boarded it and turned their backs on Norfolk, and all this in the face of an order from the provost that they were to be shot in case they were detected in any such attempt. They rowed for twenty-eight or thirty miles between two lighthouses and finally succeeded in reaching a point of safety from which they made their way to camp. Bless that boy! This is only the third time he has taken French leave of his captors. Oh I'm so glad for now he'll be home Christmas and I do think he deserves promotion for the evidence he has given of strategical abilities. What would I not give to see him and hear him talk about it all now, though he is too modest to say much for himself I know.

> *This escape by Scott Roy is described in* History of the Seventeenth Virginia Infantry, C.S.A., *by George Wise. Lieutenant Roy had been captured on November 15, 1863, while scouting for his company around Suffolk, Virginia.*

November 30, 1863
Bitter cold—up early and had the house in order betimes. Busy with my hat. Uncle Tom in to dinner. Rumors of the defeat in Tennessee.

> *On October 17, 1863, General Grant was given command of the Union Armies of the Tennessee, Cumberland, and Ohio. Thomas replaced Rosecrans as commander of the Union Army of the Cumberland. Grant arrived in Chattanooga on the twenty-third of October. Supplies and reinforcements began to arrive via a pontoon bridge across the river and the city was relieved of siege. Bragg had waited too long. He had even detached Longstreet's I Corps on November 5 and 6 to Knoxville to fight Burnside, U.S.A. Thus, Bragg weakened his army by 12,000 men. Sherman's army arrived at Chattanooga in mid-November and formed the Union left flank. Thomas was in the center, and Hooker assaulted Lookout Mountain on the twenty-fifth, Sherman struck the northern end of Missionary Ridge, only to be repelled by Confederate General Pat Cleburne's division.*
>
> *Thomas's forces on November 25 were ordered to advance on the rifle pits below Missionary Ridge. This was more of a diversion for the action on the right and left flanks, but without orders and to the astonishment of Generals Grant and Thomas the Yankees carried the Ridge. Bragg retreated in defeat.*

U.S.A.		C.S.A.	
Effectives	56,359	Effectives	46,156
Killed	753	Killed	361
Wounded	4,722	Wounded	2,160
Missing	349	Missing	4,146

> *Longstreet arrived before Knoxville on November 17, 1863,*

and Burnside retired into the city. Longstreet attacked Fort Sanders on November 29, but was repelled.

Sherman was sent north to relieve the siege of Knoxville, after the Battle of Chattanooga. Longstreet retreated into Virginia.

Hope 'tis false though. Sitting all of us before a bright fire in Grandma's room. I with Frank on my lap feeding him preparatory to putting him to sleep when we were startled by a sudden knock at the door which proved to proceed from a wagon driver who enquired if we would give lodgings to Mr. George Burwell, his wife and daughter. It was very inconvenient yet how could we refuse shelter such an inclement night? They came in almost frozen. A fine looking old gray-haired gentleman, an energetic lady in black—his wife, a ladylike looking little niece and daughter and son respectively thirteen and fifteen years of age. We proceeded to make them as comfortable as possible. Great was our consternation upon finally discovering that they were attended with a suite of twelve servants, three white drivers, eleven horses and five or six conveyances. Made the best of our bargain though and got on very comfortably, the night cold as it was.

December 4, 1863

Busily engaged putting things "to right." Sewing and talking when Uncle Tom came in—he had not long been gone when Cousin Bettie Richards came in and very soon after to our horror Miss Betsie White. Then Aunt Bettie Ashby. Miss Betsie thought fit to commence a tirade against "blockade runners" the first thing when she entered the room, denouncing them as traitors and everything that was mean. Then she commenced speaking of the report of Cousin Mount's complicity in the affair of the burnt mill but Nellie soon stopped that and so visible her displeasure that the amiable lady soon departed white with rage and eyes glittering in fury.

December 5, 1863

Both Cousin E. and M. are in deep distress and at a loss what to do for Captain Roy had told them he thought it scarce safe for them to remain in town since the Yankees might see fit to make them suffer for provocation which Cousin Mount had offered them—or was considered as offered them. They would have to leave town and yet were not able to get a conveyance to go in.

Persuaded Cousin Mary to go with me down to Dr. Leach's thinking the walk would do her good. 'Twas quite late and Miss Lizzie was not in but the doctor and little Sallie entertained us till she came in after awhile. Did not remain long after that. The doctor told us that news had come of Bragg's having been superseded by Gen. Joe Johnston—that the Battle of Rapidan was a mistake and that Bragg was certainly badly defeated.

> *General Bragg was replaced by Gen. Joseph Johnston December 1, 1863, as commander of the Army of Tennessee. Bragg was made military adviser to President Davis.*

Heard that three of Mr. Richard's servants with two horses, a mule and several of Mr. Petty's servants fled to Yankeedom.

December 11, 1863
Jacquie came in the afternoon bringing me some ivy leaves for wreaths. Working so hard preparing Nellie for Clarke—she goes with Jacquie tomorrow. Feel so distressed at her leaving—'twill be so lonely but I try not to let her know it. ... her but tonight. 'Tis after twelve o'clock—I'm perfectly exhausted and must hie to bed. Oh me! Raining hard—hope they'll not get off tomorrow. Ma heard through Harry Roy this evening that he had seen our servants in Chambersburg when he was in—that Mahala was doing finely keeping a boarding house—Eliza Ann living with her, and Martha married and settled down. Must confess I've my doubts about it though the servants will all believe it and 'twill have the effect of inducing numbers to leave home.

December 12, 1863
Rained so hard last night and the morning was so gray and chilled that we did not think our travelers would get off but it cleared off gloriously by breakfast and Orville, Nellie and Jacquie were off by ten o'clock. Oh me! I do feel so lonely it seemed as if half the household had gone off in that wagon with Nellie. Ma and I watched them from the door and then went on the house and looked after them till they were out of sight. Then settled myself to reading and writing—spent one of the most deliciously quiet days that I've known for a long time. Father came about three o'clock and said all was going on very well when he left our travelers at "Crooked Run." Read and wrote and then played and sang some hymns after dark and got Frank to sleep telling him stories. Elliott Buck came down today and brought tidings of Mr. Sampson Bailey's death. I don't want to believe it and yet it seems to come so direct from a friend of the family's who was imprisoned with him and took the oath that he might come out and inform his family of it. Poor dear Sue! How my heart aches for her, for if this news be true I fear it will almost kill her. Ma home from Rose Hill.

December 18, 1863
There came a loud "Holloa" from the yard and going out Father was confronted by a cavalryman who asked if supper could be obtained here for Major Harman, Adjutant Nott and some other officers who were coming in. Being answered affirmatively he then informed us that the

whole of Rosser's brigade was passing the house and so it was though we knew nothing of it before. Dear Walter! I thought of him immediately and remembered how—at any other time we should be looking for his coming with them and now he would never come again. Had not time for thought though for, the soldiers came pouring in and we had to attend to getting supper for them.

> *In August, 1863, General Jones was replaced by Thomas L. Rosser as commander of Ashby's brigade and renamed it the Laurel Brigade. The brigade left the Army of Northern Virginia on December 16, 1863, and rode around Meade's army by way of Fredericksburg, Sangster Station, Upperville, and entered the Shenandoah Valley via Ashby's Gap. They moved south to Front Royal where they camped for the first time in forty-eight hours. In thirty-five hours Rosser's men had ridden more than ninety miles.*
>
> *The objective of this raid was to cut behind two Union cavalry regiments moving up the Valley, but when Rosser arrived in the Valley he discovered the Federals had returned to Winchester. After resting in Front Royal, the Confederates moved up the Luray Valley.*

Poor creatures they were in all that storm night before last and in a skirmish last night—some of them were perfectly stupefied with cold and fatigue and had water in their boots which they got in crossing the river at Fredericksburg. They had come from there and gone entirely around Meade's army—were en route for Clarke or Frederick but diverted from their course by the high waters. Being at the doors on an errand I met face to face a poor fellow who had just dismounted—he limped terribly and I asked him if he were wounded—he told me that he was crippled with rheumatism. Indeed he could scarce move and we told him he must stay in the house tonight although he said it had been a year since he slept under a roof before. There were at one time twenty or thirty horses before the door at a time. All settled down by eleven o'clock.

December 24, 1863
Very busy cleaning and finishing my dress till after eleven o'clock. Then Father came in bringing a long, long letter from Alvin to Nellie of the twenty-ninth sent through Miss Kate Graves. Bless his soul! It is such a treat and he is well and cheerful as usual and he's heard from Irvie and he is after the battle. Thank Heaven! There was a letter for me too from Scott—a good long, saucy "Scottish" letter. Such nice Christmas gifts as they are! Busy down in the kitchen baking cakes till after eight o'clock. Lucie went home this evening; we hated so to give her up and she cried bitterly.

Mr. Buck hired a young white "Mountain girl," Lucie, to help with the housework, after the slaves left.

Tonight got the children washed and put to bed and after they went to sleep filled the stockings and boiled some molasses for taffy. Father attempted to attend to the boiling but after waiting till ten o'clock he gave it up in despair and left Grandma, Ma and me alone in our glory. Did not get through till after twelve o'clock. Poor children! I contrast their limited means of enjoyment now with our former happy life and it makes me sad. Ah! Dear, tomorrow will be a lonely, dreary day for me with none of the dear ones we were expecting—not even Nellie and Laura. There are only five pairs of stockings over the fireplace tonight and there are five of our house circle absent—five hearts are no doubt turning longingly this way tonight. God bless them! One of the very loneliest nights I ever saw.

December 25, 1863
Children up very early. A lovely day clear and bright. Helped the children with the contents of their stockings and then proceeded to clean up. Dressed after breakfast and went off upstairs to take a good cry for my heart was full of sad and pleasant thoughts and memories and I was so lonely—missed the dear absentees. Felt better after crying awhile and went downstairs with Ma and Grandma. Uncle Newton sick. Father went out to see him. Charlie Buck spent an hour or so with us. Cheery boy that he is—tried to play and sing for him but had to give over the attempts in despair. Then Uncle John came. He was not well and lay down. Then Uncle Tom who remained to eat our orthodox turkey and mince pies. Wonder where the poor boys got their Christmas dinners this year or if they had any poor fellows?—and Nellie and Laura and Orville?

Frank fretful and sleepy this evening and I felt really worn out. At twilight when Ma and Father were talking by the firelight—I laid on the bedside and thought, thought and cried. Ah the sad, sad changes that are more and more apparent every year! how much more they depress, how much less able I feel to bear them—our dear lost Walter! Let the seasons roll around as they will, he will never come to make glad the festive times for us. And yet 'tis wrong to grieve thus when we have so much more to be thankful for than to complain of. Our other dear ones are spared to us. I think how this house might now be shrouded in sorrow as thousands and thousands of Southern homes are—how our hearts might be writhing in anguish had a hostile bullet laid low our darling Irvie in that last miserable battle. I think of poor Mr. Smedley—of his son—so young—so cruelly deprived of his useful young life—think of the sad households there and feel that we are blessed even more than we could reasonably hope for.

We are anxious about the children but look for them tomorrow or the day after.

December 29, 1863
A bright beautiful day. Father went down to the river to hear from the children. Playing and singing and telling Gussie stories all the forenoon. Aunt Letitia here. Feeling quite unwell tonight. Aunt Letitia has letters from her son in Philadelphia who has heard from Cousin Alex. He's in Chicago. Of course he would not say if he was not well treated. They had also letters from Mack Bayly who is at Camp Chase and doing well. They had a letter from Cousin Mack and Dick but don't know the contents of them.

December 30, 1863
Had a letter from Nellie—written the twenty-fourth. She says the children were to have started yesterday so I presume they'll be here tonight. Father and Carey went down to the river to meet them. While washing up the dinner things Uncle Tom came in bringing a package of letters—some seven or eight from Alvin, Irvin and one from a Mr. Dore of Richmond to Father and an enclosure from Benton to myself, an old one. Indeed nearly all letters were old ones dating back—some of them as far as August—some were more recent and all of them welcome as could be. How we devoured their contents learning from them many little incidents which we probably could otherwise never have obtained. This outpouring of the post office is probably owing to a letter which Father wrote the P M General some time since. It's high time there was something of the kind done for we've been badly enough treated by the mailboys. The letter from Mr. Dore was written informing Father that his young son had stopped here going and coming from Maryland, that he had spoken in such warm terms of his kindness to him and this had prompted him to make the request he did of him. He said his poor boy had fallen at Williamsport and was buried in the Lee Cemetery there —his headboard bearing his name—"Leslie C. Dore." He had heard there were blockade runners constantly plying between here and Maryland and he wished to know if they could by any means procure the remains for him and bring them in. He wrote so touchingly—it made me sad to think that this was but one incident out of a hundred such occurring daily in our Confederacy and that this appeal was but one out of many heart cries coming up constantly from bereaved households. Ah me!

December 31, 1863
Uncle Tom came in about eleven o'clock bringing another pacquette of letters which came by this redundant mail—three from Irvie to Nellie and three from him to Ma and two from Benton to me—one dated 29 November, the other December 5, the latest one we've had from them. Poor fellow! he is in no happy frame of mind—so depressed by the defeat there—seems so desponding—complains of hearing nothing from home.

Read the letters all through. Suffering very much all day—towards evening felt better and took a cup of tea. Determined to watch in the new year though it was only by dint of persuasion I could get permission to do so. Filled the children's stockings after they went to bed—undressed—got my portfolio and went to writing. Grandma sat with me till eleven o'clock and then left me alone writing to Scott. It seems so lonely—so isolated sitting there waiting for the last few sands to drop from the glass and watching for the burst of another year of trial—even as I watched the advent of the last year—little knowing, little dreaming what that year the great move of time would sweep from me—how much of life's brightness it would dim—how it would sweep away to the dim shores of eternity the form of one so dear to us—one of the brightest lights of our darkened days of time. How little I had dreamed of the toil, the trials and the care that like a blight had come over me. And yet how little there was to complain of in comparison with the blessings that have been showered upon my unworthy head—and can I not trust for this coming year to the same kind hand that has guided me through the darkened paths of life heretofore? Yes, surely. It is raining and the drops fall like great drops of tears—the old year is weeping his inevitable death. Poor old year! Why should he wish to linger in a world where his eyes behold only the fading and blight of all things bright and beautiful, rather let him close his eyes to all the sorrow and care of this trying season and fold his hands softly and lay his old weary, white head down till it rests upon the bosom of oblivion's stream—thus—while we mortals turn to hail the incoming of the new "eighteen hundred and sixty-four!"

January 2, 1864

Was just bringing in the wood and chips when I saw Laura coming in the back door and then Orville and Jacquie and Dumb Mary. They had left their baggage at Mrs. Painter's and walked over having crossed the river in a skiff at Hans Ferry. Such a noise as ensued among the children—so many questions to ask and answer! Then there was a letter from Nellie. Poor thing! She was evidently loath enough to have the children go and will, I'm afraid, be sad enough. Laura our new "help" came in this evening—a delicate looking, unsophisticated individual. Hope she'll be able to do more than her appearance indicates. Very cold tonight. A great crowd about the fire. The Yankees are in town—came in very unexpectedly from Warrenton—a body of Meade's troops come to cut off Early's division and reinforce Averill at Martinsburg. From the appearance of the campfires tonight there must be infantry with them. I feel perfectly at ease tonight but am afraid tomorrow they'll commence their plundering though. Well, they won't get my "treasures" I guess.

January 3, 1864

Clear, bright, and cold. Did not get through with my work as soon as usual. Soon after breakfast we saw the Yankees filing out of the woods and forming into ranks, went out of town the way they came carrying with them one poor little prisoner. They said the mail—containing those letters I've been writing—has been captured. Ma and I were so provoked that we bundled up and went over to see Uncle Tom about getting a postmaster who would attend to his business and hide the mail when the Yankees should come. There was no church and we would spend the day with Aunt Bettie. Saw where the wretches had been in the Baptist Church killing chickens. There were the feathers and blood on the floor and everything in sickening disorder. Indeed it seems they confined themselves to warring on fowls.

It seems there was a whole division of cavalry with artillery—the greater portion of them encamping between Drs. Dorsey's and Turner's. They had come thinking to cut off our troops and reinforce Averill but the high water proved an insurmountable obstacle and they had to return as they came. They searched Uncle Newton's house for guns—taking from there one ham. Charlie had fortunately escaped up the river. Uncle Tom says they went to Rose Hill and took every turkey and ham they had besides nearly all their other meat. Poor Cousin Elizabeth. She gets it on every side and is so little able to stand these losses and annoyances. Green Samuels was at home and made his escape by adopting female costume and walking out after dusk. Dr. Leach sent his little son off to the woods with their horse. The animal refused to move after getting on the hill and as the Yankees were pursuing the child, the child had to surrender. Was taken to camp when Miss Lizzie hearing of it, went and begged him and the horse off. One of the girls then led the horse into the dining room where holding him by the reins—holding in her hand a pistol and keeping at bay the miscreants who came to take him. Dick Bayly came in about noon—said he stayed at home last night and talked across the river to the Yankee picquet on this side knowing that the river was too full for them to cross, the boat was destroyed and the night too dark to admit of his being recognized as a "Rebel."

January 12, 1864

Father took Laura and me down on the ice and gave us our first lessons in skating. It was a magnificent morning and I felt so invigorated by the bracing air, the bright sunshine and the run through the crisp sparkling snow. Then the ice formations at the dam were so exquisitely delicate and beautiful. We were there about two hours—Father predicting that we will make expert skaters—did not get one bad fall though Father did. Returned to the house with tired ankles but in a perfect glow. Read in the *Journal*. Sewed a little. Ma home to dinner.

January 14, 1864

Received a message to the effect that Mrs. Roy had gotten letters from the West and that we must go up and hear from Irvie then. Walked up about sunset—heard them read and also learned that there was an enclosure for us from Irvie which through some mistake had been sent over home before we got it. The letters were to Nellie and I felt not a little nettled at the idea of writing so many letters to Irvie and receiving no reply. So General Hardee is to be married after all and to a Miss Lewis of Demopolis.

February 11, 1864

Bright and keen. Busy after breakfast preparing Laura's costume and making a "Bonnie Blue Flag." Then writing in my diary. Ma was taken suddenly sick about noon but being better in the evening Laura, Orville, Carey and I walked over to Dr. Leach's. Met everybody there and had the greatest time selecting subjects, costumes and rehearsing. All seemed "Merry as a Marriage Bell"—but my heart was very, very heavy—thinking of Ma and all at home. Sitting at the dinner table when a messenger brought in a pacquet of letters—one a long one, from Alvin to Father—one from Cousin Mack Newton to Nellie and myself—an enclosure from Benton—a piece of General Hardee's bridal cake with names to dream on and a nice little one from Nanny dear.

February 12, 1864

Cloudy. Up and at work busily making off programmes and sending bundles. Nanny and Mollie came about eleven o'clock. Had everything prepared and went over to the Academy about four o'clock to assist Miss Lizzie in preparing for tonight—found everything bustle and excitement—went to work with the rest smiling as brightly as they did and I know not one of them suspected what a heavy heart I carried in my bosom. Quite a cavalcade came from Clover Hill—Henry, Julia and a whole party. Went with Sally down to Dr. Leach's to see them. Jule went over to our house. Annie Ford and Miss Hortensia went back to the Academy with us. Arranged the stage, pinned on the wreaths about sunset—came home and dressed. By dent of persuasion induced Ma to go with us. There were six of us. Found them waiting for us. Such a babble of confusion as I entered into behind the scenes! My name was called till I almost regretted having one and the boys were noisy but these being gradually arranged things passed off very nicely, "Drilling Conscripts," "Examining Conscripts," "None but the Brave Deserve the Fair," "Come Spin My Dearest Daughter," the "Interview between the Pickets" and above all the "Bonnie Blue Flag" sung in person were admirable. After all our dread the affair passed off quite creditably and we realized quite a nice little sum—$94.00 for the benefit of the poor soldiers. Got home about half past nine o'clock.

February 16, 1864

Very unwell. Dick Bayly tried to coax me to go down home with him as he wished to have a little social reunion but I declined not being in the spirit to enjoy myself because Aunt Betty is so sick; because

I am unwell myself, because Grandma is away and 'tis so cold. Helped him make out his list of invitations and offered my assistance in every way in my power.

February 20, 1864

Beautiful day. Spent an hour this morning on the ice. Little Leaches and then poor Charlie came in. He was in high spirits and would have me in the parlor to play for him. Father came in about two o'clock to say, if Charlie had no objections, he would ride his horse to Mr. Forney's. Before he started the children ran in to say the Yankees were coming. Charlie sprang to his feet, flung me his overcoat, mounted his horse and at Father's directions galloped across the orchard toward Green Hill. They proceeded and pursued them but he managed to elude them that time. While waiting the denouement of this move one of the children cried out "Oh they've got poor Old Sam!" *(balzed freed sorrell horse)* and sure enough Horace had started off towards the thicket with the horses and was overhauled by the Yankees and forced to give up the best of the two. We saw them cantering across the fields towards town leading with them our main dependence for future bread and fuel. It was with a mingling of consternation and anger that we saw the robbery committed. We waited some time for the main column to approach—Carey finally concluded to go over and try to get the horse returned to us. Father soon followed him and just as he started some one remarked they "did believe there was Charlie Buck upon the hill looking down upon the Yankees now." Sure enough we descried two horsemen on the brim of the hill near the thicket where Charlie should have been concealed but could not believe that it was Charlie till by looking through the spyglass we recognized him beyond a doubt. We at first concluded that he was a prisoner and the other horseman with him his captor but closer inspection convinced us that they were both of them of the same "Stripe." It was very rash of Charlie, and Laura and Orville concluded they would run across the field and give him warning but after they started we recollected the Yankees might be led to watch their transit across the plowed field in full view of town and thus their attention be attracted to Charlie when otherwise he might escape notice. Just then the whole column appeared coming over the hill and we saw Carey and Father returning from town leading "Old Sam"—we were as much surprised as delighted at the success of this expedition. When they came up to the stile where we were standing Carey told us he had asked the man who took the horse to return it to him, the man appealed to his sergeant to know what he must do and the sergeant—"Oh! give him up, he's not fit for cavalry service." "But," turning to Father—"I return him only on condition that those two men on yonder hill remain where they are: if they leave I shall take it for granted you have warned them, and in that case I will take your horse from you again. I have already sent my men to take them." And while we were hearing this account one of the servants said "The Yankees are after Mass. Charlie!" And we saw them dash on him from the thicket in his rear and all disappeared together over the hill. Presently we saw them coming back and poor Charlie with them. We ran down to the fence as he passed and I just had time to say "Oh Charlie, have they got you?" and "have you any message home?" But the tears leaped into his eyes and he could only compress his lips and shake his head. He is strong and brave and so far as the consequence to himself is involved could have borne his misfortune unflinchingly, but alas he knows the sorrow that it will bring upon his home—upon his poor old father. Laura and I determined to go to see him and if possible obtain his release from the colonel. We wrapped him up some apples and pies and took his overcoat, Carey going with us as escort. When we reached the camp heard that Misses Lizzie Leach and G. Petty had been before us and with a great deal of trouble succeeded in obtaining permission to approach to the prisoner in presence of an officer. We threaded our way through the wall of soldiers and horses and approached a group in the center of which we soon discovered the poor boy standing on his wounded foot. His eyes filled with tears as he saw us and still he seemed glad. He was surrounded by a whole bevy of little boys who were heartily abusing the Yankees and Miss Lizzie and Miss Gennie stood near besides a whole lot of his captors. When we gave him his overcoat one of the creatures remarked facetiously "he shows the 'spread-eagle', don't he?" The officer who had him under guard—a captain—seemed somewhat of a gentleman and he said "My boy if you were not in military service you should not be wearing those buttons" alluding to the U.S. buttons on the overcoat. A third chimed in with "Oh! he's put half and half Seccesh uniform with Yankee buttons. You are not much of a Rebel are you my fine fellow?" Charlie in reply positively affirmed that he was altogether a Rebel! They all then unanimously agreed that they honored him all the more for fearlessly declaring his sentiments. The captain now came forward and remarked that he was under the necessity of placing him with his guard as he should be compelled to leave him. So we kissed the poor boy good-bye and they carried him off. Miss Lizzie heard me inquiring for the colonel and went with me to find him. He had just ridden out of town, so we waited at Dr. Leach's till we saw him dash in town . Then we followed him immediately down to camp. As we were walking around looking for his colonel-ship I heard someone say "Are you looking for me, Cousin Lucy? Here I am," and peering through a group near the wagon saw Charlie sitting near one of the fires surrounded by his half dozen guardsmen. Passing him we came upon the colonel standing just in the rear of the wagon surrounded by his officers and reading what I supposed to be a letter he had purloined from the P.O. He was magnificently equipped but was one of the most cruel looking beings. Very tall, finely formed, a red head surmounted with a fine laced hat, a very red face, a beak-like nose, ugly blue-green eyes, a sinister mouth and long, red side whiskers.

He pretended not to see us approaching and resolutely turned his back but our friend the captain announced us to his Lordship and he then looked over his shoulder and growled out—"I told you might speak to the prisoner, why don't you go on?" With this he sharply confronted us, when Miss Lizzie stepping forward said "Colonel, the young ladies with me are relatives of the prisoner, we wish to speak to you about him." I then told him that Charlie was lame and would never be of any service to the Confederate states as a soldier any more. He asked then "why did he run?" We told him "for the purpose of saving his horse." "He did not act much like a man trying to save his horse—sitting there right in full view of our force and in company with another soldier too. He was spying our movements and communicating with the Rebel army." We asked him how that could be when his own soldiery occupied the town. "Why" he said, "if they are not in town they're somewhere near—you know where as well as I do and you'll know more in a few hours about them than you do now. I've been out myself reconnoitering." He was such a coarse kind of wretch and every time we attempted to combat his arguments he would arrest our speech by some lame attempt to act facetiously and then look around to his officers as if appealing to their admiration and they evidently regarded him as an Oracle. At times, he would try to entrap us into some betrayal of the knowledge we supposed to possess of our army. Finally I said "Colonel, if you are not attacked by our forces before you leave town you have no reason to suppose this young man has given them any information detrimental to you, if he has given no information he has not harmed you—surely you will release him?" The rude churl turned his back cooly upon me and thrusting his hands into his pockets shrugged his shoulders and looked oh! so mean. Finally he faced about and remarked contemptuously—"Well, my good woman, I don't think I shall take the fellow, of course I cannot decide as yet though." This was said in a manner which plainly implied a dismissal but just as we left his Lordship's presence Miss Lizzie in an ... proposed that we should invite him to our home. I felt as if this was too much of a condescension but while I hesitated she continued—(for the sake of getting Charlie off—I will!) I then turned about and remarked to the officer that if he would come to my house that evening I thought I would convince him of the truth of what I said, at the same time pointing to the house just across from camp. He muttered something about "seeing about it" and with this we were obliged to be contented and left camp. Had scarcely gotten home when the sergeant who had returned the horse marched up to the stile announcing that he had been sent by the colonel to see into the case of the young prisoner. He then went on to say there was no use talking about it for there was no hope of his release—he "felt sorry for him" had "been a prisoner himself" and "knew the sweets of captivity" and so on. At last turning to us he said "Good evening ladies. I hope the old gentleman will be able to keep his horse which I returned to him this morning. Can you give me a little bit of something to eat?" So I had to go off and get him some bread and butter and milk. He seemed determined to give us no comfort at least. We persuaded Father to go over and see the colonel himself—he went and presently returned saying they were about all starting—not having received the reinforcements from Cole's battalion which they professed to expect. He had seen the colonel, he promised to release Charlie after they crossed the river in case he was not attacked by our guerillas. There were two or three other prisoners besides Charlie and Newt Broy—the soldier who was not taken with him—young Bartlett and Mr. Sheppard. We watched the column as it left town as long as we could see it and then went into the house to canvass the day's events. Presently came a knock at the door and a request that Father would meet Aunt Jane at Dr. Leach's. He went and on his return said that Aunt J. and Nannie had come in just a few minutes too late to see Charlie and that he—poor fellow—had gone off without so much as a change of clothing. Oh, I'm so sorry. I certainly thought they would be long enough here to allow him to see them all at his home and knew that they would furnish him with everything. How thoughtless of me to let them pass by, go off unprovided for. Yet I hope he has not gone far either—surely they'll let him return as they said they would. Cousin Sue Buck and Nannie and Mrs. Armistead and Mrs. Wheatley walked on down to the river hoping to overtake them but only reached the bank in time to see them crossing to the opposite side. Poor Charlie, how much he is in our thoughts and hopes tonight. Surely he will come back.

> *Charles Newton Buck, captured in Front Royal, was not exchanged until after the war.*

February 21, 1864

My first thought upon waking this morning was of our dear Charlie. "Would he come?" I asked myself over and over again. We heard that poor Uncle Newton was well-nigh frantic and Ma concluded to go out and see him—Laura and Willie went with her.

Was surprised to see Aunt Jane at church—asked her if Charlie had returned but her tears were sufficient to give the sad negative. She said Cousin Sue Buck had proposed her going to Harper's Ferry to try if possible to communicate with Charlie—at least to send him clothing. We friends all held a council at the door and advised her to do so by all means.

Poor Uncle Newton is so almost heartbroken—indeed 'tis so ... all day I have felt almost as if the corpse of a dear friend had been carried away—miss the poor boy and grieve so for him—and if this is the case with us, how much the sorrow is augmented in the case of those to whom he was their all and all. Dear Charlie, he has grown to be such a comfort to us all—and like all who have become a consolation to us is snatched from us by these ruthless vandals. Aunt Jane and Mr. Berry are gone to the ferry and will, I hope, succeed in at least learning something concerning him. We will at least trust for the best.

February 27, 1864
Father heard that a part of the building at Capon Springs had burned a short time since and speaks of going up next week.
An alarm of Yankees—false. Three of the 120th Georgia Regiment supped here tonight. Took a nap tonight and then sat up till twelve to finish Father's coat. A part of Capon Springs has been burnt they say.

March 1, 1864
No news. Irvie enclosed me General Cleburne's autograph—like the old general's face very much—old gentleman I say but he's really much younger than I had thought for.

March 4, 1864
One of the Gilmore's men called in to get "a bite" and there was a deal of confusion. As it grew later I persauded Emma to go upstairs and dress to personate "Miss Duechenberry." While preparing her Jule and Annie Ford and Neville came; then the parlor rapidly filled. I went in with the girls and found Sallie Petty, Sallie Leach, Lottie Blathis, Lucie Overall, Mollie Barbee, Mollie and Mattie Cook, Wythe Cook and Hennie, Allie Ashby and Bob Buck, Vivian, Willet and Engie Leach, Willie Davidson and Neville. Presently Emma knocked at the door and being invited in created no small sensation. After playing a few games in the parlor they all adjourned to the basement where game after game followed each other in quick succession—"Blindfold," "Fox and Goose," "King William," "Jugging Along," "Travellers," "Pleased and Displeased," "Smiling Angel," "Clap in and Clap out," "Drunken Sailor," etc., etc. When they became uproarious below we "old fogies" as they voted us went into the parlor and had music. I thought so much about Nellie and wished for her tonight—know she would enjoy it all. Had nuts and ginger cakes. All left a little after eleven o'clock—Jule, Annie, Anice, Emma, Cousin Lucie, Jessie, Nannie, Bob, Nev, and Allie remaining with us. We had music and a game of "Lawyer" after all the others left and a snack so that it was near two o'clock A.M.

March 10, 1864
Was reading to Father a treatise on metaphysics when two wagons drove up bringing refugees who wished to get lodging for the night. They came in nearly drowned in the rain. Mrs. Ramey and her idiot son from Leesburg and Mrs. Hendricks, a young widow with her babe and their servants. Made them as comfortable as possible. They seemed to be nice people. Am afraid this rain will prevent the arrival of our travelers from Clarke.

March 11, 1864

Alternate sun and showers. Pouring down a little after five o'clock when we were sitting talking about Nellie and the first thing we knew the door flew and in walked the lady herself followed immediately by Aunt L. Buck—such a delightful surprise. Aunt L. and Jacquie went home when it cleared off but as for Nellie we have just had her singing and talking ever since she came home without a moment's intermission. Dear old thing. She looks so well. 'Tis after eleven o'clock. Oh me, I'm so glad she's come home again.

March 16, 1864

Was practicing on the piano when a stranger came in to see Father to beg lodgings for the night as their carriage had broken down. He proved to be a Methodist minister—Mr. Hammond, his wife and little baby and a nurse and driver. Was terribly put out by the unexpected invasion. We made them comfortable though as we could. The little Paul was a sweet little fellow—everything much more quiet and pleasant than could have been expected.

April 18, 1864

The anniversary ever to be remembered of the calling out of the "Virginia troops to Harper's Ferry" and the day our dear little band left us for the tented fields.

April 20, 1864

Wythe Cook came in to bid us farewell as he goes tomorrow with Uncle Tom en route for his brigade. Poor fellow!—it really grieves me to see him, the last of our old social circle, going from us into this cruel work. He too, seems sad. Nellie and I played and sang for him and he left about ten o'clock.

April 29, 1864

Aunt Betsie came home and told us about Dr. Leach's reported desertion of Mrs. Armistead and her exceeding great distress thereat. Ma went out to engage us "help" and returned about noon successful.

April 30, 1864

Very busy. Sweeping off the pavement when Dick Bayly came over to get me to go out with a fishing party to the river. Did not feel like it but they persuaded me and I had a pleasant walk. Found at the place of rendezvous Kate Green, Mollie Barbee, Sallie Leach, Jennie Jackson, Sallie Petty, Charlie Barbee, Welton Green, Allie Ashby, Henry Cooke, and a host of "lesser fry." Caught no fish of course. They would have been very daring fish who ventured to nibble a bite amid such a tumult as was kept up with tongues and oars. We soon wearied of fruitless sport and adjourned to the mill to weigh. I made out a hundred and thirteen pounds. From thence Dick took us out boat riding in detail. Sallie Leach and I were last—we sat on the grassy bank and gathered apple blossoms chattering like two magpies while Sallie's cavalier Charlie looked woefully on from a distance doubtless most jealous of my proximity to her. Had a delightful row in the boat firing a salute from Dick's revolver to the party on shore but a sudden shower cut our sports suddenly short —we landed and took refuge in the little veranda of Mr. Weston's sweet little cottage—'tis my ideal of a home. Started home after the rain abated a little but it resumed and was ... in a brisk shower when we reached Dr. Leach's. Sallie invited us in and we spent an hour chatting. Found Ma out in the garden dropping seeds. Poor little Evred scalded his foot terribly—sitting before the fire a kettle of boiling water overturned on his right foot and took the skin off. His screams of agony were awful and 'twas some time before he experienced any relief but I held him in my arms and told him stories and finally he proclaimed himself ready to sit up and take some supper. Poor child. I'm afraid he's going to have a bad time of it. Had a note from Jule and poor Tell was dead.

May 3, 1864
Father and the boys digging in the cornfield trying to make us some bread for next year. Very gloomy day and the children, Evred and Frank, almost crazed me being confined to the house and so fretful. Dick Bayly over to say good-bye. Wrote Uncle John by him.

> *Grant, the victor of the West, became commander of all Union armies, March 10, 1864. Halleck was named Chief of Staff. Meade continued to command the Army of the Potomac. Sherman was in command in the West. Thomas commanded the Army of the Cumberland. Banks was fighting along the Red River. Grant's plan for the summer of 1864 was to attack the Confederates from all sides. He and Meade's army would head for Richmond. General Sigel was to attack up the Shenandoah Valley. Sherman was to move against Joseph Johnston in Georgia. Banks was to attack Mobile and Butler was to advance on Richmond via the Peninsula.*
>
> *Grant's army, 100,000 strong, crossed the Rapidan River May 3, 1864, in an effort to turn Lee's right flank. He was faced by 60,000 Confederates. Lee's lookouts spotted Federal movements and he sent his Confederates east. Ewell's II Corps found the Federals on May 5, 1864, moving toward the Orange Plank Road in the Wilderness south of the Rapidan River close to Chancellorsville. Ewell's orders were to avoid a general engagement until Longstreet was up, but he was struck by the enemy. The attack was repulsed.*
>
> *On May 6, 1864, Ewell's corps and A. P. Hill's corps awaited attack. Longstreet's I Corps had not arrived. The Federals*

struck and the Confederates gave ground. The situation was acute, but Longstreet arrived in mid-morning and the Confederates began to push the Federals back.

This was Longstreet's shining hour, but he was wounded in the neck by a ball from his own men who could not recognize him in the dense woods of the Wilderness. It was a serious wound, but not a mortal one.

General Gordon discovered the Union right flank exposed and reported the situation to Ewell. The attack was not ordered until Lee arrived late in the afternoon and gave Gordon the go-ahead.

The Federals were caught off guard and nightfall saved Grant's army from serious trouble. The statistics from the Battle of the Wilderness, May 5–7, 1864, were as follows:

U.S.A.		C.S.A.	
Effectives	101,895	Effectives	61,025
Killed	2,246	Killed	Reports inaccurate
Wounded	12,037	Wounded	Reports inaccurate
Missing	3,383	Missing	Reports inaccurate

Fancied we saw Yankees' campfires on the north mountains. Report says they're at Winchester en route up the valley. Chatting around the fire before retiring tonight.

May 6, 1864

Father is very busy in the garden—has finished planting corn and now making great exertion to have every vegetable in the ground before another rain. The children have actually taken off their shoes and stockings, 'tis so very warm.

So many Yankee deserters passing constantly in squads.

May 9, 1864

Jule better—up at breakfast. After washing the breakfast things we adjourned to the parlor and read the *Messenger*, gossiped, sewed and played on piano till dinner time. Julia Hope up in the early afternoon to tell of the 'news that had just reached town—glorious news of a victory at Chancellorsville by our intrepid and peerless Lee! Poor General Longstreet wounded though not seriously and General Jones killed. Just one year tomorrow since one of our brightest military stars paled and faded from our firmament—our noble Jackson went to his rest! So rejoiced are we at the good tidings and yet so anxious as to its individual result.

An alarm of Yankees coming and Julia fled home. Seven of the enemy's cavalry did advance into town but made the visit brief. When the alarm somewhat subsided and while we were all of us, Ma, Nellie, Laura, Julia and I—sitting in a circle on the grass playing "Knife," Annie Ford, Annie Leach, Charlie Leach came over excepting Annie who is with us tonight. We walked to the creek with the girls and then continued our stroll down to the old mill where we spent a pleasant half-hour then back to the house for supper. Went into the parlor and had some twilight music and talked. And now in the chamber the girls are having a general romp. Do hope there'll be no more Yankee rumors. Felt pleasant and contented tonight. If there was only news from the battle!

May 12, 1864

Carey ran in to say the Yankees were coming. There was, sure enough, a regiment of cavalry and we had a time pitching about trying to get things arranged for their reception. Seven of them came to get something to eat and informed us the whole army would soon pass through. Sitting upstairs this afternoon heard someone talking in a rude voice and going to the window found a Pennsylvania Dutchman on horseback parleying with Father about corn to feed his horse with. Impudent churl! I was angry enough to shoot him when he tried to frighten Father into giving him the little corn he had saved for bread by telling him he would bring his whole company to search the whole house if he complied not with his demands. Father compromised by giving him some refuse feed for the fowls and the wretch chuckled gleefully over his success. About four o'clock they suddenly left town in a hurry, at least the greater number of them—some remained in camp and some went to Luray. Scarcely had they turned their backs on town before one of Mosby's officers rode up, then while upstairs writing to Scott in came Captain Montjoy and four comrades to tea—we had come from the table and everything was in confusion so we had to go to work and fix the things on the board and in a great hurry.

> *R. P. Montjoy was captain of Co. D. of Mosby's command (Forty-third Battalion.) This brave companion of Mosby was killed near Leesburg, November, 1864. When Mosby announced his death in his general order of December 3, 1864, he wrote, "His death was a costly sacrifice to victory. He died too early for liberty and his country's cause, but not too early for his own fame."*

The soldiers had just commenced eating when Father called me out to reconnoiter the premises with him and suddenly a troop of little boys came from town to inform the Confederates that there were a hundred Yankees in town. We gave the alarm and they made the most rapid exit I ever saw from the dining room and mounting their horses rode in the direction from which the enemy were expected. Captain M. rode off to town and presently a troop of twenty came by and we waved and cheered them so heartily. Oh! I do hope as Mosby is here he will "hurt somebody" before he's done. Great excitement. Reaction tonight and I'm low-spirited and tired. So "coming events cast their shadows before?" I wonder.

May 13, 1864
Father came in at noon and brought news of the advance on Staunton and sad news of the slaughter at Chancellorsville.

> *Following Grant's plans, General Sigel moved up the Shenandoah Valley. General Imboden, C.S.A. who had been assigned commander of the Valley on July 21, 1863, watched the advancing Federals and asked Richmond for reinforcements. General Breckinridge was sent from southwest Virginia and among his forces was the Cadet Corps of V.M.I. Breckinridge outranked Imboden and assumed command. The Confederates attacked Sigel's army at New Market on May 15, 1864, and drove them back in defeat.*
>
> *After the battle Breckinridge was ordered to bring his army to aid Lee in the defense of Richmond. Imboden was left with 1000 men at New Market to defend the Valley.*

Sallie Leach wants to get boarding here for the old doctor seems determined to marry and drive his children from home. I do wish we were so situated that we might take her indeed. My heart aches for the poor little orphan and such a dear girl as she is too. Sitting upstairs talking and dreaming tonight.

May 14, 1864
Sallie Leach came over in the afternoon to apply for a home in person—poor child! We all of us feel so deeply for her and large as is our family and inconvenient as 'twill be to have an addition to it, we must take her and make her as happy as we can. Her father is to be married tomorrow evening to that hateful woman and they're all going to scatter wherever they can find homes. 'Tis one of the saddest cases I ever knew. Have read of such things but never witnessed anything of the kind before. To think she has already commenced management of his home and making him whip Ninian like a dog. Then for her to boast of how she's going to arrange things and above all things her great impudence. 'Tis enough to disgust anyone in the world.

I was very sad tonight. Have just heard that Lieutenant Wells was mortally wounded, poor fellow. Mr. Gold of Clarke with us. Saw prisoners who were captured by Mosby's men brought in today.

May 15, 1864

Raining. Upstairs reading in Testament. Mr. G. left early. Laura and Jule intended to go to Dr. Leach's but the rain prevented. About eleven o'clock we saw them leaving home, all of them poor things and came here. Dear girl! How I wish we could do something to comfort her.

Jacquie here in the afternoon—says Dr. L. went about the streets today inquiring for his daughters. He's happy now, I suppose, as they've all gone. Poor Sallie, she is so sad. Children very noisy and troublesome.

May 16, 1864

Annie, Minnie and Lizzie Leach over in the evening and told us all the sad tale. How it made my heart ache to see those pale delicate girls in their sombre robes standing and telling to strangers the story of their wrong. They are bitterly afflicted indeed. Did not eat supper, had not the heart. Ah me! My heart is so heavy. Jule and I have been sitting at the front window in our room looking at the moonbeams gilding the aspen leaves and sparkling the creek and talking about the stars. The quiet loneliness of the scene and the talk have done me so much good.

May 18, 1864

Father came in to give us some additional particulars of the battle. It must have been a most desperate one and poor General Stuart was certainly killed. Irreparable loss to us! Five of Baylor's men came in to get dinner and told a great deal about it—they said Rosser's brigade repulsed three brigades of the enemy.

> *Grant again moved east for an end sweep towards Spotsylvania Courthouse. Lee sent Gen. R. H. Anderson, who replaced Longstreet as commander of the I Corps, to Spotsylvania. Anderson arrived to find the Southern cavalry already engaged. The fighting from the eighth to the twenty-first of May in this area was some of the bloodiest of the war. This included the Bloody Angle or Mule Shoe engagements.*
>
> *From May 5 to May 12 the Union sustained 26,815 casualties, killed and wounded. The Confederates had approximately a third as many losses, but they had few or no replacements. This was part of Grant's plan. In April he refused to exchange prisoners and now was willing to sustain high casualties at the price of Southern losses that could not be replaced.*
>
> *Gen. Phil Sheridan, who was in charge of Grant's cavalry, headed toward Richmond during the battle at Spotsylvania. On May 11, 1864, J. E. B. Stuart caught up with the Federals and in the Battle of Yellow Tavern just north of Richmond, Stuart was mortally wounded. He died in Richmond May 12, 1864, approximately twenty-seven hours later. With the help*

of the Richmond defenders, Sheridan was repulsed and he rejoined Grant.

That old villain Dr. Leach actually had the barefaced assurance to tell Father today that he would "shoot him" if Sallie were not returned to him within twenty-four hours. I can't find words to express my contempt for and detestation of him. Poor Sallie came home about noon—she and Laura and told us that her father was going to try and force her and Jessie home and that they would have to go to Clover Hill in the little wagon which was going from here after Aunt Lizzie who had been sent for to come to old Mrs. Turner's who was thought to be dying. Poor child!

Just as she was leaving she received an imperative summons from her father to come over and have an interview with him and she left pale and trembling just as a terrible storm of wind and rain came up. Miss Lizzie had to dismiss school for several days till she could make some arrangements for herself.

May 20, 1864

Pleasant very. Doing job work. Ninian Leach over to say good-bye preparatory to leaving for the army—poor boy, he looked so young for such a rough, trying life.

May 22, 1864

Horace brought news of a skirmish between Mosby's cavalry and a body of Yankees picketing over the river. Went into the garden and gathered flowers to put in all the rooms. Then went upstairs and sat by the open window breathing the air heavy with the rich fragrance of the locust blossoms and listening to the birds and leaves and waters making music. Ma, Grandma, Father and I went to church. Heard Mr. Berry. Was told that a body of Yankees having heard Major Turner was at home, went to his house last night to search it and there was no one at home but Lucie and her protectress, Miss Roberts. How frightened she must have been! The major had taken the precaution to spend the night with a friend but the thieves got his watch and boots though he escaped himself. Conflicting rumors as to the skirmish at the river.

May 28, 1864

Nev. Buck and Cousin Tom Buck rode up. The latter would not dismount but sat talking in his own noisy fashion at the stile. He seems to think there is no doubt of the western army having come on to reinforce Lee at Richmond.

The army in the west was busy fighting in front of Atlanta. However, Lee received a few troops from North Carolina and western Virginia.

Oh! If we could hear something definite.

May 29, 1864
Left Father on the porch repeating an account of the battle which he had from Lieutenant Samuels and came up to my room. I felt deeply sad all day.

> *Beauregard, who had been commanding the defenses of Charleston, was given the job of protecting southern Virginia and North Carolina in April, 1864. Thus it fell to Beauregard to stop Butler's army on May 16, 1864.*

Everyone seems to believe that our army as well as those of the enemy are massing at Richmond and that a most hideous and stupendous struggle is impending—if this be the case what vital interest we have involved in the issue, both nationally and individually—how entirely are we severed from all communication with the seat of war and in what suspense we must exist for the coming week till all is over—but knowing ... and bloody death ... of the strife. Only God can support us through the dangers and trials that await us and to Him I try to submit myself and those dear to me.

May 30, 1864
Mrs. Kiger passed on horseback—just in from town bringing tidings from Washington of a glorious victory gained by Lee over Grant last Friday in which we captured a hundred pieces of cannon. So glad!

> *Grant again slid to the left May 20 and on the twenty-third he tried to cross the North Anna River, but Lee was there necessitating another left swing to Cold Harbor. Lee's army had again arrived first and struck Grant on June 1, but was repulsed. Works were constructed and Union soldiers attacked on June 3, 1864, in the battle known as Second Cold Harbor. The Federals were slaughtered. Union losses were about 12,000 killed and wounded to approximately 1500 Confederate casualties. Grant now had lost almost as many men as Lee's entire army.*

Ninian Leach went off last night taking with him the horse which belonged to him and which his father refused to let him have. Came home tonight and Nellie and I went in to bathe in the creek.

June 4, 1864
Have heard through Laura that Major Simpson was certainly dead

and that General Cleburne had had a desperate fight and my heart ached for my poor Irvie as well as for Mrs. Simpson's family.

June 6, 1864

Busy preparing for our departure. Grandma home about eleven o'clock. Cousin Sue Buck and Belle in an hour. Sent Mrs. Roy's shawl home and sent a bouquet to Roxie Jackson.

Cousin Mary Cloud over in the afternoon. Rained. Rumors from our valiant army but nothing reliable though.

Went up after tea to tell Mrs. Hope good-bye. Got home and found Mr. Berry had been there with letters for us to carry to Yankeedom and Kattie Boone too. Nellie here. Laura and I busy preparing slips of flowers to carry Cousin Nellie. Got dear little Frank to sleep tonight for the last time.

June 7, 1864

Up at four o'clock. Flying around as busy as could be till seven. Kissed little Frank and Evred good-bye in their sleep. Thinking so much of what Cousin Mary told me last night about poor E. Jacquie down to see us off and Uncle Tom. Felt very sad at leaving. Met Aunt Bettie on the road and at Rose Hill Ginnie and Cousin Lizzie and all of them out to see us. Father went with us across the river and told us good-bye at Riverside. Had a charming ride—the sweetbriars in the road were still sparkling with their morning dew bath and looking so rosy and fresh while the perfume from the roses with the odor of the grapevines was perfectly intoxicating. The horse moved with great spirits and although the day was clear 'twas so cool that we did not have to hoist our umbrellas. At one o'clock we stopped in a beautiful grove of trees and spreading out our lunch had a most charming little picnic. Gathered mosses and flowers while the horse was eating. Left in an hour and had a pleasant evening ride. Did not meet a living soul from the time we left the river till we entered Berryville and then a very few of them. Reached Bloomfield about six o'clock and Cousin William met us at the wagon and conducted us into the house. Found old Mrs. Allen and Miss Lucie there taking tea and Mrs. Pittman staying with Aunt Cattie while Miss Julia was at the store inquiring for their tobacco. Did not go into tea but was introduced to them afterwards. Fannie and her mother have not returned yet—so sorry. Felt less fatigue than I expected from my journey. Chatting tonight and Cousin Nellie playing some for us. Up in our room early. There are no Yankees in the neighborhood. I felt so thankful and am so grateful that we've gotten through this far safely. Mack's a great boy. Wonder who got little Frank to sleep tonight—dear little fellow.

June 9, 1864

Gray and threatening. Mrs. and Miss Pittman left early. Played a game of checquers with Nev and beat him one game but he beat me twice.

Cousin William and I then had a game which proved a drawn one. Went in and made off a memorandum and wrote a note for Aunt Cattie. Nev, Irvie, Aunt Cattie out and Uncle Larue went out to hear the news. Ma, Cousin Nellie and I had the day to ourselves.

> *After Cold Harbor II, Grant moved his army south of the James River and attacked Petersburg, Virginia. He was held by Beauregard on June 13, 1864, until Lee could send reinforcements. Petersburg as well as Richmond was now under siege.*
>
> *The home, Bloomfield, belonging to Lucy's Aunt Cattie Larue, sister of William Mason Buck, is located near Berryville, Virginia.*
>
> *Lucy accompanied her mother to Bloomfield en route to Harper's Ferry to obtain provisions for the Bel Air household. A similar trip was made the previous year.*
>
> *Miss Lucy also had the objective of teaching her Cousin Walker, son of John Newton Buck. Uncle John's wife died before the war and their only surviving child, Walker, was living with Aunt Cattie.*

All returned at noon just escaping a heavy shower. Ma was all day trying to make arrangements for getting to the ferry but they told her they were very strict there and dissuaded her from going. A showery evening. Mrs. Davis and Martha called to tell Ma the difficulties to be encountered in an excursion to Harper's Ferry. I was perfectly enamoured of Martha—she's so sweet and pretty. Quite a heavy shower this afternoon. Ma is making arrangements to go to Van Cleersville tomorrow and Cousin Nellie is to go as far as Tudor Hall with her. Cousin William and Nellie playing for us tonight. Wish I could hear from home.

June 10, 1864
Bright, but cool. The travellers off soon after breakfast. Had a message from some gentleman who passed the gate informing me he had brought us a letter from home, but not knowing he would come this road had left it in Berryville. So anxious to get it but see no chance of doing so. Mrs. Luke called and spent a couple of hours this morning.

> *Hunter replaced Sigel on the twenty-first of May 1864 and immediately began another advance up the Valley. Sigel took command of troops in the Harper's Ferry area. Imboden again asked for reinforcements and Brig. Gen. William E. Jones, then in southwest Virginia beyond Lynchburg was sent to his aid. Jones joined Imboden June 4, 1864, and being superior in rank assumed command. On June 5 about half a mile northeast of Piedmont, Hunter struck the Confederates. Jones was killed and the Confederates beaten.*

Hunter entered Staunton on June 6, 1864, and formed a junction with Crook and Averell who had moved on Staunton from Lewisburg.

A report of the fall of Staunton but don't believe it. Altering my blue gingham dress. Was preparing to start to Rippon this evening when old Mr. Paige came in saying there had been a squad of Yankees at his house during the day. So Aunt Cattie sent Francis with me as a "footman" and Walker and I had a glorious canter on old Saltman through the dim cool arches of the woods. Went to Mrs. Phillips and tried to learn some news but she had heard but little save the confirmation of rumors already heard. A woman had just come in and was telling us of a reported battle which had been fought by the Yankees with some of Mosby's men in which a Confederate officer, Captain Gleson was killed, when a rushing sound was heard and presently a squadron of Yankees dashed by. Francis flew out to protect the house. They did not molest anything though and passed on to join the main column just beyond. I started back to Bloomfield after they left and had to wait some time in Mrs. Davis' meadow for Francis to come up. While Saltman was browsing on the white clover, old Mr. Strother came out and chatted till F. came. Got home, found Dr. Osborne there on a professional visit to little Black Billy—he was mad as a hornet—had met the Yankees on the pike. One inquired the time of day, he drew out his watch to obtain the desired information when a companion of the inquirer wrenched the watch away from the doctor thereby nearly jerking him from his horse. Could not get the ribbon I went for. So sorry.

Talked Walker to sleep in the lounge. Occupied the little end room for the first time tonight—it's to be my domicile while I remain here.

June 12, 1864

Cousin William asked me to walk in the park to see his wild geese and the deer. While there Walker found a little fawn only a day old—the prettiest most graceful little creature imaginable.

June 13, 1864

Cousin William was sitting with me on the porch speculating as to the cause of the detention of our absentees and proposing to go after them tomorrow when he sprang to his feet with "Hist! I hear the sound of wheels" and then hurried off into the gathering shades of evening to look out for them. Arrived all safe and well. Ma had been unable to accomplish anything by the trip both on account of scarcity of goods and difficulty of getting the check acknowledged. Was detained by news of a difficulty persons had in getting through. Had met with a kind reception at Cousin Meredith Helm's though and was perfectly charmed with her visit there. So glad they're here again. Have been uneasy. They brought some Yankee papers which I've been reading tonight. There has been

a bloody battle in N. Georgia. My poor Irvie!
Commenced teaching Walker this morning.

June 16, 1864

Aunt Cattie and Ma rode down to Mrs. Van Meter's to see about sending to Harper's Ferry leaving Cousin Nellie and William and me in charge of the house. Had scarcely gotten settled when Uncle L. called me hastily into the passage and going to the front door saw two ladies standing there, and peering into the hat of the first lady caught the merry gleam of a pair of sparkling black orbs and a glitter of white teeth and to my immense surprise recognized Maggie Mohler—the very girl of all others in Page County I would like to see. She introduced the other lady as "Mrs. Long." They were accompanied by young paroled soldier, a Mr. Foreman. We invited them in, gave a round introduction and learned that they were "running the blockade" with tobacco and had been directed here by Mr. F., they having no acquaintances elsewhere in the neighborhood.

June 17, 1864

Very warm. Sat on the porch steps after breakfast and talked with Maggie and showed her some little bits of poetry which I thought she could appreciate. Heard quite a heavy cannonading in the direction of Martinsburg. Dr. Osborne came in—brought no news. Dogs fought and frightened me. When it became too warm for the porch we adjourned to our room for a nap which we however did not take as our tongues ran away with our fatigue and we talked as if for dear life till late in the afternoon. When did ever I say as much before in as short a time? Ma got hold of my *Commonplace Book* and we had a review of it.

We came up to our rooms at ten o'clock and Ma and Mrs. Long went to bed but Maggie and I sat up reading letters when.there was heard the clatter of hoofs on the road above the house. Our first impression was that the Yankees had come after Mr. Foreman and we were consulting as to what we should do for him when Cousin Nellie came in with a shawl around her to say she did not think they were Yankees. We looked so ridiculous all of us standing up on the floor with wild, staring eyes and disheveled tresses and certainly we would have been in no costume for receiving the Yankees. My first thought was for my daguerreotypes and letters which were in a drawer in another room of which I had misplaced the key. However, we soon found that they were Confederates who had come by to get Foreman to go on a scout with them. Captain James Bailey, Jim Williams and Webb Maddox and a Mr. Brown. We went over into the room adjoining Cousin Nellie's and looked out of the window beneath which they were standing and I thought Maggie Mohler would have made us all hurt ourselves laughing at her mischievous comments upon the conversation that ensued below. Cousin Nellie and I donned our wrappers and went down to get the gentlemen something to eat, and when it was prepared, nothing would do but we must go and peep through the curtain of the dining room window to see them eat. When they came out on the porch Maggie got her satchel of luncheon and pelted them with ginger cakes. They declared that 'twas the first country they had ever visited where it "rained gingerbread." They remained so long before starting on their scout that Ma and Mrs. Long went to bed but Maggie and I sat on the garret steps by the window in the moonlight and talked of everything. Poetry, theology comicalities, human nature and the usual themes of very young ladies generally. She has always possessed the greatest fascination for me—I can't account for it unless it be the influence of a stronger, brighter nature over a weaker, dimmer one. She has more depth and warmth of feeling than any casual acquaintance would suspect her of possessing. I do love her dearly.

June 18, 1864

I made Mag a wreath of red roses which she declared made her look like a "calf looking through a rosebush." We came on the porch and Aunt C. had some cherries for us—but my head ached badly and I was forced to lie on the trundle bed and Maggie undressed and took her place beside me and she copied while I read from my book and we discussed the pieces together. Presently Ma and Aunt Cattie and Mrs. Long came up and the merry girl kept us all laughing ourselves almost sick till the dinner bell surprised us in the midst of our fun. Did not go down to dinner and Mag soon finished hers and came back to her place by me. We read and talked all evening—some time all would be with us, some time we were alone. Aunt Cattie about four o'clock made me drink two cups of tea and go and lie down quietly awhile till I felt better. In an hour's time I was ready to dress for the evening. We went into the parlor and commenced a game of draughts when Mr. Allen came in. I beat Maggie and gave her over to Mr. Allen who also beat her and then me too. Tea bell rang. After tea finished our game and then Maggie and Cousin Nellie sang and played.

June 19, 1864

After dinner Maggie proposed going under the beautiful horse chestnuts in the front yard. We took a knife and carved our names on the trunk, then sat on the grass till Aunt Cattie called us to come away lest we should take cold. We went upstairs and lay on the bed and fairly talked ourselves to sleep. Mrs. Long soon aroused us and said they must be going. It really gave me the blues to see them preparing to start—Maggie seemed almost as sorry to go. They will go to the Foreman's tonight and on to the store tomorrow, and will return here on their way home. I made them leave some of their clothing as hostage.

Aunt C. got a letter from Mack Bayly through Mrs. Van Meter. Poor fellow, he's at Point Lookout and wishes Aunt C. to send him something to eat.

VIII

EARLY'S VALLEY CAMPAIGN

June 21, 1864 - September 21, 1864

June 21, 1864
One of the first things I thought of this morning was that this was the anniversary of our poor Walter's fall. All day the recollection haunted me, making me so sad when I thought how

> "One that I loved grown faint with strife
> When dropped and died the tender bloom
> Folded the white tent of his life
> For the pale army of the tomb."

I know Nellie was thinking with me of our loved and lost and wanted so much to talk with her.

Josie Grantham came over about eleven o'clock and brought us news of Hunter's defeat and capture which news gladdened us so much. She remained till after dinner singing and playing.

June 25, 1864
Sewing steadily and finished Eliza's dress early. Was in the garden making a wreath for my hair when Walker called me in to say there was a note from home. 'Twas from Father—very brief but most welcome for it brought us tidings of Alvin and Irving—the former in Petersburg, the latter in Georgia. There was a letter from Uncle John—poor Wythe Cook and Jimmie Brown are wounded and Cousin Mount is with his command again and General Rosser is reported dead. Ah, me!

Lee again sent Breckinridge to the Valley. Hunter had burned much property in Staunton and after a few days' rest moved toward Lynchburg. At Lexington V.M.I. was burned as well as Governor Letcher's residence and other private property. Washington College was narrowly spared and Hunter moved on toward Lynchburg.

To defend the area Lee sent the Second Corps under Early. Ewell had become sick and had to be relieved of field duty. Early left Lee on the thirteenth of June and arrived on the seventeenth at Lynchburg. Hunter began to retreat on the nineteenth without giving battle and retreated toward Lewisburg. Early began to advance down the Valley unopposed with approximately 14,000 men on June 28. By July 2 he was in Winchester.

General Rosser was wounded but not mortally in the Battle of Trevilian's Station. In this battle Sheridan was defeated by Hampton's Confederate cavalry and this prevented the Union cavalry from joining Hunter at Lynchburg.

When Thomas L. Rosser was wounded at Trevilian's Station, Dulany took over command of the Laurel Brigade. Rosser returned to duty in August and when he was promoted in October Dulany again became commander of the brigade. Dulany was wounded and Funsten became commander until Dearing was given command. The latter was mortally wounded on the retreat from Richmond, and E.V. White took command until Appomattox when the brigade fought its way out and was disbanded at Lynchburg.

June 26, 1864

So warm. Up and dressed early. Thinking of Maw first thing. Cousin William informed us at the breakfast table that he had heard of their safe arrival at Mrs. Van M.'s last night. Visited the sick and helped Aunt Cattie and took my Bible on the porch but the flies and heat drove me to the sofa in the parlor. Had not been there very long when Ma came. Was so glad to see her all right again. She seemed not to regret having gone in the least as they did not propose the oath at all, not even questioning her.

June 27, 1864

Very warm. Sitting on the porch sewing. Rained a little about noon. After dinner went upstairs and undressed. Labelling some old letters, cutting out my black silk Garibaldi. Old Mr. Edmund Lee and his sons and Mr. Tompkins in to tea. These autocrats of Clarke I find refined, polite good sort of people but as a general thing intolerably stupid.

No Maggie yet—begin to think very strange of her nonappearance. Cousin William and Nell playing on the violin tonight. Harvesting today.

July 2, 1864

Walker and I mounted Saltman and rode down to Rippon. Heard from Mrs. Phillips but the Yankees who had gone up to reinforce Hunter had returned to Martinsburg. Went into the parlor after dinner and played and sang and old Mr. Lee read us a poem of his wife's. Mr. Thompson came in to tea and then Mr. Sidney Allen and both affirmed the news which we had for several days past been hearing of the advance of the army. Some of the young men from the neighborhood had already come in and reported Early twenty thousand strong marching upon Martinsburg. So enraptured to hear it! If Beauregard just be coming with Alvin now it would be too much glory.

July 3, 1864

Pleasantly cool. Awoke quite early and Uncle Larue came out in the yard and called out to me to listen to the cannonading. Sure enough discharge after discharge was heard. There was a cessation about nine o'clock but the firing was soon after resumed and more violently than before. Writing and reading. Perry quiet and very pleasant. Was lying down upstairs about twelve o'clock when the door opened and in marched Fannie Larue. So glad to see her. She heard that the firing was at Smithfield beyond Berryville—a diversion to deceive the Yankees as to Early's real intent.

July 4, 1864

We have Harper's Ferry, thank Heaven.

July 5, 1864

The Yankees have still possession of Maryland Heights.

July 6, 1864

> *The Federals evacuated Harper's Ferry July 4, 1864, but the town could not be occupied by Early's men because of the enemy artillery on Maryland Heights.*

An invitation came from Mrs. Van M. this morning for Ma and me to accompany her to the ferry. Delighted by the idea. Repaired ourselves, took a hasty breakfast, mounted old Saltman and rode down to her house. She did not get the wagon she expected and could not take us both. Ma insisted on my going. A young Reb by the name of Moore drove us. Enjoyed the drive but wished much for Ma. After passing Charlestown we came in view of the heights above the ferry and I had enough to do looking at them, tracing the road winding like silver tracery up the sides of the green purple mountain and the white tents of the Yankee camp about the summit, and thinking of all the various incidents connected with this classic ground of our ... history. There was still some firing and as we reached Hall Town a few miles this side of the ferry we met numbers of soldiers who warned us against venturing into the place telling us that the Yankees were shelling it and had already killed several ladies and torn the arms off a little infant in one of the doomed houses. Indeed, they had thrown shells into Hall Town itself. Each one we met told us the same story. Finally when we were within three miles of the ferry we met a surgeon who told us we were already further than was prudent, but on we went till met by a squad of Rebs direct from there and they told us there was momentarily expectation of an attack as the Yankees were said to be heavily reinforced and advancing to cross the river. We concluded "discretion was truly the better part of valor" and turned about to the house of an acquaintance of Mrs. Van M. Found a little musical box in the parlor and amused myself playing on it. About noon squads of Rebs commenced dropping in for dinner. There was a loquacious young North Carolinian who proceeded to acquaint me with the "situation." We have but one brigade there—Hokes—it seems. One of the four surgeons who came in was an acquaintance of Nannie Taylor's and belonged to the Winder Hospital, Third Division. There was also a nice little fellow—the facsimile of Mr. Moreton who said Mr. Moffatt was there with him. About three o'clock it was currently reported that the Yankees were advancing to the attack in heavy force and that if they did so our men would have to evacuate the place. So the wagons which could not be gotten out were arranged in close phalanx filled with fine new axes and harness and saddles—hay was spread all around them and the quartermasters stood awaiting the order to fire them. The order, however, did not come and when we left after four o'clock our sharpshooters were said to be crossing over to attack the Yankees and there was heavy cannonading heard from the Yankees on South Mountain. Had a pleasant ride home and met, to my great surprise, with Dr. Turner on the pike and heard from home. Was really glad to see him—he expects, I believe, to go home tonight. It was dark nearly when we reached Mrs. Van M.'s and looking back towards the ferry we saw two large fires near the Yankee camp in the mountain, and they were sending up rockets from there. Wonder what it all means? Found Uncle Alex waiting for us with horses and we rode immediately on home. Found the parlor brilliantly lighted and Maggie and Mrs. Long and Fannie there—so glad to see them. Felt very dusty and heated but washed and arranged my dress, drank a glass of milk and went into the parlor to hear Maggie sing and tell some of the adventures that befell them. They've been consistently successful in obtaining all they wished and seem really to have enjoyed themselves. When we came up to our room we three girls undressed, put on our night robes and laid on the floor till after twelve o'clock chattering. Old Mr. Taylor had just come in late as it is. They say our vanguard is at Gettysburg and Early's headquarters are at Boonsboro.

On July 9 the Southern army was south of Frederick, Mary-

land, where it forced a crossing of the Monocacy River. For the third time the Confederates were in Maryland.

July 7, 1864

I had a pleasant ride. Enjoyed the day very much despite the oppressive heat. Martha Davis is a gentle sweet girl and so pretty—Eliza too is interesting. In the afternoon Mrs. Albert Davis came in and after awhile Delphia came to tell us that Neville and Cousin Mary Cloud had come. We soon started home, Walker, Delphia (colored girl) and I walking. Found Cousin Mary reclining on the sofa in the parlor overcome with the ride. They had brought us a bundle of papers and letters and Ma and I sat on the porch steps and read the welcome missives then and there. One from dear Nellie to me telling about the children being sick and poor thing I know she's had a time of it with them. Then there were three from Irvie and one from Alvin—written, all of them, in good spirits. It was almost too much joy getting them all at once though.

July 11, 1864

We were invited to spend the day at Mr. Luke's. Neville drove Walker and myself in the little wagon and Aunt Cattie, Ma and Cousin Mary went in the rockaway and Uncle Larue went on horseback. Found Colonel Grantham, Mr. Shirley and Cousin George Carter and Mr. and Mrs. Enders there. Then came Bettie Moore and her brother Nicholas, a wounded soldier boy. Then Sidney Allen and Mr. Page, Mrs. Ed Monica and Annie Lee and young Miss Lee. All dinner parties are stupid and this was no exception to the general rule, though 'twas not quite so bad as I anticipated. Mr. and Mrs. Luke are so kind that they will make you enjoy yourself. They had a sumptuous dinner and for dessert there was frozen custard and cream, a thing which I've not seen before since the war.

July 13, 1864

Ma left quite early. Felt so sad about her going that I took a good cry instead of my breakfast. Felt stupid and unwell all day.

Sitting on the porch in the moonlight thinking of home and the happy faces then brightening at Ma's arrival. Old Mr. Taylor came in and said 'twas reported that our army was falling back to this side of the river. Don't believe it though.

July 14, 1864

Heard that Early was shelling Washington City at a greater rate.

By late afternoon, July 11, 1864, Early's forces were at Washington. He elected to wait until the morning of the twelfth to determine whether his small force had a chance to capture the Union capital. During the night Washington was reinforced by men from the Richmond front. General Early cancelled his attack orders and saved his force from possible destruction. His objective was completed, "We haven't taken Washington, but we've scared old Abe Lincoln like hell!"

Early recrossed the Potomac on the morning of July 14, 1864.

July 16, 1864

I suppose we're to be given up to the Yankees again sure enough for our army is leaving the Potomac. Wonder what it all means—this short and bloodless campaign in Maryland and the present return of the forces to Leesburg. General Early has an object in it, no doubt, and fully understands all he intends to do. Wish I did too. Saw some beautiful little rabbits.

July 17, 1864

Read two sermons aloud to Aunt Cattie and read in the Bible myself. Went upstairs to lie down and on coming down to dinner found six soldiers there on the porch who had come in to dinner. They belonged to Early —Hoke's division—and the army was all coming back in this direction. We were so surprised but had not long to indulge our astonishment for the poor fellows kept thronging in for their dinner and it required all our united efforts to supply them. I washed dishes, went to the garden for onions—sliced these and carried pickles from the cellar to the dining room all the afternoon. Had fifty in to dinner and then after a short respite there were ten more in for tea. Major Thornton, Dr. Bizzel, a captain on Early's staff, and a couple of young Marylanders and a young lieutenant were really the only fairly civilized specimen of humanity that we had. This one young Marylander was a nice little fellow—very much like Johnnie Wilson and a member of Bradley Johnston's cavalry. He related a good many anecdotes of the campaign in Maryland.

July 18, 1864

Soldiers in bright and early for breakfast. Had very well-behaved guests. The Lieutenant Rogers has a queer little North Carolina page who comes down every day and by whom Aunt C. sends him his meals. Today he wrote her a nice little note. Darning socks for the soldiers. Dr. McM. in to dinner and a number of others beside. Busy feeding the Rebs till three o'clock—then played and sang some for the doctor. Then wrote a little and finally put on my riding habit to accompany Cousin Kate and Cousin James by invitation down to Rippon. Had a pleasant ride, transacted our business and started home just before sunset. Heavy cannonading in direction of Castleman's Ferry. They say the Yankees have crossed to this side of the river and are charging our batteries on the mountain. We could see the folds of heavy smoke clinging about the mountain gorges and all the way home through the dim woods in the shadowy twilight the heavy boom of the cannon fell like the voice of Doom. 'Twas dusk when we reached home. All seemed to think our army will have to retire up the valley if the Yankees advance. Oh, me! Whither are we tending, I wonder. Old Hunter has burned Andrew Hunter's home in Charlestown.

> *General Hunter, U.S.A., burned the homes of Alexander Hunter, a Virginia state senator and the general's first cousin. Homes of Colonel Edmund Lee and Colonel A. R. Boteler were also fired. After General Early learned of this he decided to "open the eyes of the people of the North to this enormity, by an example in the way of retaliation." On July 29, 1864, he sent his cavalry to Chambersburg, Pennsylvania, to demand $100,000 in gold or $500,000 in greenbacks for the indemnification of the Southern people whose property had been burned by the Yankees and if they did not pay, the town would be burned. On July 30, 1864, Chambersburg was fired.*

July 19, 1864

Not all the soldiers gone yet. Seventeen came in for breakfast. Soldiers in frequently during the day and among them a poor sick fellow who remained till the afternoon. I heard that the army was falling back and Cousin James took a sudden fancy to fall back with it, so after dressing this evening I went to work and wrote home and finished my letters to Alvin to send to Warren by him. Little Charlie Lee brought us a letter from Uncle John—an old one, though.

Memorable day for Bloomfield. About midnight I dropped into a doze which was broken by Aunt Evelyn coming in with a candle to get something for Cousin Nellie who she said was sick. Felt very uneasy and did not sleep until nearly day. Was up by five o'clock and downstairs to see Aunt Cattie whom I found quite unwell. She got up though and very soon Cousin James left. Dr. Osborne and Mrs. Luke were sent for and soon came in—and when Aunt Cattie sent for Cousin Mary and me to take a private breakfast Cousin Kate met us on the staircase and told us Cousin Nellie had an "immense daughter." Was so glad she seemed to be doing well. Spent a quiet morning. Went up to see the stranger—a very fine specimen of infantile femininity.

Heavy cannonading all evening in direction of Bunker Hill.

July 20, 1864

Old Mr. Lee in this morning to tell us that the Yankees had burnt his house and he and his family were at Mr. G. Pendleton's houseless and without any of this world's goods at all scarcely. Poor old man. He wanted Nellie LaRue's but I'm afraid won't get it. Faulkner's, Butler's, Dr. Byington, Dr. Tanner, Mr. Huntley and Mrs. ... houses are all said to have been burnt and this dense smoke that fills the air seems to indicate that the work of destruction continues. Father of Mercy, where is this all to end?

Mrs. Luke left this morning and we all spent a good portion of the day in Cousin Nellie's room. She continues quite well and the baby decidedly improving. Mrs. Luke back tonight. All sorts of rumors from our army but none reliable. Reported that the Yankees have stolen all Cousin George C's Spanish dishes. Hope 'tis false, poor fellow.

July 21, 1864

The nurse Cousin Nellie had engaged—Ann Eliza—came this morning. Dr. Osborne said the other day there was a letter at his house for some of us and we expected him to bring it but he didn't and was rude when we asked him about it that in a fit of indignation I begged Aunt C. to let me ride down to Rippon and let me get it. After some hesitation with regard to Yankee troops passing up the road she consented. Mrs. Osborne met me at the stile and gave me a package telling me at the same time that an ambulance train had passed down last night with four hundred wounded en route for the ferry, said wounds having been inflicted they said in Loudoun. And a large baggage train had gone up in direction of Yankee army. Our troops were supposed to be somewhere in direction of Front Royal. Was afraid to open the package on the pike, but we turned off into the woods, I unfastened it and found within a paper of the twelfth, the ... for Uncle L. and in the envelope directed to me was a letter from Ma, one from Nellie and one from Nannie besides one from Ma to Aunt Cattie and a note from Nellie to Cousin Mary. I was so overjoyed, so bewildered with my good fortune that I scarce could sit on my horse, but for all that made out to read them before returning home.

Attending to Cousin Nellie and the baby after tea. My letters have made me almost wild but I begin to want more already.

July 24, 1864

Mr. Page, Mr. Luke and Mr. Senter in. Latter brought good news, our army again in this vicinity—Early had whipped the Yankees near Winchester and driven them back to the Potomac. Mulligan certainly mortally wounded. So delighted.

> Col. James A. Mulligan was commanding along the Baltimore and Ohio Railroad. In the battle near Winchester on July 24, 1864, he received three mortal wounds and died some forty-eight hours later. He was thirty-four years old.

August 1, 1864

Spent a pleasant day chatting and reading and watching the soldiers passing. Had an immense glass bowl of frozen custard placed on a stand in the parlor after dinner and we ate our satisfaction of the cooling refreshment.

The army is not falling back.

August 5, 1864
Soldier here getting provisions for hospital in Winchester.

August 10, 1864
Was sitting in Aunt Cattie's room after dinner when a loud holler was heard and Aunt Cattie went to the porch just in time to see a Yankee dash up to the little front gate. He instantly ordered her to bring that horse (Saltman was grazing in the yard with his saddle on) out to him in the most peremptory manner. She, as peremptorily, refused and by this time Uncle L. came out and the wretch then commanded him to bring it out. In answer to this Uncle L. deliberately led the horse around the corner of the house and Aunt C. told the Yankee she thought it was too impudent in him to talk to her in that style—if he got the horse he would have to come after it and he shouldn't have it then either for 'twas her horse and he shouldn't have it. With this the cutthroat flung the gate open and dashed up the gravel walk shouting "D—n you, I'll shoot you and the horse too" while he brandished his pistol in a frightful manner. Seeing Uncle L. leading the horse away he ordered him to stop and with an oath that made me shudder he cocked his pistol and aimed at him vowing he would shoot him down and so determined and bloodthirsty the villain looked I was sure that he would carry his threat into execution and closed my eyes to shut out the dreadful scene. Uncle L. was as bold as a lion though and resisted to the last. The villain even tried to ride over him and knocking his hat off his head endeavoring to fell him with a blow of his pistol on the head. A scuffle ensued in which it seemed as if Uncle L. must be killed and Aunt Cattie called for Cousin Will who was upstairs with Cousin M. to come down and protect his father. He came down and with Cousin M. and me in the passage Cousin N. was afraid for him to go out and entreated him not to show himself as he would augment the disturbance and at last grasped his coat to detain him. Both were pale as ghosts and I felt that my face was but a reflection of theirs. He broke from her and rushed out explaining to the Yankee that the horse was blind in one eye—still the caitiff persisted saying he was ordered to bring to headquarters all horses found with saddles on them. Uncle L. was the best man though and carried the horse off to the garden leaving the Yankee swearing that he would report him to headquarters. I never was so alarmed in my life for I was sure the fellow looked as if shooting a man would be an interesting amusement to him. After he went away I went upstairs to sit with Cousin Nellie and wash and dress. Had just completed this operation when a great slamming and locking of doors brought me downstairs and they told me the Yankees were coming and just as it commenced pouring down rain three of them rode up and demanded something to eat. One of them,

a tiny, beardless boy, was spokesman and very saucy after satisfying his appetite he turned his attention to some colts in the park and proposed going out and getting them. They found out they were unbroken colts and impracticable and they then chased the deer, and finally ended the entertainment by running after the geese and knocking them on the head with their pistols, killed four of them. It was so provoking. The infantry were in camp in the Page's yard and we had a benefit of all the stragglers that passed. We had to keep up a perfect system of picketing on the porches to watch lest they should steal something. They applied—numbers of them—for milk and butter and were refused upon plea of having none to spare. Upon sending down to get milk and butter for tea it was discovered they had broken in the back window of the spring house and rifled it of its contents. Such confusion, such excitement! I was almost crazy. Uncle Larue had imprudently left Saltman in the garden instead of the cellar where Cousin Mary and I begged him to put her and about bedtime 'twas discovered that she had been stolen through the back of the garden. I could have cried to think of them getting the poor little pony particularly after Uncle L. having struggled so for her. The baby was better tonight and the excitement and fatigue and exposure to damp air has brought on such a miserable headache that I can scarce breathe. Oh, me!

August 11, 1864

Uncle Larue finds he lost a half dozen of his sheep and one hog and I think has come off pretty well considering all things. Miss Annie Page over—says they fared very well. Mr. Luke came in the afternoon and said he had lost thirty sheep and as many swine, all his horses but one, oats, corn and hay all in one fell swoop. Felt so wretched all day—in the late afternoon Fannie L. surprised us by coming in in a state of excitement to say she had been obliged to come up from her aunt's on business and a Yankee had halted her and when she refused to do so fired twice at her. To cap the climax old George gave her a chase just as she reached here and 'twas not wonderful she should look nervous. She was so cheerful though, tonight, that she roused me from my languor and I felt better. The corps that passed us was Sheridan's and I would not be surprised if Lee's army comes through the valley again this summer and if so they will seem dear friends to home.

> Grant placed Sheridan in charge of the Union forces operating against Early and on August 7, 1864, he took command. On August 10, 1864, Sheridan's army moved out of Harper's Ferry. General Early's army was located along the west bank up the Opequon Creek. Early fell back up the Valley to a better defense line at Fisher's Hill. He was followed by Sheridan's army.

August 12, 1864

Much better this morning. Quite busy making a Garibaldi this morning. Baby not well all day and Fannie nursing it a great deal.

A Garibaldi was a kind of shirtwaist worn by women. It was named for its resemblance to the red shirt of the Italian patriot.

Heard a great rumbling of Yankee wagons on the pike tonight. Feel anxious to hear what it means. Hope Mosby is after them and will take them by surprise just to spite them for taking away all our butter and condemning us to dry bread for four days. Lovely night.

August 13, 1864
Was awakened by Fannie coming to my bedside and bidding me listen to the cannonading. Sure enough there were sound of artillery and small arms firing coming up through the still morning air. After breakfast heard that Mosby had pitched into a train of 150 wagons going up to the army and taken them from the Yankees and sending them off barehanded.

At 10:30 A.M. on August 12, 1864, a 525 wagon train with with approximately 3000 men left Harper's Ferry for Winchester with supplies for Sheridan's army. By 11:00 P.M. the train was about one mile from Berryville. The wagons were stopped at a small stream and the animals were watered and rested. At 1:00 A.M. the leading teams began to move, but by the time the sun was rising a large portion of the train had not moved. Mosby, with 300 men, attacked the train at dawn and burned seventy-five wagons, captured 200 prisoners, 500-600 horses and mules, and nearly 200 beef cattle and other valuable stores.

August 15, 1864
Aunt C. had me helping her take a comb of honey awhile after tea and then Cousin Mary and I walked out to find Fannie. She did not come back till near dusk and as we walked home she told us there was a rumor of Longstreet being at Fisher's Hill. Oh! My prophetic heart! Want to go home!

On August 6, 1864, Lee ordered Kershaw's division of infantry and Fitz Lee's cavalry to northern Virginia to aid Early. These reinforcements were under General Richard H. Anderson, Longstreet's successor after the latter was wounded. The troops under Anderson of Longstreet's corps came into the Valley and encamped at Front Royal. On August 16, 1864, Sheridan fell back toward Halltown.

August 17, 1864

Mr. Taylor told me he had brought plenty of letters but could not bring them through the picket's station near Berryville. So provoking! He only remained one day and one night in Front Royal and has been all this time gasconading about over the ridge. Left saying he would be back tonight or in the morning and bring them to us.

Old Mr. Taylor came in to a late supper and told us he was unable to return home today, the Yankees had fallen back to Berryville and infested the place refusing ingress and egress to all. So distressed about not getting my letters. Preserved some blackberries for Aunt Cattie today.

August 18, 1864

> *The Federal authorities set forth to rid themselves of the ever present attacks by Mosby's guerrillas. Sheridan wrote Grant after the Berryville wagon train raid that he would "destroy all the wheat and hay in the country and make it as untenable as possible for a Rebel force to subsist."*
>
> *As Sheridan moved back to Halltown this order was carried out.*

There was a Yankee to breakfast, quite a civil being he proved to be. Raining in torrents all morning. Was upstairs visiting when Fannie came up to say the Yankees were searching the servants' rooms. Down I went and found they had searched under their beds and in to all their little boxes for Government property and ended by demanding Alex's money, knife and comb out of his pocket and Aunt Evelyn's clothing and all of Dan's money. They then rode away without deigning to enter the house. They had not been very long gone when three cavalrymen rode in to the front gate and up to the porch where we sat. One of them remarked in an insolent tone "I want to search the house"—upon which Fannie stepped forward and inquired: "By whose authority?" One of them, a pert little stripling, answered "By authority of this officer," pointing to one of his comrades as he spoke. Officer indeed!—no more officer than Fannie herself. In they came and the little malapert commenced upon Aunt Cattie's dresser drawers, running his fingers into the little memorandum books and spool and work boxes for "government property!"—"arms" and "Rebels." Aunt C. had neglected to conceal a little casket of jewelry belonging to Aunt Millie and slipping it out of the drawer handed it to Fannie to carry away. The wretch must have seen her in the glass for wheeling about just as she reached the door he shouted "What's that you're carrying off there? Bring it here!" Not heeding him she hurried on through the hall and he went after her trying to grasp it out of her hand. She resisted and he raged threatening her in a loud voice at last drawing his pistol and taking deliberate aim he swore he would shoot her if she did not deliver it. She never quailed but facing him with her back to the parlor door held the casket behind her refusing even to let him see it lest he should wrest it from her. He then fired his pistol or rather snapped a cap right full in her face without producing any impression. Rushing forward he attempted to gain possession of the coveted box and a rough hand to hand scuffle ensued in which Fannie dealt the miscreant such a blow as sent him reeling from her. The soi disant officer who with his companion had been an amused spectator of this scene now came forward to interfere. Telling Fannie that she had better be quiet about the matter and if she would let him just notice if the box contained nothing contraband he would release her. She had told him previously that there was only some trinkets of a dead friend but to prevent further annoyance she hastily flung the lid open and giving merely a glimpse of its contents marched triumphantly off with her treasure. The wretches showed conclusively that they were looking for booty, money and the like for they did not so much as look into any place where there was any possibility of concealing arms and Rebels but drawers and trunks and desks were ransacked. Going upstairs they noticed Cousin Nellie's immense traveling trunk standing in the hall near her door. This immediately attracted their attention and they demanded it to be opened. They were told it belonged to a sick lady but it mattered not who the owner was and they were evidently skeptical of the invalid. To convince them the door of her room was thrown open and there was Dummie with the little infant on her lap just in the act of bathing it. Fannie warned them against venturing into the room lest the "little Rebel" should have some design against them. She called them poltroons and the little imp who had been most forward all the time told her if she persisted he would burn the house just as soon without as with orders. They were informed that she was not an inmate of the house only a visitor from New York. They immediately wanted to know what a New Yorker could be doing here and were informed she had come down on a visit. Something was said about her being in Middletown and they immediately mistook it for Middletown, Virginia, and told her with fiendish delight that she had not a roof to her head as they had burnt M. and would burn Berryville and Winchester too. One even went so far as to say B. had been already destroyed. Finally, after a deal of impudence from them they departed having found nothing they thought worth taking in the way of money or jewelry thanks to our foresight and their footsteps had not grown cold on the threshold before two Yankees were after the white mare in the park which Cousin Will had protected and cherished so carefully. Off he went through the falling rain and Fannie, unwell as she was, after him. After divers fruitless efforts the horse was at length secured and Fannie not being able to do anything in the park came out on the road near the carriage house endeavored to twitch the bridle out of the Yankee's hand. Both of the wretches endeavored to ride over her but she sprang into the carriage house door and picking up a rock struck the wretch a telling blow on the shoulder with it. He was angry but the captured colt was restive and he hadn't time to give vent to his anger. There was a half hour's truce during which time and indeed all the morning they were pouring in in squads. They said Mosby's having taken their wagon trains had cut off their supplies and they were starved. Some of them were civil and offered to pay. Others and the majority of them finished eating and went right out to the park to take the seven young colts grazing there. Some would ask for milk and butter and Fannie very cordially invited them down to the springhouse that they might help themselves—the milk and butter had previously been removed to a place of safety and the door flung wide open for observation. About twelve o'clock they commenced swarming in by myriads—dirty, barefooted wretches and the first thing was to break the iron bars of the meat house window and climbing up on each other's shoulders enter the place and pitch out the meat—ten and twelve pieces fell into a dark corner and those Uncle Larue and I discovered and slipping around secured and brought into the house and hid. Then while this robbing was going on others were scampering like madmen over the yard and through the porches after the fowls till the whole air for hours was sounded with cries of the poor geese, turkeys, ducks and chickens. They got all the geese and turkeys save the old gobbler and a little wild turkey and nearly all the chickens and ducks. One old rooster they pursued for a half-hour straight ahead and Fannie and I stood on the porch and laughed at him, she remarking that if he only would pursue a Rebel with as much pertinacity he might stand some chance of catching him. The fellow sullenly replied that he did not care for the rooster and he had seen the Rebs run as fast as the rooster ever did. "Yes" replied F. "You looked over your shoulder." All this while there was an excessive fire of musketry going on and we knew the sheep and hogs were suffering for it. Dinner was not to be thought of for the imps thronged the kitchen and stole the food from the fire where it was cooking. Presently Delphie ran to me for the key to the cellar press and going down with it as fast as I could I found two miserable wretches had already broken the doors down and were running their fists down into my nice preserved blackberries and raspberries and Aunt C.'s pickles. They had not finished searching when Aunt Cattie and I got there and laid hands on a box of candles on an upper shelf. Aunt C. insisted on their not removing it as it contained nothing to eat but the ringleader swore he would see in it so I said to Aunt C. "Do let him have some tallow candles—no doubt he can digest them." The fellow turned on me with a scowl and said savagely, "Don't want to eat none o' yer candles." As the wretch was stooping down to carry his investigations further I noticed an immense excrescence on either side of his backbone showing through the folds of his loose flannel shirt, which I at first imagined to be a natural deformity but the bump commenced a bitter struggling and kicking and proved itself to be a captive duck which had been consigned to his novel haversack. I could not help laughing angry as I was. After rifling the press they insisted on breaking into the other part of the locked cellar, but we diverted their attention and succeeded in getting rid of them. Coming up out of the cellar I found Cousin W. leading old Fan the last riding horse up to the house and Fannie and I concluded to put her in the cellar. It was the longest time before we could succeed in eluding the Yankees so as to lead her through the kitchen and back into the cellar. A couple of Yankees caught a glimpse of us as it was and almost hurt themselves laughing at the experiment. Providence seems to protect the horse for they did not break into the back cellar through repeatedly in the act of doing so and did not find in the house the bacon and other supplies concealed there. When remonstrated with in regard to their depredations their invariable reply was, "This is nothing to the way the Rebs did in Maryland." False cravens! They wanted honey and threatened and coaxed for it. Finally two or three of them proceeded to make a raid on the icehouse where the bee stands were. Uncle L. very quietly walked up to the doorsill and mildly suggested the propriety of evacuating the place. They answered him with oaths and jeers and he took his cane and punched into the hives stirring up the little laborers most unmercifully. Then he retreated while the Yankees were enraged at the coolness of the proceedings as well as the stings of the bees—

Lucy's writing on this date in her dairy ended abruptly.

The following insert was taken from a diary kept by Nellie.

Friday, August 19, 1864

Spent another quiet rainy day with Alvin am so glad it is so disagreeable and no one coming in to interrupt poor Alvin so stiff and sore from walking from Culpeper C. H., tells us he has thirty days furlough but means to make it a gum elastic one. Went in the parlor late in the evening laid down his pallet but we all sat and talked with him till late.

Tuesday, August 23, 1864

We all rose early and gave Ma and Cousin James an early start. I'm so glad Lu's coming home as much for Alvin's sake as for my own. He misses her so. Found after Ma left she had forgotten my letter to Lu but did not regret it as it was such a blue one.

Friday, August 26, 1864

Laura and I went on the house this morning and put out

clothes, beds, carpets and our house and porch were covered. Alvin was trying to put an old clock together and after almost putting Evred's eyes out concluded to abandon it. Just then J. T. Petty came. The two had their apples and roast corn just like two children till dinner. After dinner we all sat out under the porch laughing and talking till nearly five o'clock. I went upstairs dressed myself came down. Alvin and I went out to the big gate to watch for the absentees and there they were sure enough! Was shocked to find Lu looking so wretchedly but oh! so glad to have her back again.

August 20, 1864

Felt unwell and blue. Went upstairs to write. Helped Aunt C. hide her meat and blankets. Mrs. Van M. came in just from up valley. Told of Longstreet's corps being between here and Front Royal and of a battle near F. R. Our troops only ten miles from here. It almost set me crazy to hear of it. Went upstairs to take a cry but Fannie danced me in her arms and got me in a good humor. Sidney Allen and Edgar here—latter brought late newspapers. Had a great romp with F. in the parlor. Mr. Taylor brought my letters—one from Ma, Cousin Mack, Scott and Benton. It almost crazed me. Had no appetite at all for my supper.

August 21, 1864

Heavy cannonading all day. Yankees driven out of Berryville and Fannie and I went over to Clifton to see the soldiers pass. Had a great many Rebs to supper. Sixth Regiment suffered severely but no friends hurt. Longstreet's coming!

August 23, 1864

Cousin James came. Said something indefinite about Ma's starting down which raised me off my bed. Went down and met Chris Larue. He told he'd seen Alvin a short time since and that he spoke of coming home. Just then they said the wagon was coming and sure enough there was Ma and Orville. Was almost wild with delight at seeing them. When Ma told me I must get well because Alvin was at home I felt as if I should faint. And General Anderson and Longstreet's old staff—Major Latrobe and all.

> Anderson's forces operated in conjunction with General Early against Sheridan until recalled by Lee. On September 3 Anderson moved toward Berryville for the purpose of crossing the Blue Ridge at Ashby's Gap. Two divisions from Sheridan's army were met in a raid toward the rear of Early's army. The Federals were driven back. On September 5 Anderson moved to Winchester and on the fourteenth to Front Royal to cross the Blue Ridge. Fitz Lee's cavalry was left with Early.

August 26, 1864

Had a nervous spell last night and very unwell this morning but the thought of dear Alvin and home nerves me to make effort to come and I stood it better than could have been expected. The children met us beyond the mill and then Alvin and Nellie at the barn. Almost broke down at the meeting with all the dear ones. Alvin is thin but so natural and so cheerful and all the rest seem just as usual save that Frank is grown more saucy and intelligent than ever.

At home once more and now I feel like I could be perfectly contented.

August 27, 1864

Cool and bright. Got up and went around. Played and sang for Alvin, all went in the garden to gather grapes and finally I went to bed with another chill and fever. Got up in the afternoon and crept downstairs but tonight felt weak and when Alvin came to the sofa where I lay and kissed and caressed me I had to cry like a baby. Dear, dear fellow!

September 1, 1864

All went to spend the day at Oakley save Laura and myself. Nellie returned home to dinner. Tried to write to Scott but was too weak and unwell. There was an alarm of the approach to Yankees and after Alvin and Cousin Mack came home we persuaded them to go on up to the "Mountain" to spend the night. 'Tis too provoking to have the boys go off when there's no earthly foundation for such report.

September 2, 1864

The boys away all day. Alvin, J. T. Petty and Cousin Mack in to tea and after tea Mrs. Moffatt walked up to invite us to spend tomorrow evening at Mrs. Hope's. While sitting on the porch all of us laughing and talking a soldier walked up and inquired if Captain Irvin Buck's father resided here. He introduced himself as Lieutenant Crittenden late of Cleburne's staff and we welcomed him as a fellow officer of Irvie's—though it has been two months since he saw Irvie. Playing and singing in the parlor all of us till bedtime. It reminds me so much of the last night I sang and played for Alvin, but dear Irvie was with us then and now we miss him all the time when with him. Dear, dear boys.

September 3, 1864

Gray and damp. Chatting with Lieutenant Crittenden and repairing his coat and hat for him. He's a queer fish, seems a mixture of misanthrope, universalist, and fame-worshiper. Still he's gentlemanly and refined in manner and something about him makes me compassionate him. Lieutenant C. left after dinner. Made our respective toilettes and after a great many capers cut by Alvin we started up to Mrs. Hope's about five o'clock under a very threatening sky. Soon after we arrived Lucie Weaver came in and then Dr. Mitchell and Mr. Hutchins, a little wounded soldier.

Were having a quiet, pleasant time—had gotten up from the tea table and standing in the front parlor door when Mrs. M. rushed in and said Carey had just come from home to say the Yankees were coming and the boys must run to the thickets. We just pushed them out of the house without their hats and they waded across the creek and scampered up the hill into the cornfield in an incredibly short space of time. Alvin laughed heartily all the time. Carey went after them with their hats. 'Twas a false alarm we learned at nightfall and were chagrined enough at having our plesant party broken up and suffering such uneasiness all for nothing.

September 4, 1864
Eliza told me early this morning that Mr. Lake had come in to inform us that the boys spent last night at his house and to ascertain if the Yankees had really come. Went home early and soon afterwards Cousin Mack and Alvin came laughing over last night's adventures. Cousin M. and Aunt L. Blakemore went home and we were all alone. Alvin was tired and sleepy but could not rest for the reports constantly coming in of the approach of the Yankees. Had a little quiet talk in the afternoon and Nellie and I sang and played hymns with him but Uncle Mack came in the later afternoon and took him home with him. Oh!—how I do lament every moment when he is away from us—so little of his society have I enjoyed and he speaks of leaving the latter part of the week. Oh me!

September 6, 1864
Raining. Busy making Alvin's tobacco bag. He, dear boy, came in to dinner and we had a comfortable chat with him in the afternoon. Sat on the porch at night and Nellie told him of some of her escapades of "Camp Pickens" memory. Had a long talk in Ma's room too—could not bear to go to bed; hated so to leave Alvin. Early has given the Yankees "beans" near Berryville. Nellie's birthday.

September 7, 1864
Cousin Mack up early this morning and we concluded to spend the day at Oakley. Alvin and Cousin Mack walked out to Mountain View and Ma, Nellie, Frank and I over to Oakley. Found Aunt Bettie looking well and the baby very sweet. Boys did not get back till twelve o'clock. Spent a most pleasant day. Met Uncle Tom at the hospital and he told us of the fall of Atlanta. So sorry to hear it—no particulars given.

Gen. Joseph Johnston was replaced by General Hood, July 17, 1864. Jefferson Davis wanted to make sure Atlanta would not be lost without a fight. In Johnston's retreat from Chattanooga after assuming command from Bragg, Sherman's army had had over 10,000 casualties. On July 22, 1864, in the Battle of Atlanta, the following casualties were sustained.

Peachtree Creek

U.S.A.	C.S.A.
Effectives 20,193	Effectives 18,832
Killed and wounded 1,600	Killed and wounded 2,500

Battle of Atlanta

U.S.A.	C.S.A.
Effectives 34,863	Effectives 36,934
Killed 430	Killed and wounded 7,000
Wounded 1,559	Missing 1,000
Missing 1,733	

Hood pulled back into the fortifications of the city and Atlanta was under siege. On September 1 Hood evacuated Atlanta and Sherman entered.

Hood entered Alabama and went back into northern Georgia to cut Sherman's supplies. Hood then headed his army for Tuscumbia, Alabama, late in October to begin his invasion of Tennessee. Sherman sent a portion of his army to follow Hood, but they were soon recalled and he started his march to the sea from Atlanta November 16, 1864. Sherman did send General Thomas and the Army of the Cumberland to Nashville to defend that area from Hood's invasion.

Sat on the porch by Alvin and he drew my head to his shoulder and put his arms around me and we had a long sweet talk such as we have never had before. Darling brother!—this visit of your's will give me strength to endure much of sorrow and disappointment the coming winter. We had just gone into Grandma's room and were sitting there quietly talking when Dollie ran in almost fainting with excitement to say Mrs. Moffatt and she had come up to tell us the Yankees were coming in town. Alvin bounced and made for the cornfield and Mr. S. followed suit. Had an hour of intense excitement and then discovered it was a false alarm as usual. Dear me! I wish the authorities would shoot the wretches who make it their business to bring such exciting alarms just for the sake of raising a row. Wonder when Alvin will come back?

September 8, 1864
Raining. Making biscuits and pies for Alvin to carry with him; he leaves tomorrow. Oh dear!—it makes my heart ache to think of it. He

came in about ten o'clock. They stayed at Mr. Lake's last night. 'Twas a day of confusion and I felt very unwell and to cap the climax Mr. Shipe and Alvin were both run off about four o'clock by a new report. 'Tis too provoking, our pleasure in Alvin's visit has had nothing to mar it but these rumors so exciting and trying.

September 9, 1864

Bright. Cousin Mack up early to make preparations for leaving. Glad and sorry to see him. Busy making preparations for Alvin. He came home about ten o'clock. Mrs. Moffatt up and Alvin had a great romp with her. Eating peaches, melons and grapes. Had a little conversation with Alvin just before dinner but not near as much as I wished. I have had so little of his society since he came that I've not said half of what I wished to say to him and I shall grieve over it enough. We all sauntered about the yard under the aspens until dinner and immediately after the boys left. Dear Alvin!—his last words ring in my ears "Never mind Lou! take good care of yourself and I shall be at home again in December." This shall be my talisman against the distress against his departure. My watchword through the dreary fall. Poor fellow, he lingered as long as he could and made every excuse for turning back to look at us. We went on the house and waved to them as long as they remained in sight and then came down to the empty rooms that had late been musical with his voice and footstep and felt very much like a corpse had but just been carried forth. Had to write Irvie though and it kept me from thinking too much. Three soldiers stayed here tonight—met the boys over the mountain and Alvin directed them here. Poor Irvie I'm so sorry; very anxious about him since these late battles.

September 10, 1864

Was upstairs preparing my letter for the mail when a shout from below announced Uncle John's arrival. Glad to see him particularly as he had seen the boys nine miles from here last evening. Seems in good spirits. Got three letters from Irvie—none later than August 15 though and no news. Oh for something since the fall of Atlanta!

September 16, 1864

Ma and Aunt L. spent the day at Colonel Jacobs'. Cousin James Larue came from Clover Hill to dine here. In the afternoon the children all went with him to the mill and presently I heard Evred screaming and Father bore him into Grandma's room pale and in great agony. His leg was broken. Seeing a large beam of wood resting on a table he endeavored to climb up to it and pulled it over on him—narrowly escaping with his life for the log was heavy enough to have crushed him if it had fallen upon his body. Father went over and brought Dr. Hough to examine it. He thought both bones fractured and when Dr. Dorsey and Uncle Newton came they confirmed the opinion. Poor child. He suffered terribly and I believe my pain was almost as great as his from very sympathy. I was so weak by the time the leg was confined in its bandage that I could scarce sit up. The operation was performed though with much less trouble than I thought it would be. Ma and Aunt L. knew nothing of it all till we sent for them after tea.

September 19, 1864
Scott over about ten o'clock and sat a couple of hours. Looks thin, poor fellow. Says he's had chills and fever—perhaps this may account for his most singular behavior. He was by turns cynical and sarcastic, then sad and misanthropic and anon teasing and mischievous. His visit has chilled me so. He certainly is "a problem which he who solved dispenses with die guessing." I'm afraid I can never play Oedipus to this riddle.

Scott Roy became a physician, married Mattie Cook and lived many years after the war.

He brought me a piece of music, a new song "The Murmur of the Shells." Says he has something pretty to show me when next he comes. He saw Alvin in Petersburg, says he was writing a letter to me when he left but he had not time to call for it. Scott does not know when he will go.
Heard news this evening of the falling back of our army. Oh! me I feel so very very sad this evening. Uncle John here and a Mr. Taylor stayed all night.

Early, with 12,150 men, was pushed back from Winchester on September 19, 1864, by Sheridan and his 48,000 troops. The Confederates fell back south of Strasburg to Fisher's Hill on September 20, 1864.

September 20, 1864
The advance guard of Wickham's brigade passed here on picket this morning.

Fitz Lee was severely wounded at Winchester. The cavalry was now under Wickham and was sent to Millford Pass to hold the Luray Valley.

Our army reported on the retreat and the enemy in hot pursuit. Poor broken-down soldiers constantly coming for something to eat. Nellie, Laura and I went without our dinners that there might be the more for them. A little before noon there was rapid firing at the river and we could see the enemy very distinctly on Guard Hill. They had a battery there and shelled across this side the river—some of the shells passed quite near us—some talk of our leaving home till it was over but Nellie and I bitterly opposed the move. Grandma had to go over to Oakley as Uncle Tom sent us word he must leave home with Allie in case the Yankees caused our army to retreat as they must do, for our force is a mere handful compared with that of the enemy. She took Nannie with her. Firing ceased about three o'clock. Busy baking bread for the soldiers. We thought, of course, Scott had gone but in the late afternoon he came over to bring us a letter from Irvie which had been handed him by Miss Kate Graves and which he had overlooked. With what a mingled feeling of thanksgiving and sorrow we read his announcements of having received a slight wound in the late battle and being now in the hospital. We rejoiced that it was no worse but grieved at having to know of his suffering without having it in our power to relieve him. He writes cheerfully and hopefully—the bone of his wounded limb is untouched and the bullet extracted so I pray God it may be all well with him yet. Poor Cousin George Williams was captured with his brigadier general. His noble spirit will chafe so under the confinement. How sorry I feel for him.

> When Irving was wounded, General Cleburne wrote the doctor: "You must save Buck. He is the best adjutant general in the army."

Scott left before tea and we tried to persuade him to stay in the mountain tonight but I'm afraid he won't do it. While I write the hostile armies confront each other at the river in a menacing attitude but everything seems unnaturally still—the quiet so dull and dead broken only at intervals by the distant beating of the tattoo or the wail of a bugle. It is the calm preceding the storm. We shall not undress tonight for there's no knowing when we may be aroused to a renewal of strife. How I dread the morning no tongue can tell. Writing to dear Irvie hoping to send it out tomorrow by Scott.

September 21, 1864
Well the close of this most miserable day is at last here and we breathe again. They commenced fighting at the river by the dawn of day. Our little handful of men retreated and the Yankees with a terrific yell charged them down the hills north of town and under cover of the fog there was such an incessant firing that we thought our poor boys must be murdered by the wholesale. The Rebels retreated through the woods in the rear of town and the Yankees passed directly up the Luray pike only about a regiment remaining in town. Saw a neat capture made by two of Mosby's men right in town. Expected the Yankees would have commenced pillaging and burning first thing upon their entrance but on the contrary they behaved quite decorously.

Boys went out to the scene of conflict. Heard that there were few if any men lost on either side in the fight this morning. Everyone uneasy about Early for this evening two divisions of cavalry passed through town en route for Luray and if they cannot in some way be checked they will flank him. I believe though it will all turn out right yet. We had numbers of the Yankees for milk and bread. Some were rude and broke.

This portion of Lucy's writing in her diary ends abruptly here and is not continued until February 13, 1865.

The two divisions of Federal cavalry mentioned above were under Tobert, Sheridan's cavalry chief, and were sent into the Luray Valley via Front Royal with plans of flanking Early at New Market. Sheridan struck Early at Fisher's Hill on September 22, 1864. Early retreated and on September 28 Early reached Waynesboro near Rock Fish Gap. On September 26 Kershaw's division rejoined Early. In early October the Federals withdrew down the Valley leaving in its wake destruction. Early followed and moved to Fisher's Hill on the eleventh of October and found Sheridan's camp north of Cedar Creek. By the seventeenth of October Early's rations were short. Either he must retreat or strike a stronger army. He struck Sheridan's army by surprise on October 19 with great success but failed to follow up his advantage. The Federals counterattacked later in the day and Early's small command was driven from the field. His retreat carried him to New Market. Early had been defeated but by holding on to the Valley he delayed Appomattox.

U.S.A.	C.S.A.
Effectives 30,829	Effectives 18,410
Killed 644	Killed 320
Wounded 3,430	Wounded 1,540
Missing 1,591	Missing 1,050

Fort McAllister, near Savanah, Georgia, fell to Sherman December 13, 1864. He had completed his march to the sea leaving behind a sixty-mile wide path of destruction. He now turned north to strike Lee's army. Hood crossed into Tennessee and tried to trap General Schofield's 30,000 troops at Spring Hill, but the Federals retreated northward almost through Hood's army. Hood followed and caught Schofield in Franklin, Tennessee on the Harpeth River. The Federals threw up fieldworks while they began to cross the river. Hood directed frontal assault, one of the most dramatic of the war.

He was repulsed and Schofield retired to Nashville to rejoin Thomas.

Battle of Franklin

U.S.A.	C.S.A.
Effectives 27,939	Effectives 26,897
Killed 189	Killed 1,750
Wounded 1,033	Wounded 3,800
Missing 1,104	Missing 702

Six Confederate generals died. One was General Pat Cleburne, upon whose staff Irving Buck had served until the latter was wounded in Jonesboro. Irving later wrote a book about General Cleburne. Hood pressed on to Nashville with his battered troops and on December 15, 1864, Thomas struck Hood. On the sixteenth Hood's army was in full retreat and was being pursued by Gen. James Harold Wilson's cavalry. General Forrest, C.S.A., fought gallant rear guard actions.

Battle of Nashville

U.S.A.	C.S.A.
Effectives 49,773	Effectives 23,207
Killed 387	Killed* ....
Wounded 2,562	Wounded* ....
Missing 112	Missing* ....

*No accurate report on Confederate casualties, however approximately 4,462 prisoners were taken by the Federals.

Hood left his beaten command with Gen. Richard Taylor at Tupelo, Mississippi, January 14, 1865. Wilson's Federal cavalry raided in March and April into Elyton, Tuscaloosa, Selma and Montgomery, Alabama. They then proceeded into Georgia after much destruction.

Lee's hungry army was still holding out in Richmond and Petersburg. On January 23, 1865, Lee was appointed General-in-Chief of the Confederate States Army.

IX

DEFEAT

February 13, 1865 - April 15, 1865

February 13, 1865
My diary was laid by. Those sad autumn days my heart too sad. There was too much that... to record I had not the spirit to write. Since then what has not happened of sorrow and... with a feeling of humiliation. I'm a different being from what I was then—the change the worse. When it will end God only knows.

... of toil and apprehension—dreary and dark. Dear Aunt Lizzie died November 8. Henry left the... army.... Went to Luray in December. Expecting Irvie home all that month but our hopes were dashed and our anticipation for the winter taken from us. Last visit from the Yankees was just before Christmas when Torbert's whole corps passed on a raid as far as Madison C.H. Amusing reencounter with Lieutenant—now Captain Danner. Sallie taken sick and the next day I too had to go to bed. The girls had a week of toil during the Christmas season and I unable to help them and so much domestic trouble I felt almost deranged sometimes. Sick for two weeks—chills and fever. Horrid weather all winter—more snow than for many years past and some bitter cold days.

These unwritten pages from September 21, 1864, to February 13, 1865, were certainly "sad autumn days" in the Shenandoah Valley. Not only were the South's armies losing on distant battlefields, but General Sheridan had completely devastated the Valley. To quote General Sheridan, "The crow that flies over the Valley of Virginia must henceforth carry his rations with him."

As noted previously Mosby was a thorn in Sheridan's side and prior to the destruction by Sheridan, General Grant forwarded Sheridan the following order: "If you can possibly spare a division of cavalry, send them through Loudoun County, to destroy and carry off the crops, animals, Negroes, and all men under fifty years of age capable of bearing arms. In this way, you will get many of Mosby's men. All male citizens under fifty can fairly be held as prisoners of war, and not as citizen prisoners. If not already soldiers, they will be made so the moment the Rebel army gets hold of them." This order by Grant to Sheridan was followed by another: "The families of most of Mosby's men are known and can be collected. I think they should be taken and kept at Fort McHenry, or some other secure place, as hostages for the good conduct of Mosby's men. When any of Mosby's men are caught, hang them without trial."

On September 22, 1864, approximately 120 of Mosby's men under Sam Chapman attacked a wagon train in the vicinity of Front Royal. To Chapman's surprise the reserve brigade of Merritt's cavalry division was a short distance behind the train. Before the fight could be called off the Confederates were surrounded. The only escape was to fight their way out. In the confusion a Federal lieutenant was ridden over and his body riddled with bullets. There were conflicted stories as to the death of the Federal. The Confederates stated he was killed in the excitement of battle while their smaller force was seeking to escape. The Federals said he was killed after he surrendered and six of Mosby's men captured while attacking the wagon train were ordered by Custer to be executed in retaliation.

On September 23, 1864, four men were shot before the citizens of Front Royal. One, Henry Rhodes, was tied to a horse and dragged through the streets before being shot. His family, hearing of his capture, went to Sheridan and begged for his life, but to no avail. The other two captives were offered freedom if they would disclose Mosby's headquarters. When they refused, they were hanged on a walnut tree and a placard was pinned to their clothing, "Such will be the fate of all of Mosby's men." The following are the names of the executed Confederates.

          Lucian Love
          Thomas E. Anderson
          David L. Jones
          Henry C. Rhodes
          William Thomas Overby
          Mr. Carter (first name unknown)

On November 6, 1864, Colonel Mosby captured twenty-seven men of Custer's command. After drawing lots seven were selected to be hanged for retaliation. Mosby had captured over 700 officers and men between September and November, but had waited patiently to get men of Custer's command. Three Federals were hanged and two shot. Attached to one victim was the following note: "These men have been hung in retaliation for an equal number of Colonel Mosby's men hung by order of General Custer, at Front Royal. Measure for measure."

Mosby then sent a scout to Sheridan's headquarters with this message: "Hereafter any prisoners falling into my hands will be treated with kindness due to their condition unless some new act of barbarity shall compel me reluctantly to adopt a course of policy repulsive to humanity."

This ended the "vendetta" between the two armies.

Aunt Lizzie of Clover Hill died November 15, 1864. It is said she died of shock and distress at seeing her home invaded, pillaged and everything but the dwelling house burned and destroyed. General Custer ordered destruction of the house but the dwelling was saved by the surrender of a small bag of gold, which had been entrusted to the eldest daughter, Julia, for safekeeping. All barns and outhouses were burned and livestock driven off or killed. All food supplies were either taken or destroyed.

February 19, 1865
Up early to get the house cleaned up in time for Ma to make an early start. Busy after breakfast—felt bright. Carroll and Fettie and Bob Buck and Russell Richards here, then Aunt Letitia Buck and Jacquie. Mary Carson and Carey did not come till ten o'clock. Carey brought me two such welcome notes from Mac and Jule. Ma rode behind Father and all started a little after ten. Had a most quiet Sabbath reading, writing and talking. Nellie had a letter from Dick in which he spoke of Alvin's having been ordered to rejoin his regiment. It makes me feel uneasy. N. and I had one of our twilight talks on the stile. Russell still here—had singing tonight till bedtime.

February 20, 1865
Lovely day. Reading, writing, sewing and as this is my week —housekeeping. Eating walnuts too. Had a note from Ma. Report of a victory by Beauregard over Sherman, wonder if it can be true. A cozy quiet time we had tonight the children being all asleep and Grandma, Laura, Nellie, Clara and I having the fire and candle all to ourselves.

February 21, 1865

Still fair weather. Laura and Annie spent the day at Uncle Tom's—had a very quiet time of it. Cannonading heard from direction of Winchester. Grand alarm—reported invasion of Yankees—false rumor. No one here for a wonder. Quiet pleasant evening. Report of Beauregard's death—don't credit it.

February 22, 1865
Captain Marshall in to dinner. Willie Buck over in the afternoon—political discussion. Frank hurt himself very much with a hot iron.

> *Columbia, South Carolina fell to Sherman February 17, 1865, and was burned. Charleston was occupied on the eighteenth. Fort Sumter, a symbol of the Confederacy, had been practically demolished by eighteen months of bombardment from Federal batteries and gunboats. It was impregnable to assault and was evacuated on the night of February 17.*
> *Lee named Gen. Joseph Johnston to command the remnants of the Confederates in North Carolina in an effort to stop Sherman's northward advance.*

Rumor that Charleston and Columbia had fallen. Nothing more than I expected. Dyspeptic.

February 24, 1865
Bright and pleasant. Writing all morning. Willie came over to give me a lesson in chess. Am afraid I'm too stupid ever to learn the game. After he left enter Uncle Tom with a letter from Cousin..., and a valentine for Nellie—from Cousin Ed Buck I am sure. Busy sewing making a floral card this evening. Nellie in the parlor playing and singing tonight when a rap at the door was followed by the entrance of Charlie Brown and Wythe Cooke. So glad to see them—two fine young Rebels and two very clever ones too. Sat until ten o'clock talking over auld lang syne and singing and playing. Sitting up late tonight laughing and talking in our room.

February 25, 1865
Up early closing up my housekeeping week. Gray and cloudy. Writing all morning. Raining by noon. Mrs. Robert Turner came in about two o'clock to spend the day. Pleasant little woman. Very soon afterward a young soldier Mr. Bruner came in to stay all night. Father voted the children a frolic Saturday night though it was, so Allie and Charlie and Wythe were summoned and a right merry time we had of it. The young folks danced awhile and then we proceeded to the dining room where "tap-the-rabbit," "fox-and-goose," "blindman's buff" and similar dignified games engaged us till after eleven o'clock. Such a wild gay time as we had—hardly knew myself that I could enjoy fun as much as I

did. Ate a philopoena with Wythe and mean to ask him for his photograph. Feel quite wearied—we shall only get to bed in time to save ourselves from the charge of Sabbath breaking.

February 27, 1865
Unsettled. Upstairs reading and writing during the morning. Nannie and Mollie went home. No one here all day. Father went to Mrs. Wheatley's tonight to see Mrs. Kiger—had just gotten back at nine o'clock—says she'll be over tomorrow. Heard a confirmation of this morning's report—Generals Kelly and Crooks captured by a party of our cavalry who dashed into their camp in Cumberland and "gobbled them up."

> *Lt. Jesse C. McNeill's partisan command captured Maj. Gen. B. J. Kelly and Maj. Gen. George Crook in Cumberland, Maryland on February 21, 1865. The town was guarded by 6,000–8,000 Federal troops and the generals occupying separate hotels were awakened from slumber in the early hours of the morning.*
>
> *Lieutenant McNeill assumed command of the Partisan Rangers when his father, Capt. John H. McNeill was killed.*

March 3, 1865
Was sitting about dusk telling the children stories when a rap at the door was followed by the entrance of Dick Bayly. He told me there was an opposition party at Mr. Overall's and that there would be few at Aliza's assembly so I concluded to go with him. Found none but our party there—all around the table at cards. Willie Jacobs soon came in and after we had had our suppers I stirred them up and we had game after game of romps. Enjoyed ourselves very much till eleven o'clock when we returned home—Dick stays with us tonight.

> *Lincoln was inaugurated for the second term March 4, 1865, and thinking toward reconstruction said, "With malice toward none, with charity for all, with firmness in the right, as God gives us to see the right; let us strive to finish the work that we are in, to bind up the nation's wounds, to care for him who shall have borne the battle and for his widow, and his orphans to do all which may achieve and cherish a just and lasting peace, among ourselves and with all nations."*

March 6, 1865
Girls all went to Mr. Hope's mill to be weighed and to invite Julia and Eliza and Wythe Cook whom they found there. Sent a note to the "Mountain," one to Oakley and a message to Rose Hill and Mountain View. Had all our simple preparations made by dusk—a nice fire in the parlor and all—Belle R. and Allie, Willie Buck and Charlie R. came

first. They told me of a report in town of Rosser's having been badly defeated and that poor Sam Buck was wounded and had his leg amputated. Feel so sorry to hear it, such a noble boy and gallant soldier as he is. Mrs. Moffatt, Julia and Eliza were next, then Cousin Will Cloud, Dick Bayly, Jacquie and Gussie and last though not least Charlie B. and Wythe Cook. A wild time we have had of it and our company did not disperse till two o'clock. Nannie, Belle, Gussie, Allie, Dick and Cousin Will stay with us tonight. Oh me!—so tired.

March 7, 1865

Up late but succeeded in getting everything in order before breakfast. Sitting in the parlor chatting and singing. Cousin Will taught me "Aillien Aroon." Gussie and Allie could not be persuaded to remain till after breakfast. Jim came over early after Nannie and Nellie and Belle went with her. Cousin Will and Dick off early too. Laura and I "alone in our glory" feeling stupid and tired. Charlie Brown told us last night that he had heard from the Seventeenth Regiment and that Alvin and George Hope had arrived there. There was a mail in last night though of course we got no letters—thinking that Mrs. Roy perhaps might be able to furnish us tidings I put on my cloak and hat and "waded" over. Received a hearty welcome but no news. Benton's past letter contained no mention of either of the boys. So sorry. Saw a photograph of the colonel—looks as if viewed through a magnifying glass—so fat and rosy has he become. Read a letter from G. White—what a delightful scribe he is! Sat until after twelve gossiping and then waded back home. Dried my feet and went to bed but could not get my nap. So stupid all day. Tonight reports of the advance of the Yankees through Rappanhannock. Father and I preparing for their advent tonight by caching.

March 9, 1865

Lovely day. Reading the *Vicar* and sewing. Nellie and I went to investigate the myrtle bed on the hillside. Eliza and Julia helped us.

On March 2, 1865, Early's depleted command collapsed. Early escaped and was sent home to await orders.

Rosser's defeat and Early's stampede at Laceys Spring confirmed. Nothing from Ma—wish we could hear.

March 10, 1865

Disagreeable morning. Observing the day by fasting. Nellie went over to prayer meeting in the morning and in the afternoon I went with Russell, who had come in, and Willie to hear Dr. Hough. A large attendance of soldiers and everybody else there. One of the most solemn, impressive sermons I ever listened to—everyone—even the most frivolous seemed to feel it deeply. He scored our revellers most soundly—made me feel like forswearing dancing for the rest of the war. Have heard through Mack Bayly's letter that Henry Buck is in Phil. in business with Cousin Thos. Fayette Blakemore. Reading tonight

March 12, 1865

Most beautiful day. No services in church—after reading during the morning betook myself to my little sanctum to write to Irvie. A grand alarm of Yankee invasion—a great time we had secreting and a great time the boys had scampering out of town—all for nothing too because the alarm was a false one. Laura and Nellie went to Mrs. Hope's a little while and when they returned from there Laura went with Evred over to Oakley. Jacquie in with Julia and Father went to Belmont. After dinner Jacquie, Nellie, Neville, Willie and I went on the housetop and sat there talking over old times—then to the attic room eating walnuts. Laura and Evred home at dusk. Writing tonight. Father not at home till late.

March 13, 1865

Most delightful morning. Reading, writing and sewing. Dick Bayly in during the morning and had a romp and was off again. Nellie and I made our toilettes and strolled over to Dr. Turner's—spent a pleasant hour and missed tea and Nannie came back with us—found Julia H. and Aunt L. Blakemore here. All but Aunt L. left at dusk. We all walked up to Mrs. Hope's with Julia, sat a minute and then walked home. Laura made a black cake and sent it a parting present to Charlie who leaves tomorrow. Ellen wrote a very nice note of thanks in return. Left Aunt L. chatting with the family in Grandma's room and went out on the porch to drink in some of the tranquil loveliness of the night. The day has been one of such beauty and I've felt so light-hearted and happy. While sitting there Willie Buck rode up and very soon after Charlie Brown came in to tell us good-bye. Poor boy! He looks sad. Left at ten o'clock and we were just preparing to retire when there was an alarm of Yankees. Willie mounted his horse and went to town to hear something from them. Came back in a short time saying 'twas all false. Oh! me these excitements are terrible. Hamp Miller went down to Castleman's Ferry to hear from his wife—left this morning.

March 15, 1865

Raining. Allie Ashby over. All plaiting straw. Hamp Miller home this evening—could only hear that Ma and Mrs. M. had been for ten days in Shepardstown unable to get out but would probably be home next week. Wish we knew something more direct from them. Allie stayed all night. He and the children had a grand romp tonight.

March 20, 1865

Warm and pleasant. Kattie Samuels came in very unexpectedly this morning after Sallie Leach left. Glad to see her—very—sat till two o'clock. Nellie, Laura, Orville and I went fishing but were unsuccessful. Miss Tencie and Annie came over by appointment to walk as far as the river with Sallie. Did not feel like going 'twas so warm. Had a very delightful trip though, and got home by dusk. Met Mrs. Hamp Miller on the bridge which was the first intimation I had of Ma's having gotten home. Rounded the house and found her on the front porch surrounded with an eager throng. She looks badly—has had a most terrible time and I only wonder she's alive. Her trip has been only partially successful too. I'm mighty glad to have her at home once more. Sitting up till nearly twelve o'clock listening to a recountal of her adventures. Ah me! I feel relieved indeed. Had a note from Jule today.

March 21, 1865

Three soldiers—returned prisoners came in to stay all night—they were with Charlie Buck at Camp Chase—said he had been exchanged with them—was in Charlottesville and would be on shortly—had a ring which Charlie had made and given them. Reading and writing and playing on the piano. Wrote Cousin Mary Cloud.

March 27, 1865

Sam Buck came in unexpectedly—has resigned and is going into Mosby's command. He's a nice fellow, so like Alvin, affectionate and kind. Had a game of marbles all of us and a grand romp outdoors then into the house and some music. Sam taught me "Auralee" and "Love's Chiding." We did have such a pleasant time altogether. Ah me! "When shall we all meet again."

March 28, 1865

Sam taught us songs and copied—showed us some complimentary letters from his officers—made a half engagement to go to Luray with us, had a great romp then left.

The boys went fishing but soon came back. Jule unwell and in bed till noon. While at dinner Mr. and Mrs. Miller came in to spend the evening and not long after Mack Irwin! Such a pleasant evening we had! Mack is a great boy and laughed heartily over what I told him on the porch. Made an engagement to spend tomorrow with Mrs. Miller. She left soon after tea and then Jule, Dick, Mack and I and Nellie and Cousin James and the children walked on the river bank till after the stars came out and then Mack and I paused on the porch and talked. Oh!—he was so kind and encouraging and humbled me so by his earnest Christian conversation. If I could only be as good as he and Jule! God help me! Felt quiet and sad all evening even after going up to our rooms.

Lee's troops were supplied by the Richmond and Danville Railroad. Grant made his move to turn the Rebels' right flank and cut the supply route. Lee sent his cavalry and General Pickett's division to prevent this. The Southerners could not stop the thrust, so Lee prepared his army to evacuate Richmond and Petersburg. On April 3, the Southerners left their capital. Lee's desire was to join Gen. Joseph Johnston in North Carolina and possibly the two united armies could defeat Sherman and then turn on Grant and destroy him. Lee headed for Amelia Courthouse where supplies were supposed to be stored. Finding none, the starving troops with Federals nipping at them constantly, moved westward toward the mountains. About half of Lee's armies including Ewell's corps fell to the Union troops on April 6. The Federals were now west of Lee and on April 9 Lee tried, to no avail, to fight out of the trap. Lee felt the time had come and by a flag of truce arranged an interview with Grant.

This was Appomattox April 9, 1865. Approximately 28,356 men of the proud army of the Confederacy surrendered to Grant's 120,000 troops and were paroled.

Six days later Lincoln died on April 15, 1865. The radicals were now in power. It would be a long reconstruction and this was to leave more scars on the South than war.

Lee's farewell order issued April 10, 1865 reads as follows: "After four years of arduous service marked by unsurpassed courage and fortitude, the Army of Northern Virginia has been compelled to yield to overwhelming numbers and resources.

"I need not tell the brave survivors of so many hard fought battles, who have remained steadfast to the last, that I have consented to this result from no distrust of them; but feeling that valor and devotion could accomplish nothing that could compensate for the loss that must have attended the continuance of the contest, I determined to avoid the useless sacrifice of those whose past services have endeared them to their countrymen.

"By the terms of the agreement, officers and men can return to their homes and remain until exchanged. You will take with you the satisfaction that proceeds from the consciousness of duty faithfully performed; and I earnestly pray that a Merciful God will extend to you His blessing and protection.

"With an unceasing admiration of your constancy and devotion to your Country, and a grateful remembrance of your kind and generous consideration for myself, I bid you all an affectionate farewell."

April 5, 1865

I'm so depressed—feel like we were given up into the hands of our foes indeed. Aunt L. Blakemore was spending the day with us and just before dinner while finishing a letter to Irvie Uncle John came in pale and sad to say Richmond, our own Richmond, had fallen. I felt stunned, sick, wild. But soon the thought came that 'twas perhaps all but the best and we must bide our time. Our army has fallen back toward Lynchburg. Oh me! Light!—for this darkness! Light!

April 6, 1865
Sad all day. Ma went to church this afternoon. Bruner came in very unexpectedly, was seeming so cheerful and bright. He's en route for Clarke—wrote by him. Cousin Lucie Buck and Emma came in this evening and are with us tonight. Our army is said to be in a starving condition. Oh misery!

April 7, 1865
Up in my dormitory all morning. Cousin L. and E. left early. Reading *Bride of Lammamoor*. The story is such a sad, tragic one that it has depressed my spirit no little. Sitting out on the porch in the moonlight trying the effect of quiet and calm on my excited nerves and thinking oh so wistfully of lang syne when the gate opened and Uncle John rode in. He had heard of a sudden advance of the enemy up the Valley and the news accelerated his intended departure. He leaves tomorrow and came to say good-bye—so sorry to see him go and he's loath to leave. Old Aunt Bettie sick.

April 8, 1865
Willie Buck was over this morning talking bravely with us when Father came in to say Miss Terrill and Miss Yates were coming in. They were on their way to Rappahannock to see an invalid brother and had to stop over till tomorrow, when Mr. Harmon promised to take them down in his wagon. Nice girls—very pretty and accomplished—spent quite a pleasant evening. Nannie Buck over. Pickett's division was engaged in the fight that preceded the fall of Richmond. What of our poor boys.?

April 10, 1865
We were quietly sewing this morning when E. Hope came in with a white face to tell us Dick was mortally wounded—the man (Mr. Gannett) who brought him off the field had come with the tidings. It was such a shock—we felt almost heartbroken all day. In the afternoon Father went to Belmont and returned at dusk with Uncle Mack to say that the news more recently received from our poor boy represented him as severely but not dangerously wounded, and in the enemy hands. Such a relief to hear this much. Poor fellow if I could only be with and nurse him! We were beaten out of Petersburg but Pickett fought gloriously as he ever does. Many of our poor boys are wounded, many... we may only pray God to protect them and hope for the best.

Bruner here tonight, has returned from Clarke, brings news that all was well at Bloomfield—makes us cheerful with his news. Feel as if I'd been belabored all day, I'm so stiff and worn out.

April 11, 1865
Bruner left early. Wrote by him to Uncle John. Dick Bayly in this morning and I think did not relish something Nellie said to him about the absentees from the army for he left very suddenly.

April 12, 1865
Ma spent the day in town. Came home in the evening with news of Mr. Robert Wells' arrival from prison. Brings such cheerful news from Richmond—says our armies are in fine spirits and oh!—ever so many things to dissipate the gloom in our hearts. If we may only be free let troubles come and we'll try to bear them. Old Aunt Bettie died.

April 13, 1865
Such a day as this has been! A few more would, I believe, kill me. Father came in suddenly pale and grave with the words "Well, I fear the die is cast—Lee had surrendered"—almost torn from his lips. If the heavens had fallen there could have scarcely have been greater consternation and grief in our midst. To remember half the horrible ideas that filled my heart and brain would be impossible—the one thought—subjugation—all staked, all lost. Our dearest hopes dashed—our fondest dreams dispelled—we and our brave ones who had struggled, bled and suffered—slaves and to such a tyrant. God only knows how nearly mad I must have been. Some soldiers came in during the day and confidently denied the report and I felt cheered so much. Ma went to Mr. Hope's and returned with additional confirmation of the dreadful news. Cousins Sue and Emma over and Mr. Berry but I was too near crazy to know much of what they said or did. Oh! me I'm almost tempted to envy poor Aunt Bettie lying cold and still in death in her little cabin tonight. If it had been any but Lee—our peerless Lee! Poor fellow!—what a trial to his noble heart. God bless him and comfort him under his trial and give us strength to bear our cross. I'm desperate and wicked tonight.

> *On April 26, 1865, Gen. Joseph Johnston near Durham Station, North Carolina, surrendered his 37,047 men to Sherman on the same terms Lee had received.*
>
> *The four years had been costly. The United States dead were 360,222; wounded were 275,175. The Confederate dead were 258,000; wounded unknown. Thus more Americans died than in World War I and II combined and the population at that time was only one-fourth the present population.*

April 14, 1865
Took the children down this morning to see poor old Aunt Bettie's

remains. Did not go to the funeral. Sam Buck came in—confirmed the news but yet is so naturally cheerful that we involuntarily imbibed some of his brightness. He begged me to go to the Mountain with him. I consented—rather against my own inclination but was glad afterwards—enjoyed the air very much. He's so much like Alvin. Read tonight the correspondence between Lee and Grant relative to the surrender. "Things sad are ever true."

April 15, 1865

Raining. Young Detheridge came up this morning with news from Dick. He's in Farmville—in the hospital doing well. Dear fellow so glad! He also brings us much cheering news from our army. Johnson is said to have whipped the enemy and oh! I don't know what else. We started home and it rained so hard we were thoroughly drenched. Sam took Laura out to Mountain View—had a bad headache all evening. Have one of my nervous attacks.

(VOLUME ENDS ABRUPTLY HERE)

Lucy Rebecca Buck started her diary again in later years. She nor her sisters ever married. She died in 1918, and is buried in the same cemetery she visited so many times in Front Royal–Prospect Hill.

In studying Lucy's diaries covering her life from 1861 until her death in 1918, I noted a life filled with sadness, yet she was sustained by a power I did not understand. Few of her expectations ever materialized. She outlived most of her immediate family and was on hand as their bodies were committed to the earth at Prospect Hill Cemetery. In one week, after the Civil War, three children of her brother, Alvin, died of cholera and their bodies were brought to Front Royal for burial. After reading the events of an entire lifetime in a few volumes, I concluded life was sad–"Sad Earth." I began to search. Was there a "Sweet Heaven?" How did Lucy have the ability to cope with such sadness?

My search of history proved that God indeed has a plan for humanity. In the Bible I found a plan that includes an abundant life now.

We cannot really enjoy this abundant life because we all have fallen short of God's standard. We are sinful and separated from God because of our own stubborn self wills. The penalty of our sin is death–eternal separation from God. God's plan includes a provision for man's sin. Through His death on the cross, Jesus Christ has paid the penalty for all our sins.

Just because we know or give intellectual assent to the fact that Jesus Christ died for our sins does not necessarily mean that we are Christians. To become a Christian we must individually receive Jesus Christ as Saviour and Lord. Then we can know and experience God's love and plan for our lives.

How do we receive Jesus Christ? We must trust in, rely on, cling to the fact that when Jesus Christ died on the cross, He paid the penalty for our sins. This is what it means to believe. Jesus Christ says he will forgive our sins and come into our lives if we ask Him. Jesus says in Revelation 3:20, "Behold, I stand at the door and knock; if any man hear my voice and open the door, I will come in to him." The door refers to our heart. He wants to forgive our sins, bring peace and purpose to our lives, and give us power to live an abundant life. We open the door by prayer.

If you have never received Christ, you can ask Him into your life right now. You can pray like this, "Lord Jesus, I want you to come into my life, forgive my sins, and become my Saviour and Lord. Please make me the kind of person you created me to be."

If you prayed this prayer, believe on the authority of God's Word ("I will come in") that He is now in your life and will never leave you! Do not depend on feelings or seek an emotional experience. The Christian lives by FAITH (TRUST) in God and His Word!

Lucy was a Christian and because of her personal relationship with the Lord Jesus Christ, she had the ability to meet each situation that confronted her.

I pray that each reader, if they have not already, will discover this same pardon, peace, purpose, and power found only in Jesus Christ.

William Pettus Buck

Homes and Occupants
in the Front Royal area
(1861 - 1865)

The following were homes in the Front Royal area in 1861 - 1865. Listed under each are the occupants of the house.

CLOVER HILL (burned 1891) was located six miles southwest of Front Royal on the west bank of the South Fork of the Shenandoah River. It was the home of Uncle Fayette (Thomas Fayette Buck, 1803 - 1874) and his wife Aunt Lizzie (Elizabeth Peake, 1814 - 1864). He was a brother of William Mason Buck of Bel Air. Their children were:

    Henry, (Henry Augustus Buck) 1842 - 1888
    Julia, (Julia Catherine Buck0 1843 - 1909
    Neville, (Linton Neville Buck) 1847 - 1912
    Esten, (George Esten Buck) 1849 - 1913
    Carroll, (John Carroll Buck) 1851 - 1918
    Fettie, (Thomas Fayette Buck) 1853 - 1875
    Lily, (Lily Elizabeth Buck) 1855 - 1920

BELMONT, three miles to the south of Front Royal on the slopes of the Blue Ridge mountains, was located near the beginning of the present Skyline Drive. It was surrounded by one of the largest vineyards east of the Mississippi River. Uncle Mack (Marcus Blakemore Buck, 1816 - 1881) was another brother of William Mason Buck. His wife, Aunt Letitia, was Jane Letita Bayly. Their children were:

    Walter, (William Walter Buck) 1842 - 1863
    Dick, (Richard Bayly Buck) 1844 - 1888
    Jacquie, (Jacqueline M. Buck) 1848 - 1907
    Gussie, (Catherine Augusta Buck) 1852 - 1877
    Elliot, (Elliot Mausey Buck) 1855 -
    Mary, (Mary Richardson Buck) 1857 -
    Eltie, (Elton C. Buck) 1860 -
    William, (William Walter Buck) 1865 -

MOUNTAIN VIEW, located two miles west of Front Royal on the South Fork of the Shenandoah River. Uncle Newton (Dr. Issac Newton Buck, 1801 - 1877) was an uncle of William Mason Buck. His first wife was Susan Taylor. Their children were:

    Marcus T. (died Aug. 12, 1862)
    Cathernie B.
    Mary C.

Dr. Buck's second wife was Aunt Jane, (Janet U. Lovell, 1815 - 1893). Their children were:

> Sue (Susan R. Buck), 1836 - 1880. (Was engaged to Willie Richardson who died of wounds, May 29, 1862)
> Charlie, (Charles Newton Buck) 1842 - 1925. (Captured in Front Royal)
> Nannie, (Nannie Lovell Buck)
> James, (James C. Buck)
> Robert, (Robert Buck)
> Willie, (Thomas William Buck) 1845 - 1877. (Captured Oct. 1863)

BUCKTON, the home of John Gill Buck and his wife, Eliza McKay Buck, was located near Waterlick, Virginia between Front Royal and Strasburg. Their children were:

> Sandy, (William Alexander) "Most gallant soldier I've ever seen in action," Gen. W.E. Jones
> Meredith
> Annice
> Elizabeth
> Thomas
> Samuel Dawson, Capt. C.S.A. "Buck is the bravest man I ever knew," Gen. Early
> Mollie
> John Gill, Jr. (Born after his father's death)

RIVERSIDE was located two miles north of Front Royal at the junction of the North and South Forks of the Shenanadoah River. The locality is called Riverton. The home was owned by Maj. James Russell Richards (1806 - 1895). His wife was Cousin Bett (Elizabeth M. Blakemore Bayly Richards, 1825 - 1891). Their children were:

> Russell, (James Russell, Jr.) 1854 - 1914
> Annie, 1857 - 1925
> Henry, 1860 - 1914
> Walter, 1863 - 1904
> Thomas, 1869 - 1941

Richard B. Bayly (1844 - 1921) and Marcus (Mack) Bayly (1842 - 1886) were sons of Cousin Bett by a former marriage.

Cousin Bett's brother, Thomas F. Blakemore (1822 - 1896), lived in Baltimore. Her brothers Marcus N. Blakemore and Richard M. Blakemore (1843 - 1924), were in the C.S.A. Army. Their mother was Letitia A. Buck Blakemore who also lived at Riverside (1803 - 1885).

BLOOMFIELD was located near Berryville in Clarke Country, Virginia. It was the home of Aunt Cattie (Catherine Elizabeth Buck, 1805 - 1882) and her her husband, John B. Larue. Aunt Cattie, the only sister of William Mason Buck, had no issue, but her husband had several children by a previous marriage.

Aunt Cattie cared for Walker, the son of John Newton Buck. John's wife died in 1859. He was a brother to William Mason Buck.

OAKLEY, just west of Front Royal, was the home of Uncle Tom (Thomas Ashby) and his wife, Aunt Betty (Elizabeth Almond). Uncle Tom was a brother of William Mason Buck's wife. Their children were:

>Allie, (Thomas Almond Ashby) 1848 - 1916
>William Richardson Ashby, Aug. 8, 1864 - 1942

ROSE HILL, just north of town on the highway leading to Winchester, was the Richardson home. Mr. William Richardson died of typhoid fever in 1859. His widow, Cousin Elizabeth (Elizabeth Millar Richardson) lived there with her son and three daughters.

>Sammie died in 1860, age 10.
>Willie, (William Millar Richardson) died of wounds May 29, 1862.
>Eltie died July 29, 1862
>Belle
>Susan
>Mary died in 1849
>Ann Rebecca died in 1855

Sue Buck, of Mountain View, was the fiancee of Willie, and after he was killed she moved into their home. She never married and became sick every May 29th.

WILLOW GLEN - The Cloud family home near Front Royal.

HAPPY CREEK - Old Marshall home near Front Royal. Built by James Markham Marshall who married Hester Morris, daughter on Robert Morris.

Hester was the number two female behind Martha Washington in the Colonies. Her father financed the Revolution.

Uncle John (John Newton Buck) was a widower and youngest brother of William Mason Buck. His wife, Amelia Ann Buck (Millie), died April, 1859 leaving one child, Walker, who was raised by Aunt Cattie Larue. After the death of his wife, Uncle John made his home at Bel Air.

Aunt Calmes (Henrietta Chew Buck Calmes, 1770 - 1872) was William Mason Buck's great aunt, the widow of Spencer Calmes (1771 - 1854). She formerly lived in Kentucky, but lived at Bel Air after her husband's death. She came for a visit and remained until her death.

There were approximately twelve slaves at Bel Air. Mahala was the cook. Horace, Alex and John Henry were her son; Liza Ann, Allfair and Mary were her daughters. Dummy or Dumb Mary was the nurse who was deaf and dumb. She responded to the vibrations from a knock on the floor by a cane kept for that purpose. Allfair was a Negro baby and Rob Roy a free Negro. Gilbert, a freeman, lived near the mill. "Uncle Ben" and "Aunt Betty" were servants who lived in a cabin near the mill on Happy Creek. After the slaves deserted the family, Mr. Buck hired a white girl to help with the family chores. She was described as being a "gawky, strong, sturdy and willing to learn, country girl."

Bibliography

Alan, William
History of the Campaign, Gen. T. J. (Stonewall) Jackson in the Shenandoah Valley of Virginia, Philadelphia 1880

Ashby, T. S.
The Valley Campaigns, New York, 1914

Baylor, George
Bull Run to Bull Run, Richmond, 1900

Cammager, H. S.; edit. by
The Blue and the Grey, 2 Vols., New York, 1950

Freeman, D. S.
Lee's Lieutenants, 3 Vols., New York, 1942–1944

Freeman, D. S.
R. E. Lee, 4 Vols., New York, 1934

Gilmore, Harry
Four Years In the Saddle, New York, 1866

Hale, Laura Virginia
Four Valiant Years In Lower Shenandoah Valley, Strasburg, Virginia, 1968

Jackson, Mary Anna
Life and Letters of Gen. Thomas J. Jackson, New York, 1892

Johnson, R. U. and Buel, C. C.; edit. by
Battles and Leaders of the Civil War, 4 Vols., New York, 1884–1887

Jones, V. C.
Ranger Mosby, Chapel Hill, 1944

McDonald, W. N.
Laurel Brigade, Baltimore, 1907

Newman, Ralph and Long, E. B.
The Civil War, Vol. II: The Picture Chronicle, New York, 1956

O'Ferrall, C. T.
Forty Years of Active Service, Washington, 1904

Lucy and Nellie Buck

Figure 1, This photograph was made in approximately 1860 of the author of the diary, Lucy Rebecca Buck (1842-1918) and her younger sister, Nellie (1844-1902).

William Mason Buck, Lucy's Father

Figure 2, William Mason Buck, son of William Richardson Buck and Lucy Neville Blakemore, was born August 30, 1809 and died September 23, 1895. On April 3, 1837 he married Elizabeth Ann Ashby.

Elizabeth Ann Ashby Buck, Lucy's Mother

Figure 3, Wife of William Mason Buck, Elizabeth Ann Buck, was the daughter of William R. Ashby and Rebecca Buck. She was born September 25, 1821, and died in 1904.

William Mason Buck and Elizabeth Ann Ashby

Figure 4, William Mason Buck (1809-1895), son of William R. Buck, was married on April 3, 1837 to Elizabeth Ann Ashby, daughter of William R. Ashby and Rebecca R. Buck.

Rebecca Buck Ashby

Figure 5, Rebecca Buck Ashby, Lucy's grandmother, was the wife of William R. Ashby. Rebecca was a daughter of Anne Richardson Buck and Captain Thomas Buck, builder of Bel Air. She was born on February 14, 1792, married April 3, 1817, and died August 6, 1878.

Bel Air

Figure 6, Home of Lucy Buck, Bel Air, was built in 1800 by Captain Thomas Buck. Photographs made in 1860's and 1960's.

Bel Air

Figure 7, Pictured here is Bel Air, the home of Lucy Buck, as taken from a sketch made in 1860.

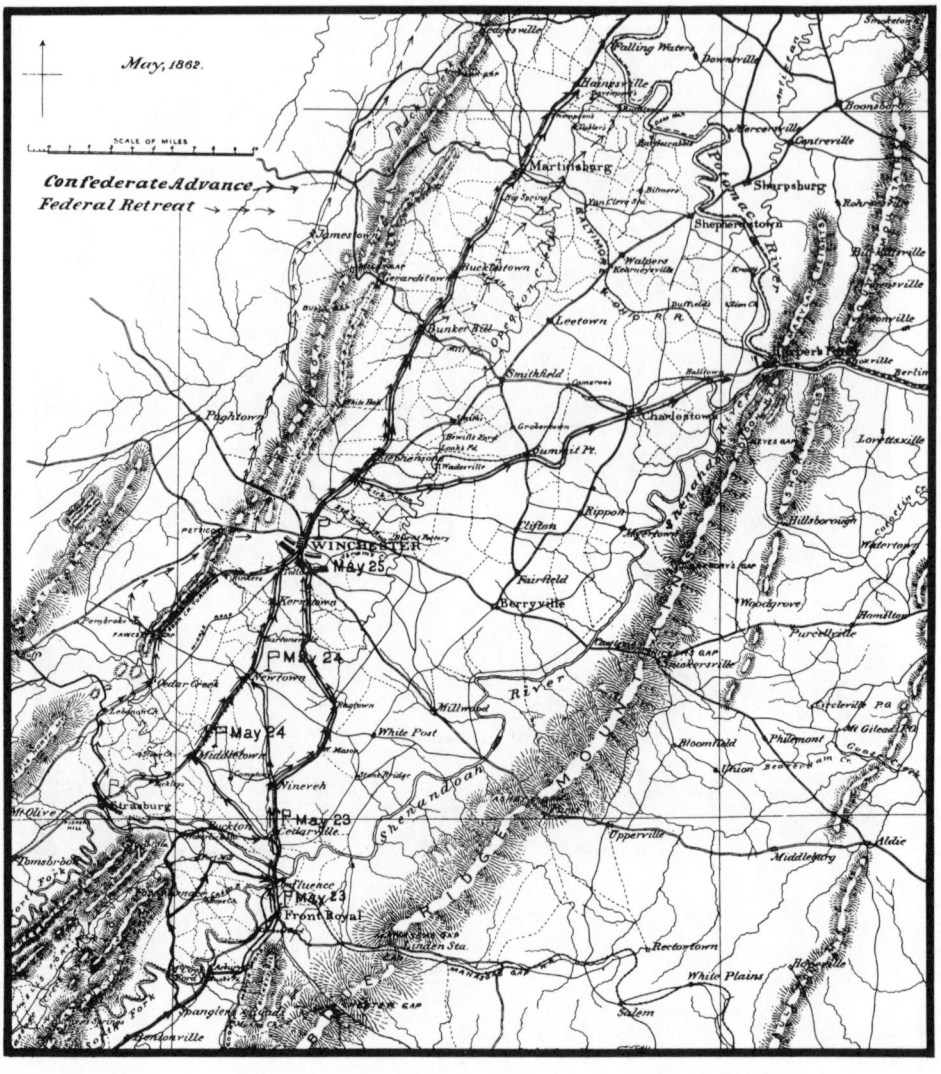

Figure 8, Jed Hotchkiss, map drawer. From the book, *"History of the Campaign of Gen. T. J. (Stonewall) Jackson in Shenandoah Valley of Virginia."*

Front Royal, Virginia — 1863

Figure 9, Pictured here is the Union Camp at Front Royal, Virginia, 1863 as depicted in a wartime sketch.

Figure 10, Front Royal, Virginia — 1963

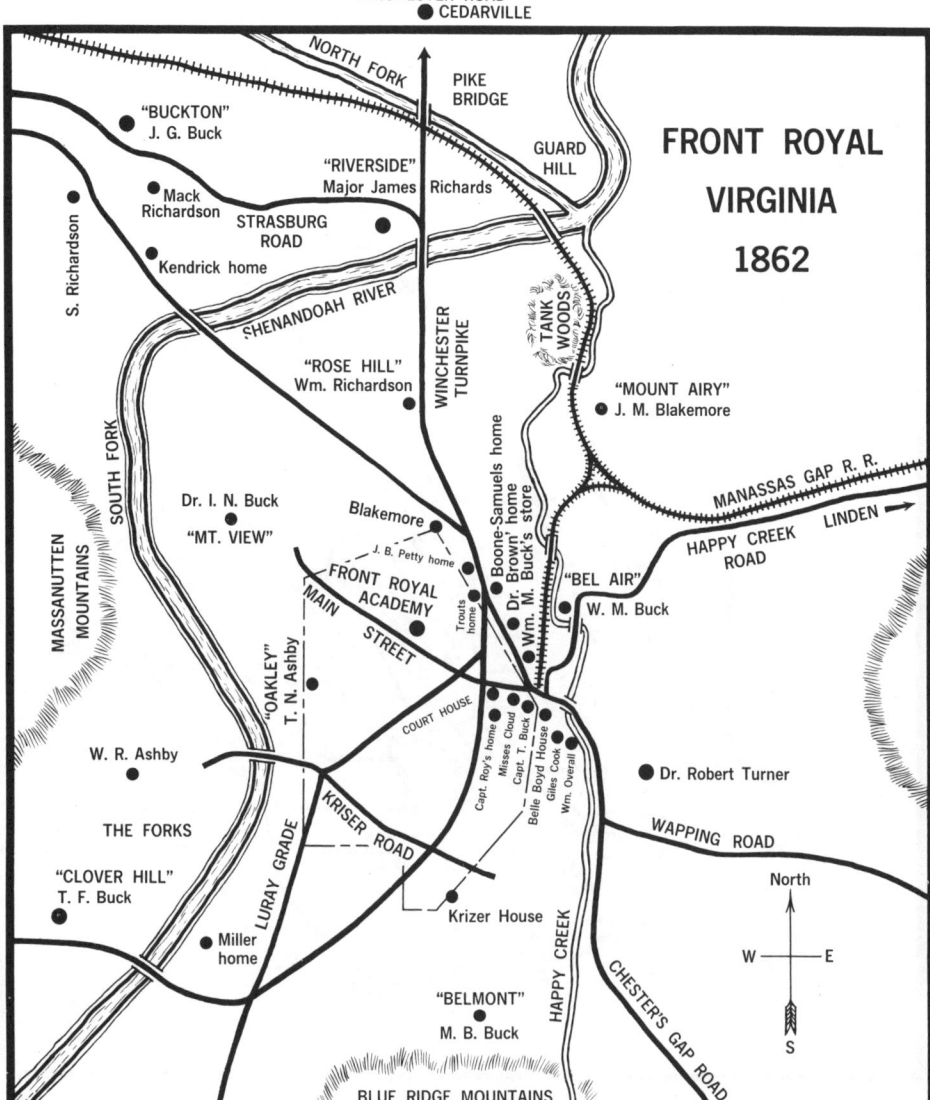

Figure 11

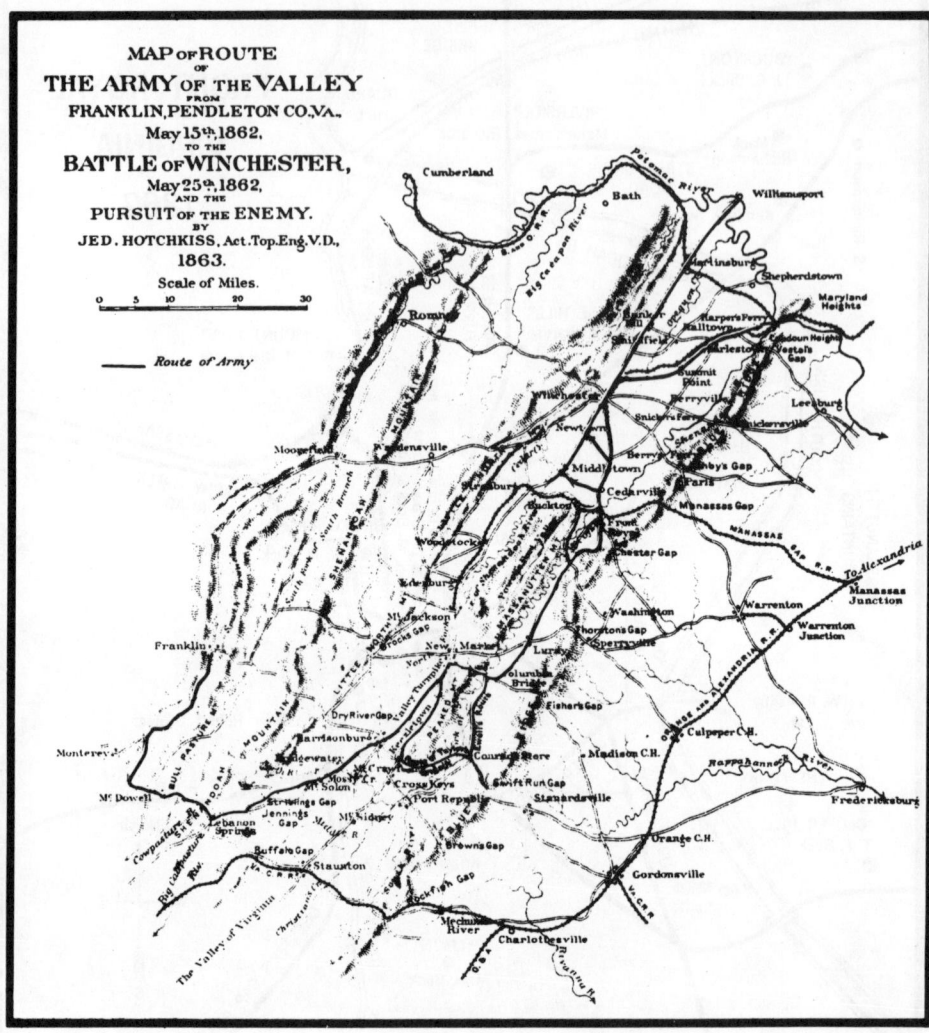

Figure 12, Jed Hotchkiss, map drawer. From the book, "*History of the Campaign of Gen. T. J. (Stonewall) Jackson in Shenandoah Valley of Virginia.*"

Alvin Duval Buck

Figure 13, Brother of Lucy Buck, Alvin Duval Buck, was born in 1838 and died in 1922.

Captain Irving Ashby Buck

Figure 14, Lucy's brother, Irving Buck, was A.A.G. of General Pat Cleburne and the author of *Cleburne's Command.* Captain Irving Ashby Buck was born in 1840 and died in 1912.

William Walter Buck

Figure 15, Lt. William Walter Buck was the son of Marcus B. Buck. A lieutenant in Co. E. 7th Virginia Cavalry, Walter Buck was killed in a cavalry charge and skirmish near Upperville, Virginia, June 21, 1863.

Figure 16, Doorknocker from Bel Air which was built by Thomas Buck in 1800.

Supplement

Page 6
"Bel Air" was built by Captain Thomas Buck (1756 - 1842) in 1795. It was named for his wife's birthplace, Bel Air, Maryland. He gave the home to his youngest daughter, Letitia Amelia Buck Blakemore in 1837. When Letitia and her husband, John Mauzy Blakemore, moved to Tennessee William Mason Buck purchased the family ancestral home for 6500 dollars. Lucy Buck was the first of William Mason Buck's children to be born there. After her husband died "Aunt Letitia" lived at "Riverside" with her daughter Elizabeth Mauzy Blakemore Bayly Richards. George Neville Blakemore (brother to John Mauzy Blakemore) sold "Rose Hill" to William Richardson when he moved West.

Page 12
Mr. Brenwood was a young student who seceded from Dickinson College, Pennsylvania. He was engaged to teach Allie Ashby. Emma Cloud of "Willow Glen" married Thomas Newton Buck of "Buckton."

Page 17
Esculopius was the Roman god of medicine. There were two hospitals built by the Confederate Army in Front Royal. After the Battle of Manassas thousands of sick and wounded were quartered there. Plus a number of doctors.

Page 21
George Williams became Colonel on General Liddell and General Govan's staff. Williams, along with Benton Roy, Irving Buck, and Alvin Buck went west with Colonel Jordan and served with the Army of Tennessee.

Page 22
Benton Roy became Colonel and General Hardee's A.A.G.. He married one of General Hardee's daughters and became a lawyer and lived in Selma, Alabama. Later they took their adopted daughter to Germany to study. He died there. Bentonville, Virginia is named for him.

It is difficult to understand why the Buck's did not like Capt. Simpson. I do not think it had anything to do with his being Headmaster of the school in Front Royal, but had more to do with city and country politics.

In the spring of 1861, Alvin Buck wrote a letter from Kentucky before he headed home to Virginia to join the army. In it he mentioned Uncle Tom Ashby, who was a city politician equivalent to a mayor, "had put Capt. Simpson in his place".

Later in the diary when Longstreet visited "Bel Air" the Bucks praised Capt. Simpson and suggested he be promoted, and soon after he was.

Kattie Boone wrote, "One of my first school teachers, Miss Augusta Brown, who could not have been much more over sixteen years old herself. About this time the Tyler sisters, Miss Tensia and Miss Annette, moved up to Front Royal from Prince William Country. I suppose, to be near their aunt, Mrs. Fayette Buck of "Clover Hill". Julia Buck had to be taught and so Miss Tensia decided to open a small day school on account of Julia. (Julia was the daughter of Mrs. Fayette Buck of "Clover Hill.") "She agreed to take Lucy and Nellie Buck, Emma Cloud, Mollie Richardson, and myself. It was a most select little school for small girls. We were taught to speak very low and to be very delicate in our ways.... When we grew old enough, Miss Tensia Tyler's pupils were sent to the new Front Royal Academy, where old Professor Smith taught the boys in the right hand room and Miss Susan Randolph the girls in the left hand room. Kate Green, Lillie Robinson, Emma Cloud, and Lucy and Nellie Buck were among my school mates."

Kattie Boone later wrote a letter, on June 9, 1860, to her mother when she was attending a private school in Woodstock, Virginia. She asked, "How is Mr. Simpson getting along? Mr. Eakin told me he had scholars of every class going to his school. I know I am very glad I stopped. It is a wonder Nellie Buck would go. She and Lucy are always so aristocratic."

Lucy Buck wrote Benton Roy on September 12, 1864, "Major Simpson's death was a shock to us all. I felt it deeply owning to the misunderstanding existing between us. I felt no unkindness toward him although there was a change from the old friendly felling, still I have reason to believe he died thinking me unkind. Heaven knows how sincerely I regret it."

Page 27
Charlie Richardson belonged to the "Waterlick" Richardsons.

Page 34
Miss Pollie Haynie, a dear old lady boarded at the hotel. She is buried at Millar graveyard at "Mountain View".

Page 35
Dr. Hanson Dorsey and his wife, Amanda Castleman lived at "Sunnyside" near town.

Page 36
Francis Pierpont was provisional Governor of West Virginia.

Page 45
On April 5, 1862 Marcus Buck wrote in his diary, "The negro stampede continues".

Allie Ashby wrote in his book, "The Valley Campaign", regarding two of his servants, "In fact but for Uncle Lewis and Aunt Susan we would have had a very hard time and I cannot recall the services of these old negroes without the tenderest of emotions.

"A few days after the surrender, when we were assured that the war was over, my father called all of the servants together under a large tree in the yard and explained to them under order of the President of the United States the negroes had been liberated and were now free to do as they pleased. He told them that he had no further control over them, that in the future he would pay them for services such wages as would be established in the community, and that if they wished to remain in his employ they could do so as long as they desired; but that if any of them wished to find new homes, they were of liberty to make a change. He assured them of his friendly interest in them and of his desire to see them do well and be happy. He told them of the altered conditions that would surround them under freedom and urged them to cultivate habits of thrift and industry, which would make them useful citizens and self-respecting men and women.

"After he had finished his remarks, which he had made in a tone of deep emotion, Uncle Lewis stood up and tried to be the spokesman for his race. In his illiterate way, but with strong sense, he said he did not wish to be free, that all his life he had been a slave in my father's family, that he had always been treated with the greatest kindness by my grandfather and after his death by my father and that in his old age he did not want to be thrown on the world to make his own living and to be neglected by strangers. He then broke down in tears and wept copiously.

"My father told him that he need not fear, that as long as he lived he should have a home with us and would receive the same attention he had always received. The other negroes assented to what Lewis had said, but, as they were younger, it was not expected that they would wish to remain indefinitely in our family. It was, however, several years after the war before they all found new homes. Aunt Susan stayed with us some three years before she went to live in her own home. She had accumulated enough money to buy a neat little house in Front Royal, and by taking in washing and doing light work she lived in comfort until she died.

"A few weeks after the incident mentioned above Uncle Lewis went to his room with an illness that soon led to his death. We waited on the old man and did all we could for his comfort, but he expressed a desire to die, for he said he was heartbroken and had nothing left to live for.

"When Uncle Lewis had passed away my father had him buried in the lot where for many years his people had been buried. He had the faithful old friends assemble under the shade trees in the yard and a short service was held over the remains. My father and I accompanied the body to its last resting place, where Lewis now sleeps. I wept then, and the tears come now into my eyes as I write these words; for this good old negro had been one of the best friends of the days of my childhood and boyhood. He had taught me the early lessons of outdoor life, how to ride, to load and shoot a gun, to hunt, and do may of the little things about the farm and home; he had entertained me by the hour in his room with stories and tales of his early life; he had told me many things about my grandfather, who died before I was born, and about other members of my family whom I had never seen, about the western country and the Valley in which we lived when he was a young man."

Page 49
On April 16, 1862 Walter's dad Marcus Buck wrote to his son Dick Buck that Walter had been home several days with the mumps.

Page 51
In Marcus Buck's diary he described his son Walter in this instant as, "Rash and thoughtless and he will not be advised." A father's remark regarding the brave action of his son!

Page 53
Mr. Cook (1812 - 1891) was an attorney and was speaker when the banner was presented to the Warren Rifles. He had two sons who fought in the war. One was Giles, Jr., who married Elizabeth Lane after the war and became a judge. The other was Wythe, who became s physician in Washington, D.C.

Page 65
Allie Ashby wrote in his book, <u>The Valley Campaign</u>, "There came to our house at this time a Federal officer, Col. Thos. C. McDowell, in command of a Pennsylvania regiment in Shield's Division, who asked for quarters for himself and staff. His request was granted and he was entertained by my parents with as much courtesy as was possible under the existing conditions. My father soon learned that he was a gentleman of culture and refinement, a Democrat, and a much dissatisfied soldier. Colonel McDowell soon became very confidential and related his history to my father with a frankness that was pathetic.

"It seems that at the beginning of the war he was editing a Democratic paper in a large city in Pennsylvania. Being a Union man and what was known as a War Democrat, he had been given a commission as Colonel of a regiment of volunteers by the Governor of his State and in this capacity he had entered the army. He was a man with a family, one of his sons being a lieutenant in his regiment. While a guest in my home he expressed to my father his dissatisfaction with the policy of the Federal Government both in its purpose and in its conduct of the war. He said he had entered the army under the conviction that the war was for the restoration of the Union, but he had discovered its main purpose was to destroy the institution of slavery. With the latter purpose he had no sympathy. He then told my father that he had decided to resign his commission in the army and resume his duties as editor of his paper which was opposed to what he conceived to be the policy of the Government. During the few days this officers was in our home we became strongly attracted to him, and when he left we had no thought of ever seeing him again. Later I will tell of a visit he made to our home a few weeks afterward."

Page 75
Allie Ashby wrote in his book The Valley Campaign ,

"During the ten days following the defeat of Shields at Port Republic my home was filled with Federal officers. General Duryee and staff were still with us and Colonel McDowell still remained a guest in our home. In addition to these guests, we had two wounded officers, one Federal and one Confederate. The Federal officer was a German of General Shield's support staff, who had been shot in the face at Port Republic. He was a handsome, dashing fellow, quite popular with his companions, an officer in the German army, we were told, on leave of absence, who had joined the Federal army to learn some of the methods of American warfare. He was severely punished for his curiosity, for his face was badly scarred by a rebel bullet.

"A singular circumstance took place in connection with his stay in our home. While confined to his room one afternoon a young woman, accompanied by a German officer, and riding a spirited horse, dashed up to the front door of the house. She sprang from her horse, rushed into the house, and asked the servant where she could find the wounded officer. When told where he lay, she rushed upstairs and, without ceremony, entered his room. This woman was the then celebrated Belle Boyd. Her history in brief may not be wanting in interest.

"She was a well-bred woman, a native of one of the northern countries of the State, and at that time had relatives in our village, with whom she was temporarily staying. She had developed a strong interest in military matters, and posing as a Rebel spy and heroine, she had already attracted considerable notice by her exploits; but she was not taken seriously by either the Federals or the Confederates. Though professing warm allegiance to the South, she played with both sides a game that inspired no confidence in either, hence she lived in either camp as it suited her purpose and, as far as I know was never under arrest. At the time I speak of she was in the Federal lines and was receiving marked attentions from the young Federal officers. On May 22nd she had ridden into the Confederate lines and had given Jackson information that proved to be unreliable.

"When she rode up to my home to see the wounded German officer she was playing the game of flirt and lowering the dignity of her sex. She was a young woman of some personal beauty, vivacious, attractive, and spirited in manner, and a skilled rider of spirited horses. Nor was she wanting in energy, dash, and religious fervor of the true heroine. She loved notoriety and attention, and was as far below the standard of the pure and noble womanhood of the South as a circus rider. Her own sex in the south repudiated her, and the true manhood of both armies was as suspicious of her character as Frederick the Great was of Madame de Pompadour. So much for Belle Boyd. Her heroism has long faded into the forgetfulness of her generation. She has found no decent place in history."

The Yankee press were particularly hard on the Southern heroine Belle Boyd. The following comes from the book, <u>Bohemian Brigade - Civil War Newsmen in Action</u> by L.M. Starr:

"Next to Jackson, the sensation of the campaign was Belle Boyd, the Confederate spy - a lady brazenly described by the Herald as 'an accomplished prostitute'. Nathaniel Paige, a Tribune reporter with General Shield's division, interviewed her at Front Royal. She admitted spying, he said, 'but resents attacks on her virtue' ... In personal appearance, without being beautiful, she is very attractive. Is quite tall, has a superb figure, an intellectual face, and dresses with much taste... She can give you the name of almost every officer in the Rebel army... Why she should be allowed to go at will through our camps, flirt with our officers I am at loss to know... She wears a gold palmetto tree beneath her beautiful chin, a Rebel soldier's belt around her waist, and a velvet band across her forehead, with the seven stars of the Confederacy shedding their pale light therefrom.

"Paige wrote Gay privately that General Shields was closeted four hours with her, but I think she is not what camp gossip charges with being. A Philadelphia Inquirer man completed the picture,

"Belle has passed the first freshness of youth. She is a sharp-featured, black-eyed woman of 25, for care an intrigue have given her that appearance. (She was 19.) Last summer (with Patterson's army) she wore a revolver in her belt, and was courted and flattered by every lieutenant and captain in the service who saw her. There was a kind of ... dash about her, a smart pertness, a quickness of retort, and utter abandon of manner and bearing which were attractive from their very unwontedness. The father of this resolute black eyed vixen is a paymaster in the Southern army ...'

"The Inquirer man considered that his colleagues had violated some canon of journalism by implying that she was 'personally impure'. Reporters who thus attack a woman, he wrote gallantly, 'exceed the license which justice and fairness allot even to outlaws.' When Belle was finally incarcerated in the Old Capitol Prison that July (only to be released and recaptured later aboard a blockade-runner) reporters mourned the passing of a lively source of copy."

Kattie Boone wrote that William Mason Buck did not allow his daughters to come into his presence until they were fully dressed to teach them modesty.

One can understand Lucy Buck's rejection of Belle Boyd especially when she waved to Yankee officers from her hotel room. And was often seen on the arm of Federal soldiers.

Page 78
Dr. Robert Cary Buck wrote, in later years, this account of the liberation of Front Royal:

"The mind of childhood and youth, like the delicate film of the camera, receives and retains impressions with a facility that is not possible in maturer year, when the weight of responsibility presses, and the lesser objects are obscured by the greater. Thus, the vivid impress of the events of 1861 to 1865 are to the writer, the most prominent of his life. Reared at Front Royal in one of the Northern counties of Virginia, where the moving panorama of war was shifted almost daily, his opportunities for viewing the moving events of the period; so pregnant with historic action, were of the best. It is not the purpose of the writer to relate his experiences in chronological order or sequence but to place on record those that appear to him to be of most interest to the public.

"The 23rd of May was a typical day. The landscape shimmered in the bright sunlight, verdue of field and forest suggested nothing but peace and tranquility and there was no outward or visible sign of the wrinkled visage of grim war. The little town seemed wrapped in a preternatural slumber. Tis true the white tents of the garrison, composed of the 1st Maryland (Federal) regiment and a section of artillery - the extreme left flank of Gen. Banks army - could be seen flapping in the breeze. The writer in company with two companions sought a sequestered and shady spot on the creek, to indulge a boys loves for a bath. While so engaged from the direction of the village is heard a scattering discharge of musketry. Across the rail-road bridge flies a dismounted cavalryman, followed by a Zouave, in his baggy red trousers, which do not appear to impede his flight. Alarmed at this rude interruption of my pleasure, I flee to my home, upon a commanding eminence; and gazing toward the town, I see the Federal soldiers pouring down the streets, filling the Court House, hospital, and other buildings and the white smoke of their guns belching from cupola and windows. A long gray line is advancing upon them from the south, their loud huzzahs drowning the din of the guns. The panic stricken Federals are now fleeing down Main and Chester streets; as they arrive at the junction of a cross street, the head of the Confederate column debouches from it, and into the faces of the former is poured a withering volley, to which they reply. A momentary stand and the discomfited Federals resume their disorderly retreat seeking the protection of their reserves and the artillery that crown the heights over looking the town and the Shenandoah river. Now the guns are unlimbered and the bombs begin to scream over my head. Yonder one drops into a herd of peaceful cows grazing. Another tears through my fathers barn, and yet another explodes under the shed of the old mill, driving the stones and gravel through the roof. I see a company of Confederate cavalry charging the left flank of the enemy. At its head rides a gallant kinsman (who later offered up his life for his country) (*Walter Buck - see Diary of Lucy Buck*) his face suffered with the joy of conflict and to the anxious inquiries of my sisters as to the strength sufficiency of the Confederate force, exclaims, 'Jackson and Ewell are here with 30,000 men and he can whip any force they may bring against him' - there was a shell tore up the turf to the left of the house, he cried, 'Go to the cellar'. We needed no second invitation for the missiles from the Federal guns were now whistling through the trees cutting off limbs. After a time there is a lull in the conflict, which is receding toward the north and Jackson's guns are firing over the heads of his advancing army and has silenced the Federal guns. We venture forth and see the Confederates advancing by the left flank over the dense wooded ridge, turning the position of Col. Kenly, the Commander of the Federals, upon that part of the field. Later when Federals have left the ridge the masses of victorious rebels pouring down the Winchester turn-pike. A band at the head of the splendid regiment strikes up the inspiring strains of 'Gay and Happy' and the men in response seem infused with new life, as they hear the lively quickstep they press to the top of the commanding ridge and on toward the bridge, spanning the Shenandoah, which the enemy has fired. Wheats battalion of Louisian Tigers are upon them before their purpose is accomplished and they kick the burning brands into the river as they cross in hot pursuit. Between the two branches of the river the enemy is surrounded and compiled to yield to the victors. A Confederate cavalryman approaches the commander of the Federals and demands his sword. Col. Kenly declines to deliver it to a private, but after the latter used his own weapon upon his head, he decided that the exigencies of the occasion permitted him to waive ceremony and he complied. As I viewed the field at the conclusion of the battle I saw an old farm house far to the right in flames and on the left a rail fence fired by the shells burning briskly.. Mounting an old farm horse I tore the fence to pieces, (it had been splintered at the point of impact to a degree that it resembled tooth-picks). I hastened then to the village to witness the return of the prisoners, from the front. There was a compact body of 1,500 in line, and their downcast mein proclaimed the depth of their humiliation. The scene above described was the prelude to Jacksons celebrated Valley Campaign, and was known as the battle of Front Royal and the brilliancy of his strategy and tactics was only to reach its acme upon the fatal field of Chancellorsville, where the frightest orb of the military galaxy was blotted out."

Page 79
General Jackson slept on the porch at Riverside on the night of May 23, 1862.

Page 81
Allie Ashby wrote this account of Colonel Kenly in his book, <u>The Valley Campaigns</u>:

"General Shields' army remained in camp only two days and then crossed the Blue

Ridge into eastern Virginia. Shortly after this the First Maryland Federal Regiment, under the command of Colonel R.J. Kenly, went into camp on a high hill one mile north of our village. It was a large and well organized regiment, made up almost entirely of Maryland men. With the regiment was a battery of artillery. Two companies were detached and stationed in the village as a guard for the Provost-Marshall, whose office was in the hotel. Outposts and pickets were stationed on the main road that led into the village. These Maryland men were well behaved, orderly, and kind to our people, and they created a good impression. At this time all private property was protected, and when needed for the use of the army, was paid for. The soldiers paid for the small things they wanted, such as milk, pies, cakes, and fruit. There was no disposition to rob or pillage. Colonel Kenly camped on land owned by an estate of which my father was the administrator, and he gave an order on the Government to indemnify the estate for the use of grass and other property taken by the men of his command. Though the Government never respected his order and has never paid for the property the men took, it was not due to any fault of Colonel Kenly. He was a gentlemen and respected the rights of the citizens; which is more than can be said for the Government for which he was fighting. His action indicated that the Federal authorities were fighting men in arms and not robbing and destroying the property of unarmed citizens. Even the Confederate authorities were not at that time more considerate of the rights of our citizens than were Colonel Kenly and his men. Had a policy like his been adopted during the subsequent years of the war, it is more than probable that peace would have been made sooner and without so fearful a waste of life and property.

"It was for the reason that the policy of the Federal Government with regard to the people of the South during the last two years of the war was so exasperating to the men, women, and even the children of that section, that no sacrifice was considered too great to make in defense of their lives and property. When it became a war of extermination few shrank from the hardships inflicted on them; for life and property seemed of less value to the Southerners than freedom from tyranny and oppression.

"And that is why fathers and mothers, wives and sisters, bore their sorrow with stoicism when their loved ones fell in battle. Only those who lived through the storm of war, who experienced the hardships and sorrows of a brutal and inhuman struggle, can fully realize the sufferings, the sorrows, and the courage of the Southern women, of the old men, and even the children of tender age when brought face to face with starvation and death. We will never know how many innocent lives were destroyed, what brilliant hopes were crushed by the conditions that surrounded the non-combatants, nor how many actually perished from disease due to starvation. Even at this late day, when I think of that time of war, and recall the many incidents that came under my personal notice, I often wonder how so many lived through them, how the spirit of men, women and children could have endured the situation presented to them."

Page 95
The whole "Bel Air" family went to "Belmont" on June 1, 1862.

Allie Ashby wrote in his book, "The Valley Campaign", regarding McDowell: "Sunday morning, June 1st, was a most beautiful day. The heavens were clear, the atmosphere was mild and balmy, the flowers were in bloom, and the birds sang sweetly in the trees around the house. All nature smiled with peace and happiness, and only man was vile and cruel. Seated at the breakfast table in my home were my parents, Colonel McDowell, General Carroll and his wife, General Duryee and his staff, and Dr. Mercer, and old physician, the uncle of Mrs. Carroll who accompanied her so that she would not be lonely when General Carroll was attending his military duties. I, the only child present, sat at my mother's side. While the meal was being served and all were conversing animatedly, we heard the slow fire of artillery in the distance. Each discharge become more and more distinct, and the reports of muskets mingled with the roll of artillery, indicated a general engagement on the Valley pike in the neighborhood of Cedar Creek. Attention was soon called to the cannonade and remarks were made by the officers present suggesting the probable cause of the firing. They decided that the engagement was between the forces of Fremont and Jackson, 12 miles west, on the Valley pike. As General Carroll had instructions to join his command that morning at 9 o'clock and march west to Strasburg, he volunteered to explain the situation.

"He told us that General Shields would march with his division to Strasburg to take a position in the rear of Jackson, who, with his advance, was at that time near Winchester 19 miles north of Strasburg, in full retreat up the Valley. Shields had a distance of 12 miles to cover, while Jackson had 19 miles, and his men were widely scattered. The artillery firing, he said, was between some of Jackson's cavalry, which was trying to hold in check the advance of Fremont from the west, and Fremont's men, who were trying to reach the Valley pike. He remarked, with some brusqueness and braggadocio, that Shields and Fremont would unite their forces at Strasburg by 12 o'clock and close in behind Jackson, thus cutting off the retreat of the Confederates. Turning to my mother, he said, 'This means, Mrs. Ashby, that before midday we will have Jackson bagged, and the backbone of the Confederacy will be broken'.

"As there was apparently more truth than poetry in General Carroll's remarks, my mother's eyes filled with tears, and she excused herself from the table. After she left General Duryee, a most courtly gentleman, remarked to General Carroll that his remarks had wounded my mother's feelings; and he tried to apologize to my father for an apparent boldness of speech that had no serious meaning.

"Very soon the company arose from the table. General Carroll took leave of his wife, mounted his horse, and left to join his command that was to march at 9 o'clock for Strasburg. General Duryee and staff also mounted their horses and rode away to their command.

"Mrs. Carroll retired to her room to worry over General Carroll's departure for active service. Dr. Mercer took a stroll around the lawn, while my father, Colonel McDowell, and I went out on the front porch. We could distinctly hear the cannon booming on the pike and the direction of the firing was gradually moving south, indicating that the Confederates were holding their ground. Colonel McDowell, turning to my father, remarked that General Carroll had stated that Shields and Fremont would unite their forces by 12 o'clock and bag Jackson, but that he did not believe one word of it. Then he said, with an emphasis and feeling that impressed me greatly, 'I hope to God that Jackson will lick them'.

"Taking a chair, he sat down and drew me to his lap, took a silver watch out of his pocket, and put it on me, with these words, 'Keep this watch, my son, to remember me. I bought it for rough use when I entered the army. I have a gold watch at home'.

"He then said to my father that he had his resignation in his pocket, and was no longer in the service of the Government and added, 'when I return home I will resume my editorial duties and will oppose the policy of the Administration, its purpose to overthrow the institution of slavery. I am a Union man, not an abolitionist'.

"It would be difficult for me to forget the words of Colonel McDowell as to forget his kindness. He remained with us for several weeks and seemed loth to part with us. After his return to his home he resumed his editorial duties and the next time we heard of him he was a prisoner in Fort Warren, for his denunciation of the policies of the Governments. After the close of the war he wrote to my father that he had been persecuted and financially ruined by his war experiences. I still have the watch he gave me."

Page 96
Captain James N. Sanderson wrote to William Mason Buck after the war. He had been captured, imprisoned, and released at war's end. He was charged by the United States authorities for being helpful to the Confederates but the charges were later dropped.

Page 101
Colonel Joseph Thornburn was the acting Brigadier General in the absence of Colonel Samuel S. Carroll, the 8th Ohio Infantry.

Page 115
Sue Buck became ill every May 29 in memory of her fiance, Willie Richardson.

Page 145
Lucy does not skip this month in her writing. The diary is unreadable on scraps of paper. The dates are unsure.

On October 15, 1862 Stuart's Cavalry passed through Front Royal with horses captured in Pennsylvania and John G. Buck died of diptheria. His son, Captain Samuel D. Buck, wrote a book, "With The Old Confeds". His other son, William Alexander Buck (Sandy) also served in the Confederate army. General W.E. Jones wrote, "Sandy was the most gallant soldier he had ever seen in action". General Early wrote, "Samuel D. Buck was the bravest man I ever knew".

Page 151
Colonel Walker was probably General J.A. Walker of the 13th Virginia Infantry. Captain S.D. Buck wrote about him on his death in the Confederate Veteran Magazine Vol. 10, page 34.

Page 153
Thomas Ashby of "Oakley" was a city official. He saved all the county papers by taking them to "Belmont" on the mountain to protect them from being destroyed by the Yankees.

Page 154
Elder Thomas Buck (1777-1862) died December 10, 1862. He was buried in Buckton Cemetery. He was a famous preacher in that area.

Page 172
Gus Tyler was a member of Company B, 17th Virginia Infantry. He survived Pickett's charge and the trenches around Richmond and Peterburg. After the war he was engaged in fur trading in Montana and died in Wyoming in 1887.

"A Diary and Refugees Life" by Mrs. Cornelia McDonald gives a full account of the state of affairs of the people in Winchester and especially the McDonald family.

Page 173
"I have yet to find any writings by Mr. Crippen of the Cincinnatti Times. Certainly he must have written about the Buck family. I am still pursuing his work." (Editor, W.P.B.)

Page 188
This description of the Marshalls and their home "Happy Creek" is given by Laura Virginia Hale in her book, "The Revolution Years":

"Perhaps the nearest thing to a baronial household in early Fredrick County was 'Happy Creek', the magnificent home of James Markham Marshall, one of the most distinguished Americans of his day. He was born in Fauquier County in 1764, with abilities equal to those of his brother, Chief Justice John Marshall, while his accomplishments were wider and more varied as a Revolutionary hero, lawyer, diplomat, land speculator, and gentleman of the old Southern regime.

"In the Revolution, James Marshall first served under his father, Colonel Thomas Marshall, then rose to a lieutenancy in the First Virginia Artillery Reg't. at the age of 16, and led what was called 'the forlorn hope' in an attack upon the fort in the siege of Yorktown.

"For his military service he received a grant of 2,666 acres in Kentucky (then Virginia), and followed his father there, where he ventured into frontier politics and was involved in suppressing the 'Spanish conspiracy' (not to mention a dual he fought with James Brown, later U.S minister to France). His avid interest in Land speculation brought him into contact with Robert Morris, the financier of the Revolution, and into the courtship of his beautiful daughter, Hester Morris, who was the second greatest heiress in America at the time of her marriage of James Marshall in 1795.

"Hester Morris was reared amid the turmoil of revolution at the Philadelphia seat of the Continental Congress and the capital of the new Republic. Her father's bounty to the Continental government, friends, and charity made him the 'real Prince of North America', host to all the prominent of Europe and America who visited Philadelphia, including George and Martha Washington, lifelong intimate friends of the Morris family.

"A true gentlewoman, Mrs. Morris ranked second only to Mrs. Washington among Philadelphia's 'Revolutionary Dames', and she and her daughter Hester, were social leader in the so-called 'Republican Court', the brilliant gathering of literati, scientists, statesman, and military heroes surrounding the President and his lady.

"Mrs. Washington noted in her diary that her Custis grandaughters had attended the marriage of Hester Morris to James Marshall of Virginia. The couple went aboard on a combined two year honeymoon and business trip, during which he negotiated for himself, his brother John, and their brother-in-law, Rawleigh Colston, the purchase of the remainder of Lord Fairfax's Northern Neck Estate - some 220,000 acres of Virginia. Acting also as Secretary of the North American Land Co., he visited all the financial centers in Europe, while seeking loans, buyers, and settlers, for the vast land holdings of Robert Morris, by that time facing bankruptcy. While in Europe James Marshall was appointed as President Washington's personal representative to the Prussian court to plead for Lafayette's release from prison.

"During those years abroad the two eldest Marshall sons were born on American ships off the Bristish coast, their patriotic parents not wanting them to be born in

England. Upon their return to America, the Marshalls lived for a time in Winchester, where he practiced law, meanwhile building on his 80,000 acre share of Fairfax Manors near Front Royal, a massive stone mansion of 16 rooms and wide halls with ceilings 20 feet high and front windows so tall a man could step upright through them. There were separate quarters for servants and tenants, porters's lodges at the entrance gates, a spring house, ice house, and bath house - all built of stone. The grounds and gardens were landscaped and tended by an English gardener. Among the drawing room furnishings were an oil portrait of Hester Marshall painted by Gilbert Stuart at the time of her marriage, and a rug and table bought by the Marshalls in France at a sale of Marie Antoinette's fabulous Versailles treasures.

"Over this courtly manor, which he called 'Happy Creek' from a nearby stream, James Marshall presided, a handsome, dignified gentleman over six feet tall, wearing a queue, stockings, and knee buckles. There he entertained distingusihed guests, among them the Marquis de Lafayette, Charles C. Pinckney, U.S. Minister to France, and Chief Justice John Marshall.

"'Happy Creek' was not just a place of regal splendor, but a 'feast of reason and flow of soul' that welled from nobility of character and intellect, grace and charm of personality. The library was reputed for such rare and classical volumes as Froisart's 'Chronicles', richly illustrated in gilt and colours.

"James Marshall's children settled on neighboring estates carved from their father's vast acreage, forming a prosperous community of hospitable, cultured, and deeply religious citizens. Three of his sons studied law, one of whom, Thomas, had established a successful practice in Winchester when he, his wife, and two children died in the epidemic of 1826. Ten of James Marshall's grandsons were Confederate Soldiers, two killed in battle. Another, Dr. James M. Ambler of the U.S. Navy, died in the cause of science and humanity on the ill-fated 'Jeanette' expedition to Siberia in 1881. He refused to abandon the sick to save his own life, and the last words in the diary found on his frozen body were a confident expression of Christian faith.

"James Marshall's progeny has included farmers, doctors, teachers, and statesmen, five civil engineers and a public school superintendent. Judge Elliot D. Marshall, of Front Royal, is a great-grandson.

"'Happy Creek' homestead remained in possession of Marshall descendants until 1921, when fire reduced it to picturesque ruins. The crumbling stone walls wreathed in vines and haunted by history, lend on old-world charm to the landscape."

Page 197
Charlie Richardson of Company E, 7th Virginia Cavalry died in Broken Bow,

Nebraska on December 3, 1910. He moved there in 1871 and served two terms as Sheriff in Custer county. (See Confederate Veteran Magazine, Vol. 19 page 134)

Page 200
R.L. McCalley was in Company I, 4th Alabama Regiment.

Page 202
Allie Ashby wrote in his book, "The Valley Campaign" the following:

"When the line of march was taken up I and several boys of about my age joined the men and went to the river to see them cross on the pontoon. We spent the entire day watching the different commands file across the bridge. It was a sight that few boys can ever see and was worth the time we gave to it.

"As we were marching along the road one of the men called me and asked me to carry his gun. This was just the thing I wanted to do and in a few minutes I was loaded down with guns. After carrying them a short distance I would give them back to their owners and in return they would give me a handful of caps. One of my boy companions was named Charlie. I called out, 'Charlie, come and get this man's gun.' In an instant the men along the line as far as we could hear took up the cry and called. 'Charlie, Charlie, come and get my gun,' so that before we reached the river Charlie had more guns and caps than he could carry and his name was known to every man in the command."

Page 203
There were seven Bucks in Captain Horace Buck's Company E, 7th Virginia Cavalry.

Page 206
Alvin Buck wrote to Lucy Buck from Hopkinsville, Kentucky on Monday, Arpil 8, 1861:

"Our meeting is still in progress with now and then a convert. Tell Walter, our friend Tom Bryant, is a seeker. O Lucy! You cannot imagine the interest I take in this young man, and when he could no longer resist the earnest appeals made to him from the puplit and went forward I had feelings which had been first stirred up upon seeing Walter take the same step. How I wish our dear father could be brought under the influence of sermons which seem daily to be thrown away upon this sin hardened and rebellious people. There is a young minister with us from Paducah who preaches the most powerful sermons I ever heard."

Dick Buck, Walter's brother trusted Christ as his Savior in the trenches around Petersburg late in the war.

William Mason Buck, the most pious and respected Virginia gentleman in Front Royal finally made Jesus Christ his Saviour in 1886.

Page 207
Walter Buck was first buried at the Buck Cemetary in Buckton, After the war his body was interned at Prospect Hill Cemetery in Front Royal where his body lies with family members.

Page 212
Colonel Marshall was later killed at Cedar Creek in November 1864.

R.L. McCalley of Company I, 4th Alabama, was wounded on July 2, 1863 and left in enemy hands. Later he was exchanged and reassigned on November 12, 1864 to his home in Huntsville, Alabama. He was a student and single when he enlisted in Cmpany I in North Alabama on October 6, 1861. He fought in sixteen battles until wounded at Gettysburg.

Page 224
According to Marcus Buck's diary, Mr. Richardson captured one of the robbers.

Page 229
Aunt Eliza was a servant from "Rose Hill". She was sent over to "Bel Air" as was recorded in the diary of Sue Richardson October 5, 1863, because "the women of Cousin William Buck's were sick".

Lucy's father had cut his foot with an axe chopping wood on September 30, 1863.

Page 232
In "The Valley Campaign" by Thomas A. Ashby, known as Allie in the diary, we read, "One of our boys, whose home was in the main road of travel between our place and Winchester, visited his home and spent several nights with his family. Early one morning a man dresssed in Confederate uniform rode up to the house and rushed in before his presence was know. Without ceremony he entered the room where the boy in grey was seated, talking with his mother (*Mack Bayly and Betty Richards*). As he entered the room the young Confederate took him for one of his companions and rose from his seat to offer him a welcome. The Federal soldier, seeing the boy, drew his pistol and demanded surrender. The boy in grey sprang on him so suddenly that he seized the pistol before it was fired. Then he grappled with the Federal soldier. In the tussell that insued, the Confederate threw the Federal and had him fixed on the floor, while the mother, who was in the room, and an eye witness to the struggle, cried out to her boy, 'Give it to him, son, give it to him'. But while the fight was still going on a great commotion was heard in the yard. The mother, going to the window to see what the noise meant, found that the yard was full of Federal cavalrymen, who were dismounted to enter the house.

Turning to her son she told him to surrender, as there was no chance to escape. Up to this time, he had the advantage, and but for outside aid would have captured his aggressor. Realizing the situation, he released his hold and allowed the man to rise. Then, still holding the pistol he told the man he would surrender. He was soon hurried off to prison. This episode took place at 'Riverside' where our cousin Beth or Elizabeth M. Blakemore Bayly Richards lived." Mack Bayly was imprisoned at Camp Chase.

Page 237
Dick Buck wrote on June 21, 1864, "Cousin Mount Cloud has a letter form the President acknowledging valuable service".

Page 240
"James Smedley was killed attempting to escape from the Yankees at Little Washington in Rappahannock County. He was an enrolling officer. When the Yankees arrived in town. They mounted their horses and fled, but Jimmy "lost his hat" and when he stopped to retrieve it he received a carbine bullet through his breast bone" (from Marcus Buck's diary).

Page 241
Mr. Dore was a druggist in Richmond and had helped Dick Buck.

"Cousin Mack" was Mack Blakemore. He moved to Van Buren, Arkansas after the war. Note Confederate Veteran Magazine, Vol. 6, page 521.

"Dick" or Richard M. Blakemore was adjutant in Morton's Artillery Battalion in Forrest Cavalry.

Page 249
Mattie Cook married Scott Roy after the war.

Page 250
Nellie Buck had been to Clark County with the LaRue's for three to four months.

Page 254
Dr. Leach married Mrs. L. Armstead on May 15, 1864.

Page 256
Marcus Buck wrote in his diary on May 21, 1864, "there was dense smoke covering the area of Front Royal from Lee's battlefield".

Page 258
John James LaRue was the second son of Uncle John Billups LaRue by his first wife, Frances Major. They were married in 1828. She died on August 21, 1836. Mr.

LaRue then married William Mason Buck's sister, Kathryn E. Buck on January 31, 1843. Aunt Kathryn died June 1882 and her husband died May 9, 1875.

Page 266
The Van Meter's were one of the oldest families in the valley. In 1730, John and Isaac Van Meter had received two grants of 40,000 acres each.

Page 267
John W. Grantham or Colonel Grantham's father had been Quarter Master in Washington's Army.

Mr. and Mrs. Luke were John Luke and his second wife Ann Louisa Grantham. Ann was the daughter of James Grantham and Phoebe LaRue.

Page 269
Cousin James was probably Uncle LaRue's second son, John James LaRue, who was born August 26, 1835 and married Katherine Grantham December 20, 1863.

The immense daughter was Eliza Frances LaRue. They have three more children: Ditt, Bunt, Warren.

Page 272
Fannie L. was probably the daughter of Samuel LaRue, Uncle John Larue's brother. She married Richard Timberlake and had three children.

Page 274
Cartmell, in his history of Frederick County wrote, "August 17, 1864 will go down as the blackest day the lower valley has ever seen. Sheridan has retired from Strasburg and Front Royal. He put a torch to the entire area. He burned everything but houses, but even burned some of them." See the description on page 400 of "Four Valliant Years" by Laura Virginia Hale.

Page 278
Chris LaRue was Christopher LaRue son of Samuel LaRue, brother of Uncle John LaRue, and his second wife Juliet Carter Collins.

Page 280
William Richardson Ashby was born on August 8, 1864. He was the son of Thomas N. Ashby and Elizabeth Almond Ashby. He was the brother of Allie Ashby. William R. Ashby died March 4, 1942 and is buried in Lowden Park Cemetery, Baltimore, Maryland.

Page 282
Colonel Jacob's son, Bayly was mortally wounded at Gettysburg and died on the retreat in Winchester, Virginia.

Page 287
Those "sad autumn days" are described in this letter written by Nellie Buck to her cousin, Dick Buck.

Bel Air October 23, 1864

"hold um tuddy Itchie." (*Dick Buck*)

And don't look too doleful when you open the envelope to find one of my "four stars" as Irvie calls them, I am only going to answer in this one the five of yours, dates of which are in my letter case but have slipped my memory. My only excuse for long silence is, in the first place, when Alvie came home (those thirty days are among the happiest in my life), I had just as much as I could do to look at and to talk to him; in the second place, ever since then we have been subjugated and I have not had the heart to write.

I do wish my dear Cousin I could recollect and tell you all we have passed through since Alvie left us; purgatory I might say is a circumstance to these last forty days and nights. You remember I wrote you about Gen.'l Anderson and Gen.'l Longstreet's old staff having dined with us when our army went down the Valley, after Early's retreat from Winchester Gen.'l Wickham attempted to hold a large force of yankees out numbered him ten to one; his men fought gallantly, sustaining but small loss in their retreat. I can never forget that morning. I rose early and was in the kitchen assisting Sallie in baking bread for a little Confed, (which he never got, poor fellow), when the firing commenced. We heard the yankees' cheer and charge across the river, and knew that we might then expect. In less than ten minutes the whole face of the country seemed covered with blue coats and the air was rent by the most hideous yelps that only a yankee can make. For three days the cavalry wagons and artillery were passing through toward Luray. We fought them all along the road to Bentonville where we made a stand till morning and then fell back to Luray and so on to Port Republic. Then we gave them their desserts and they came back, burning, destroying and stealing in the most heathenish manner. They burned all mills and barns as far as "Clover Hill', excepting Hazard's.

A negro and white yankee burned the "Clover Hill" barn, then rode up to the house and said they had orders to burn it too, but if Uncle Fayettee would give them forty dollars in gold they would not do so; if he did not they would shoot him. Jule had some money concealed on her person and becoming alarmed for her father, threw it to them. We have not heard the extent of the mischief they did there but understand they burned even all Uncle Fayette's farming implements. Some two weeks ago Aunt Susan (*servant at "Clover Hill"*) and her three children went off one night to the yankees, saying she was going to look for her husband. The last I heard from there. Aunt Lizzie had just finished churning and said it was the hardest days work she did. Did you ever dream of her coming to that? Mrs. Miller's, Mrs. Green's, Capt. Gardner's, Capt. Roy's (*servants*) and Horace have all gone to taste the sweets of freedom. Some twenty or thirty white families have also gone, a happy riddance indeed. Copp and family started last Saturday evening and there is a rumor that he was captured by McCauslin's men next day and forwarded to "Camp Lee"; I can't vouch for the truth of it. Horace left us in the day Friday, to see what he could pick up off the camp ground, returned at midnight and took his clothes which he had packed previously. We all saw from his movement several days before that he intended it. It was last night, two weeks ago we went on top of the house and witnessed the burning of Mr. Weston's mill and house; had it been the funeral pyre of Lincoln and Cabinet, Grant and his hirelings, I should have thought it the grandest, most beautiful fireworks ever seen; as it was, when I saw those terrible flames licking upward illuminating the whole face of the county and sky and thought of fiendish cowards who could not compete with our brave southerners in the field and were waging a cruel war against their helpless wives, mothers, sisters, and children at home, I felt strong enough to consume the whole of yankeedom. Starvation is now their declared purpose in the Valley, and tho' they may partially succeed, we are not more yankees now than we were when the first call of Virginia summoned them to the field. They can't burn all the dry leaves, tree branches and water. You can't imagine, my dear Cousin, what a trial it was to have them dash up and ask for bread, when they had burned our mills, taken our grain and to have to feed them and not open our lips to tell them what we thought of them. The 77th New York (commanded by Col. French of the 6th Corps) camped for three days on their return from up the Valley, in the field to the right of Uncle Tom's and between Mr. Glasscock's and the woods. Col. French was an old friend of Uncle Marcus in the old war and I give him the credit of having the best behaved men I've seen during the war. Your Pa and Jaque were obliged to leave home with the horses and for fear of their conscription, which, I am happy to say, was not put into execution. The servants betrayed your Pa; told where all the things were hid and they took every grain of tea, coffee, sugar, all Aunt Letitia's preserves, some of the best clothing and Jaque's clothes, knives, forks, and oh! Dick, the grapes were ready to gather and they took the last one of them. Just to think of it, and I don't expect my poor Coz has tasted one this session. Your Ma was very much alarmed, but Gussie fought and matched them to the last. When you come she will tell you how she cut one with a knife and kicked another from the top of the steps to the bottom, and saved a good deal by the way she managed them. I tell you she is just as spunky as she can be with them. Miss Caroline Willis and Gussie jerked Uncle Mack's overcoat off a yankee's back and pummeled him well. All Aunt Letitia's goods she got in Clarke last winter they took. They left Uncle Netwon the house and out houses and four sheep not a grain of any thing. The last we heard from Mr. Richards, his servants, two pigs, a few potatoes, a barrel of corn and three cows were all he had. And don't you think his Confederate bonds and every piece of meat were burned in the mill? He, like many others is completely ruined. Dr. Dorsey had half barrel of flour and one piece of meat; he, Dr. Dorsey nor the children have a single rag of clothes but the ones on their backs, and only enough cover for one bed. He was here and said they even took her stockings, his little dead girls clothes, and said he would have to borrow a shirt when he had his washed. Scott was here in the intervals of their invasions and can tell you of the six men of Mosby's they shot after they had surrendered, one of whom was poor Henry Rhodes whom they caught at Mrs. Jones' toll gate, tied him between two horses and dragged him past his mother's door to the field just opposite Cousin Elizabeth Richardson's, where they shot him three times. Mrs. Rhodes and Emma extracted a solemn promise from old Custer that he should be treated as a Confederate prisoner and whilst the former had taken his hand in gratitude for having saved the life of her son, he lay a corpse. Two men, a Georgian and a Virginian were hung in the woods beyond Cousin Elizabeth's. It was a horrible day to us. Jim Anderson and Ed Saffle were in the mountain with their horses. Ed was up a chestnut tree when the yankees came up and made him mount Jim Anderson's horse bare backed and trotted him all the way to Guard Hill where they pleaded "citizen" so hard they let them off. Jim started for the mountain instanter.

Cousin Elizabeth fared like all others; badly. They suffered as much from their insolence as any thing else. So far we have fared better than any of our neighbors. They killed two of our hogs, took nearly all of our corn, killed fifteen turkeys (we thought to keep them for our poor boys Christmas), tore down our fence from the wood pile to the corner, and even burned the little gate up. Tore off the carriage house door and the weather boarding off of it and the mill; but I feel so thankful that we came off so well. A drunken Irishmen was all that came in the house. One night they camped in the meadow next to Mr. Petty's shop and half past eleven we were aroused by hearing them breaking open the smoke house door. When we got up the yard was full of them. They were in the garden digging potatoes, stealing everything they could lay their hands on. We have not for five weeks laid down without all of our clothing on. We hear this evening that Gen.'l Sheridan with thirty thousand men will pass through tomorrow on their way to Culpepper; what we may suffer the next three days the Good Being only knows.

I suppose you have heard ere this of the death of poor Eddie Brown, Joe Painter, and Joe Johnston; Mack Irwin and Alfred McKay were wounded. Early captured in the fight on Tuesday over two thousand prisoners, a hundred wagons and twenty three cannon; it was quite a surprise to the yankees, as to us. We were awakened at five o'clock by the sound of cannon, and I'll tell you it was the most pleasant music that we've heard for many a long day. Our men were passing through all day and we had quite a day of rest. We laid down and slept soundly, to wake on the morrow and find our army all gone. Early at Fishers Hill and the yankees at Guard Hill again. The battle was ours up to four o'clock when our men straggled to plunder yankee camp ground and the yankees received heavy reinforcements. Rosser pitched into their rear and played the wiles with them; we have heard nothing from our friends with him, since we drove the yankees nearly to Winchester. Cousin

Mount, Willie Buck, Willie Cline and Giles Cook were on the mountain all the while and worried them not a little; and don't you think they rode into town one evening just as a squad rode out?

Scott Roy is still sick with chills and fevers at Mrs. Millers when we heard last but suppose he has left ere this. Do you know that 'tis said Dod Foster and John Ship are leading the yankees through the mountains? I hope they will yet catch it. This day two weeks ago Eliza Hope came up almost carrying her mother in her arms and said they were going to burn the mill, and we all started in great haste to try to save what we could for them, and in less time than you could imagine we had everything moved out and in the west end of our house, but fortunately they changed their minds. Mr. Hockman's and Petty's mill and house (Water Side) were burned. Mr. Hope's and Father's are the only ones left for miles around. They even burned up Uncle Tom's saw mill because a bomb shell picked up from the battle field had been laid in there and they said there was ammunition concealed in it. To think that September grapes, hardy chokes, water melons, and beans have all passed and you were not here to enjoy them with us. You don't know how much I thought of, and wished for you, especially whilst Alvin was at home. Have you seen him and Cousin Mack since their return?

Cousin Mack met with a Miss Alice Williams on his way up; rode in the wagon with her several miles; fell in love with her eyes and went to Fauquier to see her; quite a romance wasn't it? You should hear Alvin tell how one evening we were invited to spend the evening at Mr. Hope's and the cry of "yankees are coming" started them over the hill through the cornfield to Johnson Lake's bare headed, and spoiled all our fun for it was a false alarm. Mrs. Wheatly's darkies all picked themselves up a night or so since and left.

November 6th
Two week since I commenced this and we are still in yankeedom! but faring far better than at first. Orville and I walked up to "Belmont" this morning, the first time I have left home since Evred broke his leg some eight or nine weeks ago, and you don't know what a treat it was to breathe pure fresh mountain air once more; and oh! the woods; what would not you have given to have been in my stead. Surely fall is the most beautiful season of the year, more especially in this beautiful little valley. I spent such a quiet pleasant day with Aunt Letitia and Uncle Mack and of course you were duly thought of, wished for and spoken of frequently during the day. Jacque, Gussie and Elite walked as far as Mr. Criser's with us; was quite night when we arrived. Some two week ago Uncle Mack returned from his "home in the woods" and when he got up next morning found out that William, Bernard, Jim and Eveline had decamped; are you not surprised at the two last? We thought them so faithful. Margaret is in Luray and Horace was off with the horses; to think of parents leaving the only two children they had in that way. For two weeks past we have had a guard of ten yankees in town who are very faithful and have protected us well.

Our men have promised not to disturb them night or day; and don't you think last night one of our men walked in the Hotel dining room which they occupy, took his seat amongst them, conversed with them sometimes and walked out and left them. The guards have orders not to fire on them and they come in every day, some of them. We feel quite a sense of protection now, knowing that Co E and Mosby's men are all through the mountains. We can not find out whose troops occupy Milford now, but it seems to be generally understood that we have been largely reinforced and some say by Pickett's division, but it's too good news to be true; and don't you think 'twas even told your Ma that you have been there and she said she could not help looking for you a day or two. Don't you think I had some grapes yesterday, wish it had been you. Gen.'l Lomax sent a flag of truce over to Guard Hill, on Thursday evening they returned at night fall and serenaded the ladies of Front Royal with bugles, tunes so sweet, we all sat out on the West End steps and listened to them a long while. Not one word have we heard from Alvin since Scott was here; A letter from Benton to his ma of October 11th, says he had just received a letter from "Pat" who was in Americus, Ga., doing well and said he would soon be winding up his way homeward. Just suppose for one instant if it could be so; I should be almost deranged with joy!

I know how anxiously you have been wading through these pages for the following, which will be worth all the balance of the letter to you. I received a short note from Sue a month or so ago, saying that her mother was quite ill, not expected to live, and begging if I possibly could write to you and tell you ; but you know I've had no opportunity for so doing. I have heard nothing from there since, excepting that one of Mosby's men said he left there the latter part of last month and Mrs. Bayly's physicians had all given up all hopes of her recovery. I suppose she has consumption. How sorry I fell if poor Sue should be left motherless. Some in form Fauquier said that while the yankees were running the cars on the rail road down there, they took Mr. Sampson Bayly and one other prominent citizen and carried them backward and forward on the cars with them to prevent Mosby's men from firing into their trains. Did you ever hear such villainy? I wish I had something new to write you about her but I suppose she manages to get a letter or two out to you now and then through Mosby's men. About a fortnight since, the yankees went to Mr. Peter Bell's near Cousin John Buck's and found one of their men who had been killed by some of our men, and took Mr. Bell and his partner Mr. Trester with his little son out a mile form the house and shot them both in the presence of little Trester whom they tied to a tree, telling him they wished him to see his father die. After this they went back and burned Mr. Bell's house. Old Mr. John Bell have taken Mrs. Bell and her children to live with him. We have still a few hogs and flour left to live upon, and should these hateful wretches be driven from here to enable you, Alvin and Irvie to come home at Christmas, we can give you a hearty welcome and something to eat. Gussie has some grapes hung away for you. I forgot to tell you that Uncle Mack thinks Horace has gone. He came down to town this morning with Jessie and this evening we met the latter going home alone. If I just had two days conversation with you I could tell you enough to make you laugh and cry yourself sick; but dear me, when can we ever have that pleasure? It seems to me that they never intend going. Guard Hill this morning was covered with Head Quarter tents. You see Frank has added a post script to my letter, not only with pen but his finger marks, the little scamp. Aunt Letitia says Mamie was so alarmed when the yankees were around she had to send her to Mrs. Smedley's and Mrs. Simpson's. I know you are tired but I dislike to say good bye so much. Lucie, Laura and all say "give my love to Dick". Lu says be a good boy. Now won't you write me soon and tell what you have been doing with yourself all this long while.

Wishing you a good night's rest, I am as ever your affectionate, Cousin Nell
P.S. I did not tell you that for three nights while the yankees were here we had regular corn shuckings in the smoke house and invited the Hopes up to help us and we had a merry time of it, I can tell you; and when the yankees came to dig our potatoes, we every one of us turned out and dug in one patch while the yankees were digging in the other, a negro with them at that and as saucy as he could be. I got three red ears, Laura two, Ma two and Mr. Hope one, and Lucie one.

Page 288
The execution of the Confederate soldiers by General Custer is described in "The Valley Campaign" by Thomas A. Ashby. He wrote in his book, "The wagon train that General Custer had determined to send back from Millford to Winchester was presumed to have a small body-guard, and it was this train that Mosby had arranged to attacked in a narrow road some two miles south of our village. Mosby divided his command into two companies, with about 150 men in each company. It was arranged that one company would fall on the rear of the train when it passed a given point and that the other would make the attack in front when the train reached a certain place. Mosby expected to catch the wagon train in a narrow passage, walled in on one side by the river and on the other by a high bluff. In this gorge there was no way to spread, and the Federals would be held as in a vise.

"When the column of Federal cavalry with its wagons came down the road from Millford, and before it entered the gorge in the road, the command which Mosby had sent to make the attacked on the rear of the train, discovered that the train was guarded by the entire Federal cavalry, which was in retreat from Millford. The officer in command of the men that were to attack the rear sent a courier to notify the commander of the men that were to attack in front to withdraw his forces, as the Federal army was to strong for an attack. In some way the courier failed to deliver the message in time; and when the Federal advance came in sight the order for the attack was given.

"The road going south in front of my home crosses a hill about three hundred yards away and then descends along a deep ravine to the river. The road is hemmed in by this ravine on the east side and by a high, wooded hill on the west side, so there is no room for expansion.

"In the early afternoon I was playing in our front yard when I saw a company of Confederate cavalry gallop across a field at right angles to the road, I heard the officer in command give the order, "Wheel to the left. Charge!" As he gave the command the men in front turned into the road and charged over the hill. They had scarcely disappeared from sight when the air was filled with the reports of firearms.
"I rushed back to the house to tell my mother what I had seen; but before I could enter the house I saw a ambulance coming down the road as fast as horses could carry it. In a second I saw a horse running with the saddle turned and the saber striking the ground. The horse was trying to get out of the way of the saber. In less time than I can tell the story men were running in every direction and the whole earth seemed to be swarming with Federal cavalry. They came up like a flock of birds when a stone is cast into it.

"It was apparent at once what all this meant. Mosby's men had run into the wagon train, which was guarded by a large force of cavalry, and had fallen into such close quarters that the command had run in every direction to escape capture. It was stated afterward that the Federal commander had gotten information of this attack and had arranged to trap Mosby. He had placed the wagon train in advance, with a very small guard, but had a large force following, which was to come to the relief of the train when the attack was made. The front wagon in the train was an ambulance, and in this ambulance was a sick officer. The men in charge fired into the ambulance, which was the one I saw coming down the road at such speed, and unfortunately killed the officer.

"In the charge down the narrow road Mosby's men became wedged in between wagons and the ravine on one side and embankment on the other, so that it was almost impossible for them to extricate themselves. They broke in disorder and every man had to look out for himself.

"One of Mosby's men had his horse killed in the beginning of the charge. Anderson, that was his name, ran back on foot, but was captured before he could find a hiding place. Five more were captured at different places.
"As soon as the rout was over the Federals took these prisoners and, without trial, had them shot. Two young men, Love and Jones, were shot in a lot back of a church in our village; Anderson was shot under a large elm tree about a half-mile south of the village; a boy by the name of Rhodes was captured and brought through the village between two cavalrymen and taken a half-mile north and shot under a walnut tree. This boy had been a schoolmate of mine, and was only 17 years of age. He had not been in the army, and that morning he borrowed an old horse from one of our citizens to join in this raid so that he might capture a horse to enable him to become a member of Mosby's command. The old horse broke down in the retreat, and Rhodes was taken prisoner. I doubt whether he fired a gun. As he was led through the village he passed the door of the house where lived his widowed mother

and single sister; but he was not permitted to stop and say good-by to them. His dead body was left on the ground where he was shot, and afterward brought to his home by some of the citizens.

"Two men, Ogelvie and Carter, were taken a mile north and hung on a walnut tree. Rope being attached to a limb and the noose placed around their necks, they were made to stand up on their horses' backs, then the horses were removed from under them. They were left hanging to the tree all night, as our citizen were afraid to go near them and cut them down. On one of the bodies a note was attached, saying, 'Hung in retaliation for the death of a Federal major, killed in an ambulance this afternoon'.

"The following morning, September 24th, several of Mosby's men rode into the village and then went out to the place where their comrads were still hanging. They cut them down and brought their bodies into the village on their horses, a body being thrown across the saddle in front of each rider. The sight was the most ghastly incident our citizens had ever witnessed.

"The Federal cavalry did not go into camp that night at the village but hurried on to Winchester. They were greatly exasperated and it was fortunate that they were hurried on. Our people were thrown into the deepest distress by this experience, and it was made more so because of the sad death of young Rhodes who was known to everyone. He was an amiable, kind, and industrious boy, and had been most helpful to his mother and sister."

Page 289
See page 240 in the "Diary of Refugee Life" by Mrs. Cornelia McDonald.

Page 294
Captain Samuel D. Buck of Company H, 13th Virginia Infantry was the son of John Gill Buck of "Buckton."

Page 297
Dick Bayly married Mary Bird Garrett in 1876. After the war he attended Washington and Lee, studied Law and practiced in Philadelphia, Pennsylvania and in Front Royal.

Page 299
Welford Ashby Buck, a son of Robert Cary Buck, wrote,

"A faded red memorandam book loaned me by William R. Buck of Baltimore, MD., contains a history of the business life of William Mason Buck, his father, which was dictated to Irving A. Buck, another son, during an illness in 1882, and 12 years before his death. A penciled forword, written by Wm. M. Buck."

(Written are some of the episodes of an active business life -- omitting domestic, social and religious phases of it -- which may possibly interest my dear children.)
                    Wm. M. B.
                    Bel Air, Va.,
                    February 25, 1882

While confined to my room for some days past, and reviewing my early life, I found some difficulty in fixing upon dates of certain events and incidents, and concluded to make from an old Diary and papers in my possession, an outline sketch of the business portion of it, for reference, which may interest some of my children and serve to explain what was exceptionable in my manner during the darker and later periods of it, which they could not otherwise well understand.

Before I had attained my fourteenth year, I withdrew from school to accept a situation in a store, offered me by J.F. Stephenson of Millwood.

My eductation, confined to the lower branches of English, was limited and imperfect and I had scant time for improving it afterwards.

Entered upon my duties at Millwood on the 25th of April 1823. (This was a branch of the Charlestown store of J & J Stephenson). January 1, 1824, was transferred to the Charlestown store, where I remained 1st of May, 1825, when I returned to Millwood, where I continued until August, 1827, when protracted illness from bilious fever then prevailing as an epidemic throughout the Valley, caused my return to "Clover Hill", the family home, on the 25th September, 1827.

Accepted a situation offered me by L. & Reel, who at that time commenced selling goods in Front Royal, with whom I continued one year, when I accepted the proposal of Cousin John L Buck to accompany him to "Buckland", Petit Gulf, Miss. to assist him in setting up the business of several firms with which he had been connected; and in October, 1828, I set out on horse back, and reached Lexington, Ky., in three weeks; and after spending six weeks in visiting our relations in Fayette, Madison and Woodford Counties, rode to Louisville, where Cousin J.L.B., who had come by stage, met me and we took passage on the "Geo. Washington" on the 1st of Nov. and arrived at "Buckland" on the 13th, where I spent an active adventurous life in the newly settled portion of Mississippi, which the Choctaws were then vacating and among the bayous and swamps of Louisiana, with skiff and canoe voyaged from Lake Providence as far south as Natchez.

In May, 1829 returned to Lexington and spent several weeks in visiting relatives and in quest of some employment for the summer, intending to return south in the fall.

Through the influences of an early friend, A.W. Bowie, I became deputy clerk in the County Court office at Lexington on the 16th June, where I spent six and a half months of greater enjoyment than had as yet fallen to my lot. I had access through my relatives to the most refined society of the city and my posittion as clerk brought me in contact with the leading men of the state -- gave opportunity of hearing Clay, Crittenden and others and of paying a visit to Mr. Clay at Ashland.

While engaged in the clerks office at Lexington, Ky., an incident occurred that may be worthy of mention;

Your Grandpa Ashby's sister, Mrs. Elizabeth January, after whom your mother was named, owned a beautiful property near the city limits. Her deceased husband, Col, Jas. January, a lawyer, had become very reckless and dissipated and had given Judge Thruston a mortgage upon this property, and it was shortly to be sold, leaving the widow houseless and homeless. One day, while looking over some old records, I discovered that the conveyance was imperfect - - - Cousin E. J. never having relinguished her ..... . I lost not many minutes to acquaint her with the facts, which relieved her distress and anxiety, and I had the satisfaction of knowing that she had possession of her home during the remainder of her life.

In December, I received a proposal from a young friend, A. L. Shotwell, who was about engaging in business in Georgetown, Scott Co., Kentucky, to join him upon an increased salary, which induced me to accept; and on the 1st Jan., 1830, I became clerk and salesman for the firm of Turlton and Shotwell, and where I remained until the spring of 1831.

About this time I had several very flattering business offers: one of the principal merchants of the City of L (Louisville) said to A.W.B., "If your young friend, Buck has not made a positive engagement with S., I would like to have him with me, and pay him double the amount of salary he is to receive in Georgetown"; but I declined to cancel my agreement.

Professor W.H. Richardson offered me the use of any amount of capital I might want, without security, but wished me to take his dissipated son, Louis, as partner, which I also declined.

A highly respectable gentleman merchant, (Mr.S.S.) whose health was impaired, wished me to take charge of his business as a partner. If I had accepted this offer, my lot would have been permanently cast in Kentucky, and the current of my life have been comparatively smooth and prosperous.

I had, also overtures from the firm of W.&. J. which I declined.

At the solicitation of my mother and family I left for Virginia, intending only to spend a few weeks and return to Kentucky. Reached "Clover Hill" May, 1831, was detained, and in July again became a victim of the epidemic bilious fever, which had prevailed throughout the Valley, with fearful effect for more than seven years. During its prevalence I lost my father, and uncle, Charles (II) (*see writing of Rev.W.C.Buck*) and a number of young relatives and friends. Scarcely a family escaped, and nearly all lost a portion of members.

In September, I had so far recovered as to be able to visit my esteemed kinsman cousin, Marcus C. Richardson, during my stay he remarked that he had $2,000.00 on hand, and proposed my furnishing a like amount and engage in selling goods in Front Royal, where there were but two stores.

From what I had saved from my salaries and some funds from my father's estate I was enabled to raise the required sum and thus the firm of William M. Buck and Co., commenced with a cash capital of $4,000.00. Although still feeble, I started at once to Philadelphia, where I had some acquaintance with the merchants, and bought a portion of my stock in Baltimore. The business was profiable and at the end of four years our capital was doubled and I paid my partner his half of $8,000.00 and continued the business alone.

In 1835 I bought of N&J their stock of goods in Flint Hill - nearly $4,000.00 and placed this branch store under the charge of my brother, M.B.Buck, and cousin Thomas Ashby. Both were very young and inexperienced; and finding the business unprofitable removed the stock to Front Royal.

In 1838 I built the brick store house at a cost of $2,000.00. About the same time incurred a loss of over $3,000 by two men which were heavy drafts on my limited capital. (One of these was W.L., contractor for the public building - - by fraud - - and the other J. Munroc, whose wagons and teams I had bought, were destroyed by the Seminole Indians, the Government refusing to pay). But under these disadvantages I managed to keep my business and credit unimpaired.

In 1841, the old homestead, "Bel Air", was thrown upon the market, and it became evident that it must pass out of the family and into the hands of strangers unless I would incur the responsibility of heavy indebtedness This I did, and bought the property at $6500.00 and expended $1500 in building, repairs and improvements, making the entire cost $8000.00. Every building on the place and all the enclosurers were in a state of dilapidation. Rebuilt the mill, roofed and repaired dwelling, barn, carriage house, smoke house, and all outbuildings, also the enclosurers to fields and garden were removed.

Henceforward, my life was one of unceasing activity and toil. Boarding with my little family at "Locust Hill", gave a walk of two miles morning and evening - - added to the supervision and management of the store, oversight of the various sets of hands engaged upon repairs and upon the farm. I was also the executor of several estates, guardian for minor heirs, and official duties as magistrate to perform. Finding the farm in an impoverished condition, I rented the "Mt. Airy" place and other land adjoining, and kept the home place in clover for several years, until its fertitlity was restored, and from it I made large and remunerative crops, so that at end of eight years I was nearly free from debt. In February, 1846, I went to Tuscaloosa, Alabama to settle and close up the business connected with the estate of my uncle, Doct. Marcus C. Buck, in which, after some delay I succeeded, collecting in cash some $3,800 and returned to "Bel Air" in April.

Shortly after my purchase of "Bel Air", I took my brother, John N. Buck, as partner in the store, and the business was for several years profitable conducted by the firm of Wm.M. & J.N Buck, and aided in some degree in meeting my payment of the $8,000.

In 1849, my brother, John Buck was offered by Mr. John R. Ricards of Baltimore a partnership in buying lots and building the "Mountain House" Hotel at Capon Springs, he (J.R.R) to select the third partner and furnish $15,000, the other two each $7,500, making the capital $30,000.

The partners, John R. Ricards, John Buck and Thomas Blakemore became the firm of Ricards, Buck and Blakemore; and in the winter of '49 & '50 began work upon building, which was finished, furnished and ready for occupation in 18 months but at a cost of nearly seventy thousand dollars.

In order to aid my brother John in furnishing his share of the capital, I agreed to close up our business in Front Royal, and sold the stock to Fristoe and Slanker; but before the building was half complete, he (J.N.B.) became as discouraged that he returned home declaring he would sink the capital he had put in rather than have anything more to do with it. This compelled me to take his place and to buy half his share (an eighth) and finally his fourth.

I had none to leave my family and home affairs and aid in superintendence of the buildings and general management, where there were over one hundred hands employed.

Fristoe and Slanker, who bought our stock of goods, failed, and my brother, John Buck, took the goods they had in hand and resumed business with cousin Thomas Ashby as partner.

Before the expiration of three years after completion of the building, the three partners of the firm, Ricards, Buck and Blakemore, all became insolvent. From that time forward I had not only to assume the general management of the concern, but also to assume and provide for the Firm's debts, amounting to twenty seven thousand dollars.

As every possible means had been used to sell the property, but without success, the only alternative left was to rent it, and arrange with the creditors for gradual liquidation of their claims. If they pressed and brought suits, my home and all I possessed would be lost. To prevent this subjected me to many trials and difficulties for twenty years.

Three seasons, through fraud and dishonesty of lessees, were lost and seven during and after the war.

In 1867, I refurnished and repaired the "Mountain House", nearly all the personal property having been destroyed during the war.

I succeeded finally in settling all the debts of the firm, without any suit having been brought against it or myself. All my available capital was absorbed in sustaining this tottering concern; and to meet the increased expense for support of a large family, education of the children and effort to give them a start in the world caused constant anxiety and care.

Of my active duties were; management of the farm and Capon affairs, the charge and distribution of five Estates, with extensive correspondence. Altogether, they left me no time for rest or recreation.

Shortly after the close of the war, cousin M.Y. Johnson of Galena, Ill., kindly loaned me $1500 to replace fencing (all of which had been destroyed), to repair buildings and buy horses and farming implements and family supplies. A portion of this sum I applied to the planting of a vineyard. At that time nothing promised so profitable a return, as wine sold readily at $3.00 per gallon; but the time the vineyard was in full bearing, it fell to 50 cents, and the cellar stuck of nearly 7,000 gallons of fine wines finally brought under the hammer from 25 to 30 cents, and the business was abandoned.

In 1874, a period of comparative prosperity seemed before me; and in the early part of '75 I received a check for nearly $2,000 for Capon rent, which I intended to apply to payment of the Galena debt and two others of less amount, and thus relieve myself of debt and embarrassment. The day after its receipt I called at the bank and requested Mr. French to fill up three checks on Baltimore - - one for fifteen hundred dollars, and two for smaller amounts, saying I would return in an hour and bring the Capon check over.

It was known at "Belmont" that I had received it, and I had reached home but a few minutes when Julien Smith rode up hurriedly and said that Mr. M.B. Buck had gone to Alexandria, and that his note of $2,000 in the Bank of Warren would be protested if not paid before three o'clock. If I would let him have that amount it should be replaced as soon as Mr.B. returned.

I handed him the check, but the promised money was never paid, and in consequence the other debts named were only paid in part, after long delay from the trust fund, for following close on this transaction, the collapse at "Belmont" occurred, June 1875, ruining a number of relations and friends.

I was, however, the greatest sufferer, for my name was on all his paper to banks and individuals, his debts amounting to nearly two hundred thousand dollars.

I was thus deprived of the satisfaction of paying all that I owed, and was deprived of all my property, real and personal. (The old homestead, "Bel Air", store house, "Moore" house and Capon Springs interest). For the latter I was then negotiating a sale at $40,000, equal to $10,000 for my one-fourth.

My situation now (1876) was one of great trial. Suddenly cut off from means of support of myself and helpless family, there seemed only penury and suffering before us. But through it all I was singularly sustained by trust in the protection and goodness of an over-ruling Providence, and so my spirits were but little depressed.

Nearly every relative and friend who had any property was involved in M.B.Buck's failure, and among them, my son, Irving. The little capital he had accumulated by his energy and sagacity was well nigh swept away; but he had credit and the confidence of all the business men around him, and nobly threw himself into the breach by assuming a large amount of indebtedness to save the old home and keep the family in a respectable position. This task he accomplished and is enabled to see the result of his untiring industry and perseverance while now nearly released from the obligations thus incurred.

While my son, Irving, was the only one of the family who could give aid or relief, it is a pleasure to believe that either of his brothers, similarly situated, would have willingly have made a like sacrifice.

And it is a pleasure, in the retrospect of a business life so cheapened with necissitude and misfortune, to know that these were the result of the action of others, and that there is nothing in connection with them for which I can reproach myself, save, perhaps, an excess of confidence in the integrity of my fellow-man.

I do not know that I can better close this rough sketch than by using the remarkable sentences written by Patrick Henry in the conclusion of his last will and testament, in which after mention of the disposition of all his property to his family, he wrote;

> "There is one thing more I wish I could give them and that is the Christian religion. If they have that, and I had not given one shilling, they would be rich; and if they have not that, and I had given them the whole world, they would be poor."

That wish is the only legacy I have to bestow on my dear children.

W.M. Buck

SAD EARTH, SWEET HEAVEN
The Diary of Lucy Rebecca Buck
During The War Between the States

INDEX

A

Academy, 244
Alabama, 28, 281
Alabama, Huntsville, 201
Alabama, Tuscumbia, 281
Alden (See Fred Allen, 99)
Alex (cousin), 241
Alex (servant), 134, 135, 168, 183, 190, 197, 266, 274, 303
Alexander, Captain, 78
Alexander, Mr., 178
Alexandria, 33, 192
Alice, 17, 18, 27,28, 46, 88, 115, 119, 152
Aliza, 291
Alleghany Mountains, 6
Allen, Edgar, 278
Allen, Fred, 99
Allen, Mr., 112, 113
Allen, Mrs., 258
Allen, Lieut.R.O., 196
Allen, Mr. Sidney, 262, 265, 267, 278
Allfair, 192, 303
Ambler, Dr., 115, 118
Ambrose, 117, 122, 123, 168
Amelia Courthouse, 295
America, 19, 210
Anderson, Lieut. Ceneral Richard Heron, C.S.A., 201, 255, 273, 278
Anderson, Thomas E., 288
Anice, 249
Ann Eliza (servant), 270
Annie, 157, 233, 234, 255, 290, 294
Antietam, 142, 145
Appomattox, 137, 285, 295
Arkansas, 39
Arlington Heights, 136, 141
Armanda (servant, worked for Mrs. Roy), 192-195, 198, 201, 202, 224
Armistead, Brig. Gen. Lewis A., C.S.A., 210
Armistead, Mr., 215, 225
Armistead, Mrs., 225, 248, 250
Arnstead, Mr., 56
Armstrong, Captain, 196
Army of Cumberland, 251
Army of Northern Virginia, 138, 139, 145, 182, 193, 227, 239, 295
Army of Potomac, 153, 184, 216, 228, 251
Army of Tennessee, 238
Ashby, Elizabeth Almond (Aunt Betty), 12, 43, 48, 52, 60, 63, 69, 83, 100-102, 109, 110, 121, 124, 134, 135, 148, 149, 149, 152, 155-157, 162, 164, 182, 188, 191, 195, 197, 198, 211, 216, 232, 233, 235, 237, 243, 244, 250, 258, 280, 296, 297, 302

Ashby, Rebecca Buck (Grandma), 7, 15, 32, 52, 57, 58, 68-70, 72, 87, 91,93, 94, 108, 110, 115, 121, 123, 124, 149, 158, 160, 171, 173, 178, 182, 187, 188, 190-192, 196, 199, 211, 221, 231, 232, 235, 237, 240, 242, 245, 256, 258, 281, 282, 284, 289, 293, Figure 5
Ashby, Thomas (Unlce Tom), 21, 24, 27, 54, 60, 63, 73, 80, 99, 100, 104, 110, 116, 118, 119, 124, 130, 132-135, 140, 147, 148, 153, 155-157, 183, 191, 195, 208, 211, 221, 231, 236, 237, 240, 241, 243, 250, 258, 280, 284, 290, 302
Ashby, Thomas Almond (Allie), 19, 27-29, 40, 110, 133, 166, 181, 189, 192, 196, 249, 250, 284, 290-293, 302
Ashby, Brig. Gen. Turner, C.S.A., 35, 38, 39, 44, 47, 48, 52, 54, 58, 59, 69, 75, 76, 82-84, 96, 99, 101, 102, 111, 134, 175, 176, 205, 206
Ashby's Gap, 239, 278
Atlanta, 7, 256, 280-282
Atlanta, Battle of, 280, 281
Augurs, General, 121
Augusta, Georgia, 232
Averill, Maj. Gen. W.W., U.S.A., 242, 243, 260

B

B., 40
B., Cousin, 151
B., Grussie, 124
B., Kate, 120
B.,Mr., 222
B., Mrs 166
Bailey, Captain James, 261
Bailey, Mr. Sampson, 238
Baker, Major Page, 200, 201
Baltimore, 29, 45, 47, 49, 50, 81, 110, 136, 147, 151, 157, 214, 270, 280
Baltimore and Ohio Railroad, 270
Baltimore Sun, 137
Banks, Maj. Gen. Nathaniel P., U.S.A., 38, 39, 43, 57, 62, 65, 77, 84, 88, 95, 106, 112, 113, 116, 117, 131, 151
Baptist Church, 243
Barbee, Charlie, 250, 251
Barbee, Mollie, 249, 250
Barksdall, 210
Barrett, Mr., 45
Bartholomew, 37
Bartlett, Mr., 121
Bartlett, "Young", 248
Baylor, Lieut. Geoge (Author of Bull Run to Bull Run), 127, 169, 170, 232
Baylor, Mr., 170
Baylorians, 136
Baylor's Light House (Co. B., Twelfth Virginia Calvary, C.S.A.), 127, 255
Baylors. 226
Bayly, Dick, 38, 50, 86, 156, 179, 180, 181, 230, 243, 244, 250, 251, 291-293, 297, 302 (Married Bird Garrett)

Bayly, Eve (of Grafton), 209
Bayly, Marcus (Mack), 32, 82, 127, 164, 219, 232, 241, 262, 278-290, 282, 289, 293, 302 (Married Mollie B. Buck)
Bayly, Sue, 228, 233, 234, 238
Beauregard, Gen. P.G.T., C.S.A., 21, 25, 30, 33, 35, 38, 46, 47, 69, 81, 86, 96, 97, 110, 114, 121, 125, 132, 133, 159, 174, 180, 218, 257, 259, 265, 289, 290
Beecher, 191
Bel Air, 5, 6, 7, 11, 19, 20, 37, 47, 50, 58, 64-66, 68, 92, 96, 147, 149, 157, 170, 259, 300, 303 Figure 6&7
"Belle" (Walter's Horse), 226
Belmont, 46, 93, 279, 291, 293, 296, 300
Ben, "Uncle" (servant, lived at Bel Air Mill), 63, 152
Benkamin, Judah, 22, 25
Berry, Mr. (Rev. Robert T.), 19, 30, 33, 37-39, 42, 48, 54, 69, 83, 84, 96, 97, 112, 113, 147, 148, 154, 155, 172, 175, 182, 185, 187, 192, 202, 205, 210, 212, 217, 248, 256, 258, 297
Berry's Ferry, 198, 199
Berryville, Virginia, 212, 258, 259, 265, 273-275, 278, 280, 302
Betty, "Aunt" Black (servant), lived in a cabin at the mill below Bel Air on Happy Creek, 108, 152, 296
Big Springs, 97
Bizzel, Dr., 268
Black Billy, 260
Blackford, Dr., 35
Blackwater, 180
Blakemore, Alex, 83, 86, 132, 241
Blakemore, Dick, 32, 40, 86, 241
Blakemore, Jimmie, 201
Blakemore, Letitia (Aunt), 29, 74, 280, 293, 295
Blakemore, Marcus, 32, 40, 241
Blakemore, T.Fayette, 56, 131, 293
Blakemores, 40
Blathis, Lottie, 249
Blenker, 119
Blodget, 167
Bloody Angle, 255
Bloomfield, 258-260, 269, 297, 302, 303
Blue Ridge Mountains, 6, 116, 130, 193, 202, 211, 278, 300
Bogardus, Dr., 119-123, 168
Boone, John, 232
Boone, Kattie (see Kattie Samuels), 21, 30, 248
Boone, Mrs., 34, 75, 158
Boonsboro, 266
Boston, 135, 214
Boswell, Capt. J. Keith, C.S,A., 152
Boteler, Colonel A.R., 269
Bowen, 49

Bowling Green, KY, 29
Bowman, Mr., 228
Boyd, Belle, 17, 18, 34, 74, 75, 81, 97, 105, 115, 119, 121, 124, 191, 196, 226, 233, 258, 292
Boyd, Mr., 29, 31, 115
Bragg, General Braxton, C.S.A., 110, 132, 158, 159, 164, 171, 174, 219, 227-229, 236-238, 280
Brandy Station, 196
Breckinridge, Maj. Gen. John C., C.S.A., 254, 264
Brerwood, Mr., 12, 14, 19, 20, 26, 31, 33, 43, 155 (came from Dickinson College, Pa. to teach Allie Ashby)
Brigade, Laurel, 205
Bristoe Station, 136, 137
Broad run, 230
Brown, Charlie, 13, 14, 211, 290, 292, 293
Brown, Dr., 18, 163
Brown, Ellen, 84, 135, 176, 293
Brown, Jimmie, 263
Brown, Miss Carrie, 131
Brown, Mr., 261
Brown, Mrs. (hotel housekeeper), 64
Brown, Victor, 211
Brown's Cove, 127
Brown's Ferry, 229
Broy, Newt, 248
Bruner, Mr., 290, 296, 297
Bryant, 204, 230
Bryant, Major, 152
Buck, Alvin, 7, 14, 21, 22, 24-26, 31-33, 72, 87, 92, 120, 125, 135, 143, 159, 167, 171, 173, 176, 180, 189, 195, 228, 232, 239, 241, 244, 263, 265, 267, 277-283, 289, 292, 294, 298, Fig. 13
Buck, Amelia Ann, 303
Buck, Annice, 301
Buck, Annie (Nannie), 7, 157, 171, 233, 284, 290
Buck, Bob, 169, 181, 249, 289
Buck, Catherine Augusta (Gussie), 205, 209, 235, 241, 292, 301
Buck, Catherine T., 301
Buck, Charles "Charlie" Newton, 34, 36, 52, 53, 84, 88, 132, 169, 196, 197, 201, 231, 234, 240, 243, 245-248, 294, 301 (Co. B, 17th Va. Inf.)
Buck, Cornelia "Cousin", 200
Buck, "Cousin" Ed, 141, 205, 290, (Co. B, 17th Va. Inf.)
Buck, Eliza McKay, 301
Buck, Elizabeth Ann Ashby (Ma), 7, 20 ,24, 26, 32, 35, 38, 40, 43, 44, 48, 50, 52, 55-57, 59, 60, 63, 64, 67-72, 77, 78, 84, 86, 87, 91, 92, 98, 100-103, 108, 110, 116-118, 120, 123, 124, 126, 132, 134, 143, 149, 150, 152-254, 156, 157, 165-168, 171, 173-176, 180-183, 185, 186, 188, 190, 193-195, 199, 202-204, 208-210, 213, 217, 291, 221, 225, 227, 230, 232, 238, 240, 241, 243, 244, 248, 250, 253, 256, 259-262, 267, 270, 277, 278, 280, 282, 283, 289, 292-294, 296, 297 (Figure 3&4)

Buck, Elizabeth Peake (Aunt Lizzie), 55, 126, 128, 129, 143, 170, 181, 233, 234, 256, 287, 289, 300
Buck, Elliot Mauzey, 191, 238, 301 (married Delia Cloud)
Buck, Elton C. (Eltie), 110, 125, 140, 146, 205, 223, 233, 301
Buck, Evred R., 7, 123, 149, 157, 171, 205, 224, 251, 257, 258, 278, 282, 293
Buck Frank "Dixie", 7, 21, 122, 124, 149, 171, 217, 224, 231, 237, 238, 240, 251, 258, 279, 280, 290 (named after Frank Buck who was killed in war in 1863)
Buck, George Esten, 233, 300
Buck, Gray Carroll, 5
Buck, Henry Augustus, 12, 26, 31, 42, 127, 172, 175, 176, 181, 223, 244, 287, 293, 300 (served and left Army in 1864) (married Getrude Richardson)
Buck, Horace Cousin, 61, 86, 120, 179, 203 (Capt. 7th Va. Cav.)
Buck, Horace, Dr. (Mississippi), 199
Buck, I.N., Dr. (Uncle Newton), 14, 40, 52, 115, 116, 132, 134, 135, 179, 192, 240, 243, 248, 282, 301
Buck, Irving Ashby, Capt., 14, 18-26, 29, 32, 45, 70, 72, 86, 92, 99, 103, 110, 120, 140, 147, 153, 158-160, 162, 171-174, 176, 180, 181, 183, 195, 196, 201, 207, 208, 211, 219, 226, 228-231, 240, 241, 243, 244, 249, 258, 259, 261, 267, 279, 282, 284, 286, 287, 293, 296 (first in Warren Rifles then A.A.G. to Gen. Cleburne) (Figure 14)
Buck, Jacqueline M. (Jacquie), 19, 86, 103, 166, 167, 181, 203, 205, 209, 213, 238, 242, 250, 255, 258, 289, 292, 293, 301 (married Lydia Ricards, Irving Buck married Fannie Ricards)
Buck, James (cousin), 277, 278, 292, 294, 301
Buck, Janet Lovell (Aunt Jane), 40, 52, 192, 193, 223, 248, 301
Buck, John Carroll, 289, 300
Buck, John Gill, 301 (died Oct. 12, 1862) (Ever present on battlefields checking on his sons)
Buck, John Gill, Jr., 301 (born 1863)
Buck, John Newton (Uncle John), 22, 132, 134, 135, 147, 173, 176, 190, 196, 212, 226, 227, 240, 251, 259, 263, 282, 283, 296, 297, 303
Buck, Julia Catherine (Jule), 19, 33, 43, 45-48, 55, 110, 128, 130, 166-170, 181, 207, 224, 233, 244, 249, 251-253, 255, 289, 293, 294 (married Mack Erwin)
Buck, Laura, 7, 17, 21, 24, 26, 32, 35, 40, 42, 44, 50, 56, 60, 68, 70, 87, 94, 98, 110, 114, 122, 135, 149, 157, 159, 160, 168, 171, 173, 174,184, 185, 189, 190, 192, 193, 195, 196, 208, 212, 216, 224, 231-234, 240, 242-246, 248, 253, 255, 256, 257, 258, 277, 290, 292, 293, 294, 298
Buck, Lawrence Neville, 5
Buck, Letitia (Aunt) (Jane Letitia Bayly), 38, 45, 46, 61, 110, 132, 151, 203, 205, 207, 209, 235, 241, 250, 282, 283, 287, 289, 300
Buck, Lily Elizabeth, 233, 234, 300 (married Samuel Majors of Riverside)
Buck, Linton Neville ("Nevie"), 48, 127, 128, 130, 143, 167-170, 233, 249, 256, 258, 259, 267, 293, 300 (graduated V.M.I. 1870, head of class)
Buck, Lucy C., 176, 249, 296 (daugther of John Buck & Sara Catlett Buck)
Buck, Lucy Rebecca, 5, 6, 7, 14, 17, 22, 41, 46, 60, 84, 90, 105, 108, 110, 130, 136, 154, 158, 160, 168, 169, 176, 189, 191, 196, 198, 200, 207, 211, 215, 218, 223, 225, 259, 278, 282, 285, 296, 298 Figure 1

Buck, Marcus Blakemore (Uncle Mack), 27, 45, 46, 49, 54, 61, 69, 96, 97, 99, 103, 134, 142, 143, 151, 166, 170, 191, 197, 203-206, 209-213, 226, 227, 232, 234, 280, 296, 300
Buck, Marcus T., 301
Buck, Mary, 13, 48
Buck, Mary C., 301
Buck, Mary Richardson (Little Mary), 205, 233, 242, 301, 303
Buck, Mason, 69
Buck, Meredith, 301
Buck, Mollie, 198, 244, 291, 301
Buck, Nannie Lovell, 34, 169, 196, 198, 233, 244, 248, 249, 270, 291, 292, 293, 296, 301
Buck, Nellie, 7, 12, 14, 17-21, 23, 24, 26, 30, 34, 35, 38, 40, 44-47, 50, 52, 53, 55-58, 63, 65, 67, 68, 70, 73, 75, 79, 81-83, 90, 93, 94, 98-100, 102, 106, 112, 116, 117, 119, 122-124, 128, 130, 132, 133, 135, 139, 142-147, 149-152, 154, 156, 158, 160, 162, 167, 168, 171, 173, 176-178, 180-183, 185-188, 190, 191, 194-197, 199, 200, 203, 205, 207, 213, 215-219, 226, 228-231, 237-244, 249, 250, 253, 257-258, 263, 267, 270, 277, 279, 280, 283, 290, 292-294, 297 Figure 1
Buck, Orville, 40, 45, 100, 122-124, 149, 157, 168, 171, 177, 184, 189, 196, 238, 240, 242, 244, 245, 278, 294
Buck, Orville M., 5
Buck, Richard Bayly (Dick), 20, 38, 40, 42, 99, 139, 140, 154, 180, 207-209, 211-213, 215-217, 225, 226, 235, 241, 251, 289, 294, 296, 297, 298, 301, (2nd Lieut., Co. B. 17th Va. Inf.) (married Laura Grafflin)
Buck, Robert (Bob), 169, 181, 249, 289, 301
Buck, Robert Carey, 7, 33, 40, 45, 52, 53, 67, 86, 101, 123, 149, 153, 157, 162, 166-168, 171, 177, 184, 185, 188, 189, 196, 200, 223, 241, 244-246, 253, 280, 289
Buck, Capt. Samuel D. ("Sam"), 19, 42, 169, 196, 223, 230, 292, 294, 298, 301 (Co. H, 13th Va. Inf., "Buck is the bravest man I ever knew," Gen.Earl;y) (married Alice Parkin)
Buck, (Cousin) Sue, 53, 54, 110, 115, 116, 118, 131, 148, 205, 209, 248, 258, 301, 302
Buck, Thomas Fayette (Uncle), 53, 84, 128, 134, 233, 289, 300
Buck, Thomas Fayette, Jr. "Fettie", 233, 289
Buck, Thomas William (Willie), 14, 144, 150, 181, 185, 196, 214, 215, 290, 291, 293, 296, 301 (co. E, 7th Va. Cav.) (married Catherine Augusta Buck)
Buck, (Cousin) Tom, 39, 40, 142, 154, 176, 181, 212, 256, 301
Buck, Walker, 259, 260, 263, 265, 303
Buck, Welford Ashby, 5
Buck, William Alexander (Sandy), 82, 83, 212, 301 (Co. E, 7th Va. Cav. "Most gallant soldier I've ever seen in action," Gen. W.E.Jones, C.S.A.)
Buck, William Mason (Father), 7, 19-22, 24, 26-29, 31-33, 35-40, 43, 44, 48, 55-68, 70, 72, 74, 77, 84, 85, 89, 90, 91, 93, 95-100, 102, 103, 105, 109, 112, 117, 119, 122, 123, 125, 126, 128, 131, 133, 134, 135, 137-143, 146, 148-151, 153, 156-158, 164, 166-169, 171-174, 176, 179-199, 202, 203, 205, 207-209, 211-220, 222, 223, 225, 226, 228, 229, 231-233, 238-241, 243-245, 248-258, 259, 263, 282, 289-293, 296, 297, 300, 301-303 Figure 2,4
Buck, Wiiliam Pettus, 5, 7, 299

Buck, William "Walter", 28, 30, 31, 36, 37, 38, 48-52, 61, 78, 79, 86, 99, 132, 154-156, 170, 175, 176, 178, 179, 183, 203-209, 212, 213, 216, 218, 226, 239, 240, 248, 263, 300 (2nd Lieut. 7th Va. Cav.) Figure 15
Buck, "Willie" (William R.), 5, 7, 35, 45, 53 69, 93, 132, 157, 171, 181, 184, 292, 293
Buck's Company, 165
Buckton (Station), 76, 82
Buckton (home). 301
Buell, Maj., Gen. Don Carlos, U.S.A., 46, 47
Bull Run, 11, 13, 33
Bull Run, Battle of, 214
Bunker Hill, 220, 269
Bunting Captain, 67, 72, 90, 105
Burnside, Maj. Gen. Ambrose E., U.S.A., 28, 81, 153, 154, 157, 172, 236, 237
Burwell, Bob, 69 90, 91, 95
Burwell, Mr. George, 237
Bultler, 269
Bulter, Maj.Gen. Benjamin F., U.S.A., 57, 251, 257
Byington, Dr., 269

C

C., Miss, 163
C., Mr., 163
C., Mrs., 163
Calmes, Isabelle (Aunt Calmes), 149, 303
Calmes, Spencer, 303
Camp Chase, 241, 294
Camp Pickens, 212, 280
Cannon, Dr., 194
Capon Springs, 31, 37, 139, 140, 249
Carey, Captain, 202
Carlisle, Pennsylvania, 202
Caroline (servants for Miss Polly Haynie), 191
Carroll, Maj. Gen. S.S., U.S.A., 69, 101, 104
Carson, Mary, 139, 146, 163, 289
Carter, Mr., 207
Carter, Mr., 288
Carter, Cousin George, 267, 270
Castleman's Ferry, 268, 293
Catoctin Mountains, 136
Cedar Creek, 285
Cedar Mountain, 131
Cedarville, 79
Centreville, Virginia, 13, 14, 22, 24, 26, 30, 32, 33, 36, 230
Chambersburg, Pennsylvania, 238, 269
Chancellorsville, 9, 184, 251, 252, 254
Chantilly, 137
Champman, Miss Kate, 87, 156
Champman, Sam, 288

Charleston Harbor, 288
Charleston, South Carolina, 110, 112, 171, 172, 180, 182, 187, 218, 228, 257, 269, 290
Charlestown, 33, 88, 187, 265, 269
Charlottesville, 56
Chase, 157
Chattanooga, Battle of 237
Chattanooga, Tennessee, 132, 219, 227, 229, 230, 280
Chester's Gap, 78, 214, 216, 219
Chestersville, 234
Chicago, 181, 241
Chickahominy River, 113, 114
Chickamauga, Battle of 229
Chickamauga Creek 227
Chickasaw Bayou, 158
Childs, Mrs., 231
Chilton, Brig.Gen. R.H., C.S.A., 218 (senior staff officer to Gen. Lee)
Cincinnati Times, 173
Clapp, (Bostonian), 95, 97
Clara, 289
Clark, Rutherford, 178
Clark County, 33, 36, 45, 49, 52, 169, 179, 183, 226, 227, 233, 238, 239, 249, 254, 264, 296, 302, 303
Clarkson, Dr., 148
Cleburne, Maj. Gen. Patrick R., C.S.A., 7, 158, 173, 228, 229, 231, 236, 249, 258, 279, 284, 286
Clifton (near Front Royal), 184
Clifton (near Berryville), 278, 303
Cloud, Elizabeth (cousin), 40, 175, 213, 229
Cloud, Emma (cousin), 12, 19, 29, 30, 35, 36, 38-40, 51, 126, 146, 170, 181, 185, 186, 230, 231, 237, 249, 258, 296, 297 (married Thomas Newton Buck)
Cloud Family, 302
Cloud, Mary (cousin), 13, 29, 31, 34, 36, 40, 43, 44, 46, 55, 56, 63, 74, 75, 114, 122, 124, 139, 146, 163, 203, 223, 229, 237, 258, 267, 269, 270-273, 294
Cloud, Mount (cousin), 32, 42, 124, 179, 194, 237, 263
Cloud, Mr., 147
Cloud, Mr. Daniel, 147
Cloud, Mrs., 13, 56, 114, 147, 165, 166
Cloud, Newton (cousin), 39, 40
Cloud, "Cousin" William ("Will"), 24, 26, 141, 154, 203, 206, 207, 292
Clover Hill, 12, 42, 55, 126, 129, 149, 164, 169, 170, 223, 225, 233, 244, 256, 282, 289, 300
Cobb, Brig. Gen. Thomas R.R., C.S.A., 155
Coffield, 47, 136
Cold Harbor, 113, 257, 259
Cole's Battalion, 248
Columbia, South Carolina, 290
Columbus, Kentucky, 27, 32, 22, 36, 140, 290
Company B, 17th Virginia Infantry Regiment (see Warren Rifles), 211, 219

Company E, 7th Virginia Calvary, 83, 205 (there were seven Buck's in this company)
Confederate Army, 216, 221, 222, 252, 254, 255, 259, 267
Confluence, 145
Congress, U.S.S., 36
Conner, Col. Z.T., C.S.A., 89
Conrad, Santy (surgeon), 148
Conrad's Store, 57, 97
Cook, Giles, 36, 74, 180, 183, 221
Cook, Mattie, 249, 283, (married Scott Roy)
Cook, Mollie, 249
Cook, Mr., 19, 53, 163, 194, 221
Cook, Mrs., 52, 163
Cook, Wythe, 233, 234, 249, 250, 263, 290-292
Cooke, Henry, 250
Cooper, General James, 117
Corcoran, 81
Corinth, 46-48, 63, 74, 86, 87, 96, 97
Cornel, 233
Corse, Brig. Gen. Montgomery D., C.S.A., 210, 214, 215
Cramwell, Miss June, 186
Crane, Mr., 178
Creole, 201
Crescent City, 82
Crescent Street, 29
Crippin, Frank, 67, 72, 90, 91-95, 98-100, 102, 105, 123
Crippin, Mr. (Editor, The Cincinnati Times), 173
Crittenden, Lieutenant, 279
Crook, Brig. Gen. George, U.S.A., 260, 291
Crooked Run, 238
Cross Keys, 97
Culpepper Couthouse, 13, 131, 133, 146, 166, 175, 226, 230, 277
Cumberland, Maryland, 291
Cumberland River, 29, 30
Cumberland, Tennessee, 236, 281
Cumberland, U.S.S., 36
Custer, Maj. Gen. George A., U.S.A., 288, 289

D

Dale, Gen., 210
Dan (servant), 274
Danner, Captain, 287
Danville Railroad, 294
Davidson, Willie, 249
Davis, Col. B.F., 196
Davis, Mrs. Albert, 267
Davis, Jefferson, 22, 30, 40, 46, 154, 174, 238, 280
Davis, Martha, 259, 267
Davis, Mrs., 259, 260

Davis, Sally, 58
Delaplane, 287
Delaware, 127, 131
Delaware (Third), 127
Delphia (servant), 267, 276
Demopolis, Alabama, 244
Department of Virginia, 182
Detheridge, 298
Diamond Falls, 234
Dollie, 281
Donaldson, Mabel Locke, 5
Dore, Leslie C., 241
Dore, Mr., 241
Dorsey, Dr., 29, 34, 52, 74, 144, 163, 221, 243, 282
Dorsey, Mrs, 221
Dreway's Bluff, 75
Duechenberry, Miss, 249
Dulany, General, 264
Dumb Mary (see "Black" Mary, servant), 242 (servant of W.M. Buck who could not hear or speak but summoned by knocking on the floor with a stick)
Durham Station, North Carolina, 297

E

Early, Lieut. Gen. Jubal Anderson, C.S.A., 9, 49, 115, 202, 242, 264-270, 272, 273, 278, 280, 283, 285, 292
Edinburgh, 108
Edwards Ferry, 141
Eighth Ohio Regiment, 67
Eleventh Virginia Calvary, 112
Eliza ("Aunt"), 144, 191-193, 195, 196, 198, 229 (servant from Rosehill)
Eliza Ann (servant), 64, 91, 149, 190, 238
Elizabethtown, 158
Elliot, Lieutenant, 126
Elyton, Alabama, 286
Emmancipation Proclamation, 154
Enders, Mr. and Mrs., 267
England, 19, 117, 137
Erwin, Mack (Irwin), 166, 168-170, 181, 185, 224, 227, 233, 234, 294 (married Julia Buck)
Eve (Bayly) (of Grafton), 209
Evelyne, "Aunt", 192, 269, 274 (servant at Belmont)
Ewell, Lieut. Gen. Richard Stoddert, C.S,A., 62, 75, 76, 95, 137, 138, 193, 196, 197, 199, 202, 210, 218, 220, 222, 223, 251, 252, 264, 295
Eyster, Lieutenant, 151

F

F., Mr., 111, 163
F., Mr., 261
F., Mrs., 163, 209
Fairfax Couthouse, 137, 176
Falmouth, 153
Farmville, 298
Farragut, Rear Adm. David G., U.S.A., 57
Faulkerson, 190
Faulkner, 269
Fauquier, 52, 176, 226
Federals, 196, 216, 251, 252, 254, 255
First Maryland Regiment U.S.A., 73, 81
First Marlyand Regiment C.S.A., 81
Fishback Hotel, 17
Fisher, Capt., 117
Fishers Hill, 183, 272, 273, 283, 285
Flint Run, 128
Flournoy, Col. Thos. S., C.S.A., 79,111
Foote, Rear Adm. Andrew Hull, U.S.A, 27, 52
Ford, Annie (Nannie), 12, 80, 81, 223, 233, 234, 244, 249, 253, 294
Foreman, Mr., 261, 262
Forney, Mr., 245
Forneys, 131, 245
Forrest, Lieut. Gen. Nathan B., C.S.A., 286
Fort Donelson, 27, 29, 30, 32, 40
Fort Henry, 27
Fort McAllister, 285
Fort McHenry, 178, 288
Fort Mountain, 40, 152
Fort Sanders, 237
Fort Sumter, 288, 290
Fortress Monroe, 38
Forty Third Battalion, 176
Fourth Alabama, 200
Fourth Georgia Regiment, 222
Fox, Mrs., 209
France, 19, 108, 114
Franklin, Battle of, 286
Franklin, Tennessee, 285
Frederick, Maryland, 239, 266
Fredericksburg, Virginia, 45, 52, 64, 65, 72, 73, 101, 153-155, 163, 172, 183-185, 239
Freeman (Chaplain, Eighth Ohio Regiment), 67, 70, 71, 90, 91
Fremont, Maj. Gen. John C., U.S.A., 38, 62, 83, 89, 92, 95, 97-99, 108, 111, 113, 186
Fristoe, Mr., 52, 53, 61
Front Royal Academy, 29, 244

Front Royal, Virginia, 6, 7, 9, 11, 14, 18, 43, 53, 58, 59, 65, 72, 73, 78-83, 88, 89, 92, 103, 108, 116, 126-128, 130, 136, 169, 170, 178, 186, 193, 200, 205, 211, 218, 220, 239, 248, 270, 273, 274, 278, 285, 288, 289, 298, 300-302 Figure 9 & 10 & 11
Funsten, Colonel, 111, 264

G

Gaines Crossroads, 35
Gaines Mill, 113
Galena, U.S.S., 76
Gannett. Mr., 296
Gardner, Capt., 81
Garland, Brig. Gen. Samuel, C.S.A., 143
Garnett, Brig. Gen. Richard B., C.S.A., 210
Geary, Maj. Gen. John. W., U.S.A., 57, 58, 64
Gennie, Miss, 246
Georgetwon, 136
Georgia, 89, 110, 155, 232, 251, 261, 263, 281, 285, 286
Germany, 117
Germantown, 80
Gettysburg, Pennsylvania, 202, 209-211, 214, 216, 266
Gilbert, "Uncle" (servant), 191, 217, 229, 234, 303
Gillespie, Dr., 104, 105
Gillespie, Hattie, 87, 104-107
Gilmore, Lieut. Col. Harry, C.S.A., 49, 50, 51, 249
Glasscock, Mrs., 197
Gleson, Captain, 260
Gold, Mr., 254, 255
Gordon, Maj. Gen. John Brown, C.S,A., 252
Gordonsville, 124, 128, 133, 211
Gore, Capt., 146
Grafton, 209
Grandma (see Rebecca Buck Ashby)
Grant, Gen. Ulyssis S., U.S.A., 27, 29, 46, 158, 186, 189, 212, 213, 229, 236, 251, 252, 254-257, 259, 272, 274, 288, 294, 295, 298
Grantham, Colonel, 267
Grantham, Hosey, 179, 263
Graves, Miss Kate, 239, 284
Green Castle, Pennsylvania, 208
Green Hill, 219
Green, Kate, 250
Green, Welton, 250
Gregg, Brig. Gen. Maxcy, C.S.A., 155
Greg, Catpain, 201
Grimeley, Mrs., 233
Guard Hill, 80, 179, 283

H

Haines Bluff, 158
Hainie, Mr., 122
Hale, Laura Virginia, 5
Hall, Mr., 166, 169
Hall, Mrs., 126, 128
Halleck, Maj. Gen. Henry W., U.S.A., 46, 86
Halltown, Maryland, 266, 273, 274
Hammond, Mr. (Methodist minister), 250
Hammond, Mrs., 250
Hammond, Paul, 250
Hampton, Gen., 264
Hanover Junction, 208
Hans Ferry, 242
Happy Creek, 6, 14
Happy Creek (Marshall Home), 188, 302 (Burned 1921)
Hardaway, Dr., 199
Hardee, Lieut. Gen. Wm. J., C.S.A., 86, 158, 174, 231, 244
Harman, Major, 238
Harmer, 123
Harmon, Col. A.W., 111
Harmon, Mr., 296
Harper, 213
Harpers Ferry, 6, 95, 141-144, 248, 250, 259, 261, 265, 270, 272, 273
Harpeth River, 285
Harrellsville, 49
Harriet, "Aunt" (servant), 46, 126, 167, 168, 208
Harrison's Landing, 113
Harrisonburg, 6, 57, 97
Harry, 181
Hawksville, 152
Haynie, Miss Pollie, 34, 191
Hazeltein, Major, 220
Heater, Henry, 81
Helms, Cousin Meredith, 260 (married Mary Buck, sister of John Gill Buck)
Helms, Cousin R., 176
Hendricks, Mrs., 249
Hennie, 249
Henry, Charlie, 212
Henry, John (servant), 192, 303
Henry, Patrick, 173
Herbert, 200, 217
Herbert, Miss, 199
Herculaneum, 117
Hester,"Aunt" (servant), 192
Heth, Maj.Gen. Harry, C.S.A., 184, 210
Heironimous, H. Helen (cousin), 103
Hildt, David B., 56, 58

Hill, Mr., 163
Hill, Lieut. Gen. A.P., C.S.A., 144, 174, 184, 193, 201, 210, 218, 230, 251
Hill, Lieut. Gen. D.H., C.S.A., 142, 147, 148, 152
Hoblitzell, Mr., 12, 14, 29, 31, 82
Hoke, Maj.Gen.Robt.F., C.S.A., 184, 266, 268
Holly Springs, Mississippi, 158
Holman, 219
Hood, Lieut. Gen. John Bell, C.S.A., 228, 280, 281, 285, 286
Hooker, Maj. Gen. Joseph, U.S.A., 157, 172, 184, 193, 202, 210, 228, 230, 236
Hope, Eliza, 35, 38, 43, 62, 73, 84, 91, 125, 150, 177, 188, 195, 196, 224, 280, 291, 292, 296
Hope Family, 6
Hope, George, 232, 292
Hope, Julia Ann, 43, 61, 78, 96, 123, 125, 181, 223, 224, 252, 253, 258, 291, 292, 293
Hope, Mr., 38, 84, 91, 108, 110, 122, 140, 162, 168, 174, 176, 186, 188, 223, 291, 297
Hope, Mrs., 55, 61, 77, 90, 91, 98, 112, 174, 182, 186, 188, 192, 223, 231, 232, 258, 279, 293
Hopkinsville, KY., 32
Horace (servant), 134, 135, 168, 173, 192, 197, 198, 229, 245, 256, 303
Hortensia, Miss, 244
Hough, Dr., 126, 133, 143, 152, 231, 282, 292
Hough, Mrs. Dr., 181
Howard, Maj., 151
Hunter, Andrew Mr., 269
Hunter, Maj.Gen.David, U.S.A., 259, 260, 263-265, 269
Hunter, Mr., 48
Huntley, Mr., 269
Huntsville, Al., 201
Hutchins, Mr., 279

I

Illinois, 176
Imboden, Brig. Gen. John D., C.S.A., 232, 254, 259
Indian Tribes, 137
Indiana Calvary, 119
Irwin, Mack (see Mack Erwin)
Island Ford Route, 187
Island Number Ten, 36, 38, 52
Italy, 117

J

Jackson, Jennie, 250
Jackson, Julia (Stonewall's daugther), 96
Jackson, Mississippi, 219
Jackson, Mr., 163
Jackson, Mrs., 122
Jackson, roxie, 258
Jackson, Tennessee, 33

Jackson, Lieut. Gen. Thomas J. ("Stonewall"), C.S.A., 22, 33, 35, 38, 39, 45, 47-49, 52, 57, 62, 65, 73-76, 78-80, 83, 84, 87-89, 91-99, 101, 102, 106-108, 110-115, 120, 124, 128, 131, 132, 135-137, 139, 141, 142-147, 150-152, 154, 155, 174, 184, 185, 193, 194, 223, 230, 252
Jackson, Willie, 183
Jacobs, Colonel, 163, 221, 282
Jacobs, Willie, 40, 291
James River, 38, 75, 113, 259
Jefferson County, 48, 136
Jeffries, Mr., 114, 115, 119
Jenkins, Nancy, 109 (see John Smith)
Jessie Scouts, 186
Jim (servant), 144
Johnson, Brig. Gen. Bradley T., C.S.A., 220, 268
Johnson, Colonel, 80
Johnson, Maj. Gen. Edward, C.S.A., 202
Johnson, Miss Emma, 180
Johnson, John, 212
Johnston, Gen. Albert Sidney, C.S.A., 22, 29, 46, 47, 86
Johnston, Gen. Joseph E., C.S.A., 22, 33, 35, 38, 39, 45, 50, 57, 62, 75, 83, 88, 158, 220, 237, 238, 237, 238, 251, 280, 290, 295, 297, 298
Johnston Lakes, 219
Jones, David L., 288
Jones, Edgar, 85
Jones, Ginnie, 221
Jones, Mrs., 163
Jones, Brig. Gen. William E. ("Grumble"), C.S.A., 85, 111, 137, 174, 175, 183, 202, 220, 223, 239, 252, 259
Jones, "Yankee Gen.", 221
Jonesboro, Georgia, 286
Jordan, Brig. Gen. Thomas C., C.S.A., 22, 25, 103, 132, 134, 159
Journal, 243

K

Kearny, Maj. Gen. Phillip, U.S.A., 137
Kelly's Ford, 182
Kelly, B'V'T Maj. Gen. Benj. F., U.S.A., 291
Kendrick, Miss Sallie, 122, 151, 181
Kendrick, Mr., 40
Kenly, Col. John R., U.S.A., 79, 81
Kennedy, Dr., 35
Kenney, 221, 222
Kennon, Dr., 147
Kennon, Willie, 147
Kenrich,, 64
Kent, 90, 91, 101
Kentucky,, 22, 27, 29, 46, 132, 158, 181, 232, 303

Kephart, Captain, 104, 106
Kershaw, Maj. Gen. J.B., C.S.A., 273, 285
Kerstown, 34, 39, 49
Kiger, Mr., 191-193
Kiger, Mrs., 74, 227, 257, 291
Kimball, B'V'T Maj. Gen. Nathan, U.S.A., 39, 65, 67-71, 82, 90, 92, 94, 101, 122
King, Mr., 128, 130
Knoxville, 236, 237

L

L., Mr., 164
Lacey, Miss, 144
Laceys Spring, 292
Lacy, Mr., 165
Lacy, Reverend B. Tucker, 184, 194
Lacy, Rush, 212
Laird, Mr., 82
Lake, Mr., 282, 289
Lane, Maj, Henry, 134
Larue, Catherine Eliz. Buck (Aunt Cattie), 33, 124, 177, 258-262, 264, 267-271, 273, 274, 276, 278, 302, 303
Larue, Chris, 278
Larue, Fannie, 258, 260, 265, 272-278
Larue, Gilbert, 196, 233, 234
Larue, James, 33, 268, 269, 277, 278, 282
Larue, John B., 302
Larue, Kate, 268, 269
Larue, Nellie, 258, 259, 261, 262, 264, 269, 270, 271, 274
Larue, Uncle, 179, 211, 259, 261, 265, 267, 270-272, 276, 277
Larue, William (cousin), 258, 259, 260, 261, 264, 271, 275, 277
Latrobe, Lieut. Col. Osman, C.S.A., 145, 146, 147, 151, 157, 176, 215, 278, (Longstreet's AAG and Inspector)
Laurel Brigade, 137, 239, 264
Leach, Annie, 253, 255
Leach, Charlie, 253
Leach, Dr., 237, 243, 244, 246, 248, 250, 251, 255, 256 (married Mrs. L. Armistead May 15, 1864)
Leach Engie, 249
Leach, Jessie, 249, 256
Leach, Lizzie, 237, 243-247, 255, 256, 258, 289
Leach, Mennie, 12, 255
Leach, Ninian, 254, 256, 257
Leach, Sallie, 237, 244, 249-251, 254-256, 287, 294
Lee,, Annie, 267
Lee Cemetery, 241
Lee, Charlie, 269
Lee, Colonel Edmund, 264, 265, 269
Lee, Maj. Gen. Fitzhugh, C.S.A., 273, 278, 283

Lee, General Robert Edward, C.S.A., 88, 97, 113, 137-139, 142-145, 154, 174, 182, 184, 185, 193, 202, 210, 211, 213, 214, 216-218, 230, 251, 252, 254-257, 259, 264, 272, 273, 278, 285, 286, 290, 294, 295, 297, 298
Lee, "Young Miss", 267
Leesburg. 141, 249, 253, 268
Lehew, 148
Letcher, Governor, 153, 264
Lewis, Charles, 150
Lewis, Miss, 244
Lewis, Old Major, 181
Lewisburg, 260, 264
Lexington, 6, 45, 264
Lincoln, 32, 44, 61, 103, 121, 154, 268, 291, 295
Lincoln, Mr., 227
Linden, 108, 291, 223
Liza Ann, 303
Lomax, L.L., 112
London, 122
Long, Mrs., 261, 262, 266
Longstreet, Lieut. Gen. James, C.S.A., 97, 105, 106, 115, 136, 137, 145, 146, 153-154, 182, 284, 193, 198, 199, 202, 215-218, 227, 230, 236, 237, 251, 252, 255, 273, 278
Lookout Mountain, 236
Loudoun, 136, 156, 176, 270, 288
Loudoun Rangers, 136
Louisiana, 71, 82, 84
Louisiana Seventh, 100
Love, Lucian, 288
Lovel, Mr., 169
Lucie, Miss, 258
Lucie, 212, 224, 231, 239, 240, 256
Luckadoo, Capt., 145
Lucy (servant for Aunt Betty), 191, 195
Lucy (Mr. Armstead's servant), 225
Luke, Mr., 227
Luke, Mr., 267, 270, 272
Luke, Mrs., 259, 267, 269, 270
Luray, 35, 36, 87, 95, 135, 156, 165, 179, 211, 220, 221, 223, 232, 253, 284, 285, 287, 294
Luray Turnpike, 78
Luray Valley, 6. 75, 92, 97, 239, 283, 285
Lynchburg, 28, 31, 137, 259, 264, 296
Lyons, Lord, 18, 19

M

M., Cousin, 280
M., Katie, 54
M., Miss, 163, 189

M., Mr., 112, 155, 188, 189
M., Mrs., 90, 293
Macauley, Mr., 200, 201, 215 (Huntsville, AL.) (R.L.McCalley, Co. I, 4th Ala. Regt.)
Maddox, Webb, 261
Madision Artillery, 202
Madison Courthouse, 152, 211, 287
Magruder, Maj. Gen. John B., C.S.A., 35, 50, 115
Mahala, 125, 192, 208, 238, 303
Malvern Hill, 113
Manassas, 11, 14, 22, 31, 33, 34, 43, 49, 73, 103, 112, 136, 137, 147, 193, 212, 215
Manassas, Battle of, 215
Manassas Gap, 211
Manassa Junction, 32
Mankato, Minnesota, 137
Manor Grade, 78
Marblehead, U.S.S., 107
Markham, 83
Marshall (servant), 192
Marshall, Ann Maria, 189
Marshall, Betty Miss, 223
Marshall, Capt. (from Corinth), 86, 87
Marshall, Colonel, 212
Marshall, Dr., 125-127 (Surgeon, 3rd Delaware)
Marshall, Hattie Miss, 189
Marshall, Capt. James, 175, 217, 290 (son of Robert Morris Marshall, born March 9, 1823)
Marshall, Lucy S. ("Old Aunt L.") (wife of Capt. James Marshall, born March 12, 1823
Marshall, Miss Mary, 188, 189
Marshall, Misses, 157, 189 (Robt. Morris Marshall had three unmarried daughters:
   1. Mary Morris, b, 1834
   2. Anna Maria, b. 1835
   3. Hester, b. 1819
Marshall, Mrs., 55, 223, 232
Marshall, "Old Mr." Robt. Morris, 112, 188, 189, 220 (born Jan. 20 1797)
Marshall, Lieutenant Thomas, 230 (son of Robt. Morris Marshall, killed Brandywine Station)
Marshall (Salem), Virginia, 135
Martha (servant), 64, 90, 98, 117, 148, 150, 168, 192, 238
Martin, Captain, 112
Martinsburg, 142, 198, 261, 265
Mary, "Black (servant), 48, 153, 303 (see Dumb Mary)
Maryland, 39, 47, 49, 56, 73, 81, 84, 103, 117, 139, 140, 142, 143, 155, 196, 202, 210, 213, 220, 241, 267, 268, 277
Maryland Heights, 265
Maryland Regiment, 145
Maryland Volunteers, U.S.A., 117
Mason, 69
Mason, Captain, 67, 71, 90

Mason, James, 18, 19
Massachusetts, 56
Massanutten Mountain, 6, 95, 152
Massie, Captain, 87
Matilda (servant for Mrs. Moffatt), 191
Maury, Mr. (Episcopal Chaplain), 175
Mayland (New Sheet), 114
Mayo, Colonel, 234
Mc., Mrs. J. W., 162
McAffee, Lieut., 151
McClellan, Maj. Gen. Geo. B., U.S.A., 38, 39, 57, 62, 81, 83, 97, 101, 112, 113, 138, 139, 142
McClernand, 186
McCormick, Mr. (Clark County), 45
McCormick, Mr. (Washington City), 155
McCoy's Ford (see McKays Ford), 76, 156, 211, 212, 223
McDaniel, Mr., 188
McDonald, Harry, 172
McDonald, Mrs. Cornelia, 172 (authored book, "A Diary of Refugee Life in Shenandoah Valley")
McDowell, 62
McDowell, Maj. Gen. Irvin, U.S.A., 38, 39, 65, 72, 73, 83, 95, 97
McGetigen, Charley, 61, 66, 73
McGowan, General, 184
McK., Mrs., 163
McKay, Alfred, 156
McKay, Mr.D., 121
McKay's Ford, 223 (see McCoy's Ford)
McKay Neighborhood, 232
McLaw, Maj. Gen. Lafayette, C.S.A., 144, 155
McM., Dr., 268
McNeil, Lieut. Jesse C., 291
McNeill, Capt. John H., 190, 291
McWillie, Capt., 201
Meade, Maj. Gen. Geo. G., U.S.A., 210, 213, 216, 222, 223, 230, 239, 242, 251
Means, Capt. Samuel C., 136
Mechanicsville, 113
Meanfee, Dr., 225
Merrimac, C.S.S., 75 (see C.S.S. Vigrinia)
Merritt, Maj. Gen. Wesley, U.S.A., 288
Merriwether, Mr., 82
Mesod, Lieut., 103
Messengar, 189, 252
Michigan, 64, 176
Middletown, N.Y., 275
Middletown, Virginia, 121, 211, 275
Miles, Col. C.S., 143
Mill Road, 105

Millar, Mrs., 77
Miller, Mr., 294
Miller, Mrs. H., 139, 293, 294
Miller, Hampe, 13, 139, 293
Miller, Joe, 187
Millford Pass, 283
Millie, Aunt, 274
Milroy, Maj. Gen. R.H., U.S.A., 62, 74, 75, 83, 172, 186, 192, 196, 197, 198
Minnesota, 137
Missionary Ridge, 236
Mississippi, 36, 86, 114, 158, 199, 229
Mississippi River, 36, 52, 158, 212
Missouri, 35, 173, 227
Mitchell, 83
Mitchell, Dr., 279
Mobile, 110, 125, 251
Moffatt, Mr. 231, 266
Moffatt, Mrs., 43, 61, 62, 99, 114, 146, 191, 232, 279, 280-282, 292
Mohler, Fannie, 87, 266
Mohler, Maggie, 87, 261, 262, 264, 266
Monica, Mrs Ed, 267
Moore, Woodville, 40
Monitor, U.S.S., 76
Monocacy River, 267
Montgomery, Alabama, 30, 286
Montjoy, Capt. R.P., 253, 254
Moore, 265
Moore, Mr., 217
Moore, Mrs., 55
Moore, Bettie, 267
Moore, Nicholas, 267
Moore, Woodville, 40
Moorehead, Alice, 48, 88
Morehead, Mrs., 23, 32
Moreton, Mr., 82, 194, 195, 220, 266
Morgan, Brig. Gen. John H., C.S,A., 132, 158, 174
Mormons, 137
Morris, Mr., 80
Morrison, Mary Anna (Stonewall Jackson's 2nd wife), 96
Morrel, L.T., 103
Morrow, 151
Morton, 214
Mosby, Col, John S., C.S.A., 49, 176, 253, 254, 256, 260, 273, 274, 276, 284, 288, 289, 294
Moses, Maj. Raphael (Longstreet's Commissary Officer), 216
Mount Jackson, 34, 39, 48, 49, 152
Mount Solon, 75
Mountain View, 52, 110, 280, 291, 298, 301, 302

Mule Shoe, 255
Mulligan, Col. James A., U.S.A., 270
Munford, Brig. Gen. Thos., C.S.A., 111
Murfreesboro, Tennessee, 30 46, 158, 164, 174
Myers, Eddie, 40
Myers, Julia, 55

N

Nancy (servant), 198, 199
Nashville, 30, 46, 47, 158, 281, 286
Nervie, 98
Nettie (Stewart?), 152
New Market, 75, 152, 258, 254, 285
New Orleans, 57, 58, 200
New Orleans Batallion, 80, 81
New Orleans Time Democrat, 200
New Town, 136
New York, 131, 214, 275
Newport News, 35
Newtwon, Cousin Mack, 244
Newton, Mr. and Mrs. and Miss, 234
Nicholls, Brig.Gen. F.T., C.S.A., 184
Nineveh, 36, 80
Norfolk, 28, 36, 75, 235
Normal, Mrs., 191, 193
North Anna River 257
North Carolina, 28, 176, 182, 256, 257, 290, 295, 297
North Fork, 6, 79
North Georgia, 229
Nott, Adjutant, 238

O

Oakley, 21, 60, 87, 100, 124, 239, 149, 150, 157, 181, 223, 226, 232, 279, 280, 284, 291, 293, 302
O'Ferrall, Capt, C.T., C.S.A. (later Gov. Virginia), 48, 51, 155, 205
Ohio, 236
Ohio Railroad, 270
Old Dominion, 120
"Old Sam" (horse), 245
O'Malley, Charlie, 155
One Hundred Second New York Reg., 131
One Hundred Twentieth Georgia Reg., 249
Opequon Creek, 272
Orange Plank Road, 251
Ord, Maj. Gen. Edw. O.C., U.S.A., 93, 95
Orlean, Virginia, 136

Osborne, Dr., 260, 261, 269, 270
Osborne, Mrs., 270
Overall, Isaac, 169, 291
Overall, Lucie, 249
Overby, William Thomas, 288

P

Paducah, Kentucky, 27
Page, Miss Annie, 272
Page County, 107, 261
Page Valley, 6, 35
Paige, Mr. (Page), 260, 267, 270, 272
Painter, Mrs., 242
Palmetto State, 172, 194
Pamunkey River, 107
Paris, 117
Partisan Rangers, 291
Patrick, Major, 112
Paxton, Brig. Gen. E.F., C.S.A., 184
Peachtree Creek, 281
Pearce, Mr., 147
Pegram, Mr. and Mrs., 225
Pender, Maj. Gen. W.D., C.S.A., 184, 202, 210
Pendleton, Mr. (of Clarke Co.), 36, 165, 175
Pendleton, Mr. G., 269
Pennsylvania, 56, 193, 196, 202, 211
Perry, 265
Perryville, Kentucky, 132, 158
Petersburg, Virginia, 259, 263, 283, 286, 295, 296
Pettie, Dr. J.T., 115, 120, 278, 279
Pettigrew, Brig. Gen. J.J., C.S.A., 210
Petty, G., 115, 246
Petty, Mr., 238
Petty, Newt., 125, 165
Petty, Sallie, 249, 250
Petty, Tom (J.T.), 120, 143, 278, 279
Peyton, Major, 218
Philadelphia, 56, 60, 61, 241, 293
Phillips Mrs., 260, 265
Pickett, Maj. Gen. Geo. E., C.S.A., 210, 211, 215, 295, 296
Piedmont, 259
Piedmont Route, 187
Pierpoint, 36
Pittman, Miss, 258
Pittman, Mrs., 258
Pittsburg Landing, 46, 86
Plattsburg, 227

Pleasant Valley, 137
Point Lookout, 262
Point of Rocks, 146
Pompeii, 177
Pope, Maj. Gen. John, U.S.A., 52, 116, 122-124, 130, 133, 136, 137
Port Republic, 97, 100-102
Porte Crayon (see David Strother), 42, 44
Potomac, 6, 47, 84, 139, 141, 144, 202, 210, 213, 214, 268, 270
Presbyterian Church, 83
Price,Maj. Gen. Sterling, C.S.A., 35, 114, 174
Prospect Hill Cemetery, 298

Q

Quakers, 156

R

R., Miss Matty, 165
Ralph, 106
Ramey, Mrs., 249
Ramseur, Maj. Gen. Stephen D., C.S.A., 184
Rangers, 61, 147
Rapidan, Battle of, 237
Rapidan River, 251
Rappahannok, 292, 296
Rappahannock River, 135, 136, 153, 154, 182, 184, 230
Ready, Miss Alice, 174
Red River, 251
Reed, 47, 198
Reeves, Dr., 82
Reid, 136
Reid, Adjutant, 105
Rhodes, Henry C., 288
Richards, Annie, 302
Richards, Elizabeth M. Blakemore Bayly (Cousine Bettie) (Cousin Bett), 24, 32, 84, 126, 134, 144, 181, 183, 231, 237, 243, 302
Richards, Henry, 302
Richards, Maj. James Russell, 31, 53, 40, 54, 62, 64, 126, 134, 156, 179, 231, 238, 301, 302
Richards, Russell, 289, 292, 302
Richards, Thomas, 302
Richards, Walter, 302
Richardson, Belle, 118, 134, 196, 258, 291, 292, 302
Richardson, Charlie, 27, 100, 140, 175, 187, 194, 197-199, 291
Richardson, Elizabeth Millar (Cousin Lizzie & Eliz. & E.), 116, 118, 123, 124, 134, 181, 183, 194, 234, 237, 234, 237, 243, 258
Richardson, Elite, 36, 112, 115, 118, 120, 123, 124, 302
Richardson, Ginnie, 246, 258

Richardson, Mack, 19
Richardson, Susan, 22, 23, 48, 116, 118, 120, 134, 181, 183, 205, 237, 243, 297, 302
Richardson, Mr. William, 302
Richardson, William Millar (Willie), 19, 35, 74, 84, 100, 110, 115, 116, 118, 120, 124, 174, 301, 302
Richmond, 24, 25, 28-30, 32, 33, 38, 50-52, 57, 72, 74, 75, 83, 87, 88, 94, 97, 100, 101, 106, 110, 112-115, 118, 120, 121, 124, 125, 128, 132, 143, 148, 153, 157, 172, 174, 184, 185, 189, 193, 208, 213, 216, 217, 241, 251, 254-257, 259, 264, 268, 286, 294-297
Richmond Dispatch, 39, 48
Rifles (see Warren Rifles), 36, 145, 162
Riley, 144
Rippon, 260, 264, 268, 270
Riverside, 24, 144, 258, 301
Riverton, 145, 301
Rixey, Dr. (brother of Alice Morehead), 23, 88, 89, 114
Roanoke Island, 28
Robbie, 180, 223
Roberts, Miss 256
Robertson, Brig. Gen. Beverly H., C.S.A., 111, 112, 175
Robt., 138
Rock Fish Gap, 285
Rodes, Maj. Gen. Robt. E., C.S.A., 202
Rogers, Lieutenant, 268
Rogers, Major, 194
Rokett, Johnnie, 99
Rome, 117
Romney, 84
Rose Hill, 23, 28, 35, 74, 80, 110, 112, 115, 118, 123, 130, 134, 144, 148, 162, 168, 175, 176, 191, 205, 221, 231, 238, 243, 258, 291, 301, 302
Rose Hill Family, 131
Rosecrans, Maj. Gen. Wm. S., U.S.A., 95, 97, 227, 228, 236
Rosser, Maj. Gen. Thos. L., C.S.A., 239, 255, 263, 264, 292
Rouse, Lewis, 104-107
Rowe, Mary Wallace Buck, 5
Roxie, 163
Roy, Capt., 169, 181, 223, 239
Roy, Harry, 238
Roy, Lt. Col. J. Benton, C.S.A. (on Gen. Hardee's Staff), 22-25, 28, 33, 63, 86, 131, 181, 211, 219, 231, 241, 244, 278, 292
Roy, Mrs., 42, 44, 56, 63, 86, 122, 174, 192, 219, 223, 230, 231, 243, 258, 292
Roy, Rob (Negro freeman), 46, 90, 94, 103, 192, 303
Roy, Scott, 20, 24, 27, 28, 34-36, 47, 120, 124, 131, 138, 139, 143, 145, 152, 164, 172-175, 179-183, 187, 189, 211-213, 217, 219, 220, 220, 222, 230, 235, 236, 239, 242, 253, 278, 279, 283, 284 (married Mattie Cook)
Russell, Mr., 82
Rust, Willie, 35, 74

S

Salem, Virginia, 88, 114, 135, 136
Sallie (cook), 223
Saltman (horse), 260, 265, 271, 272
Samuels, Green, 30, 34, 99, 100, 158, 243, 257
Samuels, Kattie (see Kattie Boone), 34, 37, 57, 74, 75, 99, 133, 144, 157, 158, 181, 258, 293
Sanderson, Capt. James M. (of Phil.), 96, 97, (charged with being too nice to Confederates but charges dropped, wrote W.M. Buck after war)
Sangster Station, 239
Santmyers, Tom, 139
Savage Station, 113
Savanah, 285
Schlaudecker, Colonel, 117
Schofield, Maj. Gen. John M., U.S.A., 285, 286
Schweiger, 67
Scouts, Jessie, 186
Second Bull Run, Battle of, 136, 137
Second Manassas, Battle of, 112, 136, 137, 193
Second Virginia Calvary, 111
Selma, Alabama, 286
Semmes, Rear Adm, Raphael, C.S.A., 174, 210
Seven Day's Battle 113
Seven Pines, 140
Seventeenth Virginia Calvary, 111
Seventeenth Virginia Infantry (see Warren Rifles), 74, 172, 214, 236
Seventh Virginia Calvary, 35, 83, 111, 175, 176, 183, 205
Seward, 18, 19, 157
Sewell's Point, 75
Seymour, Mr., 60
Shalosse, Colonell, 102
Sharpsburg, 142-145
Sheetz, Colonel, 82-84
Shelbyville, 164
Shenandoah River, 6, 76, 300, 301
Shenandoah Valley, 6, 11, 22, 33, 38, 111, 130, 239, 251, 254, 259, 264, 272, 273, 273, 285, 287
Shepardstown, 293
Sheppard, Mr., 248
Sheppard, Young, 194
Sheridan, Lieut. Gen. Philip H., U.S.A., 255, 256, 264, 272-274, 278, 283, 285, 287-289
Sherman, Lieut. Gen. Wm. T., U.S.A., 158, 229, 236, 237, 251, 280, 281, 285, 289, 290, 295, 297
Shields, Maj. Gen. James, U.S.A., 65, 68, 69, 72, 73, 87, 88, 89, 91, 92, 95, 97-101, 108, 111, 113, 114
Shiloh, 46-48, 52, 69, 86

Shipe, Mr., 281, 282
Shirley Mr., 267
Sigel, Maj. Gen. Franz, U.S.A., 119, 251, 254, 259
Simpson, First Lt. (Rangers), 61
Simpson, John, 138
Simpson, Martha, 13, 56, 135
Simpson, Miss Mary, 230
Simpson, Mr., 163
Simpson, Mrs., 135, 163, 258
Simpson, Maj. Robt., C.S.A., 28, 29, 118, 120, 132-135, 138, 140, 146, 235, 257
Simpson, Sam, 138, 140
Sioux (Indians), 137
Sixth Massachusetts, 50
Sixth Regt., 278
Sixth Virginia Calvary (Co. D), 196
Sixth Virginia Calvary, 79, 11
Skylark (horse), 166, 169
Skyline Drive, 300
Slaughter Mountain, 134
Slidell, John S., 18, 19
Smedley, Mr., 240
Smith, Angie, 227
Smith, Governor, 213
Smith, John (see Nancy Jenkins), 108, 109
Smithfield, 265
Soldier's Rest, 20, 83
Sorrell, Brig. Gen. G. Moxley, C.S.A (A.A.G. Gen. Longstreet), 146, 215
South Carolina, 108, 110, 148, 155, 194, 201, 290
South Fork, 6
South Mountain, 142, 143, 266
Sowers, Mr., 52
Spangler, Robt., 138
Spangler, Saml., 138, 140
Spann, Capt., 201
Spotsylvania Courthouse, 255
Spring Hill, 285
Stafford County, 131
Stanton, 94
Staughton, Brig. Gen. Edwin H., U.S.A., 176
Staunton, 6, 33, 35, 39, 62, 74, 99, 157, 176, 254, 260
Steele, John 120, 124, 133
Stephens, (Yankee Officer from Wheeling, W. Va.), 151
Stephens, Captain, 103-107
Steuart, Brig. Gen. G.H. "Marlyland", C.S.A., 202
Stevens, Maj. Gen. I.I., U.S.A., 137
Stevenson, Captain (Independent Company), 190
Stewart, Alice, 17, 18, 34, 64, 115, 119, 152
Stewart, Fannie, 17, 18, 35, 120, 152, 180

Stewart, Mr. (cousin of Mr. Brerwood), 155
Stewart, Mrs., 13, 17, 152
Stewarts, the, 152
Stimpson, Mr., 163
Stimpson, Mrs., 163
Stone, Mr., 217
Stone River, 158
Stonewall Brigade, 137, 138
Strasburg, 6, 35, 37, 38, 40, 79, 82, 92, 95, 133, 150, 282, 301
Strickler House, The 17, 18
Strother, David (see Porte Crayon), 42
Strother, Old Mr., 260
Stuart, Lieut. Gen. J.E.B., C.S.A., 107, 112, 115, 139, 147, 158, 175, 176, 182, 193, 196, 202, 206, 210, 219, 255
Sturgis, B'V'T Maj. Gen. Samuel D., U.S.A., 137
Suffolk, Virginia, 75. 182, 183, 234
Summers, Maj. Gen. Ed. V., U.S.A., 101
Sumption, John, 232
Susquehanna River, 202
Swift Run Gap, 62
Switzerland, 117

T

T., Mrs., 163
Taliaferro, Mr., 144
Tanner, Dr., 269
Tattrall, Commodore J., 75
Taylor, Clara, 120
Taylor, John, 231
Taylor, Mr., 283
Taylor, Nannie, 80, 81, 120, 148, 153, 158, 160, 208, 266
Taylor, Old Mr., 266, 267, 274, 278
Taylor, Lieut Gen. Richard, C.S.A., 82, 286
Taylor, Susan, 301
Taylors, The, 174
Tell, 251
Tennessee, 30, 46, 52, 132, 158, 171, 186, 227, 228, 230, 232, 236, 281, 285
Tennessee River, 27-29, 52
Terrill, Miss, 296
The Star Battalion, 82
Third Delaware, 127
Thirty-fifth Virginia Calvary, 137
Thomas, Maj. Gen. Geo. H., U.S.A., 227, 236, 251, 281, 286
Thomas, Mr., 206 (Walter Buck killed in his yard at Upperville, VA.)
Thompson, Mr., 265
Thorborne, Colonel, 101
Thornton, Major, 268

Thorpe, Miss S., 198
Throughfare Gap, 136
Tigers (Louisiana), 82, 83
Timmerman, Lieutenant, 140
Tobert, 285
Tom, Cousin, 212
Tom Telegraph (horse), 116
Tompkins, Mr., 264
Tobert, B'V''T Maj. Gen. Alfred T.A., U.S.A., 287
Trent, H.M.S., 19
Trevilians Station, Battle of, 264
Trout, Mr. J., 163
Trout, Wilbur, 85
Tudor Hall, 259
Tullahoma, Tennessee, 158
Tupelo, Mississippi, 86, 110, 120, 131, 286
Turner, Dr., 19, 68, 72, 98, 110, 120, 148, 163, 180, 221, 243, 266, 293
Turner, Maj., 256
Turner, Mrs. Lucie, 163, 225, 256
Turner, Mrs Old, 180 (buried in garden of "Hill Crest" the Turner home)
Turner, Mrs. Robert, 163, 290
Turner, Robbie, 180
Turner, Smith, 12, 19, 120, 215
Turner's Gap, 143
Tuscaloosa, Alabama, 286
Tuscumbia, Alabama, 281
Twelfth Georgia Regiment, 89
Twelfth Virginia Calvary, 111, 127
Tyler, Colonel (brother of Miss Tensia Tyler), 37
Tyler, B'V'T Maj. Gen. E.B., U.S.A., 94, 96, 98
Tyler, Gus, 172, 213
Tyler, Miss Sue, 233, 234
Tyler, Miss Tensia (sister of Mrs. Turner who died April 13, 1863), 12, 19, 37, 180, 233, 234, 294
Tyndall, Maj., 63, 64, 73

U

United States, 19, 27, 28, 33, 36, 38, 62, 297
Upperville, 202, 203, 239
U.S. "Pierpont", 36

V

Van Buren, Colonel, 117
Van Cleersville, 259
Van Meter, Mrs., 261, 262, 264-266, 278
Vesuvius, 117
Vicksburg, 158, 189, 212, 213

Virginia, 14, 22, 29, 30, 36, 38, 42, 48, 49, 53, 57, 70, 75, 79, 83, 87, 105, 113, 115, 135-139, 145, 153, 177, 193, 205, 210, 213, 227, 237, 254, 257, 259, 269, 273, 275, 302
Virginia Central Railroad, 124
Virginia, C.S.S. (Merrimac), 75, 76
Virginia Military Institute, 45, 254, 264
Vivian, 249

W

Waldon, Major, 146
Walker, Colonel, 151
Wallace, Sir William,, 204
Ward, Frank (AAG to Col. Johnson), 80
Ward, Mrs., 151
Warinick, Maj., 84
Warren County, 29, 53, 206, 269
Warren Rifles, 19, 29, 35, 53, 56, 125, 258, 176, 211, 215, 219, 230 (see Co. B, Seventeenth Virginia Infantry Regiment and "Seventeenth" and "Rifles")
Warrenton, 124, 133, 134, 136, 145, 242
Washington, 19, 39, 50m 84, 87, 97, 108, 114, 133, 138, 139, 142, 155, 157, 202, 257, 267, 268
Washington Artillary, 199, 200
Washington College, 264
Waterford, 136
Waterlick, Virginia, 301
Waynesboro, 285
Weaver, Lucie, 279
Weaver, Mr., 163, 165, 166
Weaver Store, 165
Wells, Lieutenant, 254
Wells, Mack, 156
Wells, Mark, 61
Wells, Mr . Robert, 297
West Virginia, 38, 42
Weston, Mr., 131, 251
Wheat, Major, 80, 81
Wheatley, Mrs., 52, 229, 248, 291
Wheeling, 151, 189
White, (Miss) Betty, 78, 192, 202, 233, 237
White, Col. Elizah Viers, 136, 137, 264
White, G., 292
White, Brig. Gen. Julies, C.S.A., 143
White House Bridge, 76
White House Sortie, 107
White Oak Swamp, 113
White's Ford, 141

Wickham, Brig. Gen. W.C., C.S.A., 283
Wilderness, Battle of the, 252
Willet, 249
Williams, Dr., 155
Williams, George, 21-26, 150, 172, 230, 231, 272, 284 (Gen. Liddell's A.A.G., became Colonel)
Williams, Jim, 261
Williamsburg, 74, 83, 100, 115, 140
Williamsport, 241
Willow Glen, 302
Wilson, Maj. Gen. James H., U.S.A., 286
Wilson, Johnnie, 268
Wilson, Major, 151
Wilson, Mr., 12, 14, 19, 20, 82
Winchester, 22, 31-33, 35, 38-40,44, 52, 77, 79, 83-87, 89-100, 106, 120, 125, 139, 142, 146, 152, 154, 172, 187, 190, 191, 193, 195, 196-198, 209, 211, 239, 252, 264, 270, 271, 273, 275, 278, 283, 302
Winchester, Mr., 174
Winder, Brig.Gen. C.S., C.S.A., 95
Winder General Hospital, 266
Wise, Geo., 219, 236
Woods, Maj. Gen. Thomas J., U.S.A., 227
Woodstock, 38, 44, 158
Wough, Arthur, 100
Wright, Maj.Gen.Ambrose R., C.S.A., 219, 221

Y

Yates, Miss, 296
Yates, Mr., 178
Yellow Tavern, Battle of, 255
York, Pennsylvania, 202
York River, 38
Yorktown, 50, 52, 57, 58
Young, Capt., 146